Date D

A HISTORY OF
LATER LATIN LITERATURE

A HISTORY OF
LATER LATIN LITERATURE

FROM THE MIDDLE OF THE FOURTH
TO THE END OF THE SEVENTEENTH
CENTURY

BY

F. A. WRIGHT, M.A.

PROFESSOR OF CLASSICS IN THE UNIVERSITY OF LONDON

AND

T. A. SINCLAIR, M.A.

READER IN CLASSICS IN THE UNIVERSITY OF LONDON

NEW YORK
THE MACMILLAN COMPANY
1931

PRINTED IN GREAT BRITAIN BY THE EDINBURGH PRESS, EDINBURGH

CONTENTS

CONTENTS

PREFACE

THIS book is an attempt to deal with a large subject in a brief space. There are many excellent histories of classical Latin Literature, but when we come to later Latin the case is very different. The two great French and German histories are still far from nearing completion, and in English there is no book, long or short, which treats exclusively of Latin Literature from the fourth to the seventeenth century of our era. Hence the present volume, *pro posse et nosse nostro*.

History of Later Latin Literature

INTRODUCTION

L ATIN literature should logically be regarded as
one whole, and its history should extend from
its first beginnings towards the end of the third
century, B.C., when Plautus by an effort of genius
which has hardly been appreciated created the Roman
drama, down to the final stage of the Renaissance at
the end of the seventeenth century, when Latin at last
definitely ceased to be a universal language. There
are several reasons why such a history has never at
present been written, and one of them is the immense
amount of work which is considered necessary to satisfy
modern ideas of completeness. The standard German
history by Martin Schanz starts at the beginning, and
in seven stout volumes of some four thousand pages
carries us down to the reign of Justinian. A continuation of Schanz was begun by Max Manitius,
whose first volume, which appeared in 1909, dealt
with the period from 480 to 968 ; a second volume
of nearly 900 pages, treating of the tenth, eleventh
and twelfth centuries came out in 1923 ; the third
volume is yet to be published. A similar lesson may
be drawn from that wonderful work, the *Histoire
littéraire de la France*. Begun by the Benedictines
of St Maur in the eighteenth century and now being
continued by members of the Institute, it includes
all writers born in France after the birth of Christ,
whether they write in Latin or in French. Its first

twelve quartos bring us to 1150; its thirty-sixth is
still concerned with the fourteenth century.

Another reason is to be found in the belief, sedulously
fostered for many years by classical scholars, that later
Latin in itself is a subject scarcely worthy of serious
attention. Our teachers have always rightly insisted
on the supreme importance of the classics as giving us
a definite standard of literary value. But it is possible
for the best to be the enemy of the good, and this is
what has happened in our Latin studies. Latin for
us has begun with Plautus and ended with Suetonius :
the medieval writers have until lately been regarded
as outside the pale, deleterious stuff likely to corrupt
the palate trained to appreciate the fine vintages of
the Augustan Age. The result has been that a comparatively small amount of Latin has been intensively
studied ; the inestimably larger mass written after the
third century of our era has been most undeservedly
neglected. It will be found by anyone who reads
them that many of the later Latinists are well worth
notice ; nor are they by any means as incorrect and
ungrammatical as is frequently imagined. In this
respect the German scholars who have done such good
service in editing medieval texts are themselves somewhat to blame. The classics, as we read them now,
have been exposed to a long process of emendation ;
the errors of copyists have been carefully removed,
and the final result is in many cases very different
from the original MSS. Medieval authors have not
been thus favoured, and mistakes are frequently left
in even against the weight of manuscript authority.
A medieval author is supposed, like Habakkuk, to be
capable of anything : in reality many of them write
a Latin which, though not Ciceronian, is forcible,
vivid, and easy to read.

2

A third reason which has tempted historians to limit their period is the undoubted fact that after the death of the Emperor Hadrian in 138 there was a sudden and abrupt decline in literary production. Juvenal and Martial, Tacitus and Suetonius, left no adequate successors, and in the next two hundred years the authors of outstanding distinction can be counted on the fingers of one hand. The golden age was followed by the silver age, and when the silver age comes to an end many writers have thought it unprofitable to continue the story further. As a matter of fact, Græco-Roman civilisation during these two centuries was slowly dying, and the literature inspired by that civilisation was dying with it. At first the signs of decay were not too obvious, and the great lawyers Pomponius, Gaius, and Papinian, who wrote towards the end of the second and the beginning of the third century, still preserved some of the old Roman vigour. Yet even in their time there is only one literary figure among pagan writers of any real interest, and he is the African Lucius Apuleius, author of the *Golden Ass*.

But while pagan institutions were gradually falling to ruin, Christianity was steadily growing; and amid the anarchy of the third century it is the Christian apologists who alone redeem the literature of the age from utter insignificance. Minucius Felix, Tertullian, Cyprian, Arnobius, and Lactantius by their writings bridge the gulf between the old Rome and the new. It is hard to understand the triumphant Christianity of the fourth century unless one knows something of the trials and tribulations through which it had previously passed. It may therefore be useful here to give a brief account of the three most important of these five writers, Tertullian, Cyprian and Lactantius.

Quintus Septimius Florens Tertullianus (A.D. 155–222)

3

was born at Carthage, and after a riotous youth spent in Rome returned as a priest of the Christian church to Africa and there remained for the rest of his life. He was a voluminous writer and at least thirty books are certainly from his pen. They fall into three classes—the apologetic, supporting Christianity against paganism ; the dogmatic, expounding doctrines and refuting heresies ; and the practical, dealing with questions of conduct and morality. To the first class belongs his finest book, the *Apologeticus*, defending Christians against the charges of secret crime and open disloyalty commonly brought against them, and asserting the superiority of Christianity over all other religions. In the second class comes the longest of his works, the five books *Against Marcion*, in which he both refutes the Gnostic heresy and convincingly shows the intimate connection between the Old and the New Testaments. The third class contains the mass of his shorter writings ; among them the brilliant satire *The Cloak versus the Toga* ; the treatises on *Idolatry* and the *Theatre* ; the sermons on *Patience* and *Chastity* ; the two intimate essays addressed to his wife ; and the discourse on *Women's Dress*.

Tertullian is one of the greatest, if not the greatest, of Roman orators. Style is perhaps partly a matter of taste, and to those who are familiar with Cicero's wonderful flow of words Tertullian's African Latinity may at first seem difficult and obscure. But if the *Apologeticus* be compared with the *Second Philippic*, one cannot but realise how much higher is the plane of thought on which Tertullian moves, and to those who appreciate real originality of mind he offers an extreme fascination. Like Christianity itself, he appeals not only to the scholar but to the people ; and the language of the people, scarcely heard in Latin literature

before him save in Plautus and Petronius, is the basis
of his fabric of words. But in weaving his web he
adds many new strands of his own. His military and
legal experiences colour his vocabulary with the
technical phrases of the army and the courts ; his
controversies with the Gnostic heretics enrich his pages
with philosophical terms ; his studies in Greek and
Biblical literature supply him with an endless store of
apt quotations and allusions. And, above all, there is
the ardent strength of his spirit, warmed by the hot
rays of the African sun, which has made his admirers
compare his writing to the black ebony of his native
land.

In the records of the Church Cyprian (210–258)
holds a higher place than Tertullian ; for Tertullian
was led astray by the Montanist heresy and was never
more than a simple priest, while Cyprian was perfectly
orthodox, became Bishop of Carthage, and finally met
a martyr's death. But as a writer he is Tertullian's
inferior ; his language is clear and simple, but he
altogether lacks the fiery eloquence of his predecessor ;
he is easier to read than Tertullian but he is less worth
reading. Though his works fill some eight hundred
pages in Hartel's Vienna edition, many of them are
of slight interest, and nearly half their bulk consists
of letters written in his episcopal capacity dealing with
details of Church management. Among his other
writings three books stand out. The treatise *De Lapsis*
' On those who lapsed from the faith ' contains much
valuable information as to the conditions in which a
formal persecution of the Christians, such as that
ordered by Decius, was carried out. Even more
attractive is the dramatic monologue *To Donatus* on
the world and its vanities, a piece which shows the
influence of Juvenal but gives us a vivid picture of

the state of society in the writer's day. But Cyprian's most important work and the one that has had the greatest influence on history is the *On the unity of the Catholic Church*. Cyprian realised that the Church already ran far greater danger from internal schism than from pagan persecution, and in these pages he makes an impassioned plea, supported by constant scriptural quotations, for unity within the Church and obedience to episcopal control.

Lactantius (245–315) writes in much the same manner as Cyprian but with something more of artistic purpose. He is often called ' the Christian Cicero,' and if we confine our survey to the weaker portions of Cicero's philosophical works the title is not undeserved. He was born, a pagan, in Africa, and after studying rhetoric became a professor at Nicomedia, where he was converted to Christianity. The great persecution of 303 deprived him of his chair, but on the official recognition of Christianity he was appointed by Constantine as tutor to his son Crispus, and died full of years and honours at Trèves. A long list of writings by him is given by Jerome, but most of these are lost and his fame now chiefly rests on the *Institutiones Divinæ*, dedicated ' to the mighty Constantine, the first of Roman princes to repudiate error and to acknowledge the majesty of the one and only true God.' This is one of the great doctrinal treatises of the Catholic Church, and in the vast mass of patristic literature it is still among the most widely read volumes. Nor is its fame undeserved, for it contains not only a critical history of ancient religion but also a practical code of morals and a system of philosophy based on the divine working of Providence, framed to supersede all those Pagan systems which at the beginning of the fourth century still held pride of place. It is long, carefully written in Ciceronian style, and divided into seven books, the first three a destructive criticism of Pagan religion and philosophy, the last four a constructive effort to establish a rule of life upon the maxim— 'In philosophy is religion, in religion philosophy.' With Lactantius we pass from the third century to the fourth. The reign of Constantine ushers in a new era, and with that era later Latin literature begins.

PART I

THE AGE OF AUGUSTINE
(331–430)

THE AGE OF AUGUSTINE

THE year 313 is a vital date both in the history of the world and in the history of Latin literature, for it was then that Constantine established Christianity as a religion recognised by the State, and a few years later followed that momentous step by removing the capital of his empire to Constantinople. The effect of one of these changes was gradual, of the other immediate; but between them they gave a new direction to literary effort. Up till the end of the third century the influence of Greek upon Latin literature had always been very great. Under the Empire probably most Roman writers were bilingual and Marcus Aurelius even wrote his *Meditations* in Greek. There were few authors who were not thoroughly familiar with the great Greek masters, and the larger the number of allusions to Greek mythology a Roman poet could introduce into his verse, the more pleasing was the effect he produced upon himself and upon his readers. If a new style was to be attempted, a Greek model was ready to hand :

'Exemplaria Græca
nocturna versate manu, versate diurna,'

says Horace; and though Quintilian proudly declares 'Satura tota nostra est,' he is not satisfied until he can match a Roman against each one of their Greek predecessors.

This close connection is, of course, a well-known fact, but it is not perhaps as clearly recognised that the establishment of Constantinople as the seat of government began the long process whereby Greek literature passed out of common knowledge and had to be rediscovered by the European world. In the fourth century this process was only just beginning, but as the ages passed the Byzantine Empire with Greek for its language became more and more cut off from the West, where Latin was the only literary medium ; and when we reach the tenth century even a knowledge of colloquial Greek was a rare accomplishment in most parts of Europe, and the Greek classics had passed into oblivion. Virgil, Terence, Sallust and Cicero were still studied as models of style ; Homer, Sophocles, Thucydides and Plato were forgotten ; and so at last we have a Latin literature that is based upon Latin and upon Latin alone.

This change, it has been said, was gradual ; the State recognition of Christianity bore fruit much more quickly and may be considered the chief cause of the great revival of letters which marks the second half of the fourth century. Christianity had for many years been enlisting all the best minds in her service, but State recognition gave writers a new stimulus ; from being apologists they became assailants. Rome ceased to be the centre of the world's government and found herself instead the centre of the world's thought. It is true that Constantine's own age scarcely felt the effect of these new conditions, but the next generation saw the birth of six Christian writers, who are among the most notable figures in Latin literature and make their time one of the great periods in the history of the world.

Ambrose (340–397)

How vast was the alteration made by Constantine's enactment in the position of the Church and her ministers can be clearly seen in the life and writings of Ambrose Bishop of Milan. Aurelius Ambrosius was born about 340 of a Christian family among whose members was counted at least one martyr, the virgin Sotheris, put to death in the Great Persecution under Diocletian. His father was Pretorian Prefect in Gaul, and when he died at Trèves his widow brought her three children to Rome. There the young Ambrose, following in his father's footsteps, gained a post on the staff of the Pretorian Prefect of Italy, and after a short period of subordinate service was appointed 'Consular' of the provinces of Liguria and Æmilia and stationed at Milan. About a year after his arrival the episcopal chair in that city fell vacant by the death of the Arian bishop Auxentius; and as there was good reason to expect that the election of his successor would cause disturbances similar to those which had occurred in Rome between the partisans of Ursinus and Damasus, Ambrose himself put in an appearance at the church where the choice was to be made. He was admonishing the crowd to orderly behaviour, his biographer Paulinus tells us, "when a child suddenly cried out—'Ambrose Bishop.' The people caught up the words and the disputing between Arians and Catholics at once gave way to a marvellous and incredible unanimity." The choice was made on the spot and the assembly dispersed amid universal rejoicings.

But while every one else was satisfied, Ambrose himself was at first very unwilling to accept the bishopric. He had no canonical qualifications, and he regarded the honour as both undeserved and too great for his capacities. "You would have me begin to teach," he wrote to his people, "before I have begun to learn." This plea proved ineffectual, and

Ambrose then resorted to more drastic measures in order to convince men of his unfitness for high office in the Church. For instance, he ordered criminals to be brought to his tribunal and cruelly tortured, so that the people might see how stern and relentless he could be. He ordered women of bad character to be introduced into his private house, so that he might be proved a man of immoral life. When both devices failed and the people cried : "We will take responsibility and bear all your sins," he fled into the country and hid in a lonely cottage. But his place of concealment was discovered and he was escorted back to the city in triumph. At last he gave way, was baptised, and seven days later became bishop.

The appointment was approved by the Emperor Valentinian but fiercely resented by his Empress Justina who was an Arian devotee, and against her Ambrose soon found it necessary to use all his strength. In this struggle, as in most others, he was successful, and after Valentinian's death he gained such an ascendancy over his successor Gratian that the latter was ready to follow his guidance in all matters. For example, Gratian had begun his reign by according permission to heretics to follow their religion without molestation. Under Ambrose's influence during the next year that permission was revoked, and a stern decree published forbidding all heretic assemblies. Even more important was Gratian's law ' *qui mos*,' which enacted that all matters affecting religion in which clerics were litigants, as distinct from criminal cases (a distinction afterwards conveniently ignored) should not be tried by the civil courts but by the bishop of the diocese. This, the beginning of the process whereby the clergy was put above the common law, was one of Ambrose's greatest triumphs.

His next victory was over the Arians. Two Illyrian bishops complained to the Emperor that they had been denounced as heretics and petitioned to be judged by a council of all the Catholic Bishops both from the Eastern and the Western sees. Ambrose by this time was supreme in the West, and although he was deeply indebted to Basil and Gregory of Nazianzus, he had no wish to' see his authority questioned by the Bishops of Constantinople and Jerusalem, Antioch and Alexandria. He therefore wrote for the young ruler a treatise on the true faith and induced him to leave the case to be judged by a council of the Western bishops alone. The synod met at Aquileia in 381 and after a debate which lasted from daybreak till one in the afternoon the eloquence of Ambrose prevailed and the two offending prelates were deposed from their office.

Unfortunately Gratian was murdered in 383 and for some years Ambrose had a difficult course to steer. On the one side were the usurpers Maximus and the pagan Eugenius, whose soldiers threatened to stable their horses in Milan Cathedral : on the other the Empress Justina, guardian of the young emperor, Valentinian II, who demanded full liberty of worship for her Arian protégés. Twice imperial troops beleaguered Ambrose and his followers in the Portian Basilica for several days, the bishop meanwhile composing for his patient congregation the great hymns, *Æterne verum conditor, Iam surgit hora,* and *Veni redemptor gentium.* But his troubles ended when Theodosius defeated and killed Maximus in 388, for with the new ruler he stepped almost at once into the same position as he had held with Gratian. Theodosius was an able and experienced monarch who had a great record of achievements in the East before he ever appeared in Italy ; but, as he himself said, Ambrose soon showed him the difference between an emperor and a bishop.

The first occasion was at Milan. Theodosius, attending Ambrose's church, did not return after the offertory with the rest of the congregation to the nave but remained in the sanctuary. Ambrose at once by the medium of his archdeacon bade him withdraw from a part of the sacred edifice reserved for the clergy ; and Theodosius meekly acquiesced. The next time there was a more definite contest of wills. Some Christians in Mesopotamia at the instigation of their bishop had burned a Jewish synagogue, and Theodosius ordered that it should be rebuilt at the bishop's expense. Ambrose, jealous of any secular interference in religious matters, insisted that this order should be revoked, and when Theodosius hesitated he preached openly against him and threatened that he would refuse him the sacrament. The menace was too much for the Emperor, and the order was recalled. The third incident is one of the most famous events in history. The people of Thessalonica had murdered their governor and Theodosius retaliated by a general massacre of the population in which at least seven thousand defenceless victims perished. Ambrose was horrified at the ruthless cruelty of such a vengeance and insisted in a private letter to the Emperor that he must do penance before he could receive the sacrament again. According to one tradition Theodosius attempted to enter the cathedral, but Ambrose barred his way, and an ancient column still stands in Milan to-day marking the spot where bishop and emperor met. In any case, Theodosius was compelled finally to submit, and removing the insignia of his rank fell prostrate on the ground repeating the penitential

16

formula : " My soul cleaveth to the dust : quicken thou me according to thy word."

With an Emperor so amenable to the discipline of the Church Ambrose had no great difficulty in imposing his own will and in crushing both Arianism and Paganism. Before the death of Theodosius both were forbidden by law, and then in 397 Ambrose himself passed peacefully away, happy in the knowledge that the victory of Catholicism was assured.

This brief account may reveal the diversity and abundance of Ambrose's gifts, and how successful he was as bishop, diplomat, theologian, and administrator. But when we turn to his prose writings there is a certain feeling of disappointment. It seems almost impossible for the same person to be both a great man of action and a great man of letters. Ambrose certainly was the first, but he is not so certainly the second. He was, however, a copious writer, or rather a copious preacher, whose addresses were written down and then published. These sermons of his and his allegorical interpretations of the Old Testament are very voluminous but they scarcely would appeal to modern readers. The doctrinal books *On the Faith* and *On the Mysteries* have a considerable theological importance ; but from a literary standpoint we need only consider the hymns and the two ethical treatises *On Virginity* and on *Clergymen's Duties*. The first of these, in three books addressed to Ambrose's sister, earned Jerome's warm praise and among much other excellent matter contains the very edifying history of the maiden of Antioch. The second, which is modelled on Cicero's *De Officiis*, is a practical manual for clergymen and descends to the smallest details of behaviour, as the following extract will show :

' Some clerics walk slowly with an actor's gestures. They pace like bearers in a procession and sway their bodies as though they

B   17

were statues, and seem to be keeping time even as they put one foot in front of the other. Still, I think that a hurried walk is unbecoming, except when a case of some danger demands it, or a real necessity. If people hurry, they come up to us panting, and with distorted features : and if there is no reason which renders haste necessary we have just cause of offence. I am not talking of those who have to hurry occasionally for a particular reason, but of those who by constant use have made hurry a second nature. I disapprove of your slow walker, for he looks like a moving image : I disapprove of your hustler, for he reminds me of a shell that is just about to burst. A proper gait is one in which there is an appearance of authority and weight and dignity and tranquillity. It should be perfectly simple and plain, without any affectation or conceit ; for nothing artificial is really pleasing. Let nature fashion our movements and if there is any fault in nature let care amend it. We do not need artifice, but we may need correction.'

But though in considering Ambrose's prose some faintness of praise is justifiable, his hymns deserve, and have usually gained, unstinted admiration. Not only are they in themselves a real effort of original creation, but they have served also as an exemplar to all the hymn-writers of the western church. Hilary had certainly endeavoured to write hymns before Ambrose, but those of his attempts that have been preserved must be pronounced to be failures. Ambrose in his simple eight-stanza iambics invented a form that was exactly fitted for antiphonal singing, and we can still realise the effect produced by his melodies on their first hearers if we read Augustine's *Confessions :* " What tears did I shed over the hymns and canticles when the sweet sound of the music of Thy Church thrilled my soul. As the music flowed into my ears and Thy truth trickled into my heart, the tide of devotion swelled high within me, and the tears ran down, and there was gladness in those tears."

Ambrose's hymns form the nucleus of what is still called the Ambrosian hymnary, but the genuine

18

examples form only a small part of the whole collection.
A generous estimate would allow about twenty hymns
as possibly his ; but only the five vouched for either
by Augustine or by Ambrose himself are certain.
These are the *Veni redemptor gentium, Deus creator
omnium, Iam surgit hora tertia, Splendor paternæ gloriæ*,
and perhaps the best known of all, *Æterne rerum
conditor.*

'Æterne rerum conditor,
Noctem diemque qui regis
Et temporum das tempora
Ut alleves fastidia ;

Præco diei iam sonat,
Noctis profundæ pervigil,
Nocturna lux viantibus,
A nocte noctem segregans.

Hoc excitatus lucifer
Solvit polum caligine,
Hoc omnis erronum chorus
Vias nocendi deserit.'

' Eternal Lord the world that made,
Who hides the day in night's black shade,
And fixes hour on hour, that we
May never faint or weary be.

Hark to the herald of the morn,
Who vigil through the dark has borne,
Still separating night from night,
To travellers a pledge of light.

The day-star hears, and at the call
Looses the sky from night's grim thrall,
While roaming bandits at the word
From mischief cease and sheathe the sword.'

Symmachus (345–405)

Ambrose stands for the new militant Christianity :
Quintus Aurelius Symmachus, prefect of Rome and

19

consul 391, is one of the last champions of Paganism.
For three centuries the Symmachi were among the
most prominent of the great Roman families, and this
Symmachus is their typical representative in literature. In his writings we see clearly what Paganism
really meant for its supporters. Their true divinity
was not Jupiter nor any other of the Olympians, but
'Roma,' the personified goddess of the imperial city.
Their religion was another form of their love of country,
and it seemed to them that they were fighting against
a doctrinaire internationalism which took no account
of Rome's glorious history. The weakness of their
position was that it had no stable roots in the present
and no sure prospects in the future, and it led inevitably
to a useless brooding over the past. The huge collection
of Symmachus' letters, for example, which his son
edited, is a monument of triviality, as far inferior to
the letters of Pliny the Younger as Pliny's are to those
of Cicero. As Gibbon says: 'The luxuriancy of
Symmachus consists in barren leaves, without fruit
and even without flowers.' Nor are the panegyrics he
addressed to the various emperors of his time of much
value; there is an abundance of florid rhetoric in
them but little of reality. The only section of his
works that as literature deserve attention are the
Relationes, the reports which as prefect Symmachus
presented to the Emperor; and among them especially
the third *Relatio* dealing with the long conflict between
the Christian and pagan senators over the removal of
the Altar of Victory from the Senate House. Of
that conflict we have accounts from the other side by
Ambrose and Prudentius; but although Symmachus
was defeated on this occasion he fairly held his own
in argument, and there are passages of real eloquence
in his report:

'Let us suppose,' he says, 'that Rome is standing here, and using these words: "Most excellent princes, fathers of your country, respect my years, for I have reached them by pious worship; let me enjoy our ancestral ceremonies, for I like them well; let me live in my own way, for I am no slave. This worship brought the world under my laws, these rites drove Hannibal from my walls and the Gauls from the Capitol. Was I preserved for this, that in my old age I should be censured? I will consider what this rite is which you think should be established. But it is too late to try and correct the aged; the attempt is an insult. Therefore I ask that the gods of our country, our native deities, should be left in peace." What all men worship should fairly be considered one. We gaze at the same stars, the heavens are common to all, the same universe wraps us round. What matters the system of philosophy by which a man seeks for the truth? There is no one road that leads to the great mystery.'

Ausonius (310– c. 400)

An elder contemporary of Ambrose and living in as close connection with the imperial family was Decimus Magnus Ausonius, born at Bordeaux sometime between the years 310 and 320. If Ambrose is the first of medieval hymn-writers, Ausonius for his part may be considered the first of medieval secular poets. With him there is a definite break in the classical tradition, and we see in his verse the feature that most clearly distinguishes medieval from classical literature. As the State lost its predominant position the individual became more important, and it was the individual's life in another world rather than his short existence on this earth that seemed to deserve serious attention. Secular poetry therefore abdicated the high patriotic functions with which in the past it had been invested, and instead of instructing its readers it merely sought to divert them.

Of this new trend of thought and view of poetry Ausonius is one of the first examples. He is mildly interested in many things, but his chief interest is in himself; and the history of his life is so closely connected with the history of his writings that they may well be considered together. The poem that comes first in most editions of his writings gives us, with much superfluous verbiage, the chief facts. His father was a doctor at Bordeaux, his mother of Æduan descent; he himself after teaching rhetoric for some years was appointed tutor to Gratian, son of the Emperor Valentinian I, and when his pupil ascended the throne he, like Seneca before him, became an important person at court and was finally raised to the consulship. So far this first poem. Fuller details of his early days appear in the twenty-six poems written in honour of the professors of Bordeaux and in the *Parentalia*, a collection of thirty pieces commemorating his dead relatives, his sisters, his cousins and his aunts and even his daughter's mother-in-law. These two collections were published together in 385, late in his life, and from them we learn that the boy for some unknown reason was brought up by his stern grandmother and a maiden aunt; that he was educated at Bordeaux and after learning Greek with some difficulty passed as a student of rhetoric into the university there before proceeding to Toulouse where his uncle was professor. From Toulouse he returned as a teacher to his native town, and married the daughter of a leading citizen. To his wife Lucana Sabina the best of his hundred and twelve epigrams is written :

> ' As we have lived, dear wife, so let us stay
> Nor heed the changes of the passing day,
> And still our lovers' names of old employ,
> You be " my girl " and I remain " your boy." '

Unfortunately Sabina died after bearing three children, and Ausonius remained a widower for the rest of his days, although he seems to have found some consolation in the society of the youthful Bissula, a captive maiden given him as his share of the spoil in the German War, to which in company with Gratian and Valentinian he went in 368. To this campaign Epigrams 28 and 31 refer; Bissula appears in the six poems that bear her name, and probably also in Epigram 89 :

> ' I would have my mistress be
> Pert and pretty, gay and free.'

In 375 Ausonius became quæstor, and on Gratian's accession to the throne at the end of that year he rose rapidly to the highest offices of state, drawing after him his father, his son, his son-in-law, and his nephew. In 378 he was made prefect of Gaul, and the next year obtained the consulship, an honour which forms the theme of the third, fifth and sixth poems in the *Domestica*, and is discussed at prodigious length in the prose *Gratiarum Actio*, a letter of thanks addressed to the young Emperor in person. In 383, however, there came a change of fortune : the British legions revolted, Gratian was killed at Lyons, and the usurper Maximus ascended the throne. During his reign Ausonius seems to have lived at Trèves, where he probably wrote the *Cupid Crucified*, and when Maximus was overthrown by Theodosius in 388 the poet retired to his country estate near Bordeaux and devoted himself to literary composition. The *List of Famous Cities*, the *Technopaignion*, and the *Masque of the Seven Sages*, were all written in the following years, and to this period also belong the ' Epistles ' in prose and verse, which give us such a vivid picture of his neighbour, the country squire Theon, and his Greek bailiff Philo ' who makes himself rich and his

master poor '. Bordeaux itself he rarely visited, for, as
he says in the Sixth Epistle, ' The sight of its crowds,
its noisy streets, and its brawling cross-roads fills me
with disgust ' ; and it was in his country retreat that
towards the end of the century he died.

Most of Ausonius' chief poems have now been
mentioned : two, however, still remain to be described.
The *Mosella*, in nearly five hundred hexameters, is
his longest and most ambitious effort, and on the
whole is the most successful of his works. The piece
begins with an itinerary of the poet's journey, probably
in the course of the German War, from Bingen to
Neumagen, where he has his first view of the Moselle
with its vine-clad hills and grass-grown banks. He
bursts into eulogy :

> ' Ships sail thee as on ocean's waves,
> Thou hast a river's downward course,
> A channel's fretful speed, thy stream
> Is stainless as a fountain's source,
> And as a lake profound and deep :
> The charms we find combined in thee
> Of channel, river, fountain-head,
> Of glassy lake and tidal sea.'

An account of the two modes of navigation up and
down stream follows, and then comes a picture of the
river-bed :

> ' The golden sand in furrows lies
> As o'er it sweeps thy rippling tide,
> And water grasses in the depths
> Of emerald sway from side to side.
> The plants beneath their native waves
> Endure the buffets of the stream,
> And where red gravel stains the moss,
> Bright pebbles through its covering gleam.

Less in accordance with modern taste is the catalogue

of fish that Ausonius inserts next. But this leads up to a really beautiful description of the riverside :

> ' What colours then are on thy wave
> When evening with its shades draws nigh,
> And on Mosella's liquid stream,
> The verdant hills reflected lie.
> Upon thy rippling glass we see
> The semblance of the distant vine
> Whose tendrils with the bursting grapes
> Beneath the surface intertwine.'

This fair sight suggests to Ausonius, as it might have suggested to Wordsworth, a vision of the nymphs and the satyrs who frolic in the stream ; and then more soberly he proceeds to tell of the various aquatic sports which humble mortals there enjoy. Then we have an elaborate description of the country-villas which line the river-banks, together with a list of the tributary streams ; and so at last Ausonius brings the Moselle to the Rhine, and with one final panegyric the poem ends.

Even more characteristic of Ausonius than the *Mosella* is the *Ephemeris*, the ' Diary of a Day's Business ' ; and it is a signal misfortune that, while we have so much of his verse that we could well spare, the *Ephemeris*, owing to a gap in the manuscript, is incomplete. The first of the six pieces that remain is in sapphics, and describes the poet's awakening. He calls to his valet but receives no answer, and in the next piece changes to a livelier iambic measure :

> ' Jump up, my lad, and skip about !
> Come, bring me quick my slippers.'

After the morning ablutions, Ausonius remembers his duty as a professing Christian, and the next poem is a long prayer in stately hexameters :

25

'Almighty God, by no sense seen save by the worship of the mind,
　Thou whom the pious learn to know, but evil men can never find.'

This prayer extends to eighty-five lines, and then Ausonius, with a sigh of relief, turns again to business in iambics :

'Enough of prayer to God I've made,
　Although enough can ne'er be paid
　　By a poor wretched sinner.
Quick, boy, my coat, I must go down
In haste to greet my friends in town
　Who are coming here to dinner.'

In the fifth poem the servant is sent off with the invitations ; in the sixth, an elegiac piece, the poet has an interview with his cook, whom he reminds of some past failures ; and then unfortunately some leaves in the archetype have been torn away, and we are left to imagine the rest of the day's proceedings.

It is easy to criticise and depreciate Ausonius, for he himself sets an example. 'I know,' he says at the beginning of the *Parentalia*, 'that my readers will yawn over my poor verses. Such is their usual fate, and they deserve it.' Of the *Griphus* he writes : 'Hidden among my rubbish was a miserable little book : would to Heaven it had stayed there, and not damned itself, like the mouse, by coming into the light.' As for the *Nuptial Cento*, in which he certainly reaches his lowest level, its preface begins : 'Read this if you think fit : but it is a worthless trifle, ill-shaped and unpolished, without a spark of wit or the ripeness that deliberation gives.' Allowances have to be made for Ausonius, and it must be granted that he wrote—or rather that he published—far too much verse. But his extreme ingenuity deserves our admiration. Who but Ausonius could have written a poem

26

of forty-two lines, each consisting of five words, the
first word of one syllable, the second of two, the
third of three, the fourth of four, and the fifth of
five ? Who but he could have picked out all the
monosyllabic nouns in Latin and constructed 164 hexameters with a fresh monosyllable at the end of each ?
The *Parentalia* is a sufficient *tour de force*, but even
that is surpassed by the *Griphus*, ' A riddle of the
number three,' and to those who only look for amusement in poetry Ausonius offers it in full measure.

Prudentius (348–405)

Prudentius like Ausonius is a Christian and a poet,
but it would be difficult to find two men whose
writings are more unlike. The difference goes deep
and has its roots in temperament, training and nationality. Ausonius is essentially a dilettante and passes
through life like a child, now playing with one toy and
now with another : Prudentius is a grave and severe
artist, sure of his material and resolved to use his
talents to a high and worthy purpose. Ausonius
lived most of his life in the class-rooms of universities
and the ante-chambers of kings ; Prudentius passed
his days far from Rome and was a provincial magistrate,
' dispensing justice to the good and terrifying evil-doers.'
Finally, Prudentius was a native of Spain, the country
that is still the most religious in Europe : Ausonius
was born in Gaul, and from his fatherland to-day most
religious orders have been expelled.

Aurelius Prudentius Clemens was born 348 in the
province of Hispania Tarraconensis, his native town
probably being Saragossa. His life was uneventful
and known to us chiefly by the account he gives in
the verse preface to his poems. He tells us there how
as a child he shrank from his teacher's whizzing cane,

how he was trained in the falsehoods of rhetoric, and
how after a wanton youth he became first an advocate
and then a magistrate. Late in his life the Emperor
Theodosius bestowed upon him some court office, and
it was possibly on this occasion that he paid the visit
to Rome which inspired the admiring lines :

> ' As beasts from men, as dumb from those who speak,
> As from the good who God's commandments seek
> Differ the foolish heathen, so Rome stands,
> Alone in pride above barbarian lands.'

During that visit he realised that he was growing
old, for he was then in his fifty-seventh year, and his
gray hairs decided him to devote the rest of his life
to the service of the Most High :

> ' The end draws near : my soul, awake,
> And from thee folly's trappings shake
> And sin's foul chains.
> If works avail not, raise thy voice
> To sing God's praises, and rejoice
> In pious strains.'

So it was that Prudentius began the great series of
religious poems which supplied a new inspiration to
Latin verse. The simplest division of them is by
form, according as they are in hexameters or in lyric
metres. Which section is the more attractive is partly
a matter of taste, but most readers give the preference
to the twelve lyrics known as the *Kathemerina*, ' The
Christian's Day.' These are hymns in the Greek and
not in the English sense of the word : they are long
lyrical poems, but they are not meant, as Ambrose's
hymns were, for congregational singing. Extracts from
them, however, found their way into the Breviary and
thence into the English Hymnal. From the Epiphany

hymn, for example, come the beautiful lines on the
Innocents ' Salvete flores martyrum ' :

> ' All hail, ye little Martyr flowers,
> Sweet rosebuds cut in dawning hours !
> When Herod sought the Christ to find
> Ye fell as bloom before the wind.
>
> First victims of the Martyr bands,
> With crowns and palms in tender hands,
> Around the very altar, gay
> And innocent, ye seem to play.'

From the ' Hymn for every hour ' also comes the
well-known processional; ' Corde natus ex parentis,
ante mundi exordium ' :

> ' Of the Father's heart begotten,
> Ere the world from chaos rose,
> He is Alpha : from that Fountain
> All that is and hath been flows ;
> He is Omega, of all things
> Yet to come the mystic Close.'

And even more beautiful than these is the lovely
' Hymn for the Burial of the Dead ' :

> ' Iam mœsta quiesce querela,
> Lacrimas suspendite, matres,
> Nullus sua pignora plangat,
> Mors hæc reparatio vitæ est,'

a hymn which Archbishop Trench rightly called the
crowning glory of Prudentius' verse.

His other lyrical work is the *Peri Stephanon*, ' Songs
of the Martyrs' Crowns ' ; fourteen long pieces in
various metres, written in honour of Spanish, African
and Roman martyrs. Though this book lacks the
lyrical charm of the *Kathemerina*, it is important both
in the history of literature and in the history of the
Church. It is a combination of the epic and lyric

which foreshadows the ballad, and in it are laid down the main lines of the martyr cult, which was to spread so widely after Prudentius' time. There is perhaps rather too much rhetoric in it and too much polemical argument, but in the most successful pieces, the stories, for instance, of the Spanish saint Lawrence, of Eulalia, the child martyr of Emerita, and of Cassian, the schoolmaster stabbed to death by his pupils' pens, there are many passages of wonderfully vivid narrative.

The remaining five books of Prudentius are in hexameters and are purely didactic. The authorship of the *Dittochæon*, a series of short descriptions of pictures, has been disputed, but there is no doubt concerning the other four. The *Hamartigenia*, ' The birth of sin,' is a fierce attack, following Tertullian, on the heresy of the Marcionites, whose leader is compared to Cain. The *Apotheosis*, a poem of over a thousand lines, refutes both Jews and heretics, and seeks to establish the true doctrine of the incarnation. More important and far more popular is the *Psychomachia*, the first Christian allegory, and one of the chief source books for medieval art. The ' Soul's Conflict ' is an epic of battle between personified Virtues and Vices, Modesty against Lust, Pride against Humility, Patience against Anger, etc. : each contest is described in Virgilian manner and in each virtue triumphs. Lastly we have the poem *Against Symmachus*, inspired by the affair of the Altar of Victory, which assails the whole system of paganism of which Symmachus was the representative.

Paulinus of Nola (353–431)

One of the most striking features of this period is the diversity of countries from which its writers are drawn. Augustine and Claudian came to Rome from Africa, Jerome from Pannonia, Prudentius from Spain; Ambrose, Ausonius, and Paulinus were all Gauls by birth, the latter two both natives of the same town of Bordeaux. The story of the long association between the two compatriots and how at last it was broken has a romantic interest, but it is only one episode in Paulinus' life. The eldest son of a rich Gallic family he was marked out for an official career, and after holding many minor posts he became consul in 378 and then governor of Campania. Thus far his career differed little from that of many other wealthy Romans, but then a change came. He married a Spanish lady Therasia, and soon afterwards realised the true meaning of Christianity in a sense that Ausonius could never understand. Gradually he sold his great estates for the benefit of the poor, and at last abandoning the world settled down with his wife at the shrine of St Felix in Campania. The grateful citizens of Nola insisted on making him their bishop, and at Nola, tending his garden and his people, he lived peacefully until his death in 431.

Paulinus is not a strong character; if he had been he would not have been Ausonius' favourite pupil nor probably so fervent a disciple of Martin of Tours; but he is very attractive, and the charm of his personality is reflected in his letters and poems, which each fills one volume in Hartel's Vienna edition. It is true that opinions differ as to the literary merit of his fifty-one letters, and some critics find them verbose and tedious. But they give a vivid picture of a quiet monastic life, and the thirty-ninth letter may be taken as typical of the rest. Addressed to Aper and Amanda it is written round a verse of the prophet Joel, and is a delightful blend of piety and horticulture which scarcely needs its concluding apology: ' I am afraid that I shall weary you with my loquacity and prove a greater nuisance than any plague of locusts and caterpillars.'

Whatever we may think of Paulinus' letters, there can be no doubt of the merits of his poems, which come only second to Prudentius in Christian verse. Of them we now have thirty-three, the greater part birthday poems written each year on the anniversary of St Felix :

> ' Ver avibus voces aperit, mea lingua suum ver
> Natalem Felicis habet.'

There is also a beautiful Epithalamium addressed to two young Christians, which should be compared with the wedding songs of Catullus and Joannes Secundus. Another charming piece is the long elegy of over six hundred lines written to console the parents of the boy Celsus. Best of all is the tenth poem, a mixture of elegiac, lyric, and hexameter verse, in which Paulinus tries to explain to Ausonius the reasons for his change of life and his abandonment of his old literary interests :

> ' The heart that Christ has made his own
>   Will never of Apollo sing,
>   Nor to the pagan Muses give
>   A poet's offering.
>
>   Another impulse in my soul
>   Holds now the guiding place
>   And bids me rule my altered path
>   By a diviner grace.'

Claudian (355– c. 410)

From among the Christian poets of his time the pagan Claudian stands out a lonely and rather pathetic figure; 'Poeta quidem eximius sed paganus pervicacissimus,' Orosius calls him, 'A great poet but a very obstinate pagan.' He was born in Egypt at Alexandria some time between 350 and 360, his contemporary and fellow-townsman being Palladas the satirical poet of the Greek Anthology. His own native tongue probably was Greek, and it is possible that he is the author of the two epigrams in the Ninth Book of the Anthology which are attributed to a Claudian. But however that may be, he soon abandoned Greek and the poems that have made his name famous are in Latin, although the greatest of them is in the short epic style which the Alexandrian school always especially cultivated.

In 395, when after the death of Theodosius the court became less definitely hostile to paganism, Claudian came to Rome and began the long series of poems that deal with the disastrous wars of the ten years between 395 and 404. In them appear most of the chief characters of the time; the feeble Emperor Honorius, Rufinus the minister in charge of the Eastern provinces of Italy and his successor the eunuch Eutropius, Stilicho the great Vandal general, his wife Serena, and his daughter Maria, for whose marriage with Honorius Claudian wrote both an epithalamium and also a set of Fescennine verses. It would seem indeed that in spite of his paganism Claudian was the official court poet, and we know from an inscription found in Trajan's forum—'Claudio Claudiano prægloriosissimo poetarum '—that as a reward for his services he received patrician rank and the honour of a public statue.

In these poems, which have a considerable historical value, Claudian shows a quite uncourtier-like love of truth. He keeps closely to facts in his narrative, and only allows his personal feelings full play when it is a question of imputing motives and giving reasons for action. To Honorius he is polite without enthusiasm, but for Stilicho, the saviour of Italy, he has an un-

c

bounded admiration, and an equally unbounded hatred of Rufinus and Eutropius. There is, of course, a certain monotony in the tale of war and intrigue with which Claudian has to deal, but quite frequently he rises to real grandeur. Very striking, for example, is the scene at the beginning of the *De Bello Gildonico*. The goddess Rome has made her way to Olympus, her cheeks pale, her eyes sunken, and as she falls at the knees of Jove she utters her lamentable prayer :

> ' Great Jove, if still the auguries hold good
> That blessed my battlements when first they stood ;
> If still the Sibyl's ancient prophecies
> Unchanged remain, and thou dost not despise
> Tarpeia's rock, to-day on bended knee
> I make my prayer as suppliant to thee.
> I ask not that our consul should crush down
> Araxes' fury, nor that Susa's town
> Should bow submissive to the lictor's rod,
> Nor that our eagle's wings outstretched should nod
> O'er the Red Sea. All this before you gave :
> To-day it is for mercy that I crave.
> Great Father, give us food, nor let us die,
> Wasted and spent by famine's misery.'

This poem was written in the summer of 398 when preparations were being hastily made for war against Gildo. From it we see only too plainly the straits to which the imperial city was reduced. ' If we must perish,' cries the poet, ' let us at least perish by the sword, not by slow starvation.'

Fortunately even in the midst of war and turmoil there are some bright spots, some people who live quiet lives, and Claudian himself supplies a corrective to his darker pictures in some of his shorter poems. Among these is the account of the old farmer of Verona, ' Felix qui patriis ævum transegit in agris,' a piece which

in versification equals Tibullus, and in sentiment recalls
the Tarentine gardener of the Fourth Georgic :

' Happy the man whose hopes and fears
    A few paternal acres bound,
    Who lives in childhood and in age
        On his own ground.

    The staff that helps him marks the sand
    Where as a babe he used to lie,
    And from his cottage porch he counts
        The years go by. . . .

    Unskilled in lawyer's arts he stays
    A stranger to the neighbouring town,
    And free from smoking chimneys calls
        The sky his own.

    He reckons, not by consuls' names,
    But by the crops the seasons bring,
    He knows the autumn by its fruit,
        By flowers the spring. . . .

    He and the monarchs of the wood
    Together in their age agree ;
    The acorn that he planted once
        He sees a tree.

    But still his limbs are firm and hale,
    And though he is a grandsire now
    His children's children at his knee
        His strength allow.

    Let others sail to distant lands
    And seek for gold 'mid toil and strife,
    They waste their days upon the road ;
        He lives his life.'

As this piece is an ' idyll,' a sketch in miniature, so
the ' Rape of Proserpine ' is an ' epyll,' a miniature
epic. Most of Claudian's poems can be dated, but it
is uncertain whether the *Raptus Proserpinæ* should be
put early or late, whether Claudian brought it with

him to Italy as part of his literary baggage or wrote
it at Ravenna to please the Emperor's court. It is
possible even that it was composed when Claudian
returned to Egypt in 405, after his marriage with a
rich lady of Alexandria, which is the last event in his
life of which we know. The poem is unfinished, but
that is no certain evidence of date ; on the whole, in
spite of its astonishing metrical skill, it seems a young
man's work.

As we have it now the ' Proserpine ' extends to
about eleven hundred lines divided into three books,
and its story is briefly this. Pluto in the nether world,
growing weary of single bliss, threatens to rebel against
his brother in heaven unless he be provided with a
wife. Jove acknowledges the justice of his complaint
and decrees that Proserpine, daughter of Ceres, shall
be his bride. Ceres for the moment has left her child
unguarded in Sicily while she is paying a visit to
Cybebe in Asia and Jove seizes the opportunity. In
the next book we see Proserpine gathering flowers on
Mount Henna, attended by Venus, Minerva, and Diana,
who have been sent down from heaven. Pluto appears
in his dark chariot, and in spite of the two virgin
goddesses, carries off the tearful maiden below the
earth. The third book opens with a council of all the
divinities of earth and sky, who are forbidden by
Jove to reveal to Ceres her daughter's dwelling-place
until she bestows on mortals the gift of corn. Meanwhile Ceres in a dream has seen her child languishing
in prison and returns in haste to Sicily. There she
discovers her loss and begins her search, which is still
continuing when the poem breaks off.

It will be seen that Claudian adds little of his own
invention to the Greek legend. The charm of the
' Proserpine ' depends not so much on incident as on

the beauty of its descriptions, the extreme art of its versification, and the rhetorical force of the speeches with which the narrative is diversified. It would be hard, for instance, outside Virgil to surpass the speech in which Pluto tries to comfort his unwilling captive.

> ' Her words, her comely grief that proud heart took,
> And Pluto felt the first faint throb of love.
> He wiped away her tears with his dark cloak
> And by soft speech in gentle pleading strove
> The pain of her sharp sorrow to remove.
> " Dream not of death, dear Proserpine," he cried ;
> " Nor people with vain fears this silent grove.
> A greater sceptre waits upon my bride
> And no unworthy lord shall sleep thy breast beside.
>
> Great Saturn's son am I : my lightest breath
> The fabric of the world must e'er obey :
> My power extends through all the void beneath.
> Think not that thou hast lost the light of day
> Or that no more thou wilt see the sun's clear ray.
> Stars of our own have we, and orbs more bright
> Than those that shone upon thy earthly way ;
> And thou wilt wonder at the Elysian light
> Wherein the pious dwell and ever know delight.
>
> Here is a golden age that doth surpass
> All that earth holds : what men gained once is ours
> For ever and a day. Soft meadow grass
> Will greet thy coming, and ambrosial flowers
> Fostered by balmy winds and vernal showers
> Through all the year, more beautiful, I trow,
> Than any thou didst pluck in Henna's bowers.
> And for thee, too, a wondrous tree doth grow
> Whose living metal gleams and curves the bending bough.
>
> It stands apart in darkness, and to thee
> Is consecrate for ever : thou shalt take
> Its autumn harvest for thy treasury
> And from its branches golden guerdon shake.

Nor is that all thy dowry. I will make
All living creatures thy commandments keep,
And 'neath thy will in dumb obedience quake ;
All that earth breeds, and air, and marshes deep,
And where the rushing tides of sea and river sweep.

Kings clothed in purple at thy feet shall fall,
Stripped of their pride and mingling with the host
Of squalid paupers. Death makes equal all.
The guilty then to thee shall pay the cost
And penalty of crime, in darkness tossed
And torment ; but the pious thou shalt save
And give them the repose they yearn for most.
Thou shalt be all-supreme : grim Fate as slave
Shall bend subservient to thee, and black Lethe's wave." '

The nearest thing to the ' Proserpine ' in Latin is
the ' Peleus and Thetis ' of Catullus ; the nearest
thing in English perhaps is Keats' ' Hyperion '; and a
comparison of the three poems may be recommended.

Donatus and the Grammarians

Claudian was the last in time of the fourth-century
poets, the last close follower of the ancient tradition,
and it will be appropriate to pass immediately from
him to the group of learned scholars who spent their
lives in the critical studies of the earlier Latin master-
pieces. Chief among them is Jerome's teacher, Ælius
Donatus, and with him come Victorinus, Servius,
Charisius and Diomedes. Victorinus was a philosopher,
a rhetorician, and, after his conversion to Christianity,
a theologian ; but his chief work is his long treatise
on metre. Servius is best known for his commentary
on Virgil, a vast repertory of mythological and historical
knowledge, which has come down to us in two versions ;
and he also wrote on grammar. Charisius and Diomedes,
whose writings fill nearly six hundred pages in Keil's
Grammatica Latini, were near contemporaries, and

38

as they both depend largely on Varro and Suetonius for their materials, they are often in verbal agreement. Their treatises, though valuable in themselves, are now only of technical interest ; but the *Ars Grammatica* of Donatus has a greater and more permanent value.

Upon Donatus all our Latin grammars are based and his *Ars* was in so unique a sense the medieval Latin text-book that a ' Donat ' in Chaucer's English is synonymous with a grammatical lesson. We have the book now in a longer and a shorter form ; the longer, the *Ars Grammatica* proper, in thirty-five pages, the shorter in eleven. The longer edition pays more attention to syntax and less to accidence, and concludes with ten pages on barbarisms, solecisms, the seventeen figures of speech, and the thirteen tropes. The shorter edition, *De partibus orationis Ars minor*, is severely practical, and an admirable guide : ' qui nescit partes in vanum tendit ad artes.' It begins thus :

' Partes orationis quot sunt ? Octo. Quæ ? Nomen, præ-nomen, verbum, adverbium, participium, conjunctio, præpositio, interjectio.'

Then follow declensions of *hic magister*, etc., and the conjugation of the verb *lego*, active and passive, which fills two pages. The other parts of speech are then taken and the last paragraph is this :

' De Interjectione.
' Interjectio quid est ? Pars orationis significans mentis affectum voce incondita. Interjectio quo accidit ? Tantum significatio. Signi-ficatio interjectionis in quo est ? Quia aut lætitiam significamus, ut evax, aut dolorem, ut heu, aut admirationem, ut papæ, aut metum, ut attat, et si qua sunt similia.'

Macrobius (fl. 375)

Macrobius is a scholar of another type from the grammarians ; a polymath, but one nearer to Athenæus than to Aristotle, a Robert Burton rather than a Richard Bentley. His *Saturnalia* is a Latin equivalent of the *Deipnosophists* and the *Anatomy of Melancholy*, and though it is inferior to those vast mines of miscellaneous knowledge it contains a very large amount of interesting information. Its framework is the same as that used by Plato, Athenæus and Aulus Gellius, and it purports to be the record of the conversations that took place at the table of the Roman patrician Prætextatus during the days of the Feast of Saturn. The interlocutors are the host himself, an antiquarian of some distinction who may have written the treatise ' On the ten categories ' sometimes attributed to Augustine ; Servius the commentator on Virgil, then quite a young man ; Albinus, the grandfather of Jerome's little friend Paula ; Arienus, translator of the ' Phænomena ' of Aratus ; Arianus, author of a Latin metrical version of Æsop's Fables ; Symmachus, Flavian, Evangelus, and several others. Macrobius himself does not appear, and of him we know very little. He may have been the Macrobius who was prefect of Spain in 399, but he may not. All that is certain is that he flourished towards the end of the fourth century, and that he was not an Italian by birth ; for he says in his preface that he would excuse himself for the lack of native elegance in his style were it not that he remembered Cato's advice : " Never apologise for a thing which you are not obliged to do."

As we have it now the *Saturnalia* is incomplete, and its seven books fall into two divisions. The middle section, Books Four, Five and Six, is literary, and deals with Virgil under various aspects. Book Four discusses his pathos, Book Five compares him with Homer, Book Six gives a list of his borrowings from earlier Latin poets, especially Ennius and Lucretius.

All these three books are illustrated by copious quotations in Latin and Greek. The other four books are antiquarian and historical in their interest. Book One begins with a discussion of the Feast of Saturn, from which the work takes its name. This leads to the topic of slaves, who at that feast had special licence, and is followed by a long account of the Roman Calendar, the months of the year and the notable days in each month, the book concluding with an elaborate disquisition on the various names of Apollo. Book Two consists chiefly of a collection of impromptu witticisms, attributed mainly to Cicero, Augustus and his daughter Julia. None of them are quite as good as Cæsar's ' nunquam fugiens respexeris,' but some are very clever. The best perhaps is a classical example of the biter bit. A certain young provincial was noticed to bear a remarkable likeness to Augustus. The President summoned him to his house and jestingly asked if his mother had ever visited Rome. ' No,' replied the youth, ' but my father came here frequently.'

Book Three is more serious, and begins by examining the meaning of the words ' sacer,' ' profanus,' ' sanctus,' ' religiosus,' before describing different aspects of Roman religion. Its second theme is the luxury of the ancients, and especially the luxury of their feasts. Book Seven, after a digression on jests with many examples, turns to natural science, and a series of questions occupies the rest of its space. The first three may serve as examples : ' Is a simple or a varied diet the better ? ' ' Is wine naturally hot or cold ? ' ' Are women by nature warmer than men ? ' This last is answered in the affirmative, the convincing proof being that women wear less clothes. This brief analysis will show the diversity of subjects in the *Saturnalia*, which make it the best Latin miscellany

41

after the 'Attic Nights' of Aulus Gellius. We have also by Macrobius a long commentary on Cicero's *Somnium Scipionis*, but this is comparatively uninteresting.

Martianus Capella (fl. 375)

Of Macrobius we know little; of Martianus Capella we know even less. When we have said that he was an advocate, that he had a son, and that he lived in Africa before the Vandals overthrew the Roman Government in 429, we have said all. Even his date is quite uncertain. He is usually put in the early fifth century, but Adolf Dick, his latest Editor, inclines to place him in the later years of the third. The evidence, however, on which Dick relies is mainly negative; he is not mentioned by any author earlier than Fulgentius (480–550), who took him as his model in his *Mythologicon*; and on the whole it seems safer to put him with Macrobius at the end of the fourth century.

In the fame of his one book Martianus finds more than adequate compensation for the obscurity of his life. The *De Nuptiis Philologiæ et Mercurii*, 'The Marriage of Business and Learning,' was in medieval times the foundation of all teaching; and when Latin had once been learned from Donatus, it was the chief, and often the only, school book. Upon it was based the Trivium and the Quadrivium of the seven liberal arts which constituted education :

'Gram. loquitur; Dia. vera docet; Rhet. verba colorat;
  Mus. canit; Ar. numerat; Ge. ponderat; Ast. colit astra.'

The *De Nuptiis* is written in the form of an allegory in nine books, representing the marriage of Mercury and Philologia, the bridesmaids being the seven liberal arts. On the analogy of Varro's *Satura Menippea* it is in prose and verse, and the framework is briefly this. Mercury resolves to marry, and, after rejecting several fair ladies, on the advice of Virtus consults Apollo, who warmly recommends a *doctissima virgo* named Philologia. The bride is carried up to heaven, where each of the nine Muses in turn welcome her with a song and then, attended by Prudence, Justice, Temperance and most of the other virtues, she appears before the heavenly Senate, receives deification, and enters into the married state. All this occupies the first two books ; the remaining seven are ostensibly a description of the seven bridesmaids, Grammar, Dialectic, Rhetoric, Geometry, Arithmetic, Astronomy, Music ; in reality they are a rather dry enumeration of technical details concerning the seven arts which the bridesmaids personify.

Martianus meant his book to be a handbook of useful knowledge, a practical help to teachers : and all teachers after his time welcomed his aid. The *De Nuptiis* on its business side is only a compendium ; but it was the compendium which survived, while the original authorities were allowed to perish. As for the allegory and the verse, they form the honey which Martianus meant to disguise the taste of his medicine ; and if the honey has now lost most of its flavour that is partly the effect of time.

Vegetius (fl. 375)

What Martianus Capella does so copiously for the liberal arts Vegetius Renatus attempts to do on a much smaller scale for the art of warfare. His *Epitoma Rei Militaris* is a short book, about the same length as the Greek treatise by Æneas Tacticus and our manual of infantry training. Vegetius is not a genius, but he is practical and quite instructive. The first of his four sections deals with the recruit, his enrolment and training in the use of weapons and tools; and then proceeds to the situation and fortification of camps. The second section describes the organisation of the legion, its cohorts and auxiliaries, together with the duties of its various officers and subordinate ranks. In the third we come to armies, their sanitation, commissariat and discipline; the precautions to be taken before fighting a battle and the conduct of a battle itself. The fourth gives directions for fortifying cities, withstanding a siege, and constructing the different engines used in siege warfare; and the book ends with a brief account of naval tactics. Vegetius takes as motto for his book the sentence ' In battles it is not numbers and untrained valour so much as skill and training that give victory '; and he honestly tries to instruct his contemporaries in military matters. That he does not rise to the height of his subject is not altogether his own fault; but his book would be more useful to us if he had gone more fully into historical details.

Eutropius (fl. 370)

There are two sorts of historians, those who are read for their facts and those who are read for their style; and of both kinds the fourth century supplies us with good examples in Eutropius and Ammianus Marcellinus. Eutropius, who flourished in the reign of the Emperor Valens (364–378), is an author simple in his elegance, and for many generations of schoolboys he has served as an introduction to Latin prose. His *Breviarium ab urbe condita* is a brief account in ten short books of Roman history from the beginning to the death of the Emperor Jovian in 364, the first six taking us from Romulus to Julius Cæsar, the last four dealing with the Empire. The materials are drawn from one of those abridgements of Livy which had at this time largely superseded the original work, from Suetonius and from the *Scriptores historiæ augustæ;* and they are used with considerable skill. Eutropius contributes little to our historical knowledge, but his narrative is always clear, and when he comes to his own times he is commendably impartial. He was a pagan and accompanied the Emperor Julian on his Parthian campaign, but the portraits he gives of Constantine and Julian in his tenth book show little bias. Of Constantine he says : ' In the first period of his reign he deserves to rank with our best emperors, in the second with those of the middle kind. In him shone forth countless virtues of mind and body. He was most ambitious of military fame, and fortunate in his wars ; but his own energy was equal to his good fortune.' Of Julian this : ' He deserved to be deified, for he was a man of extreme calmness of mind. In the first years of his rule he showed great moderation, although somewhat inclined to severe measures if he suspected treachery. Otherwise he was of gentle character and more fortunate in civil than in foreign war.' The practical character of the *Breviarium* ensured its popularity from the first. It was almost immediately made the basis of a similar history by Festus ; it was translated into Greek ; Jerome and Orosius drew freely from it ; and in the eighth century it served Paul the Deacon as the foundation for his long *Historia Miscella.*

Sulpicius Severus (365–425)

Less familiar to us than Eutropius, but of equal merit with him as a stylist, is Sulpicius Severus, who wrote a life of St Martin of Tours and also a Christian universal history from the creation of the world down to his own time. Both books are good, although they are of very different character. The biography of St Martin, at whose bidding Sulpicius took up the monastic life, with its supplementary dialogues, gives us a vivid picture of the great Gallic saint, his struggles with the Devil in person, his miracles of healing and resurrection, and his visions of the approaching end of the world. How far the account is based on reality we need not now consider, nor is it necessary to follow Gibbon in his surprise that 'facts adapted to the grossest barbarism should be narrated in a style not unworthy of the Augustan Age': as a work of art the ' Life ' is undeniably a success. So also in a milder way is the ' History ' (*Chronicorum Libri duo*), an epitome of Scripture history, together with a brief account of the ten persecutions of the Church under the Empire and of the troubles caused by Arius and Priscillian. It is clear and lucid, accurate and concise; in fact a model of historical narrative for general reading.

Ammianus Marcellinus (330–400)

The third historian of this period, Ammianus Marcellinus of Antioch, lacks the graces of style which Eutropius and Sulpicius possess, but in other qualities is far their superior. After a long and honourable career in the Roman army, where he served with distinction in Gaul, Germany, and Persia, he employed his later years in writing a continuation of Tacitus' *Histories*, beginning with the reign of Nerva in 96 and ending with the death of Valens in 378. His work was originally in thirty-one books, but of them we now have only the last eighteen, which deal fully with the events of the twenty-five years between 353 and 378, while the lost thirteen books must have given a much more summary account of two and a half centuries. What remains is a record of the writer's own times, a record of the highest value, sober, impartial, and based on personal knowledge. He himself gives its true character in his last words : ' All this I, a soldier in my day and a Greek, have set forth according to the measure of my strength. My work professes truth, and never wittingly, I think, have I dared to corrupt it by silence or falsehood. Let others write of what I have left, better men than I am, in the flower of life and learning.'

To all lovers of military history Ammianus may be heartily recommended, for his accounts of sieges, marches, and battles have that touch of intimate reality which can only be given by an experienced soldier. The description, for example, of Roman artillery in Book 23, the catapult, the scorpion and the ram, is a model of accurate observation. Equally good, and less technical, is the narrative in Book 18 of the siege of Amid by the Persian King Sapor, whose ' iron cavalry filled the plains and hills around, so that every place in sight glittered with starry arms.' Ammianus himself was in the town with two Celtic legions, but when at last the Persians burst in and the carnage began, he was fortunate enough to escape in the darkness. As a pendant to this may be put the description of the evacuation of Nisibis by its terrified inhabitants ; and, as an example of the judicious impartiality which so commended Ammianus to Gibbon's favour, the account which our pagan author gives of the Christians' internal dissensions.

' Damasus and Ursinus went beyond all human bounds in their eagerness to seize the bishop's chair. A fierce partisan contest

47

ensued, and the supporters of either faction boldly faced the danger of wounds and death. The palace intendant Viventius was not strong enough either to check these disturbances or abate their violence, and was at last compelled to retire from Rome to his suburban estate. In the final struggle Damasus won the day, for his partisans proved to be the superior in strength. It is a certain fact that in the church of Sicininus, which the Christians use as a meeting place, one hundred and thirty-seven dead bodies were found in one day, and it was with difficulty that the long protracted fury of their congregations was appeased. For myself, when I consider the display that is made in Rome, I cannot deny that candidates for the bishopric have some justification in straining all their powers of abuse when it comes to securing the object of their ambition. Success brings with it security and riches ; the bishop of Rome receives the offerings of wealthy ladies, he rides through the streets in a carriage, he wears magnificent clothes, and he keeps so lavish a table that his banquets surpass the entertainments of kings. These men, however, could be really happy, if, instead of making Rome's grandeur an excuse for their faults, they took pattern by some provincial priests that I know, who by their frugal diet, their humble dress and their downcast eyes are commended as pure and modest souls to the eternal deity and his true worshippers.'

This passage in the original is a fairly typical example of Ammianus' style, and perhaps even a translation may show that he is not so utterly unreadable as some critics have asserted him to be. His Latin can well be compared to Polybius' Greek : it lacks charm and ease ; and it is rather difficult to read because, we may imagine, the author found it rather difficult to write. But its difficulties have been exaggerated, and when Ammianus forgets his Greek and does not attempt to rival the rhetoricians of his day, he often succeeds in producing a clear and straightforward narrative.

Damasus (305–384)

It will be clear from the account in Ammianus that Damasus was not one of the most spiritually minded of bishops. He played, however, a magnificent part in the life of his age, and was both a versifier of some skill himself and also a munificent patron of all the arts. His enemies with some reason gave him the nickname of ' auriscalpius matronarum,' ' the matrons' eartickler,' and from the donations he received from his wealthy female devotees he was able to undertake a whole series of costly architectural schemes. He drained the Vatican hill, constructing for its flood water the channel that is still in use. He built the church of S. Lorenzo in Damazo and adorned it splendidly with gold and marble. He collected the relics of the martyrs from every land, and giving each its own shrine made the Catacombs of Rome the spectacle they are to-day. For these shrines he composed a set of epitaphs in verse, which were written out in the finest of hands by one of his protégés, Philocalus. He also composed longer poems, many still extant, in honour of particular saints and martyrs ; but his greatest literary merit is that he encouraged Jerome to translate the Bible, and to Jerome we may now turn.

Jerome (377-420)

Jerome—or to give him his real and highly significant name, Eusebius Sophronius Hieronymus, ' The pious puritan, the man of the Holy Word '—was born A.D. 345 at Stridon in Dalmatia, a small town near Aquileia, which was partly destroyed by the Goths during their invasion in 377. Like most young provincials of talent he was attracted to Rome and there studied rhetoric under Donatus, returning to Aquileia in 370. In that town he established his first society of ascetics, which lasted for just three years. Then some event—referred to by him variously as ' a sudden storm ' and ' a monstrous rending asunder '—broke up

D 49

the fellowship, and Jerome with a few of his closer associates went eastwards to Antioch. The adjacent desert of Chalcis was already full of hermits and Jerome soon joined their company, living in a bare cell, submitting himself to vigorous penances, and giving all his days to study and devotional exercise. He himself describes his experiences in a later letter :

' Oh, how often, when I was living in the desert, in that lonely waste, scorched by the burning sun, which affords to hermits a savage dwelling place, how often did I fancy myself surrounded by the pleasures of Rome. I used to sit alone ; for I was filled with bitterness. My unkempt limbs were covered in shapeless sackcloth; my skin through long neglect had become as rough and black as an Ethiopian's. Tears and groans were every day my portion ; and if sleep ever overcame my resistance and fell upon my eyes, I bruised my restless bones against the naked earth. Of food and drink I will not speak. Hermits have nothing but cold water even when they are sick, and for them it is sinful luxury to partake of cooked dishes. But though in my fear of hell I had condemned myself to this prison house, where my only companions were scorpions and wild beasts, I often found myself surrounded by bands of dancing girls. My face was pale with fasting ; but though my limbs were cold as ice, my mind was burning with desire, and the fires of lust kept bubbling up before me when my flesh was as good as dead.'

This went on for five years, and then Jerome returned to Antioch, was ordained presbyter by Bishop Paulinus, with him journeyed to Rome for the Church Council of 382, and in Rome remained for three years. There he became the friend and trusted adviser of Pope Damasus, who constantly consulted him on points of Biblical scholarship and commissioned him to write a revised version in Latin of the Psalms and the New Testament. He also found amid the wealth and luxury of the great city a few ardent souls, most of them women, who were ready to embrace and follow his ascetic teaching. One of his pupils was Paula the heiress of the great Æmilian family, who brought over her two daughters Blesilla and Eustochium. Another was the wealthy Marcella, at whose palace on the Aventine the little company used to meet for the study of Hebrew, to pray together, and to sing psalms. During this interval Jerome was perhaps as happy as he ever thought it right to be ; but the death of his protector Damasus unchained against him all the enmities that his rigorous virtues had challenged and his bitter sarcasms provoked. The new pope Siricius regarded him as a dangerous rival ; the mob were enraged by the sudden death of Blesilla, which was believed to have been caused by her prolonged fastings and penances ; the cry was raised ' The monks to the Tiber ' : and Jerome left Rome and Europe for ever.

Thus the second period of Jerome's life begins. He resolved that he would no longer sing the Lord's song in a strange land, and taking Paula and Eustochium with him he went once more to the East and settled down in Judea at Bethlehem, where he remained for the last thirty-four years of his existence. At Bethlehem he built a monastery and a convent, a church where both communities assembled for worship, and a hospice to lodge the pilgrims who came from all parts of the world to that holy ground. The administration of these various activities must have occupied a portion of his time, but the greater part of his energy was given at Bethlehem, as everywhere, to writing and study, and in the history of his later years the chief events are the innumerable books that flowed from his pen. Not that his life was peaceful, or that he passed his days in quietude. His own character always ensured a certain amount of friction ; his health was never of the best ; and the calm of his retreat was continually broken by rumours of wars and by the actual shock of barbarian invasion.

The sack of Rome in 410, for example, spread terror even in Palestine ; and it is from Jerome perhaps that we get the clearest idea of the consternation caused throughout the world by the fall of the imperial city. In the preface to his Ezekiel he writes : ' I was so stupefied and dismayed that day and night I could think of nothing but the welfare of the Roman community. It seemed to me that I was sharing the captivity of the saints and I could not open my lips until I received some more definite news. All the while, full of anxiety, I wavered between hope and despair, torturing myself with the misfortunes of others. But when I heard that the bright light of all the world was quenched, or rather that the Roman Empire had lost its head and that the whole universe had perished in one city: then, indeed, "*I became dumb and humbled myself and kept silence from good words.*"' And even two years later we see that the impression of horror had scarcely abated. Writing to Principia in 412 he says : ' A dreadful rumour came from the West. Rome was besieged and its citizens forced to buy their lives with gold. Then thus despoiled they were attacked a second time, so as to lose their lives as well as their substance. My voice sticks in my throat and even as I dictate this letter sobs choke my utterance. The city which had taken the whole world was itself taken ; nay, more, famine anticipated the sword, and but few citizens were left to be made prisoners. In their frenzy the starving people had recourse to hideous food and tore each other limb from limb that they might have flesh to eat. Even the mother did not spare the babe at her breast.'

Still, however troubled at heart Jerome might be, neither public calamity nor private sorrow could stop his labours for long. Paula passed away, her great fortune spent to the last penny in good works ; Marcella only survived the barbarities of the sack of Rome by a few days ; even Eustochium, although she was of a younger generation, succumbed to the rigours of the ascetic life. But the old man, nearly blind, and over seventy, was still working at his commentary on Jeremiah when his last illness came. He died 20th September, 420, and his body was buried beside Paula near the grotto of the Nativity at Bethlehem, in later days to be transferred and to be the cause of many a miracle at the church of Santa Maria Maggiore in Rome.

The works of Jerome, which fill eleven volumes in Migne, may be classed as follows :

(1) Bible translations from the Hebrew, Greek, and Chaldee.
(2) Commentaries on the Bible, either original or translated from the Greek of Origen.
(3) Books on Biblical subjects, such as the ' Glossary of Names in the Old Testament ' and the translation of Eusebius' ' Names of Hebrew places.'
(4) Biography : the ' Lives of the Hermits ' and the ' Book of Illustrious Men.'
(5) Controversy : ' Dialogue with a Luciferian ' ; ' Against Helvidius ' ; ' Against Jovinian ' ; ' Against Vigilantius ' ; ' Against Rufinus.'
(6) History : a translation, with additions, of the ' Chronicle of Eusebius.'
(7) Letters.

Of these seven sections the first includes the Vulgate, which is perhaps the most permanent memorial of himself that any one writer has ever left. Quotations from it should be unnecessary ; but the following few verses from the Zephaniah will show how great was its influence on Later Latin :

' Iuxta est dies Domini magnus,
iuxta est et velox nimis :
Vox diei Domini amara,
tribulabitur ibi fortis.

Dies iræ, dies illa,
 dies tribulationis et angustiæ,
 dies calamitatis et miseriæ,
 dies tenebrarum et caliginis,
 dies nebulæ et turbinis :
Dies tubæ et clangoris super civitates munitas
 et super angulos Excelsos.'

The second and third sections are chiefly of theological interest, but the fourth contains one very useful book in the *De viris illustribus*, and one very delightful book in the lives of the three hermits Paulus, Hilarion, and Malchus. Whether these biographies should be regarded as records of actual facts or religious romances written for the sake of edification is a question that need not here be discussed. Considered purely as literature they prove that Jerome had all the qualities necessary for a great story-teller ; above all, as he shows in the *Malchus*, the power to make small events interesting.

    ' A long time passed, and as I sat alone one day in the desert with nothing in sight save earth and sky, I began quietly to turn things over in my mind. Among other things I called back to memory the monks with whom I had lived, and especially the look of the father who had taught me, detained me, and lost me. While busied with these thoughts I suddenly noticed a crowd of ants swarming over a narrow pathway. You could see that the loads they carried were larger than themselves. Some with their mandibles were dragging grass seed along ; others were throwing the earth out of pits they had made and banking it up to prevent an overflow of water. One party, mindful of the winter's approach, were cutting off the tips of the grain they had brought in, so that the damp might not turn their store into grass. Another company with mournful ceremonies were carrying out the bodies of their dead comrades. And, what is especially strange in such a host, those who were coming out did not hinder those who were going in ; nay, rather, if they saw anyone sink beneath the weight of his load, they would put their shoulders to it and assist him. To be brief, that day gave me a delightful entertainment.'

This literary skill is equally evident in Jerome's controversial treatises and in his correspondence. Of his letters we have 154, written between the years 370 and 419, a collection which will stand comparison with the letters of Cicero. Some of the later epistles are of great historical importance, but there are very few that are not interesting in themselves. There are the glowing eulogies on the three saintly women Marcella, Blesilla, and Fabiola ; the two discourses on girls' education ; the letters of admonition to widows and divorced women ; above all the series in which rules of life are laid down for virgins, monks, and the secular clergy. To this last class Jerome is inclined to be sarcastic, as the following portrait will show :

' There are other men—I speak of those of my own order—who only seek the office of presbyter and deacon that they may be able to visit women freely. These fellows think of nothing but dress ; they must be nicely scented and their shoes must fit without a crease. Their hair is curled and still shows traces of the tongs ; their fingers glisten with rings ; and if there is wet on the road they walk across on tiptoe so as not to splash their feet. When you see these gentry think of them rather as potential bridegrooms than as clergymen. Indeed, some of them devote their whole life and all their energies to finding out about the names, the households, and the characters of married ladies. I will give you a brief and summary portrait of the chief practitioner in this line, that from the master's likeness you may recognise his disciples. He rises with the sun in haste ; the order of his morning calls is duly arranged ; he takes short cuts, and importunately thrusts his old head almost into the bedchambers of ladies still asleep. If he sees a cushion, or an elegant table cover, or, indeed, any article of furniture that he fancies, he starts praising and admiring it and takes it in his hand, and so, lamenting that he has nothing like this, he begs or rather extorts it from the owner, as all the women are afraid to offend the town gossip.'

Augustine (354–430)

Jerome was a great man and a great writer; but Augustine is even greater, for although he was not perhaps so profound a scholar, he possessed in a supreme degree some qualities of genius that Jerome lacked. His character is a medley of contradictions; he is both a poet and a philosopher, a casuist and a rhetorician; he can be tender-hearted and compassionate, and then again ruthless and implacable; sometimes he seems a mere controversialist arguing fiercely against all opponents, at other times he is the most zealous of preachers intent only on saving his fellow-men. He studied, more deeply perhaps than any other writer, the mysteries of the human soul and the laws that should govern conduct; but while in one place he insists on freedom of judgment, in another he demands implicit obedience to authority. The variety of his moods is reflected in the style of his books, which is now beautifully clear and precise, now verbose and over-elaborate. But taken all in all Augustine is a marvellous genius and one of the most fascinating of Latin writers.

Aurelius Augustinus was born 13th November 354 at Thagaste, a small town in Numidia, his mother, Monica, being a very fervent Christian, his father, Patricius, a pagan. He learnt Greek at Madaurus, and when he was seventeen proceeded to Carthage to finish his education. His university course there, consisting chiefly of the study of Virgil and Cicero, strengthened his natural taste for literature, and when he was twenty he returned to his native town as a professor of rhetoric. But while living at Carthage he had, to his mother's great grief, been attracted to the Manichæans, and for some years he was inclined to support at least two of their heresies ; one, the existence of two co-eternal Principles, the Principle of good and the Principle of evil ; the other, the corporeal existence of God as a form of highly subtilised matter. He had also formed a connection with a woman, and by whom he had a son Adeodatus, and was living in sin with her, so that at this time of his life neither his faith nor his morals were beyond reproach.

In 383 he left Africa for Italy, and taught first at Rome and then in Milan, where Ambrose was then bishop. In that town in 386 the crisis of his life came, and he renounced all the errors of the past. In 387 he was baptised together with his son and his devoted friend Alypius, and at the end of the year, after a short stay at Ostia, where Monica died, he returned to Africa. Giving his small inheritance to the poor, he lived quietly for three years with an association of friends at Thagaste, and then became assistant-priest to Valerius, the aged Bishop of Hippo. On Valerius' decease in 395 he was elected bishop in his stead, and remained in that office till his own death at the age of seventy-six, 28th August 430.

It will be seen that the outward incidents of this career are simple enough, and they have been clearly narrated for us in the biography of Augustine written by his friend Possidius, Bishop of Calama. But Augustine's character is by no means a simple one, and his inner life was never illumined by a clear light, but was rather one long struggle, firstly against himself and those human instincts which he came to regard as man's deadliest temptation, and secondly against all the various forms of heresy that in the fourth and fifth centuries distracted the Church. There were the Manichæans, with their recruits from the old Gnostic sects, who sought to establish some connection between

Christianity and rationalism. There were the Donatists, stiff-backed puritans who maintained that the Sacraments had no efficacy unless the minister was duly ordained and in a proper state of grace. And, most dangerous of all in Augustine's view, there were the followers of the British monk Pelagius, who maintained that Adam's sin was purely personal, that men were born into this world good, and that they had a free choice in the direction of their lives.

Against these ideas Augustine fought with all the strength he possessed, and it is probable that a weaker man would have succumbed to the stress of thought and emotion that these fierce controversies involved. But Augustine is perhaps the greatest mind revealed to us in Latin literature, and not only did he emerge triumphant from all his difficulties, but he succeeded in imprinting his mark more deeply than any other writer upon the life of the Middle Ages. He is the only Roman who can for a moment be compared with Plato ; and for the medieval man he took Plato's place and stood side by side with Aristotle as the guiding beacon of truth. ' From his distant Africa,' says Duchesne, ' Augustine shed his light over the whole of Christendom. To the men of his own time he uttered profitable words. He knew how to explain their own souls to them, to console them for the calamities of the world, and to guide their understanding through mysteries. Even now, after the inevitable attrition of so many centuries, he is still the great authority in theology. It is through him in a special manner that we have intercourse with Christian antiquity. In certain aspects he is for every age.'

Augustine's writings are very numerous, for in the assiduity of his pen he is only equalled by Cicero, and there are no less than one hundred and eighteen

separate titles in the list of his works. A rough classi-
fication will divide them as follows: *First*, the controversial books, directed against Manichæans, Donatists,
Pelagians and Arians, and establishing his own stern
doctrine of predestination. *Secondly*, the doctrinal
treatises, concerned with Church teaching and administration, the two most important being the *De
Doctrina Christiana* and the *De Catechizandis Rudibus*,
'On the art of catechizing novices.' *Thirdly*, the
philosophical and rhetorical essays, a comparatively
unimportant section, and mostly early works. *Fourthly*,
volumes of Biblical exegesis, such as the commentaries
on the Book of Job, the Psalms, and the Epistle to the
Romans. *Fifthly*, the sermons and letters, each class
containing a large number of examples of very varying
length and interest. *Sixthly*, the *Retractationes* the
work of Augustine's old age, in which he reviews and
frankly criticises most of his previous writings and
amends such statements in them as seem to his mature
judgment incorrect.

Into one of these sections nearly all Augustine's
writings will fall. But from the mass of his work
there stands out a pair of great books, the *Confessions*
and the *City of God*, the one an epitome of fifth-
century feeling, the other an encyclopædia of fourth-
century knowledge. The *City of God*, that amazing
work, occupied thirteen years of Augustine's life, and
he himself in the 'Retractations' gives his own summary of its contents. 'The great work on the city
of God was at last completed in twenty-two books.
Of these the first five were occupied with the refutation
of such persons as believe that human prosperity
depends upon the worship of the pagan gods, and that
the prohibition of their worship is the cause of our
present misfortunes. The next five are directed against

those who admit that troubles have always been the attributes of humanity, but argue that the worship of many gods possesses a value in relation to the life after death. In these ten books those two futile opinions, which are antagonistic to Christianity, are refuted. But as I did not wish to be accused of having merely controverted the doctrines of other people, without enunciating my own, this is the object of the second part of this work. The first four of its twelve books contain the origin of the two cities, the city of God and the city of this world ; the second four contain their process or progress ; the third four, the final books, their appointed ends. So, while the twenty books are all occupied with the description of both cities, yet they derived their title from the better city, and were called by preference *The City of God*.'

The actual occasion of the book was, of course, the sack of Rome by Alaric in 410, a disaster which made not only the pagans but many Christians also believe that the end of the world was rapidly approaching. Every one was filled with uneasy apprehension, and Augustine realised that it was absolutely necessary to restore men's confidence. How far he succeeded is now a matter of history, and the *City of God* was one of the strongest bulwarks of faith all through medieval times and one of the chief sources from which the temporal organisation of the Catholic Church drew its inspiration. As Dean Weldon says in his excellent edition of the Latin text (S.P.C.K. 1924) :

' The *De Civitate Dei* has been one of the great books in human history, greater even in its effect or influence than in itself. For it is a book which breathed hope into a despondent, and faith into a sceptical, society, and which turned men's eyes away from the grave of a dead or dying world to the resurrection of a living and conquering Christ. The *De Civitate Dei* made its appeal at its publication, and may make the same appeal now, to an age crying aloud for reconstruction.'

To appreciate the *City of God* thoroughly one should do as Charlemagne was wont to do in his old age, and read it through again and again from beginning to end. It contains all Augustine's accumulated wisdom, and there are few who could not learn something from the immense variety of his knowledge. To theologians, of course, it is indispensable, and all who are interested in Roman history and religion will find in it a mass of curious details. Students of science may turn to Augustine's notes on the salamander, on peacock's flesh, on charcoal, lime and salt, and on the diamond and loadstone. Believers in the supernatural will have their faith strengthened by the many tales he tells from his own experience : how in some parts of Italy landladies of inns, by giving their guests a piece of drugged cheese were able to turn them into beasts of burden ; how a doctor of Carthage suffering from gout was preparing to be baptised, when in a dream he was visited by black woolly-haired demons who tried by torture to prevent him, but persisting in his pious purpose he found both gout and torments instantly vanish ; how a certain youth was possessed by a devil, who entered into him from a river and on being exorcised at a martyr's shrine tore out one of his eyes and left it hanging by one fibre, and yet in a week's time the eye was perfectly sound again. As for psychologists, they may be especially recommended to the great passage in the fourteenth book, where Augustine propounds his theory that sex is the punishment of Adam's sin.

' We may fairly ask ourselves the question whether our first parent or first parents (for there was a marriage of two) experienced in their animal body before their sin such emotions as we shall not experience in the spiritual body when sin has been purged away and ended. If they did, how could they have been happy in Paradise, that wondrous land of bliss ? Who that feels fear or pain can be called absolutely happy ? And what could they have to frighten or hurt them amid such abundance of blessings, where neither death nor any sickness was to be feared, and where nothing was absent that a good will could desire, nothing was present that could vex a man in body or mind and disturb his happiness ? Their love to God was unclouded, their love for each other was that of partners living in sincere and faithful union ; and from this love there flowed a wonderful delight, for the object of their love was always theirs to enjoy. Their avoidance of sin was tranquil ; and so long as it was maintained no other ill could attack them from any quarter and bring sorrow. Or did they perchance desire already to touch and eat of the forbidden tree, but feared to die : and so even then in Paradise were they vexed by fear and by desire ? '

The *City of God* is a very long book; the *Confessions* is shorter but equally rich in matter. Into the *City of God* Augustine put all his intellect ; into the *Confessions* he puts all his soul, and as a spiritual autobiography it has never been surpassed. The first four of its thirteen books tell the story of his childhood, youth and early manhood, the narrative being so arranged as to develop Augustine's cardinal doctrine of original sin. He describes how as an infant he offended against the moral law by crying too insistently for the breast ; how as a boy he offended again by loving play more than books and for the sake of play neglecting his parents' admonitions to study ; how as a youth he committed the sin of theft, going into his neighbour's garden by night with a company of lewd fellows and out of pure wantonness stripping a pear-tree of its fruit. This offence, which weighed heavily on his conscience, was committed in his sixteenth year, and soon afterwards he left home to pursue his studies at Carthage, where ' a whole frying-pan of abominable loves crackled round about me and on every side. I was not in love as yet, but I loved to be in love.' During his twelve years at Carthage he went sadly astray ; he frequented loose company, visited the theatre, took a mistress, and was perverted by the Manichæan heresy ; then in his twenty-eighth year, despite his mother's tears and entreaties, he sailed with his mistress from Africa to Italy. In the next four books we find him teaching rhetoric, first at Rome and then at Milan, where he was joined by his mother and his friends Alypius and Nebridius. His mother arranged a marriage for him with a young girl, and at her bidding his mistress was sent back to Africa while her son remained with his father. Gradually, however, under the influence of Ambrose and Monica the whole group of young men drew nearer to the true Christian faith, and the eighth book closes with the great scene in the garden, where Augustine hears a child's voice crying ' tolle, lege,' ' take up and read.' ' And so I returned in haste to the place where Alypius was sitting, for there I had laid down the Apostle's book when I had risen from thence. I snatched it up, I opened it, and in silence I read the chapter that first met my eyes—" Not in rioting and drunkenness, not in chambering and wantonness, not in strife and envying. But put ye on the Lord Jesus Christ, and make not provision for the flesh, to fulfil the lusts thereof." No further did I want to read, nor needed I. For instantly, even with the end of this sentence, a light of confidence poured into my heart, and all the darkness of doubt vanished away.'

Soon after his baptism by Ambrose, Monica died and the ninth book is chiefly concerned with her praises and her son's grief. But the interest of the remaining four books is general rather than personal.

Book X sets forth the benefits that confession brings to the soul and then discusses the power of memory and the influence of the senses on men's minds. Book XI contains an elaborate analysis of time in its relation to the eternal, and the last two books deal with the creation of the world and the true meaning of the Scriptures. The last words of the *Confessions* are these :

> 'Thou, O God, art the Good, and needest no good. Thou art at rest always, because thyself thou art thy rest. And what man shall teach another man to understand this ? Or what angel another angel ? Or what angel man ? Let it be begged of thee, sought in thee, knocked for at thee : so, so shall it be received, so shall it be found, so shall it be opened.'

In the history of Christianity Augustine holds a place only second to Saint Paul. Strong as his influence was in his own age, it grew even stronger as time went on, and it persists to-day. Whether that influence has been an unmixed blessing, and whether Augustine's views of man's destiny truly represent the teaching of his divine master, are questions that need not be discussed here : the fact remains that Augustine succeeded in impressing his sincere beliefs on future generations. If any one wishes to trace the development of European civilisation and European morals, from this author and from that he will derive a certain amount of information ; but until he has made a serious study of Augustine's writings he has scarcely begun his task ; Augustine is the foundation-stone.

PART II

THE FIFTH, SIXTH, & SEVENTH CENTURIES
(430–732)

E

THE FIFTH, SIXTH, & SEVENTH CENTURIES

THE three centuries that follow after Augustine's death in 430 form a backwater in the stream of European history. The Byzantine Empire in this period under Justinian reached its highest pitch of magnificence, and in the Near East we have the unique personality of Mahomet, whose followers were destined for so many years to be a menace to European civilisation. But in the West there is a striking absence of men of genius : the only great man of action who appears is Pope Gregory the First, the only great writer is Boethius. The fifth century was for Europe a time of storm and stress, of destruction and barbarian inroads ; and by the middle of the sixth century, when the Teutonic migrations at last ceased, it seemed as if the one thing to be desired was repose. The countries that had been the mainstay of Rome were in the hands of barbarian invaders, and it was still uncertain whether these new-comers would prove to be mere destructive forces, like the Huns and Vandals, or would settle down, as the Franks and Saxons eventually did, into orderly governments.

Orosius (fl. 417)

But so great is the vitality of the human spirit and so strong the impulse which urges men to commit their thoughts to writing, that even in these centuries there is a constant succession of authors who are worthy of study. First in time among them is Orosius, the pupil of Augustine and the author of the *History against the Pagans*. He was a Spaniard by birth and

came to Augustine at Hippo about 414, soon earning
the affection of his famous teacher who calls him
' Orosius, a youthful cleric, my brother in the Catholic
faith, my son in years, my fellow-presbyter in clerical
rank.' In spite of his ignorance of Greek, Orosius was
sent by Augustine to Jerome at Bethlehem to help
him in controverting the Pelagian heresy. And the
historical work by which he is remembered was the
outcome of Augustine's advice, together with a desire
to present to Christian people a history of the world
as they should know it from the time of Adam to
A.D. 417. Hence it is not surprising that he is prone
to interpret historical events in the light of his own
preconceived opinions. His chief authorities are the
Bible, Livy, Tacitus, Suetonius, Justin, Florus, Eutropius, and possibly Jerome's Eusebius. Book One deals
with events from the creation of the world down to
the founding of Rome ' ab orbe condito ad urbem
conditam.' Books Two to Six relate the history of
the four monarchies, Babylonian, Roman, Macedonian
and Carthaginian, the larger space being given naturally
to Roman affairs. Book Seven is concerned with the
Roman Principate down to the author's own time, with
special reference to the affairs of the Christian Church.
Generally the historical value of the work is slight ;
only for the events after 387 has it any independent
authority. In spite of his alertness and enthusiasm he
is hardly an attractive author, for his style, strongly
coloured by Virgil and Lucan, is diffuse and rhetorical,
but for many centuries he was widely read.

Rutilius (fl. 416)

A close contemporary of Orosius, but in other respects
so different that he appears to belong to another
world, was Rutilius Claudius Namatianus. While

Orosius was inspired by his great teacher's City of God, Rutilius' love was still the City of Rome. Many to whom he may be no more than a name will be familiar with the lines :

'Dumque offers victis proprii consortia iuris,
Urbem fecisti quod prius orbis erat (I. 65-66).

He was born in Gaul of that Gallo-Roman stock which was the flower of the civilisation of Provence. He does not tell us the place of his birth, but wherever it was he left it early in life, when his father Lachanius became governor of Tuscany, and does not appear to have returned to his native land until 416—the occasion which prompted the poem *De Reditu suo*. Like his father, who left behind him a good name and an honourable record of service, Rutilius followed a public career and held office under the Emperor Honorius, being for a short period in 414 ' præfectus urbis '. Two years later he left Rome for Gaul. There has been much discussion about the reason for this departure. One thing at least is clear, when one reads the *De Reditu suo*, that he was very unwilling to go. The reason given by himself is that duty called him to his native land ravaged by long wars, but it seems surprising that he should not have heard the call of duty earlier. Hence it is a fair surmise that there was some other reason not so suitable to appear in his poem and that he left Rome because he had in some way incurred the Emperor's displeasure.

His only known poem is that already referred to— ' On His Return,' and it is not complete. The abrupt beginning ' Velocem potius reditum mirabere, lector,' suggests that something must have gone before ; but while this book is complete in 644 lines of elegiacs, of the second and final book we only have sixty-eight lines. The poem opens with the praise of Rome and the delights of life there ; they are so great that nothing but the need of his country could induce him to leave the city. He takes his leave in the famous passage, from which we have already quoted, and which begins :

> ' Exaudi, regina tui pulcherrima mundi,
> Inter sidereos Rome recepta polos ;
> Exaudi genetrix hominum genetrixque deorum ;
> Non procul a cælo per tua templa sumus.'

For more than a hundred lines he continues to apostrophise the Eternal City, to praise her temples, aqueducts, and military and engineering skill, to call on her to rise again and punish the Goths, as she had punished the Gauls who had dared to sack Rome eight hundred years before. The farewell over, he describes the journey by sea, the wind and the weather and the various stopping-places. He shows a pleasing contentment with nearly everything he sees. But a ' nasty Jew,' ' querulus Iudæus,' who was a hard land-lord arouses his indignation, as does also a Christian monastery. He speaks with contempt of the monks ' lucifugi viri ' who wish to live alone and be seen of nobody : ' Munera fortunæ metuunt dum damna verentur.' But for the rest he writes in pleasing elegiacs about any thing or person that aroused his traveller's interest : how a channel through the shallows of Volterra was marked with two rows of stakes with laurels tied at the top to make them more visible, and how salt is obtained in the salt marshes near the house of his friend Albinus. He sees at Pisa a statue erected to his father, and rejoices that the name of Lachanius is still honoured ' numinis instar ' among all the Etruscans.

Rutilius was a thorough-going Roman patriot and

pagan. No doubt he knew that there was a difference between Jews and Christians but he was not interested in it. The asceticism of the monks was to him foolish nonsense, but he does not waste words on Christianity in general. He seems scarcely aware of the vast changes that had taken place since the first century, and speaks of things Greek and things Jewish in much the same way as Juvenal. His religion was Rome, not the old Roman gods, and Stilicho's betrayal of the city and his burning of the Sibylline Books are together both a base outrage and a base treachery to the imperial destiny of the Eternal City.

Leo the Great (c. 400–461)

Although not chiefly remembered for his voluminous writings, which occupy three volumes of Migne's *Patrologia*, Pope Leo I cannot be passed over even in a brief survey of fifth-century literature. Both his Sermons and his Letters are chiefly interesting for what they tell us of the controversies of his time and the part which he played in them. The year of his birth is uncertain. It is probably shortly before the close of the fourth century, since Augustine, writing in 418 (Epist. 104), mentions him as a young acolyte sent by the Pope on a mission to Carthage. We know little of his life before 440 when he became Pope. According to the growing practice of using officials of the Church for civil tasks requiring skill and diplomacy, Leo had been sent to Gaul to settle the quarrel between Ætius and Albinus when the news of his election came. On Sunday, 29th September 449, he was consecrated forty-seventh Bishop of Rome, and on that occasion delivered the address which now stands at the head of his collected Sermons. During the twenty-four years of his Papacy, Attila appeared in northern

Italy, capturing Milan and Pavia (452), and neither Emperor nor Senate could devise any means of stopping his advance to Rome. So the courageous Pope himself went to meet the Scourge of God, and by his words induced him to retire beyond the Danube. There is no reason to doubt the story, though Leo with characteristic modesty does not refer to it. His writings are more concerned with the safety of the Church and especially the famous Eutychian controversy, which raised issues more important than itself. A certain Eutyches, in his zeal to oppose the heresy of Nestorius that Christ on earth was only born man of his mother, went to the other extreme and denied that humanity could be born of the Virgin; Christ was God only (the Monophysite heresy). For this he was expelled from the Church by a Synod of Constantinople. He appealed to the other great Bishops and to the Pope. Leo's decision explaining the via media of Catholic orthodoxy is embodied in letter 28, the famous ' Tome ' of Leo. Another Council held at Ephesus in 449 took no notice of the Tome and reinstated Eutyches. This, as Leo saw, brought the affair far beyond the domain of theological dispute. The supremacy of Rome and the authority of the See of St Peter were directly affronted, and Leo's prime service to the Roman Church was the firm stand which he made on this point. He regarded the acts of both the previous Councils as null and void. At the famous Council of Chalcedon in 451, Leo's Tome, which the ' Robber' Council at Ephesus had not even looked at, was now read and the heresy of Eutyches condemned. The ruling was accepted and the right to make it. Leo spoke with the voice of Peter. True, Eutychianism survived and is to be heard of again; moreover, after the Papal delegation had left, a resolution was passed exalting the Byzantine Patriarch. But future Popes did not allow it to be forgotten that the Council of Chalcedon had confirmed the supremacy of Peter's successor—'nec præter illam petram quam Dominus in fundamento posuit stabilis erit ulla constructio.'

Sedulius (fl. 470)

About the life of Sedulius, poeta Christianissimus, author of one of the most famous Christian Latin poems, the *Carmen Paschale*, we know next to nothing. Italy, Ireland, Spain have all been claimed as his birthplace. We do not know when he was born or when he died. He lived much of his life at Athens where he had a school of some sort. There he was converted to Christianity under the influence of a certain Macedonius to whom he dedicated the Easter Poem in a prose introduction. To the reader is addressed a short prologue in Elegiacs. The rest of the poem, consisting of five books, is in hexameters totalling about seventeen hundred verses. It is accompanied by a parallel narrative in prose, the *Paschale Opus*, intended to supplement and develop the theme of the poem. The title Easter Song sometimes used in English is even more misleading than its own Latin title; for its theme is not merely the Resurrection but the whole life of Christ, together with incidents from the Old Testament. The aim of the work is evangelical. He calls on the Athenians—sons of Theseus as he names them—to forsake the darkness of Paganism and its literature and turn towards the light. In a fine passage he recounts the glory of God, then turns to refute heathenism and heresies. The second book tells of the Fall and brings the narrative down to the birth, baptism, and tempting of Our Lord, and the remaining three books tell of the miracles, Passion and Resurrection. Sedulius was well versed in Pagan literature and his poem borrows whole passages from Virgil. The influence of Ovid, Lucan and later poets is also clear. In poetry he far outstrips his one predecessor in this field—Juvencus. The opinion of the Council of Gelasius (494), which decided what Scriptures were genuine and generally what Catholics ought to read, still stands. 'Venerabilis viri Sedulii paschale opus quod heroicis descripsit versibus insigni laude præferimus. Item Iuvenci nihilominus *laboriosum* opus non spernimus sed miramur.' Not only was his Easter Poem widely read in every library in Europe, but his less known *Elegia* is cited by Bede, and part of his Ambrosian hymn was translated even by Luther.

Apollinaris Sidonius (c. 430–480)

The outstanding literary figure in the fifth century was Sidonius, who was born in Lyons about 430 and died some time after 480. Thus he began his life a Roman citizen and ended it under Visigothic rule in Gaul. Like Rutilius he was of that cultured Gallo-Roman stock among whom traditions of learning and literature were still alive and, though he became a bishop of the Catholic Church, his writings are often quite pagan in tone. He was brought up a Christian but it was only after failure and disappointment in political life that he entered the Church. His poetical works belong mainly to the earlier period of his life, for when he became bishop he resolved to abandon verse. But he did not keep his resolution, and his letters contain much verse, while he is always glad of a good excuse, such as the dedication of a church, for writing a poem. But his earlier ambitions were more political than literary, and he found his skill in verses a useful aid.

He pronounced a panegyric on three different Emperors and obtained some advancement on each occasion, but the rapid rise and fall of Emperors in those days of Ricimer meant that he had to start afresh every time. The first panegyric was in favour of his father-in-law, Avitus, who became Emperor in 455 ; like the others it is built up on the old framework of classical mythology relieved occasionally by more modern allusions. When Majorian overthrew and slew Avitus, Sidonius after a decent interval addressed a poem to the new Emperor (Carm. V) and came again to Rome, only to meet with another fall. He once more retired to Gaul, but six years later (c. 467) he accompanied a deputation to congratulate the new Emperor Anthemius (Panegyric, Carm. II). This time he rose to high office but met with many difficulties in its tenure. He foresaw a breach between Anthemius and Ricimer, and remembering his two previous falls voluntarily retired about 470. Shortly after, he entered the priesthood and was at once appointed Bishop of Clermont Ferrand (urbs Arverna) and his life enters on a new phase. The Goths invaded Auvergne. Rome was powerless to assist, but the patriotic Bishop of Clermont organised and inspired a stubborn but unsuccessful resistance. In 475 Auvergne was abandoned by Rome, whose province of Gaul was now reduced almost to nothing. But the victorious Goths do not seem to have misused their power. Many of the Gauls had been in favour of peace and they prospered under the new régime, but Sidonius was imprisoned. For the rest, the Goths though Arians did not interfere with the Church, and in a year or two we find Sidonius restored again to his see at Clermont. But he felt keenly the loss of his nationality and sought solace in his episcopal duties and in the composition of those letters which are his most valued contribution to the history no less than the literature of his century.

His book of poems, as we have seen, belongs to the earlier half of his literary career. Besides the panegyrics already mentioned it contains poems on various subjects and in various metres. Their poetical value is not high, but they show skill in the handling of metre, and he is well versed in practice of allusion to classical mythology. The two Epithalamia (IX and XV) stand out from the rest, not by reason of any poetical superiority or because they are good examples of their kind, but because the treatment is less orthodox. The bridegroom in XV is the philosopher Polemius, and the bride Araneola, who is skilled in weaving. A temple of philosophy is described, in which the Seven Sages and Pythagoras, the Socratics and other philosophers are honoured. The Academy and the Stoa are there, but the Cynics only get as far as the door, and the Epicureans cannot get in at all. In the other temple Araneola weaves wonderful tapestries depicting famous heroines, but when she shows Lais pulling the beard of Diogenes she is rebuked by Pallas for her disrespect to philosophers—unseemly behaviour in a lady about to be married to one of them.

Sidonius, however, lives more by reason of his later work, especially the letters. Like his predecessor, Symmachus, he models himself on the younger Pliny. Writing always with one eye on the public he succeeds in imitating the vanity and artificiality of that precious but attractive writer, but falls far beneath him in elegance and style. Still if we do not like his Latin, we cannot but be grateful for all he tells us of his contemporaries, of himself, of life and culture in fifth-century France. And if he reveals to us much of his vanity and extravagance, we must make allowance not

76

only for the conventions of the society in which he moved, but also for the fact that letter-writers always appear vain to the public who read them. Against the Sidonius revealed by his letters must be set the Sidonius who bravely resisted his country's enemies, who was loved by his family as a good father, by his flock as a worthy bishop, and by his many friends. He was good at games, both indoor and outdoor. He had a lively if somewhat episcopal sense of humour and enjoyed a good story. On one occasion he had been deceived by a traveller who had pretended to be more than he was. When he discovered the imposture and the man's life history, Sidonius instead of being angry was greatly amused by the fellow's cleverness, especially his skilful wooing of a young and pretty heiress, and tells the whole story to his friend the Bishop of Marseilles—a tale, he says, ' as good as a play ' (Ep. VII. 2). Another good letter in the same light vein is I. 11. It recalls an incident of his earlier life under Majorian. A wealthy upstart called Pæonius had been greatly annoyed by a stinging satire. He proved to his own and every one else's satisfaction that Sidonius was the author. Now Pæonius was not popular, and Sidonius, who was innocent of the whole affair, found his reputation greatly enhanced, and try as he would he could not convince anyone that it was undeserved.

But the bishop's letters are not all so light. Although his theological works have not come down to us and his correspondence shows little evidence of his interest in such matters, yet many of his letters are deeply religious. A good example is VIII. 13, which contains not merely the conventional expressions of piety but shows a breadth of mind in the commendation of a young Jewish convert, for Sidonius had no love of

77

Jews (III. 4). The letters contain many poems, some old ones which he had found among his papers, some new. Sometimes he tells of a verse made on the spur of the moment, *e.g.* V. 17, an interesting letter of Gallic life. Often he praises his friends in an exaggerated manner, as in a poem to Mamertus Claudianus, a priest of Vienne, himself a writer of some repute and the only one of the correspondents whose own letter appears in the collection (IV. 2). Sidonius' letters were much admired in his own day and imitated by later writers. Ennodius of Arles, a poet of the sixth century, shows the influence of his poetry also.

Salvianus (c. 400–480)

Detailed information is lacking about the life of Salvian of Marseilles. He was a very voluminous writer, but we possess only the *De Gubernatione Dei* in eight books, *Timothei ad ecclesiam libri quattuor*, in which Timotheus is only a pseudonym for himself, and some letters. He is chiefly known for the first of these : ' On the Governance of God.' It can scarcely be called a work of theology proper, so much does it bear the impress of the troublous times in which it was written. When the empire was being constantly invaded by Goths and the Vandals had already overrun Africa, Christian people naturally raised the complaint that God was neglecting his own people. Salvian's book is an attempt to answer that complaint, and he does so with little sympathy towards the complainers. With no great philosophic knowledge or gifts but with plenty of vigorous rhetoric and quotations from the Bible he defends God as Ruler and Judge. If Romans were everywhere distressed it was because they deserved it for the sins and heresies that abounded. Indeed the Barbarians, he says, are

78

more moral and more Christian than the Romans. They agree among themselves while the Romans persecute each other. And did not the Vandals purify the morals of Africa while the Romans ' scortatores quidem ab alienis uxoribus removerunt, ad omnes autem solitarias passim admiserunt, adulteria vetantes, lupanaria ædificantes ? ' Salvianus had no hesitation in assigning a reason for the crumbling of the Empire : ' Nemo sibi aliud persuadeat nemo aliud arbitretur : sola nos morum nostrorum vitia vicerunt.' Christian historians have been disposed to agree with him ; but it is not surprising that Salvian was not a popular writer in his day.

Among the other fifth-century writers, most of them living in Gaul, may be mentioned Mamertus Claudianus, extravagantly praised, as we have seen, by Apollinaris Sidonius, Ruricius of Limoges, another friend of Sidonius. A useful *De viris illustribus* is ascribed to Gennadius of Marseilles about the end of the century. Among sermon writers may be mentioned Cæsarius, Bishop of Arles, Maximus of Turin, and Petrus Chrysologus. Of greater interest is Patricius or St Patrick, who lived in the fifth century but whose life has become wrapped in legend and mystery. Of the works ascribed to him the *Confessio* and the *Letter to Coroticus* are the most certainly genuine. But his place in Latin literature is doubtful. The language was to him a foreign medium and it was only in his later years that he felt able to write in it. Even then it is a case of translation, ' as you can tell,' he says, ' by the taste of my writing,' *ex saliva scripturæ meæ*. At the very end of the century we have two other Gallo-Romans. Avitus, Bishop of Vienne, evidently a member of the same family as Sidonius' father-in-law, the Emperor, wrote an epic poem on the Old

Testament, numerous letters and sermons, and a poem to his sister, a nun, on the consolations of virginity. Ennodius too is a prolific and varied writer if not a great one. Panegyric, biography, works on theology, speeches, letters and poems came readily from his pen, and in the early Middle Ages were greatly esteemed. He lived well into the next century (d. 521), so was really a contemporary with Boethius.

Boethius (c. 480–524)

While Sidonius was living his last years in Gaul, important changes were taking place in Italy. The western empire had collapsed, Odovacar had risen and fallen, and by 493 Italy was ruled by the Ostrogothic king Theodoric the Amal, who had his capital at Ravenna. It should not be forgotten that these Ostrogoths had already been living some forty years within the territory of the Eastern Emperor in Thrace. This contact had caused them to lose some of their warlike spirit, and Theodoric at any rate greatly admired the *civilitas* of the empire. The king who put Boethius to death was something different from the Germanic chieftain in Tacitus. He was both more autocratic and more civilised. He performed the difficult task of governing Italy and keeping the peace between his Gothic and his Roman subjects. With Rome, the Church and the Senate, he interfered as little as possible before the unhappy affair of Pope Symmachus. Himself an Arian heretic he gave his dominions such an example of religious toleration as was long denied to them afterwards. But, alas, he failed to live up to his principle—'Religionem imperare non possumus quia nemo cogitur ut credat invitus,' and when in the East Justin persecuted the Arians, Theodoric began to persecute the Catholics, and with malicious pleasure employed the aged Pope John on a mission to Justin demanding the restoration of the Arian churches. On his return the Pope was put in prison, where he died not long before Theodoric himself. This was the king under whom Boethius grew up and held high office, by whom he was cruelly put to death for treason. Had he died younger his name would have been less blackened and his greatness better recognised, but had he not put Boethius in prison, the world would have lost the *Consolatio Philosophiæ*.

Anicius Manlius Severinus Boethius was born in Rome about the year 480. His father was consul in 487, but died soon after, and Boethius was educated by Q. Aurelius Memmius Symmachus, the historian, afterwards his father-in-law and closest friend, who also was put to death by the king. He became *patricius*, for the old ranks and offices of the empire still remained, and by the year 505 was in high favour with Theodoric as well as Cassiodorus. He was consul in 510 and held important posts under the king. But about 523 there was growing discontent between Theodoric and his Roman subjects, aggravated as we have seen by religious persecution. Things went so far that a plan was conceived of inviting the help of the Emperor in overthrowing Theodoric. How far such a plan was acted upon we cannot say with certainty, but when a certain Albinus was accused of treasonable correspondence with Constantinople, Boethius at once defended him. This brought upon him the anger of the king, and at his bidding the Senate, whose interests Boethius had been defending, condemned him to death, on what precise charge we do not know, nor did the unfortunate man himself. 'I am blamed,' he says in the *Consolatio*, 'for having prevented an accuser from giving information which would prove

F   81

the Senate guilty of treason,' and again, in words strangely recalling the last years of the Republic more than half a millennium before, ' Senatum dicimur salvum voluisse.' It looks from this as if Boethius and other senators were actually privy to a treasonable plan, but the others failed to support him at the last. But Boethius himself says later that the evidence was forged, and that the whole affair was concocted by Theodoric with the intention of ruining the Senatorial order. At all events Boethius was put to death for his political views and was not a victim of Theodoric's religious persecution. He is to be regarded as the heir not of St Stephen but of Cato.

All through this busy life Boethius had been a keen student and prolific writer and had done more than any man since Cicero to make Greek philosophy known to Latin readers. Beginning with mathematics and mechanics he passed to the study of philosophy and conceived the immense plan of translating with commentary Plato's *Dialogues* and the whole of Aristotle's scientific and ethical works. Only a small part of this plan was carried out, but in addition he popularised the works of Pythagoras on music, Ptolemy on astronomy, Euclid on geometry, Archimedes on mechanics and Plato on theology, and wrote numerous original or partly original works on philosophy. Better known are his theological writings, the *Tractates*. These are in complete accord with Catholic orthodoxy, and, especially the book on the Holy Trinity, were highly valued in the Middle Ages. They are interesting chiefly because theology is treated after the manner of philosophy. He uses logic and philosophy to refute the heresies of Nestorius and Eutyches, and Scholastic Philosophy is indebted to him no less than to Augustine. His definition of Person, so vital in discussions affecting the Trinity, was important — Naturæ rationabilis individua substantia.

Boethius is known to the general reader chiefly as the author of the *Consolatio Philosophiæ*. The *Consolatio* is one of the great things in world literature, and it was as comforting to medieval men as Bunyan's *Pilgrim's Progress* was to our forefathers. Both books were written in prison, and although Boethius was one of the most learned of men and Bunyan was an unlettered tinker, their opening pages are curiously similar. They both begin with a verse preface, Boethius :

> ' Carmina qui quondam studio florente peregi,
> Flebilis heu mæstos cogor inire modos.'
> ' I that with youthful heat did verses write
> Must now my woes in doleful tunes indite.'

Bunyan :

> ' When at the first I took my Pen in hand
> Thus for to write ; I did not understand
> That I at all should make a little Book
> In such a mode.'

They then both proceed to an imaginative description. Bunyan : ' As I walk'd through the wilderness of this world, I lighted on a certain place where was a Den, and I laid me down in that place to sleep ; and as I slept I dreamed a Dream.' Boethius thus :

' While I ruminated these things with myself, and determined to set forth my woful complaint in writing, methought I saw a woman stand above my head, having a grave countenance, glistening clear eye, and of quicker sight than commonly Nature doth afford ; her colour fresh and bespeaking unabated vigour, and yet discovering so many years, that she could not at all be thought to belong to our times ; her stature uncertain and doubtful, for sometime she exceeded not the common height of men, and sometime she seemed to touch the heavens with her head, and if she lifted it up to the highest, she pierced the very heavens, so that she could not be seen by the beholders. . . . This woman, seeing the poetical Muses standing about my bed, and suggesting words to my tears, being moved for a little space, and inflamed with angry looks : " Who," saith she, " hath permitted these tragical harlots to have access to this sick man, which will not only not comfort his grief with wholesome remedies, but also nourish them with sugared poison ? . . . Rather get you gone, you sirens, pleasant even to distraction, and leave him to my Muses to be cured and healed." '

(Tr. ' I.T.,' 1609.)

At first he does not recognise her. She is Philosophy, his first nurse. He tells her of his woes, compares his fallen state to the comfortable library in which he had first made her acquaintance and describes somewhat vaguely the unhappy incidents that led to his imprisonment and denounces those who wrongfully accuse him. Breaking into verse he calls upon his Creator to explain why it is that he makes all heavenly bodies and the seasons of the year obey his laws but seemingly allows the acts of men to be governed by chance.

> ' For why should slippery chance
> Rule all things with such doubtful governance ?
> Or why should punishments,
> Due to the guilty, light on innocents ? '

This age-long question is the main subject of the work and is more closely dealt with later. At the moment Philosophy begins her task in the Socratic manner of question and answer. Boethius does not deny his belief in God, both Creator and Governor. Hence the world is ruled not by chance but by the Divine Reason of God. The first book ends with Boethius pondering this. In the second Philosophy reminds him of Fortune's notorious fickleness, that no man has a right to all her gifts and Boethius has had his share. But this, he answers, only makes his present distress greater. This leads to a discussion of

84

happiness which is said not to depend on possessions, advancement or office. Boethius protests that it was not mere ambition that had guided his life, rather ' I desired matter of action, lest old age should come upon me ere I had done anything.' ' Ah,' says Philosophy, ' the last infirmity of noble minds.' Hoc unum est quod præstantes quidem natura mentes . . . allicere possit, gloriæ scilicet cupido. But what is the fame of one man in a world which is itself but a point in space ? Thus she descants in prose and verse on the vanity of Fame, on Fortune and Adversity, which discovers true Friendship and true Love. Love which guides the motions of the very stars, and by which

> ' All holy laws are made and marriage rites are tied ;
> By it is faithful friendship joined. How happy mortals were,
> If that pure love did guide their minds, which heavenly spheres
>   doth guide.'

The opening of Book III finds Boethius spell-bound by her words like Socrates before Protagoras—me audiendi avidum stupentemque arrectis auribus carminis mulcedo defixerat. For the time he is refreshed and consoled and urges Philosophy to tell him wherein true happiness consists. She consents ; her reply is largely taken from Plato, especially the Gorgias, and some passages are skilful paraphrases of Plato's own words. But this enhanced rather than diminished the value of the Consolatio in the Middle Ages, for the debt to Plato is freely acknowledged. Philosophy discusses in turn the different roads by which happiness is said to be attainable—riches, honour, power, pleasure, all are tried and by familiar arguments found wanting. There must be something else in which happiness consists, a summum bonum, not any of these things.

Let Boethius pray to God that he may find it. And Philosophy thus begins :

> ' O qui perpetua mundum ratione gubernas
> Terrarum cælique sator qui tempus ab ævo
> Ire iubes stabilisque manens das cuncta moveri,
> Quem non externæ pepulerunt fingere causæ
> Materiæ fluitantis opus, verum insita summi
> Forma boni livore carens, tu cuncta superno
> Ducis ab exemplo, pulchrum pulcherrimus ipse
> Mundum mente gerens similique in imagine formans
> Perfectasque iubens perfectum absolvere partes.'

> ' O thou that dost the world in lasting order guide,
> Father of heaven and earth, Who makest time swiftly slide
> And, standing still Thyself, yet fram'st all moving laws,
> Who to Thy work wert moved by no external cause :
> But by a sweet desire, where envy hath no place,
> Thy goodness moving Thee to give each thing his grace,
> Thou dost all creatures' forms from highest patterns take,
> From Thy fair mind the world fair like Thyself doth make.
> Thus Thou perfect the whole, perfect each part dost frame.'

This and the rest of the prayer are a skilful adaptation of part of Plato's *Timæus*. The lady Philosophy is clearly not a Christian and one is tempted to ask whether Boethius had abandoned his faith. There is no mention of Christ in the *Consolatio*. All examples are taken from Classical History and Mythology, not from the Scriptures, and God, as we see, was the God of Plato not of the Christians.

There follows an argument in prose in search of the *perfectio felicitatis*, and the conclusion is reached that ' God and true blessedness are one and the selfsame thing,' and that ' the substance of God consisteth in nothing else but goodness.' But if God be goodness, Boethius cannot but raise again his old plaint (Book IV), ' for wickedness bearing rule and sway, virtue is not only without reward but lieth also trodden under the wicked's feet and is punished instead of vice. Quæ fieri in regno scientis omnia potentis omnia sed bona tantummodo volentis dei, nemo satis potest nec admirari nec conqueri.' All this Philosophy refuses to allow. The wicked are not powerful, the good are. God is all-powerful and God can do no evil. Her argument follows closely Plato's *Gorgias*. 'And it is manifest that the sentence of Plato is true : that only wise men can do what they desire, and that the wicked men practise indeed what they list, but cannot perform what they would. For they do what they list, thinking to obtain the good which they desire by those things which cause them delight ; but they obtain it not, because shameful action cannot arrive to happiness.' And later, ' Seest thou then in what mire wickedness wallows, and how clearly honesty shineth ? By which it is manifest that the good are never without rewards, nor the evil without punishments. . . . We have showed that blessedness is the selfsame goodness for which all things are done. Wherefore this goodness is proposed as a common reward for all human actions. For he shall not rightly be any longer called good, who wanteth goodness ; wherefore virtuous manners are not left without their true rewards.' Such quibbling is no worse than may be found in Plato. But Philosophy continues to enlarge upon the miseries of the wicked until Boethius is moved to reply : ' I see what felicity or misery is placed in the deserts of honest and dishonest men. But I consider that there is somewhat good or evil even in this popular fortune. For no wise man had rather live in banishment, poverty, and ignominy, than prosper in his own country, being rich, respected and powerful. . . . Wherefore I much marvel why these things are thus turned upside down, and the punishments of wickedness oppress the good, while evil men obtain the rewards of the good.' Boethius asks how, if God be Governor, the world can be ruled in such a haphazard way. Philosophy replies that God's method is not haphazard. He does not rule by chance but by Providence and Fate. A new and important phase in the argument here begins (IV. 6), showing deeper thinking than the earlier books. God uses both *providentia* and *fatum*. They are thus distinguished. 'For Providence is the very Divine reason itself, seated in the highest Prince, which disposeth all things. But Fate is a disposition inherent in changeable things, by which Providence connecteth all things in their due order. For Providence embraceth all things together, though diverse, though infinite ; but Fate putteth every particular thing into motion being distributed by places, forms and time ; so that this unfolding of temporal order being united into the foresight of God's mind is Providence, and the same uniting, being digested and unfolded in time, is called Fate. Which, although they be diverse yet the one dependeth on the other.' Further discussion of Providence and Fate concludes Book IV.

The fifth book raises the question, 'What then is *Chance ?*' It is not, says Philosophy, 'an event produced by a confused motion, and without connection of causes,' but rather, as Aristotle (Phys. II. 4) says : 'When anything is done for some certain cause, and some other thing happeneth for some reasons than that which was intended, this is called chance.' 'Have we then any free-will ?' is his next question. When Philosophy answers that we have, Boethius in a long discourse shows how he can hardly believe in free-will and at the same time in an all-foreseeing God. This is clearly the most difficult part of the argument and

Philosophy's long and intricate answer cannot be summed up in a few words. But let not the reader shirk the fifth and crowning book of the *Consolatio*. For amid the terms and expressions of Latinized Aristotelianism we can see Boethius groping after that same secret which still baffles us to-day. At least he understood that Eternity is not mere endless succession of time—the very lesson, if a layman read it aright, that modern science is now teaching us. 'Wherefore, whatsoever suffereth the condition of time, although, as Aristotle thought of the world, it never began nor were ever to end, and its life did endure with infinite time, yet it is not such that it ought to be called everlasting (æternum). For it doth not comprehend and embrace all the space of its life together, though that life be infinite, but it hath not the future time which is yet to come. . . . For it is one thing to be carried through an endless life, which Plato attributed to the world, another thing to embrace the whole presence of an endless life together, which is manifestly proper to the divine mind.' God is *ever* present, not present at one moment from which to look towards the future. 'Itaque si præsentiam pensare velis qua cuncta dinoscit, non esse præscientiam quasi futuri sed scientiam numquam deficientis instantiæ rectius æstimabis ; unde non *prævidentia* sed *providentia* potius dicitur.' A distinction is then drawn between events which are of themselves necessary and inevitable and those in which free will may have play. But this does not lessen God's omniscience. Such events, before they took place in time, *need* not, as we see it, have taken place, that is, they are not *necessary*. 'But what importeth it that they are not necessary, since that by reason of the condition of the divine knowledge they come to pass in all respects as if they were necessary ? ' Finally, 'All which being so, the free will of mortal men remaineth unviolated, neither are the laws unjust which propose punishments and rewards to our wills which are free from all necessity. There remaineth also a beholder of all things which is God, who foreseeth all things, and the eternity of his vision, which is always present, concurreth with the future quality of our actions, distributing rewards to the good and punishments to the evil. Neither do we in vain put our hope in God or pray to Him ; for if we do this well and as we ought, we shall not lose our labour or be without effect. Wherefore fly vices, embrace virtues, possess your minds with worthy hopes, offer up humble prayers to your highest Prince. There is, if you will not dissemble, a great necessity of doing well imposed upon you, since you live in the sight of your Judge, who beholdeth all things.'

Cassiodorus Senator (c. 480–c. 570)

Born about the same time as Boethius, but long outliving him, was Magnus Aurelius Cassiodorus Senator. He came from Bruttium in S. Italy and owed some of his advancement to his father, who was Prætorian Prefect to the king in 500. He himself became Quæstor to Theodoric about 507 ; the office was now like that of private secretary. A Gothic king in Italy had much need of such a secretary to write in Latin his letters and proclamations. Later he held the consulship and was Master of the Offices both under Theodoric and under his daughter Amalsuntha, who acted as regent for her son Athalaric. But so great was his value as Latin secretary that he continued, as it seems, to write the official correspondence after ceasing to be Quæstor. His letters which he published in 537 are most valuable historical documents. After their publication he retired from public life, for what reason it is difficult to say. But when Belisarius, general of Justinian the Eastern Emperor, had crushed the Vandals in Africa and subdued the Gothic kingdom in Italy, Cassiodorus had already begun to spend the last thirty-five years of his long life in retirement devoted to learning and literature. Thus his literary career falls into two parts. The letters belong to the earlier half and to the published collection he gave the name *Variæ*, 'quia necesse nobis fuit stylum non unum sumere, qui personæ variæ suscepimus admonere.' He excels most in the honorific style so necessary for royal correspondence, as for example when he writes for Theodoric to the Emperor Anastasius, or when he writes an official letter to himself announcing his elevation to the Patriciate. A really fine series of letters occurs in the third book, to Alaric the Visigoth, Luduin the Frank, and Gundobad the Burgundian, urging peace between them. This to Luduin (Clovis) : 'Adeo inter reges affinitatis iura divina coalescere voluerunt ut per eorum placabilem animum proveniat quies optata populorum. Hoc enim sacrum est quod nulla permittitur commotione violari. Nam quibus obsidibus habeatur fides si non credatur affectibus ? . . . Miramur animos vestros sic causis mediocribus excitatos ut cum filio nostro Alarico rege durissimum velitis subire conflictum, ut multi qui vos metuunt de vestra concertatione lætentur. . . . Virtus vestra patriæ non fiat inopinata calamitas, quia grandis invidia est regum in causis levibus gravis ruina populorum.' ' Let not your valour be an unforeseen calamity to your country ; for it is an exceeding great reproach to a king if heavy disaster befall a people for trivial causes.' The mind of the great Theodoric may be seen in those words no less than the pen of Cassiodorus. By no means are all the letters so elevated in style ; some chat in a naïve manner about a variety of unimportant things, in some dignity and triviality are so mixed as to produce an almost laughable effect. But for the stylist no less than the historian the twelve books of the *Variæ* have a value of their own.

When Cassiodorus retired he founded a monastery, which, if it did not actually belong to the Benedictine order then newly established, was inspired by its founder with the same devotion to study that was the distinguishing merit of those who followed the rule of St Benedict. At all events the world owes Cassiodorus a great debt ; for it was he who introduced among his monks the practice of copying manuscripts, without which the bulk of ancient literature would have been lost to us. He himself continued writing until he had passed his ninetieth year works on theology, history and grammar. An extremely long commentary on the Psalms, *Expositio in Psalterium*, was greatly esteemed in the Middle Ages and a treatise *De Anima*. As a historian he cannot be ranked very high. But what was probably his best work, a *History of the Goths*, has only come down to us in an abridgement by Jordanes (*q.v.*). The *Historia Ecclesiastica vocata Tripartita* runs from Constantine the Great to the younger Theodosius, and was based, he tells us, on a Latin translation of three Greek historians, Sozomenos, Socrates and Theodoretus. The *Chronicon*, based chiefly on Eusebius, Jerome, Aufidius Bassus, and Livy, is a list of kings, Assyrian, Latin and Roman, and of Roman consuls for 1031 years. At the beginning he says ' From Adam the first man down to the Flood, which took place under Noah, are 2242 years. The Flood took place on account of the great fierceness of the giants who by reason of their excessive size and ferocity to match had thrown into confusion all law and order among humanity.' These historical works are spread over his whole career and it is probable that at least the *Chronicle* and the *History of the Goths* belong to the time when he held political office.

Cassiodorus had hoped to found a theological college at Rome, but the fall of the Ostrogothic kingdom caused him to abandon the project. But he was keenly interested in the general education of the monks under his care and compiled for them a book of instruction which goes by the name of *Institutiones*. It is divided into two parts, the divine and the secular. In the former he deals chiefly with the Scriptures, the manuscripts thereof contained in the monastery library and the methods to be followed by the monks in copying them including the principles of emendation. There are notes on theological questions with references to various Fathers of the Church for further study. It also contains a vivid description of the monastery, Vivarium, and the daily work of the monks. Gardening is recommended for those who are not good at copying, and text-books on the subject recommended. But the needs of the scribes are his especial care, and in addition to the spelling instruction in the *Institutiones* he afterwards wrote a treatise *De Orthographia*. In the second part of the *Institutiones* he dealt with Dialectic, Music, Rhetoric and the other liberal arts.

Priscian (fl. 500)

Like all who since have written grammatical works, Cassiodorus owed a debt to his older contemporary, Priscianus of Cæsarea (in Spain), author of the famous *Institutio de arte grammatica* in eighteen books. At a time when learning was just beginning to degenerate into an affair of notes and summaries, Priscian is

93

conspicuous as one who for all his defects was well acquainted both with his subject and with earlier authorities on it. He is a worthy successor of Donatus and Macrobius, but his own chief sources are the Greek grammarians Herodian and Apollonius Dyscolus and the Latin Flavius Caper. For the *Institutio* is almost a work of Comparative Grammar and deals with Greek alongside Latin. Priscian was a student of language by profession and when he left Spain became a professor of Latin at Constantinople. He has a wide acquaintance with the Greek and Latin literatures and illustrates his lessons with copious and valuable citations. Though his Greek illustrations are not always happy, yet he saw clearly many of the connections between the two languages even in the domain of syntax, which he treats in the last two books ; as for example the kinship between the Greek optative and the Latin subjunctive moods. Aiming as he did at correcting common faults in the uses of forms, he is a valuable source of information on declensions and conjugations, to which most of the work is devoted. But we must not expect and do not find any rational historical treatment. He may deal usefully enough with *filiis* and *filiabus*, *penetralis* and *penetrabilis*, with the seventy-eight different terminations which he finds in the third declension, but the important has to be sought from among such remarks as ' The genitive plural of the first declension is formed by adding the syllable *-rum* to the ablative singular. . . . It is the only case which has not the same number of syllables as the others ' : or ' verbum autem quamvis a verberatu æris dicatur. . . .' But this great work did fulfil much of its purpose and remained for centuries the chief authority on correct Latin. Naturally it was especially prized by those western people, such as

Alcuin, Bede, and Sedulius Scotus, to whom Latin was an acquired tongue.

In addition to some other grammatical works Priscian also wrote (about A.D. 518) a panegyric on the Emperor at Constantinople, *De laude Anastasii Imperatoris*. It consists of a preface in twenty-two iambic lines and the panegyric itself in some three hundred hexameters, which are often reminiscent of Virgil and Lucan. To the historian the poem contains useful information, but the general reader soon wearies of that kind of exaggerated flattery which ascribes to Anastasius the combined virtues of the best Roman Emperors :

> ' Est iustus, sapiens, castus fortisque piusque,
> Est clemens, stabilis, moderatus, mitis, honestus,
> Et, loquar ut breviter quod sentio corde sub imo,
> Possidet hic veterum quidquid laudatur in ullo :
> Antoninum huius pietas, sapientia Marcum,
> Et mitem Nervam lenissima pectora vincunt,
> Promeruitque Titus non tantum mente benigna ;
> Gloria magnanimi Traiani cesserit isti.'

Longer and still more tedious is a geographical poem, or rather a metrical translation and amplification of the *Periegesis* of Dionysius.

Maximian the Elegist

If Priscian had not been famous as a grammarian, few would ever have read his poems. But Maximian's reputation rests entirely on five poems in elegiac metre totalling only some 700 lines. That Maximian was more nearly a poet than Priscian is true enough, but the real reason for his immense popularity, especially among medieval students, lies in his unblushing descriptions of the most intimate things. We know little of his life beyond what he tells us in his elegies, much of which may be only a literary pose. He belongs to the earlier half of the sixth century. It would appear from his references to himself that he was a native of Etruria, and that, when already advanced in years, he was an emissary to Constantinople. At all events the poems profess to be written by an old man, and there runs through them all a constant lament for his past youth, when he was a keen hunter, wrestler and swimmer, who never caught cold in any weather, and who astonished Bacchus himself by the amount he could drink. Then he could pick and choose among the girls, though he never found any of them worth marrying, but now

> ' Si modo non possum, quondam potuisse memento :
> Sit satis ut placeam me placuisse prius ' (II. 57.)

Benedict of Nursia (c. 480–c. 544)

The founder of the old and famous monastic order which bears his name deserves mention here because of the influence of his work *Regula Monachorum*, popularly known as the Rule of Saint Benedict. It is not certainly known when it was written, but its author lived in the first half of the sixth century and the monastery at Monte Cassino was founded during that period. The high standard of conduct which Benedict's *Rule* demanded from his monks is well known—constant, unremitting toil, but quiet and unhastening, whether in praising God or studying His Word, or in work in the fields ; for like Cassiodorus' monks each was to do the work for which he was best fitted. The *Rule* is marked by great reasonableness and sanity throughout. The abbot is warned against overworking his monks, who are to be allowed proper sleep and proper food. There is a pleasing absence of that extravagant asceticism which was common at the time. The *Regula Monachorum* was revised and amplified by more than one hand after the original author, the final text is supposed to have been established by Charlemagne in the year 787.

Jordanes (c. 516–573)

We have two historical works written about the middle of the sixth century by Jordanes, a writer of Gothic or Alan extraction. One, the *Summa temporum*, deals with Roman history in the barest outline, and is based on the usual sources. The other is a History of the Goths, called by a confusion of names *Getica*. Owing to the loss of Cassiodorus' work on the Goths and the general obscurity of early Gothic history, this book has acquired a value due chiefly to our lack of other sources. Jordanes' own preface is sufficient to make us hesitate to accept him as a historian. For not only will he summarise Cassiodorus' twelve books *De origine actibusque Getarum* in one only, but he will do so from memory, having at one time borrowed the book for three days: he complacently remarks, ' quamvis verba non recolo, sensus tamen et res actas credo me integre retinere.' ' Though I do not remember the words, I think I can accurately recall his meaning and the events that took place.'

Gildas (c. 516–570)

Not a whit better as a historian but more interesting to English readers is Gildus Badonicus or Gildas of Bath. Little is known of his life, and that little is obscured by a confusion between him and Gildas Albanius, a monk of the previous (fifth) century. Alcuin, late in the eighth century, calls our Gildas *sapientissimus*, but it is hard to see why. His book on the Britons falls into two parts, the *Historia* and the *Epistola*, which is the larger but less interesting part, consisting as it does chiefly of denunciations of the Britons, accompanied as a relief, he says, by many Scriptural quotations. The *History* too is full of such abuse of his countrymen that it is very likely that the writer was of Roman not British extraction. With little regard for truth and still less for lucid Latin he tells us how the Romans came to Britain 'and without opposition imposed their laws, by edicts extended obedience to themselves, and subdued the weak and faithless people not by sword, fire, or engines of war as other nations, but by mere threats, by the hand of the law, the mere looks on the faces of the Romans being enough to strike terror into their hearts.' The Romans left governors for the island but these were slain by 'the crafty lioness,' *leæna dolosa*, which seems to mean Boadicea. Again, when the Senate (!) 'hastened to take vengeance on the wily foxes,' the Britons were incapable of fighting and held out their hands to be bound. 'Ita ut in proverbium et in derisum longe lateque efferatur quod non Britanni sint in bello fortes nec in pace fideles.' There are vague and inaccurate references to the two Roman walls, also to towers on the south coast to keep out the Saxons. We owe to Gildas the report, quoted by Bede, of the appeal sent by the Britons to Rome to protect them against Picts, Scots and Saxons. 'Aetio ter consuli gemitus Britannorum. Repellunt nos Barbari ad mare, repellit nos mare ad barbaros. Inter hæc oriuntur duo genera funerum, aut iugulamur aut mersimur.' But for Gildas the Britons were wicked and obstinate, and if they were miserable they deserved to be. One true statement of Gildas is that he did not use local works as evidence for his history, because if there ever were any, they had long perished; instead he got his information *transmarina relatione*, whatever that may really imply.

Arator (fl. 545)

To the middle of the sixth century belong also Arator, poet and orator, and Corippus, poet and grammarian. Epic hexameter verse based on the Scriptures had a natural attraction for a Christian poet, and Arator follows in the footsteps of Juvencus, Sedulius, and Avitus. But his methods are mostly his own. His poem is called *De Actibus Apostolorum*,

'Versibus ego canam quos Lucas rettulit actus.'

But it is not a mere metrical version of St Luke's *Acts*. He singles out Peter and Paul to be the twin heroes of his poem, while the other characters are of little account. He is praised by Fortunatus, and still more in the Carolingian age by Johannes Fuldensis, who sets him above Virgil thus :

' Virgilius paleas, frumentum præbet Arator ;
Hic mansura docet, ille caduca refert.'

Corippus (fl. 565)

Quite different is the epic poem by the African Corippus, entitled ' John or the Libyan Wars.' The Vandal kingdom had already in 533 fallen before Justinian's general Belisarius, but in 547 the eastern Emperor had to deal with an invasion of Africa by the Moors. He appoints to the task Johannes a former lieutenant of Belisarius. This John is the hero of Corippus' epic of eight books, the writing of which brought advancement to its author. Though its interest is mainly historical, the poem is not without merit, indeed it compares very favourably with the mixture of versified history and myth which in a much more classical age was written by Silius Italicus. A panegyric on the new Emperor Justin II is the only other known poem. Like that other grammarian-poet Priscian, Corippus wrote a hexameter more nearly correct by classical standards than most of his contemporaries.

Gregory of Tours (538–593)

As in the fifth century so also in the sixth, many important bishoprics in Gaul were held by members of the old Gallo-Roman aristocracy. But there had been many changes, and a much less pleasing picture of society is given us by Gregory of Tours than by Apollinaris Sidonius of Clermont. For, quite apart from the differences in character between the two bishops, conditions had so changed in the fifty years that elapsed between the death of Sidonius and the birth of Gregory that the two were called upon to lead entirely different lives. Sidonius had unsuccessfully defended his country against the Visigoths. By 507 the Visigothic and Arian kingdom in France had been conquered by the Frankish and Catholic king Clovis. But France was not long united. The kingdom was divided on the death of Clovis and there were three Frankish kingdoms in the sixth century. Nor were the boundaries between them fixed for long. The kings disputed among them the possession of one city or another and gave or received them as gifts, dowries, and patrimonies. The city of Tours, from its central position belonged sometimes to one king, sometimes to another. Bishop Gregory therefore played a large part in the history which he himself wrote. For the bishop of a diocese was no mere appanage of the civil authority, but himself had power equal and in some ways superior to that of the Count (comes), who represented the king. And, however much the Frankish kings may have slaughtered their own and each other's subjects and ravaged each other's land, they generally respected the bishops. But they did not always, Catholics though they professed to be, honour the sanctity of churches or church property. Hence it is not surprising that much of the *History of the Franks* makes sorry reading, with its record of murder, intrigue and torture. Only exceptional faith and devotion enabled Gregory to persevere in the work of the Church, surrounded as he was by personal enemies no less than political difficulties.

Born in the year 538 Georgius Florentius belonged to a distinguished Gallo-Roman family, many of whom had been bishops. After his maternal great-grand-father, Bishop of Langres, he called himself Gregorius. In 573 he was appointed to the bishopric of Tours, a see which had previously been occupied by thirteen of his kindred. For the remaining twenty-one years of his life he held this see under one king or another, constantly watchful of the interests of the Church at a time when those were often neglected. Though certainly much loved by his people both young and old, and honoured far outside his own diocese, he seems to have led a somewhat lonely life. He tells us little of his friends, even of Fortunatus, and appears always to be fighting a lone battle. Yet he was not solitary by nature ; he was an affectionate and sensible man, fond of congenial company, glad when he is well and able to take his food and wine. Not self-indulgent, he honoured true self-denial, but rebuked that extreme asceticism which is a form of self-glorification. But for social intercourse among his equals he had little time or opportunity. The leisured days of Roman

Gaul were gone; bishops no longer lived like country gentlemen able to play games and enjoy society. Life was more serious and more dangerous. Death lurked everywhere working by murder or by mysterious disease, and fear and superstition followed in his wake. The indifference of the Arian Visigoth had affected but little either Church or civilisation; the Catholic Frank, out of sheer ignorance, rapacity and quarrelsomeness, came near to destroying both entirely.

During this politico-ecclesiastical life Gregory wrote many books, of which he himself says at the end of his *History of the Franks*, 'Decem libros historiarum, septem miraculorum, unum de Vitis Patrum scripsi, in Psalterii tractatum librum unum commentatus sum; de Cursibus etiam ecclesiasticis unum librum condidi.' The *historiæ* are the ten books of the *History of the Franks*. The seven books on *Miracles* are as follows: four on the miracles of St Martin, one *De Gloria Martyrum*, one on the miracles of St Julian and one *De Gloria Confessorum*. To Gregory St Martin was something more than a favourite saint; he was the inspiration of his whole life, and the two men had more in common than being both bishops of Tours each in his day. St Martin is constantly in his mind and references to him abound in the *History*, no less than in the four books especially devoted to him. These four books, like the *History*, were written at different periods of the author's life. The first deals with those miracles, or 'virtues' as he calls them, performed by the saint in his lifetime or by his relics after his death and down to Gregory's own time. Then at the beginning of the second book he says: 'We wish also to tell those deeds of our own time at which we wonder, leaving no slight material for more eloquent writers, while yet choosing the greatest of the miracles for my work; so that whilst my skill is unable to spin out the matter over pages, the great number of miracles may give it bulk.' We may be glad that Gregory's talent was not for long-winded writing. The description of the miracles in these books is vivid, and gains much in effect by the brevity of the narrative. In seven books of miracles some monotony was unavoidable and there is much similarity between the stories. Hence we read with added pleasure those which depart from the succession of healings by dust from tombs and similar things. For example, how St Ambrose of Milan, a contemporary of St Martin, fell asleep on the altar just when the Old Testament lesson was about to be read. There he remained two or three hours, none daring to waken him or to leave the church. Finally the people, being ' valde iam lassus,' awakened him. ' Do not,' he says, ' be alarmed. It hath greatly profited me that I thus fell asleep, such a marvel hath the Lord deemed fit to shew me. For know ye that my brother Martin hath departed from the body and that I attended his funeral and duly read the service, yet did not quite finish the chapter because ye wakened me.'—In astonishment and admiration they mark the day and the time and make careful enquiries. They found that the day and time of the passing of Holy Martin were the same as those in which the blessed Confessor Ambrose had said he had conducted the funeral. (Mart. I., 5.)

Gregory himself never tires of miracles; he spent his life collecting them, that such supports of faith might not perish. This absorbing interest is characteristic of the age no less than the man, and we may well believe that many read the *Historia Francorum* for its miraculous stories who cared little for the history. The author himself attached great importance to them, and the *History* should be read in the light of what is said at the end of the book of the miracles of St Julian: 'Ergo his miraculis lector intendens intelligat non aliter nisi martyrum reliquorumque amicorum Dei adiutoriis se posse salvari.' 'Therefore let the reader mark well these wonders, and understand that he cannot attain salvation by any other means save by the help of the martyrs and others beloved of God.' And again in the *History* itself (Book II, init.): 'Following the order of time,' he says, 'we tell indiscriminately both the miracles of holy men and the calamities of peoples. For I do not think it can be considered unreasonable to tell of the happy lives of blessed men among the miseries of the wretched, for it springs not from the writer's heedlessness but from the chronological order of events.' Hence it would be unfair to judge the *History of the Franks* from the standpoint of a historian only. Gregory was a bishop and interested primarily in the Church, especially that of St Martin of Tours. He rightly saw that the Church's chief enemy was the ignorance and barbarity of the time; and he felt that the history of his age ought to be written because it showed plainly both the wickedness of man and the goodness of God. He undertakes this task with great diffidence; he was not skilled in the art of letters, which indeed seemed to him to be already dead, but he was encouraged by the remark, 'philosophantem rhetorem intelligunt pauci, loquentem rusticum multi.'

The ten books of the *History* were composed at different times during his life and much of the later portions must have been written down soon after the events described. Book I is a summary of history from Adam and Eve down to the passing of St Martin, that is about A.D. 398, though Gregory says more than once that the passing of Martin took place

412 years after the Passion of Our Lord. But his early chronology is hopelessly disordered. This book is based mainly on Eusebius, Jerome, and Orosius. The second book continues the history to the death of Clovis in 511, but in it he tells us little of fifth-century history or the Visigothic kingdom. He is interested in Sidonius as a bishop more than in his defence of Clermont ; still more interested in a certain heretic bishop who, wishing to perform a miracle, bribed a man to feign blindness that he might heal him. But the man was suddenly smitten with true blindness, and the heretic could do nothing for him, until a holy Catholic bishop came and restored his sight. But with the accession of Clovis the Frank Gregory warms more to the historical work, especially after the well-known incident of Clovis' conversion to Catholicism because Christ answered his prayer and allowed him to defeat the Alemanni. The third book (A.D. 511–547) is less attractive, covering the quarrelsome careers of Clovis' four sons. The fourth book carries the narrative of the Frankish kings down to 575. He is now dealing with men nearer his own time and at one point pauses to remark, ' In telling this story I am reminded of a saying of Sallust (Cat., 3) against those who attacked writers of history. " It is a hard thing to write history, first because what is said and what is done must be made to fit, second because when you condemn any crimes, most people think you have spoken out of hatred and ill-feeling." ' Then he tells a good story of a wise abbot who, when one of his monks performed a miracle by his prayers, punished the young man severely lest his head be turned (IV, 34). The remaining six books (575–591) are a valuable detailed account of contemporary history, any summary of which would be out of place here. They give us a vivid picture

of the times; of the ruthless but not always ignoble kings of the Franks; of Sigibert, perhaps the best of them (Bk. IV), of his wife Brunhild, a beautiful Spanish princess, thus extravagantly praised by Fortunatus:

> ' Pulchra modesta decens sollers grata atque benigna
> Ingenio vultu nobilitate potens.'

who after her husband's death married his nephew Merovech, son of a rival king Chilperic, and lived to play a stormy part in Merovingian history; of her sister Galswintha, ill-fated wife of Chilperic, succeeded by the vile Fredegund, ever Brunhild's bitterest foe; of himself, arguing successfully on theology with Arian heretics, with Priscus a Jew (yet ' numquam compunctus est miser ad credendum'), and even with Chilperic, who had also taken part in the argument with Priscus. For this extraordinary king, who had murdered his wife Galswintha to marry his former mistress Fredegund, who is frequently seen as oppressor of his people and as a ravager of churches, who sent Leudast, Gregory's worst enemy, to be Count of Tours, was at the same time an admirer of Gregory and had a taste for theological disputes. At one time he ventured to lay down the law about the true doctrine of the Trinity. His ideas were quite heretical, and when Gregory convinced him of this he ' gnashed his teeth but said nothing.' So he turned to writing poetry instead after the manner of Sedulius. For this he was praised by the arch-flatterer Fortunatus, but Gregory coldly remarks, ' Sed versiculi illi nulli penitus metricæ conveniunt rationi.' ' But his verses conform to no system of metre whatever.' Then like a second Claudius he attempted without success to add Greek letters to the Latin alphabet. He was faithful and affectionate towards Fredegund who even in that age was notorious for her cruelty. Brunhild might be stern but, as compared with her enemy, she was kind and virtuous, as the following incident will show. ' When Queen Fredegund had retired to the afore-mentioned house in the country, she was in very low spirits, for much of her power had been taken from her, and thought Brunhild had more than her share of good luck. So she secretly sent a priest who was very well known to her, that he might by guile get round Brunhild and so be able to do away with her. The plan was that, when he had craftily wormed his way into her service and won her trust, he should then strike her down privily. So the priest came and by various means commended himself to her, " I am fleeing before Queen Fredegund and beg your help." He begins to make himself humble, kindly and obedient to all, and indispensable to the queen. But after a short time they learned that he had been sent on a mission of treachery. He was bound and flogged, and when he had confessed his secret was allowed to return to his patroness. But when he revealed what had happened and admitted that he had been unable to perform her commands, she punished him by cutting off his hands and feet.'

Yet Gregory often wearies of his own unhappy narrative and has grave doubts, happily falsified, of the ultimate unity and prosperity of his country, ' Tædet me bellorum civilium diversitates quæ Francorum gentem et regnum valde proterunt memorare.' ' It's weary I am of telling the ups and downs of civil wars that greatly crush the race and kingdom of the Franks.' Sometimes, though rarely, he sees signs of better things, as in the charitable deeds of Guntram of Burgundy. More often he turns towards anything bearing on his religion, miracles, prodigies and conversions. There are stories of impostors too (Bk. IX). One of them ' in public abstained from food and drink, but in private when he came to an inn so kept stuffing himself that the servant could not keep pace with his constant demands.' Another, less subtle, was put in prison, but escaped, got drunk, and went to sleep in a church. Here Gregory and the other clergy found him, but could not come near him without holding their noses, ' tantus fœtor egrediebatur ut omnium cloacarum atque secessuum fœtores fœtor ille devicerit.' And of hermits : one unfortunate and unbalanced youth, while yet a boy of twelve succeeded in persuading his master to let him enter a narrow hermit's cell for the rest of his days. He slowly became insane ; claustrophobia and a persecution mania, or, as Gregory puts it, an evil spirit, had done deadly work (VIII, 34). His own city of Tours figures frequently ; he successfully maintained its immunity from taxation against King Childebert, but riots and feuds among the people themselves gave him much trouble. He had personal enemies too who tried to bring this proud aristocratic bishop to a fall. Nor could he always look with satisfaction on his allies, his brother priests and bishops, many of whom had little regard for their people or for justice. One of these Badegisil, a mayor of the palace (major domus) appointed bishop by a whim of a king, and like the more illustrious Sidonius rushed through the ecclesiastical grades in a few weeks, is thus depicted (VIII, 39). ' In that year many of the bishops died : among them Badegisil bishop of Le Mans, a very cruel man among his people, robbing and confiscating property of different persons. His wife, more savage than he, added to his cruel and harsh nature, kept goading him by the most infamous suggestions into committing crimes. Not a day or a moment passed but he took some step either in the despoiling of citizens or in his various quarrels. And every day he would argue cases with judges and conduct secular business ; he was always raging against some, harrying others with floggings. Many he even went so far as to whip with his own hands, saying "Am I, because I have become a cleric, not to be the avenger of my own wrongs ? " But why should I speak of strangers since he did not spare his own brothers but robbed them the more. They could never obtain justice with him over their mother's or their father's property. Now after the fifth year of his episcopate, when just beginning the sixth, he prepared a very elaborate and abundant feast for the citizens. He caught a fever and by dying suddenly put an end to the year thus begun.'

His successor had much trouble with the widow, who claimed as hers what Badegisil had given to the Church, and generally won her point. ' She was a woman of unspeakable cruelty ; nam sæpius viris omnia pudenda cum ipsis ventris pellibus incidit, feminis secretiora corporis loca laminis candentibus perussit. Many other wicked deeds she also did, of which I have judged it better to say nothing.'

Gregory frequently apologises for his Latin ; for example thus : ' Non me artis grammaticæ studium imbuit neque auctorum sæcularium polita lectio erudivit.' ' I have not been soaked in the study of grammar or educated in the polished diction of secular writers.' Apart from the evidence of his own writings whose language is often uncouth, such remarks are too frequent not to be genuine. He does not deny his inability to get all his cases and prepositions right. Yet Latin is his mother-tongue ; he says nothing, unfortunately, of any other language in France. We do not know what constituted good Latin in sixth-century Gaul, but Gregory's language can only be considered incorrect when judged by the standards of literary Latin, that is by standards quite inapplicable to it. The cleavage between the *lectio polita* and the *sermo rusticus* was rapidly growing; and it would appear that Gregory, who had certainly read some Latin authors, knew enough about the literary language to be aware that its grammatical rules were not those of his everyday speech, but not enough to enable him to write after that manner.

Fortunatus (c. 535–600)

Among those poets who have been frequently praised beyond their deserts, and who have in the end suffered considerably thereby is Venantius Fortunatus. He was born at Treviso in North Italy some time after 530, and educated at Ravenna, whose schools were then at the height of their fame. But before the Lombard invasion, while still a young man, he left Italy, crossed the Alps and visited the Rhenish towns. The ultimate object of his travels was the shrine of St Martin of Tours, by whom he had been once miraculously cured. After Tours he visited Poitiers, an event which determined the trend of his whole life and work. For here he made the acquaintance of Radegund, a Thuringian princess, who had been married to a Frankish king (Clothar I), but left him, sorely against his will, to found a monastery. She adopted as a daughter Agnes and made her abbess. These two women, afterwards canonised, were the chief influences on the work of Fortunatus. He did not leave Poitiers till after their death (587), and then, after visiting the valley of the Moselle and, like Ausonius, celebrating it in verse, returned to Poitiers to become its bishop. During most of his former sojourn there he does not seem to have been even a priest. Among other influences on Fortunatus must be counted Gregory of Tours, another devotee of Saint Martin.

Apart from a life of St Martin in four books of hexameters and a number of lives of other saints, including St Radegund, in prose, Fortunatus' work is comprised in eleven books of *Miscellanea*, nearly all poems, and the majority in elegiacs. Many of these, especially in Books III, V, VII, IX, are letters in verse. Book IV is mainly epitaphs, while Book VI, in spite of much flattery, is of interest historically. It contains the well-known poem, suggested to him by Radegund, on the ill-fated Galswintha. Her murder is glossed over and much of the poem is taken up with the princess and her mother taking leave of each other in Spain.

There are some neat occasional poems in Books X and XI, but Fortunatus' best work is inspired by his religion and the entourage of Radegund and Agnes (Agnus Agnen dedit Radegundo). Reminiscences of Virgil and others are there less frequent and the verse has a more genuine ring. The beauty and blessings of Virginity had long been a favourite theme especially among the Fathers, and Fortunatus, sometimes with more enthusiasm than good taste, praises it in a long poem in the VIIIth Book, addressed to Agnes as the Bride of Christ. From this piece come the following lines :

' Templa creatoris sunt membra pudica puellæ
    Et habitat proprius tale cubile Deus.
Quantum sponsa potest de virginitate placere
    Ipsi cui genetrix non nisi virgo placet.
Sarra, Rebecca, Rachel, Hester, Judith, Anne, Noemi
    Quamvis præcipue culmen ad astra levent,
Nulla tamen meruit mundi generare parentem.
    Quae dominum peperit, clausa Maria manet.
Intemerata Deum suspendit ab ubere natum
    Et panem cœli munere lactis alit.'

> ' A maiden's body is her Maker's shrine,
> A couch whereon He loveth to recline.
> A virgin bride to Him is ever dear
> Who chose a virgin as His mother here.
> Sarah, Rebecca, Rachel, Hester, Anne,
> Judith, Naomi—when He came as Man.
> On none of this blest host was He revealed,
> Mary His mother was a virgin sealed.
> On her pure breast she laid Our Lord at even,
> And nurtured with her milk the Bread of Heaven.'

This is one of the best pieces in the *Miscellanea*; too much of the collection consists of mere tours de force, such as acrostic and cross-word poems, inept attempts at punning, and harmless but trivial verses on dinner-plates, etc. If anyone had the patience to read through the *Miscellanea*, he would rise from the task with the feeling that the author's reputation as a poet was ludicrously undeserved. But by something of a miracle Fortunatus also wrote two of the most glorious of Latin hymns, the ' *Pange lingua gloriosi* ' and the ' *Vexilla regis prodeunt*,' and as a corrective it may be well to give a few lines of each. Both were written to celebrate the arrival of a fragment of the true Cross sent to Radegund at Poitiers by the Byzantine Emperor Justin II. The first is in trochaic tetrameters :

> ' Pange lingua gloriosi prælium certaminis,
> Et super crucis tropæo dic triumphum nobilem,
> Qualiter Redemptor orbis immolatus vicerit.'

The second is in iambic dimeters with slight traces of rhyme :

> ' Vexilla regis prodeunt,
> Fulget crucis mysterium
> Quo carne carnis conditor
> Suspensus est patibulo.'

' The standards of the King advance,
The Cross mysterious shines on high,
Whereon our bodies' Maker hung
His body stretched in agony.'

It is by these two hymns that Fortunatus lives.
They were adopted, albeit in a truncated and altered
form, by the Church, and have never ceased to be
popular. Instead of the laboured artistry of elegiacs
we have natural, quickly-moving verse, which made
these hymns great favourites among French and
Spanish soldiers all over the world. So well known
were they that they were actually parodied in England
in the thirteenth century, not from irreligious motives
but as political skits on one of Edward II's favourites.

The weakness of Fortunatus in the mass of his
verse lies in the absence of any genuine poetical inspiration. To cavil at his metrical and grammatical
faults, false quantities and non-classical forms, is to
err on the side of pedantry and to ignore the changes
in grammar and pronunciation which the language
had undergone. Such things do not demean a great
poet and should not be allowed to warp our judgment
even of a very second-rate one such as Fortunatus.
As long as he looked back towards ancient models,
Virgil and Ovid, Claudian and Sedulius, he could do
no better than follow haltingly, but when we see
him at the threshold of Medieval Latin poetry, we
recognise him as a forerunner in that field rather than
a late-comer in the other.

Gregory the Great (540–604)

The great Christian Latin writers of the fifth and
sixth centuries have been generally and rightly regarded
as standing as it were astride the confused and imaginary

border between ancient and medieval times. But this cannot be said of Pope Gregory I, the spiritual founder of the Middle Ages. A comparison of Gregory's works with those of Boethius and Cassiodorus will soon show that we have passed into a different world. Externally we have seen the same kind of change taking place in Gaul, but in Italy the contrast is even more striking, since in Gaul Sidonius and Gregory of Tours are more widely separated in time than Cassiodorus and Gregory I, who were almost contemporaries. Gregory was born about the year 540. He came of a wealthy Roman family and began by embracing a political and administrative career at Rome. But about the age of thirty-three he sold nearly all his property to give to the poor, and with the remainder founded a monastery of St Andrew, in which he himself was an ordinary monk. We may perhaps fairly conjecture that this decision to abandon secular life was hastened by the fact that Pavia and the whole of Northern Italy had fallen into the hands of fresh invaders, the Lombards. It is true that Rome itself and other parts of Italy were free, that is were subject only to the Emperor at Constantinople. But peace with the Lombards was still very far off and Gregory was destined to play an important part in the life of politics and statecraft which he sought to avoid. From 579–585 he was *apocrisarius* or, as we should say, Papal Nuncio at the Court of the Emperor. He there wrote the *Magna Moralia*. He returned to Rome to become abbot of his own monastery of St Andrew, and five years later was brought forth thence to be made Pope, very much against his will. His election is described by his namesake in Tours. Gregory's reluctance to become head of the Church was probably no mere cry of *Nolo episcopari*. The life of a Pope, especially at such a time, was not the contemplative life for which Gregory, a man of infirm body, believed himself fitted. But his great practical abilities were badly needed and in the fourteen years of his pontificate he ruled State as well as Church and bravely opposed the Lombards, a more dangerous and more lasting foe than the Ostrogoths a hundred years before.

But it is not only because of his pontificate and political power that Gregory stands out as the founder of the Middle Ages. It is also by virtue of his attitude of mind as revealed in his writings. His great intellectual powers were so concentrated on the Church and its teaching that everything else was excluded. The arts and sciences and usual intellectual interests of an educated man did not exist for Gregory, or were of such slight importance that it was a waste of time, at any rate for a bishop, to study or teach them. The attack on grammar, his indignant refusal to have the Word of God bound by the rules of Donatus, has received more than its share of publicity, and we fail to understand it if we see in it only an episcopal idiosyncrasy. We should rather see therein how widely separate for the religious mind are the things which count and those which do not. This concentration of effort and narrowing of interest meant added power. Nor is Gregory's range of interests so narrow as appears at first sight. The intellectual may think them narrow, but the intellectual had almost ceased to exist, and was of no importance to Gregory and his Church, whereas nothing in the whole field of ordinary human conduct is outside his province as priest. Hence it comes that Gregory's writings, in addition to their historical and ecclesiastical importance, had an appeal both widespread and authoritative, and can still show us the most complete and exact system of conduct that the world has ever seen. He himself disclaimed all credit ; he would have liked the later legend which depicted the Dove of the Divine Spirit whispering in his ear as he wrote.

The most important of Gregory's voluminous works are the *Letters*, the *Dialogues*, *On the Pastoral Charge*, the *Magna Moralia*, this last being in the form of an extended commentary on the Book of Job. He also wrote other Bible commentaries and liturgical works and greatly reformed Church Music. In literary and general interest the fourteen books of letters hold first place. They cover the fourteen years of his papacy ; touching on a great variety of topics and situations with which the Pope was called upon to deal, they form a great storehouse of information about the man and his life and times, such as his difficulties with that curious and unhappy affair known as the Istrian schism, his hopes of converting the Arian Lombards. He rebukes an intolerant bishop for excommunicating an aged and infirm abbot, another for conniving at a Jewish convert who desecrated the synagogue he had just left. He often has occasion to write to the Emperor or the Empress, to kings and queens among Lombards and Franks, as well as to bishops who everywhere sought his advice. Thus Augustine of Canterbury, through whom he had converted Anglia, asks him many questions about his new charge, the ordination of its bishops, its relation to the bishops in Gaul and other more intimate and personal questions. Most important of all Augustine asks, ' Cum una sit fides cur sunt ecclesiarum consuetudines tam diversæ ? ' Gregory replies, ' You know, my brother, the custom of the Church of Rome, remembering that you were reared therein. But I desire that you should carefully select whatsoever in any church, whether in Rome or Gaul, may better please Almighty God, and by sound teaching instil into the English Church, which is still new in the Faith, all that you have gathered from many Churches. For institutions are not endeared to us by the places where they are, but the places by their institutions. Therefore choose from each Church whatsoever things are holy, whatsoever things are religious, whatsoever things are right and, gathering them together as into a bundle, set them down in the minds of the English to be the way of their Church.' (This correspondence is preserved for us by Bede, *Hist. Eccl.*, I, 27.)

The *Dialogues*, written in Rome in the early years of his papacy, were hailed with delight as soon as published, even in Lombardy, where Queen Theudalinda prized them greatly. They deal with many subjects but chiefly ' de vita et miraculis patrum Italicorum.' In his love of miracles Gregory was thoroughly characteristic of his age ; for in Italy as in France the collapse of Roman civilisation, the invasions and the seeming impotence of the Church demanded strong and convincing remedies for the doubters of the Faith. Of Paulinus, Bishop of Nola (pp. 30–2), he tells the following tale. Paulinus had given away in alms all that he possessed when a poor widow came to him, whose son had been carried off as a slave to Africa by the Vandals. She asked for money to ransom him, but Paulinus, having none, offered the only alms he could—himself. The widow was with difficulty persuaded to consent ; they crossed to Africa where they found the young man in the service of the king's son-in-law. An exchange was effected and the handsome bishop became a gardener to the prince. By the excellence of his gardening, his interesting conversation and finally by his true prophecies Paulinus won favour, and, when asked to name

117

a gift for himself, asked for the release of all his captive countrymen. 'And so it came to pass that Paulinus, servant of Almighty God, foretold the truth and by surrendering himself alone to slavery returned from slavery to liberty along with many others, after the manner of Him who took upon Himself the form of a slave, that we might not be the slaves of sin.' The *Dialogues* contain much beside stories. The supposed interlocutor, Peter the Deacon, asks many questions, especially on theological points, but Gregory's answers on prayers, predestination and compunction are chiefly of ecclesiastical interest. But the *Dialogues* were extremely popular. They were copied and summarised and translated, first into Greek, thence into Arabic, and also into French and Old English in time of Alfred.

It remains to speak of the *Liber Regulæ Pastoralis*, which in spite of its title contains much that will interest the general reader. For nowhere is better seen Gregory's human interest and observation of character, combined with his complete inability to see anything except through ecclesiastical eyes. The admonishment which the parish priest will administer will differ according to the habits and character of each person, the habitual sinner and the occasional, the ignorant and the knowing, the good- and bad-tempered, people who are always beginning good works but never finish them, people who seem to get all they want and those who get nothing—quibus omnia ex sententia succedunt et quibus nulla—people who have no very great sins but many little ones so small that they think they do not count. Married people are to be especially cautioned ; marriage is only as it were a safe city where the weak may take refuge ; 'quia coniugalis hæc vita non quidem in virtutibus mira est, sed tamen a suppliciis secura.' 'For this wedded life is certainly not remarkable in virtues, but at least is free from damnation.' *This*, the right, wedded life means 'nisi fructum propaginis in carne non quærere.'

Isidore of Seville (570-636)

The *Origines* or *Etymologiæ* of Isidore, Bishop of Seville exercised an influence far beyond its real value. His other works are not important but *Origins* remained for centuries the standard encyclopædia from which learned and unlearned alike gathered unquestioningly the fruits of a very much decayed tree of ancient knowledge. Except in the tenth book, which is a dictionary, the arrangement is not alphabetical, but kindred subjects are generally gathered into the same book. His aim is to deal with the whole sum of knowledge, the world in general, its peoples and languages, the liberal arts and all the sciences, especially medicine and anatomy, the animal world, navigation, astronomy, geography, agriculture; religious knowledge, Church organisation and heresies, sixty-eight of them. The chief impression of reading Isidore is surprise at the amount of erroneous or half-correct information which he conveys. His ridiculous etymologies, which he is always bringing in and which have given a title to the book, must be pardoned, though they are ludicrous even for that age of ignorance —'Surdus, a sordibus humoris aure conceptis.' 'Fornax ab igne vocata; φῶς enim ignis est.' Can he really have known Greek and Hebrew as tradition said? He remarks somewhere that no one is so utterly stupid that he does not know at least his own language. Yet he seems to think *haud* and *aut* are the same word! But, apart from language, we find him vague and inaccurate even when dealing with sciences well advanced before his day. Sometimes he intermingles correct and incorrect so convincingly that it is not surprising that an uncritical age should have made an authority of this careless compiler. Thus : ' Now the names of the seven sons of Japhet are ; Gomer, whence Galatæ, that is Gauls ; Magog, from whom they think Scythians and Goths took their origin . . . ; Javan, whence the Ionians, who are also Greeks. . . . The sons of Javan are Elisa, whence the Elisæan Greeks, who are called Æolians ; whence also the fifth Greek dialect is called Æolic.' The passage is no less interesting for what is right than for what is wrong, and the method employed, ' they think the Scythians, etc.,' is very characteristic of Isidore. His record for veracity is so bad when we have the means of testing him, that we hesitate to listen when we have none. The uniting of the Scythian horsemen with the Parthian peasants in the Sassanid kingdom becomes distorted thus, ' The Parthians owe their origin to the Scythians. For they were exiles from among them, as is shewn by their name. For in the Scythian tongue exiles are called *parthi*.' Obviously not all his information is wrong, indeed he occasionally surprises us. He knows that the Book of Job was almost entirely in verse in the original Hebrew. About minerals and precious stones he either knew a good deal, or was able to find a better text-book than usual to copy from. He knows that Corinthian bronze is an alloy of gold, silver and copper, and adds that it was so called because in the sack of Corinth all the gold, silver and bronze statues were cast into the fire, and *æs Corinthium* was the result. It is a pity that he ascribes the sack of Corinth to Hannibal !

Such was the encyclopædia used in the Middle Ages, which earned for its author the title of ' gran doctor de las Españas.' But rather than always make merry at his expense, let us remember that even Boethius and Cassiodorus were compilers, that Isidore was no less industrious than they, and that it was his misfortune to live at the end of a period when secular learning was rapidly disappearing.

Columbanus (c. 550–c. 621)

If science was dead, literature was still alive and destined soon to make a happy recovery in the days of Charlemagne. Already in 613 there had been founded at Bobbio in North Italy a monastery which became one of the great centres of learning and played an important part in the preservation of manuscripts. Its founder was the Irish monk Columbanus. Many other monasteries were founded by Irishmen about the same time, the best known being that of St Gall in Switzerland, founded by Gallus. That the impulse which led to the study and preservation of so many Latin Classics should have come entirely from Irish monks with a taste for travel may seem at first surprising. But in reality nothing was more natural; for in the seventh century men looked on Ireland as the only true seat of learning, which at the time was no more than the truth. If St Patrick was but a poor Latin scholar, he at least had no prejudice against the ancient Classics, and his successors made Ireland renowned not only for Latin but for Greek learning. Yet it still remains something of a mystery why Columbanus and his twelve companions chose to spend their lives on the Continent. One thing is clear; they came as apostles not of learning for its own sake but of the gospel and a stricter monastic rule.

The date and place of Columbanus' birth are uncertain; but the former is put about A.D. 550, the latter was somewhere in Leinster. He studied at the famous monastery of Bangor at the mouth of Belfast Lough, a prolific mother of scholars. Having there equipped himself with sacred and profane learning he and twelve others went abroad, where most of his life was spent, first in the Vosges, where he founded several monasteries, and finally, being expelled from Burgundy, at Bobbio in Italy. His *Regula cœnobialis* is strict and his *Table of Penitences* severe, but his sermons, *Instructiones*, have an almost familiar ring ; there is little theology but much moral teaching and comfort for the soul. Here as in his poetry the thought of the shortness of this life as compared with eternity is constantly present. His letters, including an un-answered one to Pope Gregory, are of historical interest, but his interest for literature lies in his poetry. There is little of it, but it shows on the one hand skill in handling the hexameter not so much in narrative, as in single lines. There are nearly 200 monosticha, such as :

> ‘ Contra verbosos noli contendere verbis.
> Quod tibi vis fieri hoc alii præstare memento.
> Plus tua quam alterius damnabis crimina iudex.
> Una dies quales fuerint ostendit amicos.
> Exsuperat numerus iustorum regna potentum
> Diligit hic natum virga qui corripit illum.’

So addicted is he to this not unpleasing gnomic manner that the rest of his hexameter verse is full of proverbs too. At the end of his life, being about seventy years old, he wrote the *Epistula ad Fedolium*. He would be very much astonished to find that students of literature remember him for this poem, obviously only written as an amusement. It is not great poetry ; its subject, the snare of wealth, is banal, but it is formally, metrically and verbally perfect. The verse, which was used by Boethius, is Adonic, each line being equivalent to a hexameter ending or the fourth line of a Sapphic-stanza.

> ' Hectoris heros
> Vendidit auro
> Corpus Achilles.
> Et reserari
> Munere certo
> Nigra feruntur
> Limina Ditis. . . .'

Aldhelm (c. 640–709)

In England the seventh century saw the beginnings of Anglo-Latin literature associated chiefly with names of Aldhelm of Malmesbury, Bishop of Sherborne, and in the north the Venerable Bede. The Church founded by Augustine of Canterbury under Gregory the Great at the beginning of the century did not prosper, partly perhaps because it had no intellectual and educational background. In the north the reconversion was done by Irish monks from Iona. But a dispute about the right ascertainment of the date of Easter caused a coolness between the Northumbrian and Irish Churches, especially those in Ulster and Iona. The Synod of Whitby in 664 decided finally in favour of the Roman method against the Celtic. This adherence to Rome on the Paschal question determined the whole allegiance of the English Church, and when the kings of Kent and Northumbria jointly decided to ask for missionaries to complete the conversion of the South of England, it was not to Ireland but to Rome that they appealed. First came Abbot Hadrian, an African by birth, then Theodore of Tarsus, who became Archbishop of Canterbury (669–690). These men had evidently been chosen for their learning no less than missionary zeal, possessing just those qualities which Augustine had lacked. Both were learned in Greek, especially Theodore, who founded a school at Canterbury, the first step towards that fame for Greek learning of which England is justly proud. Aldhelm, a young Wessex nobleman, had already pursued Latin studies, very probably under Irish teachers at Malmesbury ; now from Theodore he learns Greek also. His twelfth-century biographer, Faricius, tells us that he could both speak and write it like a native. This may be almost true, since Greek was doubtless Theodore's mother-tongue, but when he goes on to say that he knew Hebrew too, we are inclined to doubt his word. At all events he was well versed in the Classics, and was the first of a long line of English aristocrats who have had a taste for writing Latin verses.

Bede said of Aldhelm that he was ' et sermone nitidus et scripturarum,' but however charming his conversation may have been, the writings that we know are stilted and affected. He makes a parade of his knowledge by using Greek words in the most unnecessary places. His prose is especially unpleasing, and it is strange to find so great a master of lucid Latin as Bede praising him. He can hardly have intended the words to apply to the prose of a man who could write in a letter : ' Primitus (pantorum procerum prætorumque pio potissimum, paternoque præsertim privilegio) panegyricum pœmataque passim prosatori sub polo promulgantes, stridula vocum symphonia, ac melodiæ cantilenæque carmine modulaturi, hymnizemus, præcipue quia tandem almæ editum puerperæ sobolem (ob inextricabile sons protoplastorum) piaculum priscorum chirographum peccaminum oblitteraturum terris tantumdem destinare dignatus est, luridum qui linguis chelydrum trisulcis rancida virulentaque vomentem per ævum venena torrenda tetræ tortionis in tartara trusit.' It is very nearly as bad as the *Hisperica Famina*.

The Epistle to Acircius comprises first a handbook on metres arranged in the form of questions and answers, then a book of riddles in verse with his usual acrostic prologue, and lastly notes on metrical feet. This study of metre enabled him to write verse with little trouble and no distinction. His longest and best known poem is called *De Laudibus Virginum* (nearly 5000 lines), on which he also wrote in prose. The best that can be said of it is that it is very much better than his prose. Bede admired this poem for pious reasons and it was read and liked by his contemporaries. But however carefully Aldhelm may have gathered the fruits of his reading of Virgil, Lucan, Sedulius, Ausonius and nearly every other Latin poet before he sat down to write this poem, few will derive any pleasure from reading it. It is useless to give quotations, for they could not convey an impression of interminable dullness. Slightly more interesting are some of his lesser poems, *On the Eight Chief Vices* and *On a Church built by the Princess Bugga*.

It is doubtful whether Aldhelm also wrote in that rhythmical syllabic verse often with rime which is characteristic of Celtic Latin hymns. His training as we have seen was more Classical than Celtic. Anglo-Saxon was his mother-tongue and he is said to have written poems in it. On the other hand his interest in metre may have led him to try experiments. He probably knew the *Altus Prosator* of St Columba and the Irish *Liber Hymnorum*, while the Antiphonary of Bangor was compiled in this century. Moreover, his pupil Ætheluald certainly wrote verses of this kind which have come down to us, as did also St Boniface

(Wynfirth) Saxon missionary to Germany and his pupil Lul.

Riddles in Verse. Tatwin (ob. 734)

Riddles in verse lie only on the very fringe of literature but they are an outstanding feature of Anglo-Latin verse of this period. Puzzles have always appealed to Teutonic minds and in England to the clergy in particular. Aldhelm, Bishop of Sherborne, Huadbert (Eusebius), Abbot of Jarrow, and Tatwin, Archbishop of Canterbury, all composed riddles. But they were not written merely for amusement; they were intended to be educational. Those of Aldhelm as we have seen were included in a work on metre, while Tatwin in his dedication speaks of ' hoc monitorium opus.' Aldhelm's riddles are more numerous and more metrically correct than Tatwin's, but the archbishop's are rather more amusing. Many are descriptions of animals and birds, and by learning them the student was expected to fix in his memory their names and habits ; similarly with plants, celestial bodies and common objects. Our manuscripts always give the answer at the head. This from Tatwin :

> ' De Oculis.
> Discernens totum iuris Natura locavit
> Nos pariter geminos una de matre creatos
> Divisi haud magno parvi discrimine collis,
> Ut nunquam vidi illum, nec me viderit ipse,
> Sed cernit sine me nihil, illo nec sine cerno.'

Still less literary are the *Hisperica Famina* or *Western Sayings*. They belong really to the sixth century and are a mere curiosity in very strange Latin which, even when it can be translated, seems to give no rational sense : ' Sophicam stemicate coloniam, ac litterales speculamini apices.

The Venerable Bede (c. 670–735)

The seventh century would indeed be a barren field if its close had not been marked by the birth of the Venerable Bede. He was born about 670 in the Tyneside neighbourhood. Left an orphan while still a child he came to live with Ceolfrid, abbot of the recently-founded monastery at Jarrow. The plague which stripped Jarrow of many of its monks in 686 spared him, and he became deacon at the age of nineteen and priest at thirty. He lived and worked a simple monk in the same monastery. He was never abbot. For when Ceolfrid departed on his ill-fated journey for Rome, he appointed another successor, Huadbert called Eusebius, wisely sparing his learned protégé the administrative duties of abbot, that he might continue his studies. Study in English monasteries must have been hampered by lack of books, though Benedict Biscop, when he founded Jarrow and Wearmouth, gave them handsome gifts of manuscripts from the Continent; and when provision for daily needs, gardening, farming and the like, occupied so much of the monks' time and labour, there was much less study and copying of manuscripts than in the more favoured climates of France and Italy. Bede's learning is therefore the more remarkable. But if contact with Italy was difficult, Ireland was at hand, whence through Iona had come the reconversion of the apostate Northumbria. Bede reminds us that the debt did not end there; English monks frequently went to study among the Irish doctors, who welcomed them kindly and asked no fee (*Hist. Eccl.* III, 27). Till his death in 735 Bede remained at Jarrow, and appears rarely to have left the neighbourhood and never to have left England. But he was no recluse. His duties in the monastery were not merely those of a student but of a teacher too, and to both he devoted himself with equal pleasure, 'semper aut discere aut docere aut scribere dulce habui.' Indeed his influence as a teacher is no less important than his written works. For it was one of his pupils, Egbert the Archbishop, who founded the school of York whence came Alcuin. (See Part III.)

It was to the needs of his students that Bede's earliest works were directed. Among these are (1) the *De Orthographia*. This is not really, like the work of the nonagenarian Cassiodorus, a treatise on spelling, but rather a glossary of Latin and occasionally of Greek words. Needless to say it is not always correct and the etymologies are usually fantastic ; but a Latin dictionary of some kind was a necessity in an Anglo-Saxon speaking country and the *De Orthographia* was valuable at the time. (2) *De Arte Metrica.* The study of Latin, though pursued only for a better understanding of the Scriptures and the Fathers included the art of metre, 'quæ divinis non est incognita libris,' as Bede says. Hence most, but by no means all, of the examples cited in his essay are taken from Christian poets. He himself is the author of several hymns and poems. His more mature work (he provides us with a list at the close of the *Ecclesiastical History*) includes (1) long Biblical commentaries with many allegorical interpretations. Though outside the scope of this book these works should not be overlooked in any estimate of the Venerable Bede. All his other works, to us more interesting, were to him of secondary importance compared with the understanding of God's Word and the necessity of salvation. (2) Scientific works, such as the *De Natura Rerum*, which is based largely on the elder Pliny and Isidore. Chronology, especially the date of Easter, in which he held the orthodox Roman view, interested him greatly, and the *De Temporibus* and its fuller version *De Ratione Temporum* are a survey of the universe, sun, moon and planets, with explanations of their motions and of our time-reckoning based thereon. He appends (chap. 66) a chronological table of world history, using St Augustine's division into six ages, and finally warns his readers not to suppose that a knowledge of chronology will enable them to foretell the end of the world; such attempts are ' hæretica et frivola.' The warning fell on deaf ears. (3) Historical and biographical works, such as the *Historia Abbatum*, that is the abbots of Jarrow and Wearmouth, a *Life of Saint Cuthbert*, both based on recent work of others, the latter being written first in hexameters and then in a prose version, and above all the Ecclesiastical History or *Historia Ecclesiastica Gentis Anglorum*.

It would be superfluous to praise the *Ecclesiastical History*. Even if it had not been written by a master, it would still have been indispensable for the study of early English History. Written by Bede it is one of the finest historical works in Latin. Though Bede tells many stories and miracles, yet compared with him Gregory of Tours seems little more than an earnest gossip. We have already noted that Bede, here most unlike Gregory, was an expert in chronology. This knowledge stood him in good stead in his historical work, and fortunately for us and his successors he applied it with such care and exactitude that his dates *ab incarnatione Domini* formed the basis for the chronology of all subsequent English History. But care for dates does not of itself make a historian, and Bede's claim, which he himself would never have put forward, rests on far more than that. He was in the habit of examining and weighing his authorities. Moreover, he acknowledged his debt to them and added marginal notes, giving the sources of many of his statements. He earnestly requests that these be preserved, ' lest I be said to steal the sayings of my predecessors and write them as my own.' Unfortunately the scribes ignored this advice, and apart from those borrowings which modern scholars have detected, we know only of those whose names are mentioned in the text, Albinus, Nothelm, the anonymous life of Saint Cuthbert and many others, chiefly Anglo-Saxon. For the introductory sketch of British History from Julius Cæsar to Gregory the Great (Bk. I, chaps. 1–22) he did not consider it necessary to state that he was indebted to Orosius and Gildas.

The subject proper begins at I, 23, with the sending of Augustine to England, his correspondence with Gregory the Great (see p. 116) and the founding, apparently on an older Christian site, of Christ Church, Canterbury. The mention of Gregory's death (II, 1) leads him to describe his life and work, and to tell the story of how he came to send the mission to England. The story is well known but usually only half told. Finding some fair-haired Yorkshire boys for sale in the Forum the Pope asked who they were. 'Responsum est quod Angli vocarentur. At ille "Bene" inquit "nam et angelicam habent faciem, et tales Angelorum in cælis decet esse coheredes. Quod habet nomen ipsa provincia, de qua isti sunt adlati?" Responsum est quod Deiri idem provinciales. At ille "Bene" inquit "Deiri; de ira eruti, et ad misericordiam Christi vocati. Rex provinciæ illius quomodo appellatur?" Responsum est quod Ælli diceretur. At ille adludens ad nomen ait "Alleluia, laudem Dei Creatoris illis in partibus oportet cantari."'

The conversion of England is described and reversion to heathenism after Augustine's death. In Northumbria there was a temporary revival of Christianity under King Edwin (d. 633), but it had not penetrated deeply, and after his reign the people lapsed again. The real Christianisation of the North of England took place under the saintly King Oswald, who invited the Irish monks of Iona to send one of their number to convert his people. They sent Aidan, who became Bishop of Lindisfarne. In telling of the lives of King Oswald and St Aidan, Bede has a task congenial to him. He enjoys, as we do, the picture of the king himself acting as interpreter to the Irish missionary, who when he first came, 'Anglorum linguam perfecte non noverat.' Oswald is his ideal king. One Easter Sunday he and the bishop were about to sit down to a sumptuous meal on a silver tray when word was brought that the poor were at the gate craving alms. Oswald at once ordered the whole meal to be given them and the silver tray to be broken in pieces and distributed. The bishop was so impressed with this charity that he seized the king's right hand saying : ' May this hand never grow old.' ' And so indeed it came to pass even as he had prayed. For when the king was slain in battle and his hands were severed from the rest of his body, they have remained uncorrupted to this day. Now in the royal town called after a queen named Bebba (Bamborough) they are kept enclosed in a silver box in the church of St Peter and are venerated by all with due honour ' (III, 6). Bede's praise of St Aidan is tempered by his dislike of his Celtic practices in the matter of Easter, a subject he could never long forget ; but for the rest of his character he has nothing but the highest praise, ' quasi verax historicus, simpliciter ea, quæ de illo sive per illum

131

sunt gesta, describens, et quæ laude sunt digna in eius actibus laudans, atque ad utilitatem memoriæ commendans ; studium videlicet pacis et caritatis, continentiæ et humilitatis ; . . . industriam faciendi simul et docendi mandata cælestia, solertiam lectionis et vigiliarum, auctoritatem sacerdote dignam, redarguendi superbos ac potentes, pariter et infirmos consolandi, ac pauperes recreandi vel defendendi clementiam. In short, as far as I have learned from those who knew him, he omitted none of all those things which he knew from gospel, apostolic or prophetic scriptures ought to be done, but strove to fulfil them all in deed after the measure of his strength.'

What Aidan did in Northumbria was done in East Anglia by Fursa. He too came from Ireland, ' vir de nobilissimo genere Scottorum, sed longe animo quam carne nobilior.' For frequently, ' raptus e corpore,' he would have wonderful visions. In one of these, after beholding many things in the unseen world and hearing the words of other holy men of his own race now among the saints, he has to pass through the fire where those who died in their sins are being burned. An angel makes a pathway for him through the flames, but some of the devils, seizing one of those whom they were burning, threw him at Fursa, hitting him on the shoulder and jaw and burning him badly. Fursa recognised the man who had been thrown at him and remembered his death. Afterwards, ' when restored to the body, he bore all his life on his shoulder and jaw, visible to all, the mark of the burning which he had undergone in the spirit. So in a miraculous manner what the soul suffered in secret the flesh declared openly.'

Good Latinist though he was, Bede did not despise the language of the people. He recognised the poetical and untranslatable qualities of Caedmon, the cow-herd bard of Whitby, who knew no Latin but ' when the divine teaching was interpreted to him, soon after set it forth in his own language, that of the Angles, in poetry of great charm and feeling. After him others too among the Angles tried to make religious poems but none could equal him.' A passage from the story of how Caedmon, late in life, came to be a poet will serve to illustrate both Bede's Latin and his regard for Anglo-Saxon. Caedmon was asleep in his byre, whither he had slipped away to avoid his turn to take the lyre at a banquet. ' Adstitit ei quidam per somnium, eumque salutans, ac suo appellans nomine " Caedmon " inquit " canta mihi aliquid." At ille respondens " Nescio " inquit " cantare; nam et ideo de convivio egressus huc secessi, quia cantare non poteram." Rursum ille, qui cum eo loquebatur " Atta-men " ait " mihi cantare habeas." " Quid " inquit " debeo cantare ? " Et ille " Canta " inquit " princi-pium creaturarum." Quo accepto responso, statim ipse cœpit cantare in laudem Dei conditoris versus, quos numquam audierat. . . . Exsurgens autem a somno, cuncta quæ dormiens cantaverat memoriter retinuit, et eis mox plura in eundem modum verba Deo digni carminis adiunxit ' (IV, 24).

PART III

THE CAROLINGIAN AND THE OTTONIAN REVIVALS
(732–1002)

THE CAROLINGIAN AND THE OTTONIAN REVIVALS

IT was in 732, three hundred years after the death of Augustine, that the tide of European affairs began to run again. In that year two things happened, which eventually led to the establishment of the Holy Roman Empire and to the revival of letters which accompanied that great event. Firstly, Leo III the Iconoclast definitely abandoned the idea of winning Italy back for the Eastern Empire by force of arms, and henceforth Western Europe was allowed to go its own way with very little interference from Byzantium. Secondly, Charles Martel at Poitiers dealt the Saracens such a hammer blow that all fear vanished of Christianity in Europe being displaced by Mohammedanism. Moreover, the victory that Charles then won so strengthened his people's position as defender of the faith that his son Pepin in 751 was crowned King of the Franks with the Pope's full approval, and left to the second Charles, born ten years after his grandfather's triumph, a kingdom not only stable in itself but capable, as was afterwards proved, of immense expansion. Charles the Great (Charlemagne) came to the throne in 768 and died in 814 : the Holy Roman Empire was established in 800, and for the last fourteen years of his reign Charles, besides being King of the Franks, was also Roman Emperor of the West. Of the process of conquest and organisation by which he created a new Europe this is not the place to speak ; but the revival of letters that marks the latter half of the eighth century was so largely due to his personal influence that even in this record he has a place.

Charles is certainly one of the most attractive figures in all history. Tall, handsome, and robust he was a great man in every sense of the word : a great fighter, a great statesman, a great builder, and a great lover of women. His amorousness is the one weakness, if it was a weakness, that can be discovered in his character. He was generous and just, a kind father and a dutiful son of the Church. Upon learning he set the highest value, and though he could not write he was an ardent reader and a most liberal patron of all the arts. Conquest was his trade but education was his hobby : at his Court at Aix-la-Chapelle he gathered round him every sort of talent from every country, and in the literary diversions which occupied so large a space in his home life he took a leading part. The literary circle at Aix included Alcuin, Einhard, Theodulf, Angilbert, Peter of Pisa, and Paul the Deacon ; and although their achievements scarcely justify the comparison that they sometimes made with the Age of Augustus, they at least equal in brilliance that other company which seven centuries later we find at the Court of Lorenzo de Medici at Florence.

Alcuin (735–804)

Of these men the scholar who in Latin is called Albinus and in English Alcuin was first in the time of his arrival and first in the influence which he exercised. Alcuin was born about 735 of a noble family of Northumbria, and received his early education at York, where the traditions of Bede's learning were a strong influence sedulously fostered by Archbishop Egbert, who made York what we should call a university town. While still a youth Alcuin accompanied Egbert's successor Ælbert to Italy, and in 767 himself became the head of the York cathedral school. On Ælbert's death he again made the journey across the Alps to receive from Rome the *pallium* for the new archbishop Eanbald, and it was probably on this occasion that he met Charles at Parma and was invited by him to take up his home at the Frankish Court. He joined Charles in 782, after obtaining leave from his own archbishop, and with him he remained until 796, acting both as head of the palace school and as chief literary adviser to the great king. In 796 he asked permission to retire to the monastery of St Martin at Tours, and there spent the last eight years of his life, dying on 19th May 804.

Alcuin was the guiding force behind the educational reforms which are among the most important results of Charles' reign, and he was probably responsible for the famous Capitulary *De litteris colendis*, which definitely laid the duty of teaching upon the clergy. 'We have had letters sent us,' says the encyclical, 'from church dignitaries which show a painful weakness in composition'; and it goes on :

'On reading these letters and considering their lack of skill, we began to feel afraid lest the writers' knowledge and understanding of the Holy Scriptures might also prove to be much less than it ought to be. Wherefore we now exhort you. Do not neglect the study of literature, but with a humble effort well pleasing to God seek learning with all your might, so that you may be able the more easily and correctly to penetrate the mysteries of God's Book. In its sacred pages you will find inserted many figures of speech, turns of rhetoric, and such like things ; and there can be no doubt that the more fully a man has been instructed in literary knowledge the more quickly will he understand the spiritual meaning of what he reads. So let such men be chosen for this task as have the will and power to learn, and also have the desire to teach others.'

This letter was sent round to all the cathedrals, churches, and monasteries in Charles' realm; and we know how effective it proved. The monasteries that during the seventh and eighth centuries had been established on the Continent by Irish and Anglo-Saxon monks—St Gall, Corbie, Péronne, Fulda, Reichenau, Lorsch, and many others—became centres of scholastic activity in close communication one with the other. In their writing-rooms copies of all the Latin classics then extant were carefully made, and the Carolingian minuscule gradually superseded the Merovingian, the Visigothic, and finally the Beneventan script.

The new educational organisation, whereby the Church took the place of the State, was Alcuin's great achievement, and it was in the scholastic field also that he did his best literary work by his *Compendia* of grammar, rhetoric, and dialectic, written in dialogue form, which were soon being used in all the schools of Europe. In pure literature he is less successful. In prose we have from his pen a few Lives of the Saints, two moral treatises *On virtues and vices*, and *On the relation of the Soul to God*, four long Biblical commentaries, including one on Genesis and one on Revelations, and a mass of dogmatic writings directed chiefly against the heresy of the adoptionists. None of this, however, has to-day much interest for us, and it is with some relief that we turn to his Letters. Of these we have nearly three hundred, falling into three groups, and almost all of social and historical value. The first and earliest section consists of letters written to friends in England, exhorting the nobles to struggle boldly against the Danes and not to give way to drunkenness, recommending the clergy to avoid all luxury and to devote themselves to the moral education of their people, calling on all alike to practise virtue, if they wish to escape the judgment of God. The second section contains his correspondence with Charles and dates mainly from the time when he left Court and retired to Tours. Many of these letters are extremely interesting, and they range over a very wide field, from problems of chronology and astronomy to questions of high politics, such as the treatment of the conquered Saxons and the organisation of the new Empire. Their weakness is an extreme prolixity and a florid extravagance of compliment, which is intensified in the third section addressed to Arno Archbishop of Salzburg and Alcuin's former pupil. Arno is usually ' Aquila,' the eagle, and this is how one letter to him begins :

> ' Alcuin sends greeting to his Eagle, dearest of all birds upon the Alpine heights. O that I might be translated, like Habakkuk of old, into your presence ! With what a firm embrace would I then clasp your neck, my sweetest son ! However long the summer day I would never grow weary. I would press my breast to yours, join our lips together, and with the sweetest greetings kiss every limb of your body.'

Such fervid language as this is usually reserved for poetry ; but Alcuin's verse although it is very copious is somewhat mediocre in quality. The graceful piece ' The contest of Winter and Spring,' which is sometimes attributed to him was probably written by an Irish monk of his time ; and Alcuin's own poems on the cuckoo, which come before and after it, are of quite a different character. His two most important poems are both long and serious. The first is *De patribus, regibus, et sanctis Eboricæ ecclesiæ*, a piece in nearly two thousand hexameters, inspired by Alcuin's youthful love for Virgil, which gives the history of the See of York from 627 onwards. The second is the elegiac *De clade Lindisfarnensis monasterii*, a rather dull lament for the destruction of Lindisfarne by the Danes in 793. The mass of Alcuin's poetry, however, is of the lightest and most occasional character; letters in verse, inscriptions for buildings of every kind, including a latrine, verse riddles such as that on ' magnus, agnus, manus, magus, mus, anus,' and epigrams of rather forced humour upon his friends' personal peculiarities. To read through the collection is not a very enlivening task, and such poems as the pretty lines for a bed are rare :

> ' Bless him who sleeps upon this bed
> And on him, Christ, Thy presence shed.
> Make void the furtive snares of night
> And keep him safe till morning's light.
> For to the servants 'neath Thy ward
> Thou, Christ, art Father, King, and guard.'

As a specimen of the poet's wit we may take the epigram on Einhard. Alcuin himself was a big, burly man fond of the pleasures of the table; Einhard is ' Nardulus,' the little spikenard which goes a long way, and the piece ends thus :

> ' Small is the bee but honey sweet it gives :
> Small is the eye, but while the body lives
> It rules its movements. So our tiny Nard
> Rules all his household. Therefore pay regard
> And cry " All hail to Nard." '

Einhard (770–840)

Einhard was of very small stature, as is shown by Alcuin's epigram and by the apocryphal story that the Emperor's daughter Emma, who had a weakness for the little man, used to carry him on her back over the snow so that her father might not detect his clandestine visits to her room. But to his contemporaries he was always known as Einhardus Magnus, and his work, both as builder and writer, makes the title well deserved. Born on the banks of the Main about 770, Einhard had his early education at the monastery of Fulda, whence in 791 he passed into Charles' 'Palace School.' His promotion was probably due to Alcuin, who speaks of him in a letter to Charles as ' Beseleel, vester immo et noster familiaris adiutor.' Einhard, like the Biblical Bezaleel, was a man ' skilled to devise cunning works, to work in gold, and in silver, and in brass, and in cutting of stones for setting, and in carving of wood '; and he was no doubt responsible for the decoration of the great cathedral at Aix-la-Chapelle. After Alcuin he was one of the Emperor's most trusted advisers, and it is said that it was upon his suggestion that Charles in 813 appointed Louis the Pious as his consort in the empire. After the death of Charles in 814 Einhard remained for a time in high favour at Court ; but in 830 he retired to Mulinheim, taking with him the relics of St Marcellinus and St Peter, source of the miracles which he describes in his *Translatio SS. Marcellini et Petri*. In 836 he composed another treatise, *Libellus de adoranda Cruce*, dedicated to Servatus Lupus, and four years later he died.

It was probably at Mulinheim also that Einhard wrote the life of his great master which is his chief title to literary fame. The *Vita Karoli* is that rare thing, a model biography, perfect in form and in length, in spirit and in substance. The monastery at Fulda where Einhard was educated possessed the only manuscript of Suetonius then extant, and Einhard, using the same method as that followed by the author of the *Lives of the Cæsars*, fairly equals the Roman in his own field. His Latin is not the *lingua mixta*, which was the ordinary medium for the writers of his time, but something much more artificial and to modern scholars much more familiar, a Latin based on a careful study of the classical authors and yet written with an ease and fluency which makes it delightful reading. In length also the *Vita* exactly hits the golden mean. Its thirty-three short chapters offer a pleasing contrast to the huge bulk of some modern biographies, but in their brief space they give us as vivid a portrait as anyone could desire. The chief facts of his subject's life are given in the first seventeen chapters, and here the truth and frankness of Einhard's narrative shines out in comparison with the contemporary *Lorsch Annals* and with the other ' Life ' written by the monk of St Gall in the early years of the tenth century. Einhard does not disguise the cruelty that Charles displayed in his dealings with the Saxons and the Avars ; and although he has been accused of suppressing some awkward facts, allowance must be made for the genuine affection which he felt for the Emperor.

The second part of the book, with its life-like picture of Charles' habits and disposition, is even more attractive than the first. Einhard has the advantage of intimate and first-hand knowledge and the description he gives of Charles could hardly be bettered :

' In person he was stout and robust, and of a tall stature, which however did not exceed due proportion ; for we know that his height was just seven times the measure of his foot. The top of his head was round, his eyes very large and bright, his nose somewhat over the ordinary size, his hair a beautiful gray, his expression merry and cheerful. Whether he was sitting or standing the dignity and authority of his carriage was very great. His neck might seem thick and somewhat short, his stomach too prominent ; but these defects passed unnoticed owing to the just proportion of his other members. His gait was firm and his bearing manly ; his voice though clear was not quite so strong as you would expect from his appearance. He enjoyed good health, except that in the four years preceding his death he suffered several times from feverish attacks, and at the end limped slightly with one foot. Even then, however, he preferred to please himself rather than follow the advice of his physicians, whom he regarded almost with dislike since they urged him in his diet to give up the roast dishes to which he was accustomed and to habituate himself to boiled meat. He constantly took exercise in the form of riding and hunting, the latter sport being native to him as there is scarcely any people on earth who in it can match the Franks. He also greatly delighted in the warmth of natural hot springs, and frequently practised swimming, in which he was so expert that no one could fairly surpass him. It was for this purpose that he built the palace at Aix, which in the last years of his life and till his death was his permanent residence. He not only invited his sons to the bath there, but also his nobles and friends, and sometimes even a crowd of attendants and guards, so that there were occasions when a hundred men or more were in the water together.'

Angilbert (fl. 790)

Angilbert, known to his friends as Homer, completes the inner circle of Charles' court, making a quartette with Emperor-David, Einhard-Bezaleel, and Alcuin-Flaccus. Alcuin had the true schoolmaster's love of inventing nicknames, and was never satisfied until he had fitted each of his intimates with a sobriquet : but in the case of Angilbert he was hardly well inspired. Angilbert's poems in fact are rather poor stuff, and his life is much more interesting than his verse. He was brought up almost from infancy in the royal palace and even as a young man was entrusted with important diplomatic missions. Three times he went as envoy from Charles to Rome, and accompanied the young Pippin to Italy as one of his chief counsellors. On his return he was made Abbot of St Riquier, a monastery which he so enriched and adorned that he was afterwards honoured there as a saint. His private life, however, was not as saintly as it might have been. His fondness for the theatre was a source of great anxiety to the good Alcuin, and when he became Charles' confidential secretary—'*Homerus noster auricularius*'—he used his opportunities to win the affection of Princess Bertha. They had already had two children when Charles allowed their marriage : but as Angilbert was a priest, the marriage was even more sinful than the intrigue. Four years later the pair committed a fresh offence by taking monastic vows and entering the same house. Then they quarrelled and separated. Bertha returned to court and found new lovers : Angilbert resumed his duties as arch-chaplain to the Emperor, and stayed with him until his death in 814.

Of Angilbert's surviving poems the most important is the *Carolus Magnus et Leo Papa*, perhaps only a portion of a longer work. After a glowing panegyric of Charles, 'the Light-house of Europe,' the poet proceeds to dilate upon the glories of Aix-la-Chapelle, and then gives an elaborate description of a hunting party in the royal park, the fair Bertha being singled out for special mention. The hunting party is followed by a banquet and the banquet by a dream, in which Charles sees a vision of Pope Leo covered with blood. He sends envoys at once to Rome, and after subduing the Saxons marches south with his army. The King and Pope meet, Charles promises to reinstate Leo in the chair of St Peter ; and the piece ends. This is Angilbert's most ambitious effort, although even here his authorship is not quite certain. Another poem celebrates the return of Pippin from Italy in 796, and pictures his happy reunion with his father, stepmother, brothers, sisters, and aunt, all of whose emotions are separately described. A third, a mixture of eclogue

146

and epistle, is devoted to the praises of Charles, and a few lines from it may serve as a specimen of Angilbert's Latin verse :

> ' Surge, meo Domno dulces fac, fistula, versus :
> David amat versus ; surge et fac, fistula, versus.
> David amat vates, vatorum est gloria David.
> Quapropter vates cuncti concurrite in unum
> Atque meo David dulces cantate camœnas.
> David amat vates, vatorum est gloria David.'

Theodulf (fl. 790)

Theodulf, the ' Pindar ' of the court circle, is a far more considerable poet than Angilbert, even though he is quite unable to emulate the flight of the Theban eagle. There is some doubt whether he was born in South France or North Spain ; but it is certain that he was of Gothic race and that he passed his youth at Narbonne. Thence about the year 781 he travelled northwards to Charles' court, and by his elegant verses soon won the royal favour. We have now seventy-nine of his poems, mostly descriptive and marked rather by sound sense and moral earnestness than by any strong poetical inspiration. In 798 he became Bishop of Orleans and that same year was appointed by Charles as ' *missus dominicus*,' to hold synods and execute justice in the province of Gallia Narbonensis. Of this commission he gives an account in his best poem, the ' *Contra judices*,' a long piece of nearly a thousand lines, in which he describes all the procedure of a provincial court :

> ' Magna catervatim nos contio sæpe frequentat,
> Ætas quod dicat sexus et omnis habet,
> Parvulus, annosus, iuvenis, pater, innuba, cælebs,
> Maior, ephebus, anus, masque, marita, minor.'

When Alcuin retired to Tours, Theodulf seems to have taken his place at court as adviser on ecclesiastical matters, and when the two men in 801 had a sharp dispute over a right of sanctuary, Charles decided in Theodulf's favour and strongly condemned Alcuin's action. So all went well with the Bishop of Orleans until 814; and then there came a change of fortune for the worse. Most of Charles' men died before their master; Theodulf to his sorrow survived him. For a time indeed he exercised his former influence at court, but in 818 Louis with his usual folly listened to a false charge of conspiracy and imprisoned him at Angers. With this captivity the poem by which Theodulf is now best known is connected. According to the story, while he was in prison he composed the elegiac verses beginning :

' Gloria laus et honor tibi sit, rex Christe, redemptor,
Cui puerile decus prompsit Hosanna pium.'

It happened that on Palm Sunday Louis visited Angers, and as he passed the prison tower he heard a voice singing these lines. He asked who the singer was and was told that it was his own prisoner Theodulf : ' then the merciful and gentle monarch was moved with compassion, and from that hour he delivered and pardoned him and sent him back to his church.' The tale may be a pious legend, but the poem is a certain fact. From its seventy-eight lines a cento was made which passed into the breviary as a Palm Sunday processional, and thence into our hymnal :

' All glory, laud and honour
To Thee, Redeemer, King.
To Whom the lips of children
Made sweet Hosannas ring.'

Paul the Deacon (725–799)

Alcuin brought to Aix-la-Chapelle the traditions of Anglo-Saxon scholarship as they had been established at Jarrow and York. The three Italians, Peter, Paulinus, and Paul contributed the Lombard learning of the monasteries of Bobbio and Monte Cassino. Of these three Peter of Pisa and Paulinus of Aquileia were primarily grammarians and belong rather to a history of education than to a history of literature : but Paul is so much the most attractive of the authors of his time that a full account of his writings is necessary.

Paul was born about 725 of an old Lombard family which had suffered many vicissitudes of fortune in the past and was fated to suffer more. His father Warnefrid was a man of some consideration, and the future historian was probably sent as a page to the Lombard court at Pavia, where he received a good education including some knowledge of Greek. When his first patron King Ratchis retired to the monastery of Monte Cassino in 749, Paul in all likelihood remained at court, and it was while holding some minor office there that he came under the spell of Princess Adelperga, the beautiful and accomplished daughter of King Desiderius. Paul was about twenty-five at that time and between the two young people, united by their common love of art and literature, a close companionship began. Marriage was impossible, for a Lombard's King's daughters were invaluable pawns in the game of diplomacy, and Desiderius had marked out Adelperga for Arichis, Duke of Benevento, who was destined for many years to be the strongest bulwark of Lombard power in South Italy. Their union took place in 757 ; but when Adelperga left Pavia with her husband and went to Benevento she took Paul with her, and there for nearly twenty years he remained. Arichis was a sensible man, often away from home and greatly occupied with affairs of State; Adelperga was a good wife who found solace in her husband's absence in literary intercourse with her girlhood's companion; so to both of the royal pair Paul was indispensable.

This idyllic existence lasted for a considerable time; but unfortunately for Paul the days of Lombard dominion in Italy were drawing quickly to an end, and Desiderius was destined to be the last of their kings. In the autumn of 773 Charles the Great, who had repudiated his Lombard wife Desiderata, marched into Italy with a Frankish army, laid siege to Pavia, and after an eight months' blockade took the town. Desiderius and his wife were allowed to retire to the monastery of Corbie in Picardy, his son and co-regent Adelchis escaped to the court of Byzantium, and there spent the rest of his life, like James II at Versailles, making occasionally an abortive effort to regain his ancestral throne.

Paul was too closely connected with the royal family to remain a passive spectator of their downfall. He left the delights of Benevento, and both he and his brother seem to have been implicated in the conspiracy against Charles which Hrodgaud, Duke of Friuli, planned in 776. The plot failed, Paul himself retired to the monastery of Monte Cassino, his brother was thrown into prison, and their property was confiscated. For six years the family was in sad distress and then they were rescued by Paul's fame as a man of letters. In 782 he was invited by Charles to come to him; and as such an invitation was in fact a command, Paul at once made the journey across the Alps to Aix-la-Chapelle. There he was received with enthusiasm, and it is practically certain that his verse petition on his family's behalf, which we still possess, was favourably answered by his new patron. In any case after the year 782 Paul appears as a prominent member of Charles' brilliant court circle, his knowledge of Greek giving him there a special distinction. With Charles he remained for several years, and then was allowed to return to his beloved Monte Cassino, where he lived for the rest of his life, dying peacefully there just before the end of the century.

It is, however, as a writer rather than a man that Paul is of importance, and it is time now to turn to his works. Like most of his contemporaries he wrote a considerable amount of occasional poetry, most of it graceful verse enough, such as the acrostics addressed to Adelperga, the epitaph on the little girl who died in childhood, and the beautiful lines on Lake Como. But there is one piece commonly attributed to Paul which is far better known than these, and is for two reasons famous. The hymn to St John the Baptist begins thus :

> ' Ut queant laxis resonare fibris
> Mira gestorum famuli tuorum,
> Solve polluti labii reatum,
> Sancte Johannes.'

It will be seen that it is in sapphics, the first hymn written in the metre that the Lesbian invented to express the ecstasy of love ; and from the first syllables of the words at the beginning and middle of its lines are derived the names of the notes in our musical scale.

Paul is perhaps something of a minor poet, but he is a major historian and his prose works are both valuable in substance, and considerable in bulk. The *Homilies*, a collection of religious discourses drawn from the writings of Ambrose, Augustine, Jerome and the other great doctors of the Church, fills nearly four hundred closely-printed pages in the ninety-fifth volume of Migne's *Patrologia Latina*. Even more extensive is the *Historia Miscella*, an expansion and continuation of the history of Eutropius, which gives a continuous narrative of Roman affairs from the days when Saturn ruled in Italy down to the reign of Justinian. To these two long books must be added the *Life of Gregory the Great* and the *Record of the Bishops of Metz*; and most important of all, the history of his own people, on which Paul's fame as a writer now chiefly depends.

The *Historia Langobardorum*, which tells the story of the Lombards from their migration southwards under King Audoin in 546 down to the death of King Liutprand at Pavia in 744, is one of the most entertaining books in later Latin literature. It has many merits : it is not very long, but it gives in a comparatively brief space a clear record of the events of two centuries ; it is well written, and even if Paul's Latin is not that of Livy and Tacitus he has a style of his own which exactly suits his material ; it is composed in the heroic vein and offers many examples of the Teutonic idea of chivalry ; finally, though it deals with a single subject it is never monotonous, and each of its six books is diversified by an extraordinary number of good tales. In its opening chapters, for instance, after Paul has remarked that Germany is so called because people germinate there very freely, he continues thus :

' I think it will not be inexpedient, now that my pen is occupied with Germany, to postpone the order of my narrative for a moment and to give a brief account of a miracle which in that country is the theme of universal talk. In the extreme north of Germany, on the very shore of Ocean, a cave may be seen sheltered by an overhanging rock. In that cave lie seven men who have been fast asleep there for no one knows how long. Their bodies and even their clothes are uninjured, and the ignorant barbarians of the land hold them in the utmost veneration, seeing that through the course of so many ages they have endured without corruption. As far as may be judged by their dress, they appear to be Romans. A certain man, it is said, urged on by greed tried to strip one of the bodies, but his arm immediately withered ; and his fate so terrified the rest of his countrymen that no one since then has ever dared to touch them. You might well consider for what end God's providence has kept them all these years. They certainly are thought to be Christians, and it may be that the heathen there are destined some day to be saved by their preaching.'

After this northern variant of the Seven Sleepers of Ephesus we have immediately the vivid narrative of the descent into the Maelstrom, which Paul heard from the lips of a Gallic nobleman and Poe used as the basis for his tale. Next comes what Paul calls the ridiculous anecdote of the god Wotan and the Lombard women. The Lombards, who were then called Winnils, were fighting against the Vandals, and Wotan had promised victory to whichever nation he saw first on a certain morning. On the advice of his wife Frea the Winnil women tied their long hair under their chins so as to look like a beard and stood under Wotan's window to attract his attention. Wotan looked out and said 'Who are these long-bearded creatures ? ' Then Frea told him the truth, and the Winnils, changing their name to Langobardi, were given the victory. This story, followed at once by the tale of Lamissio, second king of the Lombards, occurs in the early pages of the *History*, and before the first book ends we begin the epic of King Alboin, who came to the help of Narses against the Goths, was invited by the great Byzantine general to occupy North Italy, and finally led his people across the Alps from Pannonia into the district which ever since has borne the name of Lombardy. The account of their settlement, together with a description of Italy itself, occupies all the second book, which ends with Alboin's death, while the third book proceeds, somewhat more soberly, with the general history of the Lombards during the sixth century. But whenever Paul finds an opportunity he brings in a romantic tale. There is, for example, the episode of the adventurous wooing of Theudelinda by the gallant Prince Autharis, a tale that rouses even Gibbon to enthusiasm ; and a little later the story of Gunthram's strange experience, introducing the element of the uncanny which was later to play such an important part in medieval legends. It happened that Gunthram, King of the Franks, when out hunting became separated from his followers and found himself accompanied by only one attendant. Wearied with the chase he threw himself down by the side of a rivulet, put his head in his squire's lap and went off to sleep. As he lay, a little creature something like a lizard ran from his mouth and made as though it wished to cross the stream. The squire, without disturbing his master, laid his sword over the water and the animal hurrying to the other side disappeared into an opening in the neighbouring hill. Presently it emerged again, ran back to Gunthram, and vanished once more in his mouth. Soon afterwards the king awoke and told his attendant that he had just dreamed that he had crossed a river on an iron bridge and made his way into a mountain where he had found masses of gold. The squire for his part told him what he had seen, and pointed out the opening in the hillside ; and later, when excavations were made, a treasure of gold beyond all counting was discovered. From the precious metal Gunthram made an altar canopy which he presented to the shrine of the martyr Marcellus at

Chalons ; ' and,' concludes Paul, ' it is there even at the present day, and nothing ever made from gold can be compared with it.'

Even more curious than this is the story in Book Six of King Cunincpert and the fly and the man with the wooden leg. One day Cunincpert was discussing with his groom of the chamber how best to get rid of two obnoxious subjects named Aldo and Grauso. As they considered ways and means, a particularly large fly— *una de majusculis*—entered the room and began buzzing round the window. The king, irritated by the noise, struck at it with his dagger, but, though he cut off one of its legs, the fly escaped and soon afterwards disappeared. Meanwhile Aldo and Grauso, ignorant of the king's intentions towards them, were on their way to pay him a visit of respect, when they were met by a man with a wooden leg, who told them that if they entered the palace they would assuredly not come out alive. Prudence counselled retreat ; and they at once sought refuge in the nearest church. Later in the day Cunincpert was informed that they had taken sanctuary, and accused his groom of revealing his plans. The groom replied that, as the king knew, he had not been out of the royal presence since their conversation, and therefore could not have given information to anyone. Accordingly a messenger was dispatched to the pair in the church asking the reason of their conduct, and by them was told that they had met a stranger with a wooden leg outside the palace who had warned them that the king meant to put them to death. Then Cunincpert realised that what he thought was a fly had really been an evil spirit, one of Beelzebub's myrmidons, and sending for Aldo and Grauso he pardoned them all their offences and took them again into favour.

Such tales as these give us a better idea of the medieval mind, its vagaries and its limitations, than could be got from pages of laborious analysis. And though Paul is a pious and cheerful soul, he does not shrink from describing the darker side of life. He tells us of the wicked Romilda, who first exacted from the King of the Huns a promise of marriage and then betrayed to him her husband's city of Friuli, finding her reward after one day's wedlock in being handed over to his soldiers and finally transfixed upon a pole. He tells us too of Queen Rosamund, wife of Alboin ; and that story is so good an example of man's cruelty and woman's faithlessness that it deserves a full translation :

' The circumstances of Alboin's death were as follows. One day at Verona he was making merry at a banquet. He had been sitting at table longer than he ought, and at last he called for the cup which he had had made from the skull of his wife's father Cunimund, and bidding it to be handed to the queen challenged her to drink to her father's health. (This may seem to some incredible, but I speak the truth in Christ : I myself once on a feast-day saw this cup in the hands of King Ratchis who was showing it to his guests.) When Rosamund realised what she had to do, she conceived a fierce resentment, and unable to forget the insult determined to avenge her father's death by killing her husband. She therefore plotted to murder him with the help of Helmechis, his foster-brother and armour-bearer, and Helmechis persuaded her to enlist also the help of Peredeo, who was a man of great valour. Peredeo, however, refused to agree to her wicked proposal ; and so the queen one night took the place in bed of one of her chamber-maids with whom Peredeo was accustomed to have illicit relations. Peredeo came in ignorance and lay with the queen ; and when the deed was done she asked him who he thought she was. He gave the name of the girl whom he supposed her to be, and she replied—" It is not at all as you think. I am Queen Rosamund, and you now have done such a thing, Peredeo, that you will either yourself kill Alboin or his sword will put out your life." At that Peredeo knew the crime he had committed, and though till then he had been unwilling, he was compelled to agree to the king's death. Accordingly Rosamund waited until Alboin was taking his midday siesta, and commanding silence in the palace removed all his other weapons, and tightly fastened his sword to the head of his couch, so that it could not be lifted or drawn from its scabbard. Then following their plan with more than a tiger's ferocity she let the murderers in. Alboin starting up from sleep saw the danger that threatened him and made a dash for his sword. It was fastened too firmly for him to move it, and for a time he defended himself with a footstool. But alas—O grief!—that stout and gallant warrior could not prevail against his enemy and met a craven's death. He who had risen to the height of fame in war amid the carnage of the foe perished by the treachery of one miserable woman.'

Hraban (780–856)

The splendour of Charles' reign was not maintained either in politics or in literature. Louis the Debonair who followed his father in 814 was a pious man but a feeble ruler, and under his sons the fabric of Charles' empire fell completely to pieces. Quarrel followed upon quarrel, and at last in 841 the Frankish nation brought about its own ruin on the fratricidal field of Fontenoy. Still, while warriors were fighting monks were writing, and although no one in the middle years of the ninth century can compare with Alcuin or Paul, a fair amount of good literature was produced. There is in particular a gentle stream of poetry tracing back to Alcuin and marked by the names of Hraban, Gottschalk, Walafrid, and Sedulius Scotus; and with these four we may begin.

Magnentius Hrabanus, surnamed Maurus by his master Alcuin, was the greatest Churchman of his time. As a boy he went to school at Fulda and for twenty years from 822 he was abbot of the famous monastery there. In 842 he retired in order to devote himself to study, but in 847 he was persuaded to undertake the charge of the Archbishopric of Mainz, and there he laboured, defending sound doctrine and combating social disorder, until his death in 856.

Even for a theologian Hraban was a very voluminous writer, and his prose works fill some seven thousand closely-printed pages in Migne. Most of this, however, consists of sermons, homilies, and Biblical commentaries which for the purpose of this book may be disregarded. We have left some educational treatises, such as the *De inventione linguarum*, and the *De clericorum institutione;* the controversial essays *De oblatione puerorum*, *De reverentia filiorum erga patres*, and *De consanguineorum nuptiis;* and, most important of all, the encyclopædic *De Universo*, a treatise based on Isidore of Seville, in which he explains the universe of things both in a mythical and a historical sense.

There remains his verse, which is of two kinds, the lighter chiefly in the form of poetical epistles to his friends, the more serious consisting of theological poems, such as the *De Catholica Fide* and the *De Laudibus sanctæ crucis.*' These are marked by a severe and simple piety but are somewhat lacking in literary grace, and Hraban's poetical fame depends on one hymn, the *Veni, creator spiritus.* Even of this the authorship is disputed, but a tenth-century Fulda manuscript definitely assigns it to him, and there seems little reason to doubt this evidence.

> ' Veni, creator spiritus,
> Mentes tuorum visita,
> Imple superna gratia
> Quæ tu creasti pectora.'

> ' Come, Holy Ghost, our souls inspire
> And lighten with celestial fire.
> Thou the anointing Spirit art
> Who dost Thy sevenfold gifts impart.
> Thy blessed unction from above
> Is comfort, life, and fire of love.'

Gottschalk (810–869)

Gottschalk was a pupil of Hraban at Fulda;
but whether from ill-treatment there or from a
desire for freedom he left the monastery, and in 829
obtained a dispensation from a synod at Mainz which
released him from his vows. This, of course, was
highly displeasing to Hraban, who had the dispensation
revoked and forced Gottschalk to enter the monastery
of Orbais. Thence, about 840, he emerged as an
itinerant preacher spreading the doctrine of double
predestination, *i.e.* predestination to evil as well as to
good. To Hraban this teaching seemed a detestable
heresy, and Gottschalk, summoned before the archbishop's court at Mainz, was severely whipped, banished
from the diocese, and handed over as a prisoner to
Hincmar, Archbishop of Rheims. At first, though
kept in close confinement, he was allowed to write;
but when he used this permission to spread his views
by the pen, he was again whipped and sent for the
rest of his life to the monastery of Hautvillers. Even
on his death-bed he refused the absolution that was
offered to him if he would recant, and as Hincmar said:
' Sic vitam morte digna finivit et abiit in locum suum.'

Such is the lamentable life-story of a monk who
dared to think for himself and brave the authority of
his superiors. But it is possibly his sufferings that
made him the remarkable poet that he is. We have
not much of his verse, but what we have is both in
form and in contents of great interest and beauty.
One piece for example, a letter, is rhymed :

> ' Tenearis ac decora
> Videas sodalis ora.
> Bis enim venis ab illo
> Speciosa iam magistro,
> Adimens fel,
> Imprimens mel.'

Another is the first example we have of a long poem written in leonine hexameters, and a third, even more striking than these, is the lament in ten six-line stanzas monorhymed on the letter e.

> ' O quid iubes, pusiole,
>   Quare mandas, filiole,
>   Carmen dulce me cantare,
>   Cum sim longe exsul valde
>   Intra mare ?
>   O cur iubes canere ? '

> ' Why bid me sing, my pretty one ?
>   Why bid me sing, my little son ?
>   How can I sing ?
>   I live in exile far away,
>   Penned by the waves. Ah lackaday,
>   Why bid me sing ? '

Walafrid Strabo (809–849)

Another pupil of Hraban, but one far happier in his fortunes, was Walafrid Strabo. Walafrid was the child of humble parents who devoted him from his early years to the Church. He received his first training in the monastery of Reichenau under Jatto and Wettin, and when he was only eighteen he composed the long poem of some thousand hexameters, *The Visions of Wettin*, in which he describes the dreams of hell, purgatory, and paradise which his beloved master had just before his death. We have brought before us the fires of hell incessantly tormenting those who have committed such deadly sins as fornication and sodomy : we have purgatory with Charles the Great himself atoning there for his fleshly lusts before passing to heaven : we have the bright palace with its golden walls where the blessed dwell in paradise. Considering the poet's youth the ' *Visions* ' is a really wonderful work; and in literature it is of extreme interest, for it is the first of those imaginary pictures of the next world which culminate in the *Divina Commedia*.

After Wettin's death in 824 Walafrid apparently was sent to Fulda to complete his studies under Hraban, and at Fulda he met Gottschalk to whom he became warmly attached. But the friends soon had to separate, for Walafrid was recommended to the Emperor Louis as tutor to his son Charles, and at court soon won the favour of the Empress Judith, whose learning and beauty he celebrates in many poems. To this period probably belong the two verse lives of St Blaitmac and St Mammes, and the curious piece *Scintilla*, a dialogue between the poet and his muse before the statue of Theodoric, in which the cruel tyrant is contrasted with the pious Emperor Louis. For this and for his tutorial services Walafrid was rewarded by being made Abbot of Reichenau; and though for a time he was expelled by Louis the German he was reinstated in 842 and remained there as abbot until his premature death in 849.

It was in these last years that Walafrid wrote the delightful *De cultu hortorum*, or, as it is sometimes called *Hortulus*, 'My little garden.' The *Hortulus* is about the length of one Georgic, and though a comparison would be unfair, it has a simple charm of its own which all lovers of Virgil will appreciate. It begins with an account of how Walafrid chose his plot of ground, broke up the earth, and put in the seed; and then comes this picture of the gardener abbot:

> ' Meanwhile my little crop by vernal showers
> Was sprinkled, and the kindly moon in turn
> Fostered the delicate leaves. But then there came

A time of drought and all the earth grew dry.
I feared the slender roots would die of thirst
And, loving well my task, with eager zeal
I filled big jars with water clear and cool,
Wherein I dipped my hands and drop by drop
Gave moisture to my nurselings.'

Then each of the twenty-two herbs and flowers in the
garden is described, the catalogue ending with the
roses and lilies which the Church has chosen for its
martyrs on earth and its saints in heaven :

'Sanguine martyrii carpit quæ dona rosarum,
Liliaque in fidei gestat candore nitentis.
O mater virgo, fecundo germine mater,
Virgo fide intacta, sponsi de nomine sponsa,
Sponsa, columba, domus regina, fidelis amica,
Bello carpe rosas, læta arripe lilia pace.'

Sedulius Scotus (fl. 850)

It may be thought that Gottschalk took too gloomy
a view of religion ; but this reproach cannot justly be
brought against Sedulius Scotus. Sedulius is the real
'wandering scholar,' always thirsty and generally short
of money, a cleric but a cleric of a very different kind
from the gentle Walafrid, the passionate Gottschalk,
and the learned Hraban. Of his early life we know
nothing, but he arrived at Liége from Ireland with
two companions in 840, and by Bishop Hartgar was
given a lodging and employment in the cathedral
school. His lodging, as he tells us, had neither windows
nor fastenings to the door, but it was a shelter for the
poor Irishmen from the bitter cold of the northern
town, and by dint of frequent verse petitions they
gradually extracted from the bishop the meat and

drink for which their souls craved. A spring poem begins thus :

> 'The year is at its fairest : corn shows green,
> Vines burgeon fast, and with a verdant sheen
>   The fields are gay.
> The songs of birds re-echo in the air,
> Earth, sea, and sky a smiling visage wear
>   On this glad day.'

But, as the poet proceeds to remark, nature's gladness is impossible for poor scholars without the gifts of Bacchus ; and Hartgar is requested to oblige. Another similar piece is addressed to a Count Robert :

> ' " Bonus vir est Robertus,
> Laudes gliscunt Roberti,
> Christe, fave Roberto,
> Longævum fac Robertum,
> Amen salve, Roberte,
> Christus sit cum Roberto "—
> Sex casibus percurrit
> Vestri præclarum nomen.'

Robert is indeed the head stone of the corner : he must not, however, be stony but send the poet a drink. It is probable that the knowledge of music which Sedulius possessed—he calls himself Orpheus, and Calliope is his *musica coniunx*—soon ameliorated his position ; and in a few years we find him in favour not only with Hartgar's successor Franco but with Iado, Archbishop of Milan. Finally he won the notice of Charles the Bald and his queen Irmingarde, and the tone of his poetry altered with his change of fortune. He is now a court official with a due regard for the proprieties, and perhaps his last work is the prose discourse *De rectoribus christianis*, in which each of the twenty chapters enumerating the virtues of a Christian prince ends with a piece of exemplary verse.

Lupus Servatus (800–863)

As Walafrid is Alcuin's worthy successor in verse, so Lupus equals, if he does not surpass, the Anglo-Saxon in the art of letter-writing. Lupus Servatus was born near Sens and passed from the monastery of Ferrières, where he received his early education, to Fulda, which was then under Hraban's direction. In 837 he appeared at court, and in 842, at Judith's instigation, was made Abbot of Ferrières by Charles the Bald, whose counsellor in ecclesiastical and literary matters he soon became. With Charles he went on the unfortunate expedition to Aquitaine : he was responsible for the decrees of the Synod of Verneuil ; he undertook the reformation of the monasteries of Burgundy and was sent as ambassador to the Pope ; and lastly he was Charles' chief adviser at the Diet of Meersen.

But in the midst of all these political activities Lupus always kept his love of literature. His own writings make only a small volume, and with the exception of two Lives of Saints and one theological treatise, they consist entirely of letters. But in spite of, or even perhaps because of, his brevity Lupus is one of the most entertaining writers of his age. He was among other things an ardent collector of manuscripts, and never lost an opportunity of adding to his library. For example, in one letter he writes to the Pope himself and asks for a Jerome, Cicero, Quintilian, and Donatus ; all of which he promises to return when copies have been made. But like a true book lover, when Hincmar asks for the loan of his Bede, he finds excuses for not sending the precious treasure. It is too large to put in one's pocket ; it will not go in a wallet ; and the roads are very dangerous. Hincmar must wait until he can come in person. It is indeed this sly humour that gives Lupus his charm, and Letter 68 addressed to Abbot Marcward may be taken as a specimen :

> ' I am setting out on a pilgrimage to Rome where there are some ecclesiastical cases in which I am interested. I will explain the details, reverend father, when I see you on my return. To settle my business properly I shall need an introduction to the Pope, and as that cannot easily be secured without pecuniary intervention, I fly now as a suppliant to your paternal, or rather maternal, breast. You have never failed me in my need before : therefore deign to help me to-day ; and, if you possibly can, send me back by my messengers two blue cloaks and two white ones, the German " glitza " ; for I understand that His Reverence is particularly fond of these kinds. If the totality of my request seems somewhat steep, I shall not turn up my nose at half ; for I am so well versed in this world's wisdom that I always ask for more and hope for less than I receive.'

Johannes Scotus Erigena (815–877)

Theology was the chief preoccupation of writers in the ninth century, and such Churchmen as Hraban, Hincmar, Radbert, Ratram, Claudius, and Agobart devoted most of their energies to the composition of doctrinal works. But, curiously enough, the greatest theologian of them all was a layman, and when Hincmar had got Gottschalk in safe custody, he thought it advisable, in dealing with so stubborn a heretic, to call in John the Scot otherwise known as Erigena. Erigena's life is something of a mystery. He was probably born in Ireland about 815, and there is a tradition that in early manhood he travelled in the East and made himself acquainted with Greek, Arabic, and Chaldean. We know that he was head of the court school under Charles the Bald in 847, and that he died about 877, but whether in his old age he visited England at the invitation of Alfred the Great and taught at Malmesbury is exceedingly doubtful.

Erigena's first book was a translation from the Greek, the *Celestial Hierarchy* of Dionysius the Areopagite, and for Hincmar he wrote in 851 the *De divina prædestinatione*, which asserts (*a*) that philosophy and religion are fundamentally the same ; (*b*) that as God is independent of time predestination cannot involve with Him any notion of necessity ; (*c*) that predestination could only be predestination to happiness, for God knows no evil ; (*d*) that if God knew evil He would cause it, for His knowledge and His will are identical. This, of course, went far beyond Hincmar and the treatise was condemned by the Council of Valence in 855. Erigena, however, being a philosopher and under royal protection, was not greatly disturbed by the anger of the Church. He returned to his study and gave the next ten years to the *De divisione naturæ*, a book five times as long as its predecessor, and one of the most subtle pieces of theological reasoning that we possess. An analysis of it here is impossible, but the four heads of Erigena's division of the totality of all things may be given. The first is that which creates and is not created, God as the source of all things : the second is that which is created and creates, the Platonic ' idea ' : the third is that which is created and does not create, the visible world of things and individuals : the fourth is that which neither is created nor creates, God as the final end. Erigena is a striking example of the fact that true genius is independent of time and circumstance. He lived in a profoundly unphilosophical age ; but he is the greatest thinker we have met since Boethius, the greatest theologian since Augustine.

Ermoldus Nigellus (fl. 850)

Of the two historians living in the first half of the ninth century one wrote in prose, the other in verse. The prose chronicler is Nithard, son of Angilbert and Bertha daughter of Charles the Great, who gives us a short, clear, and rather colourless account of the years between 814 and 843 and died in 844 defending his monastery against the Normans. The poet is Ermoldus Nigellus, and from a literary point of view he is considerably the more interesting of the pair. Ermoldus was a monk by profession and a soldier by inclination. An Aquitanian by birth he accompanied King Pippin of Aquitaine on his expedition against the Bretons in 824, and encouraged him afterwards in rebelling against his father Louis the Debonair. As a punishment Louis had him banished to Strasbourg; and it was while living there that he composed his verse history *In honorem Ludovici Cæsaris*, hoping thereby to secure his pardon from the Emperor. Besides this piece Ermoldus is also responsible for two elegies addressed to Pippin; but these are unimportant in comparison with the longer poem. The *In honorem Ludovici*, written in elegiac couplets, is valuable both as history and literature. It is in four books, and the first, which has William of Orange for its real hero, contains a most vivid account of the siege of Barcelona undertaken by Louis on William's advice. One episode will serve as an example. The Moors had captured the mother of a Frankish soldier named Datus, but offered to release her if Datus would give them his war horse:

> ' Then Datus made reply—the words sound ill—
> " I care not; slay my mother, if you will.
> But my brave steed shall never leave my side;
> He is too good for dastards to bestride."

> Then swift the cruel foemen to their wall
> His mother dragged : and Datus saw her fall.
> Her breasts and head at him they dared to throw,
> And taunting cried : " Behold your mother now." '

The second book is less interesting and is concerned chiefly with the coronation of Louis by the Pope and the Emperor's Church reforms. But in the third book we get back to fighting again in Louis' campaign against the Breton prince Morman, and there is a very lively account of a duel between the two champions Bera and Sanila. Book IV tells us of the efforts made by Louis to convert the Danes to Christianity. King Harald comes with his fleet to the imperial palace at Ingelheim and is baptised ; and the poem ends with a personal appeal to Louis for forgiveness.

Abbo of Paris (Cernuus) (fl. 890).

In his preface to Einhard's *Life of Charles*, Walafrid sighs over the decadence of his own time. ' Charles rendered his kingdom radiant with the blaze of new learning ; but now men's minds are turned away, and the light of wisdom is dying out.' Of Walafrid's generation the words are somewhat pessimistic, but they certainly are true of the last third of the ninth century. The literary merit of such writers as Hucbald, Odo of Cluny, and Saxo Poeta is very small, and the only books produced in this period which require notice are one verse history and two prose biographies. The first of these three is the hexameter poem *De bellis Parisiacæ urbis*, written by Abbo, a monk of the abbey of St Germain des Prés. Abbo—who must not be confused with the tenth-century theologian Abbo of Fleury—is a writer of the same kind as Ermoldus, and the first two of the three books of his poem, which contain a narrative of the siege of Paris by the Normans in 886, are as vigorous as his predecessor's *Siege of Barcelona*. The arrival of the Norman fleet and their fierce attacks upon the Isle of France are described in the most lively fashion, while the long recital of the miracles wrought during the siege by St Germain and St Geneviève makes the poem a curious compound of history and martyrology. This effect of quaintness is emphasised in the third book, which, though it is ostensibly a continuation of the narrative, has nothing to do with history, but is a series of maxims for clerics written in the strangest mixture of popular Latin and Greek, with copious glosses.

Asser (850–909)

Of the two biographies we have mentioned, one is the *Life of Alfred the Great*, written by Asser in 893. Asser was a Welshman who became Bishop of Sherborne, and his book, of course, has considerable interest for English readers. Considered as a piece of literature, however, its merits are not very striking. Moreover, our present text depends upon Archbishop Parker's edition, printed in London, 1574, the only surviving manuscript on which that edition was based having been burned in 1731 ; and it is in such an unsatisfactory condition that only those portions of it which are quoted by Florence of Worcester (1118) can be regarded as above suspicion. The first chapter traces Alfred's descent through his father Æthelwulf to Adam ; the second continues with his mother's genealogy, which ends, somewhat abruptly, with her father Oslam who settled in Guuihtgaraburhg. We then have an account of Alfred's reign, the facts being drawn from the Old-English Chronicle ; and it is only in the biographical chapters 22–25 and 72–105 that Asser depends upon his own knowledge. Of these, chapter 23, quoted by Florence, may be taken as an example of Asser's curious vagueness :

> 'One day his mother showed him and his brothers a book of Saxon poems she was holding and said : " I will give this manuscript to whichever one of you can learn it first." Alfred, spurred on by her words, or rather by divine inspiration, and charmed by the beauty of the book's initial letter, replied to his mother : " Will you really give the book to that one of us who can first understand and repeat it in your presence ? " His mother smiled and said : " Yes, I will." Thereupon he at once took the book from her hand, went to his master and read it, and having done so brought it back to her and repeated the contents.'

As we have just been told by Asser that the young Alfred could not read, it will be seen that an explanation of this passage calls for some ingenuity.

The Monk of St Gall (fl. 890)

About the same time that Asser was compiling Alfred's biography a certain monk at St Gall—*balbus et edentulus*—almost certainly the same Notker with whom we shall later be concerned, was amusing himself by writing a second, and what he doubtless considered an improved, life of Charlemagne. Einhard is an historian and is only concerned with facts ; Notker is a moralist whose chief aim is edification. His book was planned to consist of three parts, dealing with Charles as a Churchman, as a warrior, and as a king in private life ; but of the three sections we now only have the first and part of the second. The idea was apparently suggested by Charles III, who visited St Gall in 883, and Notker got his information chiefly from an old priest named Werinbert, and from Werinbert's father Adalbert, who had fought under Charles in several of his campaigns. The first book consists mainly of a series of anecdotes about Charles and his bishops. 'I am afraid the bishops will not like me,' says Notker, ' *sed non grandis est mihi cura.*' We have the drunken bishop who lost his see ; the too agile bishop who was called up for the army ; the bishop who fell for a woman ; and the bishop who was tempted by the devil. We have the trick played on the stingy bishop by the hairy imp who stole his wine ; and the trick played on the dilettante bishop by the Jew merchant at Charles' instigation : ' comprehendens unum murem domesticum diversis aromatibus condivit et præfato episcopo venalem apportavit.' The second book opens with an account of the campaigns against the Huns and Saxons and the reception of Greek and Persian ambassadors, and proceeds to a very imaginary account of the siege of Pavia in 773, which is shortened from eight months to two days. Charles appears always as a figure of heroic courage, and two of the many stories are these. On one occasion he was just going to swim in his new bath at Aix when the devil attacked him. Without hesitation he drew his sword and thrust him through. The shadowy form was so substantial that the whole bath was infected ' *tabo et cruore,*' but Charles merely ordered fresh water and proceeded with his swim. At another time he heard that his captains had disparaged his courage, and so he ordered a huge bull and a terrible lion to be set face to face. When the lion had got the bull down Charles cried : ' Save the bull and kill the lion.' The captains replied : ' There is no man under heaven who would dare to attempt it.' Then Charles drew his sword and did the deed, while the captains, thunder-struck, fell on the ground before him.

Notker wrote in a time that was exceptionally unfavourable to the peaceful pursuit of literature.

Charles' dream of a universal empire had faded away, and the West, lacking any strong central government, was again exposed to barbarian invaders on every side. Normans burned the cathedral of Utrecht, Danes in their long ships sailed up the Rhine to sack the palaces of Aix, Saracens crossed the water from Africa and Spain and fixed their robber nests in South Italy and Provence, Hungarians swarming in from the East ravaged all central and southern Europe, and in 924 set fire to Pavia, then the richest and most flourishing city of Italy. In the midst of this turmoil the monasteries were the only refuge of learning, and even the monasteries were not immune from pagan attacks, for St Gall itself was plundered by the Hungarians in 926.

But once again civilisation triumphed over barbarism, and relief came to Christian Europe from the people whom Charles had compelled at the sword's point to embrace the true faith. On the death in 919 of Conrad, the last of Charles' line, Henry of Saxony was appointed as his successor, and at once began the work of pacification, which was completed by his son Otto the Great (936–973). The Hungarians were crushed, the Germans formed into a strong kingdom, and in 962 when Otto was crowned at Rome by Pope John XII, the Holy Roman Empire was established for the second time. Otto was not so ardent a lover of letters as Charles had been, but like all great rulers he recognised the importance of literature, and his reign was marked by a definite revival, called by German scholars 'Die Ottonische Renaissance,' in which the two brightest stars are Liudprand and Hroswitha. But before we come to the Ottonian revival there is one work of genius that must be mentioned.

Ekkehart I (900–c. 970)

Notker died in 912 and perhaps just missed seeing the boy who was destined to be the chief of the St Gall poets and Dean of the famous monastery during the latter half of the tenth century. Ekkehart I, the first of the four of that name, was born near St Gall of a noble Alsatian family in 900, and received his education at the abbey under Gerald. While still a youth he wrote as a school exercise the *Waltharius*, an epic poem of 1456 hexameter lines; and although in later life he was chiefly esteemed for his religious verse it is on this youthful essay that his fame rests. As we have it now the text of the poem represents a double revision, the first by Gerald, the second, three generations later, by Ekkehart IV, who in 1030 undertook—'*pro posse et nosse nostro*,' as he says—to correct its Latinity; but in essentials there can be little doubt that we have it as it was originally composed.

The story is laid in the days of Attila, King of the Huns. Walter, Hagen, and the Princess Hildegund are held by him as hostages for the Aquitanians, Franks, and Burgundians respectively. Walter and Hagen are close friends, Walter and Hildegund have been betrothed from childhood. All three are well treated by Attila and his queen, but when Hagen escapes Walter and Hildegund decide to follow his example. Walter, who has just returned from fighting valiantly for the Huns, invites the king and his chiefs to a banquet, where he takes advantage of their love of wine :

> ' Therewith he gave the goblet, wrought of old
> With deeds of valour done by warriors bold.
> The king drank once, and lo ! the cup was dry ;
> And loud he cried to all the company :

173

" Drink, lads, with me." The pages to and fro
Run with the brimming beakers, nor allow
One empty to remain, while king and host
Cheer on the feast with many a jovial toast.
A drunken warmth begins the hall to fill
And takes men captive. To their owners' will
Tongues answer not, but stammering words repeat,
And stalwart heroes scarce can keep their feet.'

Consequently the young pair escape unseen, and
when Attila the next morning totters from his bedroom
' holding his head with both hands,' he finds Walter
gone and none of his own men bold enough to pursue
him.   From Pannonia Walter and Hildegund make
their way to the Rhine, where their arrival is reported
to Gunther, King of the Franks.   Hagen, who is living
at Gunther's court, recognises his comrade from the
description, but Gunther determines to rob the pair
of the treasure they have with them, and in spite of all
remonstrances orders Hagen and his eleven other
champions to come with him in pursuit.   Meanwhile
Walter has reached the Vosges mountains, and leaving
Hildegund to keep watch from the top of a defile
sleeps peacefully until his assailants arrive.   On Hagen's
entreaty Gunther sends an envoy to demand the
peaceful surrender of the treasure ; but when Walter
refuses the great fight begins.   One by one Gunther's
champions advance up the rocky path and are in
turn defeated.   When eight have been killed and
Hagen still refuses to fight, the king joins with the
last three in a combined attack ; but this also fails,
and at nightfall only Gunther and Hagen are left
alive.   Hildegund again goes on guard, singing to keep
herself awake ; but the next morning after one more
attempt Gunther gives in, Walter and Hildegund are
happily married, and the poem ends with the bard's
apology :

174

' Forgive, good reader, all that here is wrong.
Rough is the music of a cricket's song,
And nestlings, when they fly, must face a fall.
So ends my book : may Jesus save us all.'

The *Waltharius* is a very pretty example of the influence of Virgil on a youthful genius, and it is also of considerable importance in the history of literature. It is the child of classical Latin, but it is also the father of medieval German epic, for Ekkehart shows plainly that the German legends afford subjects eminently suitable for poetical treatment. Metrically, of course, the poem, in spite of the two revisions, is very rough, and Teutonisms like *Wah, quid dicis* give it occasionally an odd appearance ; but it has one very great merit ; it can be read with enjoyment, and Ekkehart is as able to communicate to others his own gusto as is the first of Otto's men, Liudprand, Bishop of Cremona.

Liudprand (920–972)

Liudprand was born 920 at Pavia of a wealthy Lombard family whose members were closely connected with the royal service, and when Hugh of Arles, King of Italy, decided in 927 to send an embassy to Constantinople, Liudprand's father was chosen as envoy. Soon after his return he died, and his son was taken into Hugh's household as a singing page, by the sweetness of his voice winning the especial favour of the king, who was a passionate lover of music. In his teens Liudprand must have studied zealously, making himself acquainted with the great classics of Latin literature, and when the time came for him to decide upon his career, he chose the pen rather than the sword, the cloister in preference to the camp, and became a deacon at Pavia. The clerical profession, however, in the tenth century did not preclude a vast amount of worldly activity, and Liudprand's parents were both fully alive to their son's literary talents and also determined that he should use them to advantage in State service. Accordingly Berengar was approached and, if we may believe our account, was induced by lavish gifts of money to appoint the young man as his private secretary and chancellor, ' *secretorum conscius ac epistolarum signator*,' whatever the words may mean. King Hugh was dead and Berengar reigned in his stead.

For a time all went well; and then there was a rift. It became necessary for Berengar in his turn to send an embassy to Constantinople, and being ' a man stuffed full of cunning ' he looked about to see if he could find an envoy who would make the voyage at his own expense. Liudprand's stepfather was very anxious that his talented stepson should add a knowledge of Greek to the Latin he already possessed. Berengar easily persuaded him that a visit to Constantinople was the very thing necessary. The stepfather supplied the money for the journey, and Liudprand set off down the Po from Pavia on 1st August 949, reached Venice in three days, sailed across the Adriatic in company with an envoy from Otto of Saxony, who was bound for the same destination, and finally arrived at Constantinople on 17th September.

The embassy was largely a matter of formal courtesy, and the envoy should have been supplied with handsome gifts for the Greek Emperor. But when Liudprand came to examine his baggage, he found that all Berengar had thought necessary in the way of complimentary presents was a letter to Constantine, Porphyrogenitus, ' packed with lies,' and that therefore he would be obliged to make the customary offerings from his own private store. This he did when the time came for him to be received by Constantine, the presence of other envoys from Spain and Germany compelling him to a generosity he scarcely felt. But it is plain that the mean trick which he considered Berengar had played on him rankled bitterly in his mind, and we need hardly look for any other reason than this to account for the ill-feeling between master and servant that arose after the latter's return to Italy.

The young Lothair died in November 950 and Berengar secured the election of himself and his son Adalbert as joint kings. But, as so often happened in this period, no sooner had he reached the summit of his ambition than his power began to fail. His own avarice and the cruel greed of his wife Willa alienated many others beside Liudprand, and soon a steady stream of malcontents began to make its way across the Alps into Germany, where Otto of Saxony was in course of consolidating his position and already thinking of adventures in the south. Among these voluntary exiles was Liudprand, who must have left his native land some time before 956, since we know that in February of that year he made the acquaintance at Otto's court of the Spanish bishop, Recemund of Elvira, envoy of ' Abd-ar-Rahman III,' the greatest of the Umayyad princes, who was then making Cordova a rival in splendour to Baghdad. Between the Spanish and the Italian cleric a close friendship soon sprung up, and it was Recemund who advised Liudprand to solace the griefs of the exile, which he so often compares to the captivity of the Jews in Babylon, by composing a history of his own times. In response to this suggestion the *Antapodosis* was begun at Frankfort in 958, reached its third book in 960, and was still in progress in 962. But meanwhile Liudprand had added a knowledge of German to his Latin and Greek, and by his varied accomplishments had commended himself to the favourable notice of Otto the Great. As early as 960 it would seem that he undertook a mission to Constantinople on Otto's behalf, halting for a time on his way back at the island of Paxos off the coast of Epirus. As a reward for this and similar services he was given the bishopric of Cremona towards the end of 961, and accompanied Otto when the latter at last decided that the time was ripe for him to enter Italy. In Liudprand Otto found a skilful and devoted instrument for his Italian policy, in Otto Liudprand gained a staunch and powerful protector ; and the result of this combination of German vigour and Italian subtlety was seen on 2nd February 962, when Otto with his queen Adelaide was crowned as Emperor of the West by Pope John XII at St Peter's, and the Holy Roman Empire came again into existence.

After 965 we find the name of the Bishop of Cremona continually occurring in the records of the time. He was again with Otto in South Italy, when the Emperor made his unsuccessful attack upon the Byzantine dominions in Apulia, and it was very probably at his own suggestion that he was sent to Constantinople in June 968 to conclude a treaty of marriage between Theophano, daughter of the late Emperor Romanos, and Otto II, the Emperor's son. This embassy, rendered fruitless by the obstinate cunning of Nicephorus Phocas, kept Liudprand in the East for some time, and soon after his return, in 972, he died.

Rejecting as spurious two or three books that have been wrongly attributed to Liudprand, we have three genuine works from his pen, the *Antapodosis*, the *Gesta Ottonis*, and the *Legatio*. Of these the *Legatio*, an account of Liudprand's second embassy, gives us a brilliant picture of Constantinople, with its palaces, parks and churches, its troops of State officials and its gorgeous State ceremonies, but from it also we derive a clear idea of why it was that there was so little real intercourse between Constantinople and Western Europe during medieval times. It is plain that Liudprand and his companions cordially disliked Byzantine food, Byzantine drink, Byzantine dress, and Byzantine manners; that they were not allowed to ride on horseback through the streets seemed to them an insult; that the palace in which they were lodged admitted the air freely was an intolerable hardship : Byzantine splendour they thought extravagance, Byzantine simplicity meanness. Evidently also in dealing with a rough soldier like Nicephorus the cultured Italian prelate was at a disadvantage, and his punctilious regard for ceremony and readiness to take offence go far to explain the failure of his mission. The *Legatio* therefore has a psychological as well as an historical interest, and as a narrative it is a wonderful production. The pen picture of Nicephorus may be quoted as an example :

'A monstrosity of a man, a dwarf, fat-headed and with tiny mole's eyes; disfigured by a short, broad, thick beard half going gray; disgraced by a neck scarcely an inch long; piglike by reason of the big close bristles on his head; . . . a big belly, a lean posterior, very long in the hip considering his short stature, small legs, fair-sized heels and feet; dressed in a robe made of fine linen, but old, foul-smelling and discoloured by age; shod with Sicyonian slippers; bold of tongue, a fox by nature, in perjury and falsehood a Ulysses.'

As regards the *Gesta Ottonis*, the only fault that can be found with it is its brevity, and the fact that in spite of its title it deals fully with but one episode in Otto's reign. That episode, the deposition of Pope John XII, is, it is true, highly important in itself, and moreover is connected with one of the cardinal events in history, the crowning of Otto as Emperor at Rome in 962. To this the opening chapters briefly refer, and then pass on to the main subject. In the year 963 Otto received evidence that John had summoned Adalbert to Italy and was trying to stir up the Hungarians to invade Saxony, and he determined to depose his former ally from the papacy. He therefore summoned a synod of the Church under his own presidency, of whose members Liudprand gives a long list, beginning with the patriarch of Aquileia, and descending by way of archbishops, bishops, cardinals, minor clergy and Roman magnates to the one solitary representative of the common people. At this synod charges were brought forward against the Pope of simony, sacrilege, fornication, drunkenness, and many minor misdemeanours; and he was summoned to appear and clear himself in person. John's answer was a threat of excommunication, and even when the synod deposed him he forced his way back to Rome. Finally after much bloodshed he was expelled, and the record closes with the reinstatement of Otto's nominee as Pope Leo VIII.

The *Antapodosis* is considerably the longest of Liudprand's works, and contains a history of Italian affairs from 887 to 949, the first three of its six books being concerned with events that happened before the author's time. Its title 'Tit-for-Tat' is explained in a preface, which Liudprand, with his usual dislike of the obvious, places at the beginning of the third book:

'The aim and object of this work is to reveal, declare and stigmatise the doings of that Berengar, who is now not king but rather despot of Italy, and of his wife Willa, who because of her boundless tyranny is rightly called a second Jezebel, and because of her insatiate greed for plunder a Lamia vampire. . . . In return for the troubles I have endured at their hands I will unveil to present and future generations their *sacrilège infâme*, that is, the abominable impiety of which they have been guilty.'

Liudprand does not even pretend to be impartial, and although the *Antapodosis* is in form a history, the many passages of original verse, the frequent quotations from classical authors, and the curious habit that Liudprand has of interlarding his Latin with Greek words and phrases, give its pages a strange effect. Liudprand, like our own Froude, is rather a novelist than a historian, and the chief charm of the *Antapodosis* lies in the numerous stories which enliven the narrative. There is the tale of Pope Sergius, who had the corpse of his predecessor Formosus exhumed, and after dressing the body in pontifical vestments threw it insultingly into the Tiber. There is the tale, told half in Latin and half in Greek, of Romanos, afterwards emperor, who killed a monstrous lion and was rewarded by being made admiral of the fleet. There is the Ingoldsby Legend of the trick played by the wicked Bishop Hatto, the very Rabelaisian anecdote of Willa and the hidden belt, and the Arabian Nights fantasies of the adventures of the Emperor Leo with the venal policeman and the sleeping guards. The last of these, which is comparatively short, may serve as an example of the rest.

'Another prank which this emperor played I think it foolish to veil in silence. The palace at Constantinople is guarded by numerous companies of soldiers in order to secure the emperor's safety, and every day a considerable sum of money is spent upon these men's pay and rations. Now it happened once that twelve of these guards were resting in one room from the heat of the day during the siesta hour, when it was Leo's custom to wander about the palace. On this occasion, when the twelve men I have mentioned had abandoned themselves to Lethean slumber, the Emperor came into the room, artfully opening the door latch with a small piece of wood. But one trickster can trap another. Eleven of the men were really asleep: the twelfth was awake although he made a pretence of snoring, and with his face covered by his arms he carefully watched what the emperor was doing. Well, the emperor came in and seeing that the soldiers were all asleep put a pound bag of gold coins into each man's bosom. He then went out again quietly and shut the door behind him, expecting that when the men woke up they would congratulate each other upon their gains and wonder how on earth they got there. But as soon as he had gone, the one soldier who was awake jumped up, took the bags of gold from the sleepers, and stored them in his wallet. Then he went quietly to sleep.

'In the afternoon the emperor, anxious to know the issue of his prank, bade the twelve guards to appear before him and addressed them thus: "If any one of you has been frightened or cheered by a dream vision, my authority bids you declare it. Moreover, if any man on waking saw any strange sight, I order you to reveal that also." To this the soldiers replied that they had seen nothing (as indeed was the truth) and surprised at the emperor's order " silent stood with faces set intent." Leo, however, thought that it was not out of ignorance but from cunning they were keeping silence, and flying into a passion threatened them with dreadful punishments if they did not speak. Thereupon the one man of the company who knew the truth put on a very humble and suppliant tone of voice and addressed the emperor: " *Votre gracieuse majesté*," that is " Your gracious majesty, I do not know what these men saw; I myself had a most delectable dream; I only wish it would come often. I dreamed, while my comrades, unfortunately for them, to-day were really asleep, that I was awake, and, as it were, not asleep at all. And lo and behold, Your Imperial Grandeur secretly opened the door, as it were, and entering quietly put a pound bag of gold in each of my comrades' bosoms. In my vision I saw your majesty go out again while my comrades were still asleep, and jumping up at once for joy I took the bags of gold from the eleven sleepers and stored them in my wallet where there was only one. I did not want them to go beyond the Ten Commandments and be just eleven, but to join with mine and make twelve in memory of the twelve apostles. May it please you, august emperor, this vision up to now has not frightened me but rather made me cheerful. I hope your majesty will not prefer another interpretation for it. It is a well-known fact that I am *un prophète et vendeur de songes*, that is, a prophet and dream pedlar."

At this the emperor burst into a loud guffaw, and admiring the fellow's skill and caution said at once : " I have never heard before that you were *un prophète et vendeur de songes*, a prophet and a dream pedlar. But it is plain from what you say that you are a prophet, and you have not beaten about the bush. You could not have the power of keeping awake or the skill to draw auspices, unless it were given you by divine grace. So whether your interpretation is true—as I hope and believe—or false, *ainsi que Lucien*, that is, as Lucian tells us of a man, that in his sleep he found a great treasure, but when the cock woke him there was nothing there ; in either case, anything you saw or noticed or discovered, you may regard as yours." With what confusion these words filled the sleepers and with what joy they filled the watcher, anyone can easily imagine if he puts himself in their place.'

Hroswitha (fl. 965)

Liudprand lived a very full life and makes good use of his experiences in his writings. Hroswitha the nun of Gandersheim, born 935, is a finer and more subtle genius, for she draws her material from her own inner consciousness and in spite of some crudities is the most sympathetic of all the Latin dramatists. She has not the boisterous humour of Plautus nor the urbane wit of Terence, but she has other qualities which they do not possess. Her dialogue with its curious effects of rhymed prose is more lifelike than theirs ; she has a deeper insight into character than they usually show ; above all, her Christian charity puts to shame the one's careless levity and the other's cynical indifference.

Gandersheim is now a quiet little town nestling in a wide Brunswick valley, and is chiefly known for the excellent beer which it brews. But in the tenth century it was a place of importance, the seat of an authority, both spiritual and temporal, which, though always in a woman's hands, gave that woman power of life and death over all the males of the district. The Abbess of Gandersheim held direct from the king ; she had her own law courts, her own mint and coinage, and her own men-at-arms. As a feudal baron she had a right to a seat at the Imperial Diet—a right which was exercised as late as 1803 by Dorothea Augusta of Brunswick—and on many occasions she was a member of the royal house of Saxony. But she was also the head of a great religious and educational establishment where the rule of St Benedict was strictly observed and all worldly luxuries prohibited. Her nuns, as a medieval chronicler tells us, ' were forbidden to eat away from the common table at the appointed times, except in case of sickness. They slept together and came together to celebrate the canonical hours. And they set to work together whenever work had to be done.' To preside successfully over such a community required qualities of a very high order, and we know from Hroswitha herself that the abbess in her time—Gerberg, niece of the Emperor Otto—was not only a good woman and a great administrator, but also a sound classical scholar : ' Younger in years than I, but far older in learning.'

The phrase comes from the preface which Hroswitha wrote for what seems to have been her first literary production, the set of poems on the Christian martyrs. These pieces, which include an account of Christ's nativity and ascension, are mostly in leonine hexameters with internal rhyme, and to all lovers of martyrology they are of great interest. One of them, moreover, is of importance in literary history, for the tale of Theophilus, the priest who made a compact with the devil, is the earliest poetical treatment of the Faust legend. The material is usually drawn from ancient records, but Hroswitha adds many touches of her own. Her story of the martyrdom of St Agnes, for example, whose presence purified the house of ill-fame to which she was consigned and whose chastity shamed its frequenters into repentance, is a most vivid piece of writing. Even more striking is the tale of Pelagius, which Hroswitha heard from an eye-witness. Pelagius lived at Cordoba in Hroswitha's time, and was so comely of person that the Caliph Abderrahman, who then ruled in Spain, wished to make him his minion. The Christian youth, of course, indignantly refused, and was thereupon handed over to the executioner. He was first shot from a catapult, but escaped unhurt ; then he was beheaded and his body thrown into the river. The manner in which fishermen found his head and the miracle that followed form the conclusion of the poem.

The third section of Hroswitha's works, also in verse, is less exciting than this, but possesses considerable historical value. It consists of two long hexameter poems, the first containing a history of the Abbey of Gandersheim from its foundation in 850 by Liudulf and his wife Oda down to the writer's own times ; the second, now incomplete, relating in epic style the chief exploits of the Emperor Otto I. But Hroswitha's poems, whether mystical or historical, are not her true title to fame. They are chiefly important as showing that a woman in the tenth century, without any distinct poetical gift, had sufficient training in literature to write better verse than most of our contemporary bards can achieve. Her real genius is revealed in the six prose plays that come second in the manuscript found by Conrad Celtes at Ratisbon in the fifteenth century, the *Gallicanus, Dulcitius, Sapientia, Calimachus, Pafnutius* and *Abraham.*

Of these, the first, and least significant, three deal with the conflict between Christianity and Paganism, and their plots are briefly as follows : In *Gallicanus* the hero, one of Constantine's generals, claims the Emperor's daughter in marriage as the reward of his military services. Constantine dare not refuse him openly, but knows that his daughter has taken the vow of virginity ; and finally, at her suggestion, he delays his answer and sends her two chaplains to attend the general on his next campaign. Their ministrations are successful. Gallicanus becomes a Christian, and on his return regretfully abandons his plans of marriage and allows his intended bride to remain a virgin.

The second play in this group, *Dulcitius*, differs from the rest in being distinctly humorous in parts. Dulcitius, a governor under Diocletian, has three Christian virgins handed over to him for examination. Enraptured by their beauty, he orders them to be confined in his scullery among the kitchen utensils ; and when night falls he, with the worst of intentions, pays them a secret visit. Fortunately, in the darkness he mistakes the round pots upon the walls for the virgins' swelling bosoms, and, embracing them tenderly, covers himself with soot and grime. So changed, indeed, is his appearance after this amorous encounter that his own soldiers fail to recognise him, and he is driven off as a vagabond. Thus far the play is broadly comical, but the later scenes are serious. The virgins still refuse to renounce their faith, and two of them are burned alive, while their younger sister, rescued from shame by angelic intervention, is shot on the mountain to which she escapes, and dies praising Christ.

If Hroswitha shows some levity in *Dulcitius*, she makes full amends when she brings the lamentable story of *Sapientia* upon the stage. The scene is set in Hadrian's palace at Rome, and the action begins with a complaint laid before the Emperor by a Roman patrician. A certain foreign woman, it appears, named

186

Sapientia, 'Wisdom,' has come to Rome with her three daughters—Faith, Hope and Charity—and is persuading the Roman matrons to refuse all their marital duties. Hadrian summons the foreigners into his presence, but on questioning the mother about her daughters' ages, he himself has to submit to a long and highly ingenious lecture on the qualities of numbers. Brushing this information aside, the tyrant orders the three young girls to offer sacrifice to his gods, and on their refusal has them put to death by the most cruel tortures. Their dead bodies are given to their mother, and in the last act Sapientia lays her children in the grave, and then, in a magnificent speech, prays that she also may die and falls lifeless by their side.

The three remaining plays deal with another conflict, the eternal struggle between the spirit and the flesh, and show, to the best of Hroswitha's ability, the evils that unlawful love brings in its train. Their aim is entirely moral, but the author thinks it prudent to write an apologetic preface :

'You will find some Catholics, and I cannot entirely hold myself guiltless, who, attracted by the charm of a polished style, prefer the empty foolishness of pagan literature to the useful lessons of the holy scriptures. There are others who, although they cling to the sacred pages and despise most pagan authors, yet too frequently peruse the plays that Terence invented, and while they find pleasure in his delightful dialogue, pollute themselves with the knowledge of things unspeakable. Therefore, I, the Strong Voice of Gandersheim, have not hesitated to imitate, on the stage, an author whom others cherish in their studies. He deals with the shameless profligacy of wanton women : I, to the best of my poor ability, use his method to glorify the laudable chastity of Christian virgins. One thing, however, has often embarrassed me and brought a hot blush to my cheek—the form of my work has compelled me to set forth the detestable madness of unlawful love and the poisoned sweetness of such lover's talk. These things, which we are forbidden even to mention, I have had to imagine for my plays and give as

187

themes to my dutiful pen. Still, if from modesty I had passed all
this by, I should not have fulfilled my purpose nor should I have
set forth to the best of my power the praise of innocence. The
more seductive a lover's blandishments, the more sublime we prove
the glory of our heavenly helper and the more wonderful the
triumph of our victory. And this is especially true when it is
female weakness that wins the day and manly strength that is put
to confusion.'

Of these feminist dramas *Calimachus* is the most
tragic and has the strongest plot, although it is not
written in Hroswitha's most characteristic manner.
Fired by love for the saintly Drusiana, Calimachus
confesses his passion to her, and Drusiana, who has
even refused her husband's lawful embraces, in her
horror prays to Christ that she may die. Her prayer
is granted ; she is laid in her tomb, and one of her
servants set to guard her. Calimachus, still maddened
with desire, comes to the grave, and, bribing the
servant, is about to take the dead body in his arms
when a monstrous serpent appears and kills both men.
Their corpses are found by the husband and the
Apostle John, who, in a final scene, revives Drusiana
and recalls Calimachus to life and repentance. Even
the wicked servant has the same mercy shown to him,
but on returning to life he refuses to repent and is
handed back again to his master, Satan.

Pafnutius opens with a school scene. His disciples
ask their master Pafnutius why he looks so sad, and he
tells them that it is because of the injuries that are
done to God by His creatures. The greater world is
obedient to the Creator, but the microcosm Man is
out of harmony with the divine law. 'What is harmony ? ' ask the disciples, and Pafnutius then gives
them a delightful lecture on music before he informs
them of the particular offender against God whom he

188

has in mind. This is the notorious Thais, and Pafnutius announces his resolve to disguise himself as a pleasure-seeker and to win her repentance. He goes to her house, and we have the wonderful scenes in which the courtesan accepts Christ and humbly follows her new guide to the convent where she is to pass the rest of her days doing penance for her sins. Three years elapse, and in the last act Pafnutius, assured of the sinner's pardon, returns to the convent, finds Thais dying, and stays by her side until her soul has winged its way to heaven.

The plot of *Abraham* is in some respects similar to that of *Pafnutius*, but there are subtle points of difference. When the play opens, Mary, the niece of the hermit Abraham, is a child of eight living in the desert under the care of her uncle and his old friend Effrem. Ten years pass, and a stranger beguiles her away. Then, after long searching, Abraham is informed that Mary is living a life of shame in a neighbouring city. He therefore disguises himself, borrows a horse and some money, and goes to save the lost sheep. He finds her in the pimp's house, and a recognition scene follows which is equal to any in classical drama.

'ABRAHAM. Now the time has come to take off my disguise and show her who I am. Mary, my adopted daughter, you who were half of my soul! Do you recognise the old man who reared you like a father, and betrothed you to the Son of the King of Heaven?

MARY. What shall I do? It is my father Abraham, my teacher, who speaks.

ABRAHAM. What has come to you, daughter?

MARY. Bitter trouble.

ABRAHAM. Who deceived you? Who led you astray?

MARY. He who ruined our first parents.

ABRAHAM. Where is that angel's life you once led on earth?

MARY. Gone, gone to perdition.

ABRAHAM. Where is your maidenly modesty? Where your lovely chastity?

MARY. Lost, lost.

ABRAHAM. If you do not come to your right mind again, what reward can you expect for all the toil of your fastings, prayers, and vigils ? You have fallen from the heights of heaven and plunged yourself in the depths of hell.

MARY. How wretched am I !

ABRAHAM. Why did you not trust me ? Why did you leave me ? Why did you not tell me of your fall ? My beloved Effrem and I would have done a worthy penance for you.

MARY. When I was fallen and sunk in sin I did not presume to approach your holy presence in my filthiness.

ABRAHAM. Who ever lived that was free from sin, save only the Virgin's Son ?

MARY. No one.

ABRAHAM. To sin is human, to persist in sinning is devilish. We cannot justly condemn those who fall unawares : we should rather blame those who refuse to rise as soon as may be.'

It is difficult to represent in English the stark simplicity of Hroswitha's Latin, but even a translation will make plain the manner in which she deals with a situation which has led many a modern author into false pathos and mawkish sentiment. *Humanum est peccare, diabolicum in peccatis durare :* such is the moral of the play, and Mary is no hardened sinner ; she leaves the city, goes back with her uncle to the desert, and in repentance finds happiness.

Flodoard (894–966)

Of the other writers who flourished under Otto and his immediate successors a brief account must suffice. Flodoard of Rheims is a more sober but a less entertaining historian than Liudprand. An excellent man, first a priest and then a monk, the chief facts of his life are given in the old French epitaph :

> ' Si ti veu de Rein savoir li Eveque
> Lye le temporaire de Fladoon le saige.
> Y les mor du tam d'Odaldry eveque,
> Et fut d'Eparnay ne pâr parentaige.

Vequit caste Clerc, bon Moine, meilleu Abbé,
Et d'Agapit ly Romain fut aubé.
Par sen histoire maintes nouvelles sauras,
Et en ille toutes antiquité auras.'

'If you wish to know of the Bishops of Rheims read the annals of wise Flodoard. He died in the time of Bishop Odaldry and was a native of Epernay. In life he was a chaste clerk, a good monk, and a better abbot, and was consecrated by the Well beloved Pope of Rome (Leo VII). By his history you will get knowledge of many new things and will find all antiquity in it.'

As a writer, both in prose and verse, Flodoard possessed immense industry. In prose his *History of the Church of Rheims* fills three hundred pages in Migne, and his three verse books *On the Triumphs of Christ and the Saints in Palestine, Antioch, and Italy* run to nearly twenty thousand lines. To read the lives of the many saints and martyrs recorded by Flodoard in hexameter and iambic verse requires some perseverance; and to most the *Annals* will seem more attractive. This is a brief and accurate record of events in France taken year by year from 919 to 966. The style is clear but not very lively, although occasionally some curious details are given. Under the year 944, for example, we find :

'In that part of Germany north of the Rhine there was a certain man whose hand had been cut off. Fourteen years later, as those who know him declare, one night while he was asleep it was suddenly restored whole to him. In some villages of the same district balls of fire were seen rushing through the air, which in their flight set houses and farms ablaze; but when they were faced by the Cross and the bishop's blessing and holy water, they were driven away. . . . In Paris this year there was a violent storm with a furious hurricane, which completely destroyed the walls of a very ancient building constructed of strong cement that for many years had stood on Martyrs' Mount (Montmartre). It is said that on this occasion demons were seen there in the shape of horsemen, who first destroyed a church close by and then used its timbers to batter the aforesaid walls until they brought them down.'

Widukind (fl. 975)

Of the life of Widukind, the monk of Corbie who wrote *Res gestæ Saxonicæ*, we know nothing; of his character we learn little from his writings, except that his frequent apologies for the *tenuitas* of his style reveal a self-distrust more suitable to the cloister than to the rough business of life. He lived at the same time as Liudprand, deals largely with the same country and period and has the same hero in Otto the Great : but when he is treating of contemporary affairs his narrative sadly lacks the spice provided by Liudprand's malicious humour. His book is dedicated to the Emperor's daughter, ' *Flore virginali cum maiestate imperiali ac sapientia singulari fulgenti dominæ Mathildæ*,' and is mostly a sober and very succinct account of the reigns of Henry the Fowler and Otto I, ending with the latter's death in 973. Descriptive passages are few, and among the best is the eloquent account of the death of the Emperor's mother Matilda at the nunnery of Quedlinburg, which ends thus :

> ' If I were to try to tell of all her virtues, time would fail me : if I had the eloquence of Homer or Virgil, it would not suffice. Full of days, full of honour, full of good works and almsgiving— for she had given away all her royal wealth to the servants and handmaids of God and to the poor—she rendered back her soul to Christ on March 13th.'

In a different style is the vivid description of Immo's stratagems : how he collected swarms of bees and at the proper moment let them loose upon the enemy's cavalry, so that both men and horses had to take to flight : how on another occasion he captured a large herd of swine passing before his town by waving a little pig from the walls, and as the herd rushed towards the noise, getting them inside the gates before their guardians could arrive : both of which tricks, as Widukind says, were very annoying to his opponent.

But in the main history passages like this are rare, and Widukind's best stories all come in the first half of the first of his three books, where he is concerned with Saxon origins. His people, he thinks, were descended from the remnants of Alexander's army, who after their great leader's death scattered to all parts of the world, and of early Saxon legends he gives several good specimens. The best perhaps is the tale of Iring :

> ' Irminfrid was called in and flung himself down at the feet of Thidriacus. Then, while he lay, Iring, who as the royal armour-bearer was standing near, drew his sword from its sheath and slew his master. The king at once said : " By such a deed as this you, who have slain your lord, have incurred the hatred of all men. The way is open to you ; take your departure ; we will have no lot or part in your wickedness." " Deservedly have I incurred all men's hatred," replied Iring, " but it was to your guileful words that I listened. Before I go I will purge my crime by avenging my master." So, as he stood with sword unsheathed, he cut Thidriacus down, and taking his lord's body laid it on the top of the other corpse, that he who was conquered in his lifetime might be conqueror in death. Then, making a way with his sword, he left that place.'

Rather (890–974)

Liudprand never mentions Widukind, but he speaks twice of Rather in the third book of the *Antapodosis :* ' A certain monk named Rather, who because of his piety and his knowledge of the seven liberal arts was made Bishop of Verona ' ; and later : ' Verona was handed back to King Hugh, and Bishop Rather being taken prisoner was sent into exile at Pavia. There he wrote a book describing in witty and elegant language the sorrows of his banishment. Those who read his tale will find in it many polished thoughts suggested by that occasion, which will afford them as much pleasure as benefit.' Rather was indeed a man after Liudprand's own heart : irritable, argumentative, and satirical, but with all his faults very likeable. His life was long and stormy, and his writings reveal the reason of the enmities which he constantly aroused. Born at Liége in 890 he came into Italy with Bishop Ildoin and was appointed by Hugh of Arles as Bishop of Verona. Against Hugh, however, he soon turned to support Arnold of Bavaria, and when Arnold was defeated he naturally had to pay the penalty, and as a prisoner at Pavia wrote the book to which Liudprand refers.

The *Præloquia*, otherwise the *Meditationes Cordis*, otherwise the *Agonisticum*, is a very curious work, purporting in its six books to give rules of life for all classes, conditions, and ages of men. The first book takes nineteen trades, beginning with the soldier and ending with the beggar : the second takes the various stages of life, husband, wife, father, mother, grandfather, etc. Then there is a change of treatment, and the next two books are a long discourse on the duties of kings, from whom finally we pass to the clergy and especially to the bishops. Rather has no very high opinion of his Italian colleagues, and his account of their ordinary mode of life makes very pungent reading :

' They prefer actors to priests, stage folk to clerics, drunkards to scholars, rogues to honest men. They give a warmer welcome to mimes than to monks, and love the glories of Greece, the pomps of Babylon, the splendour of foreign lands. Their cups are of gold, their dishes of silver : their mixing bowls are of gold plate heavier and larger than any previous age has ever seen ; their drinking vessels are bright with colour, but they leave their churches begrimed with smoke. As for the crowd of dishes served at their banquets, they are as wonderful by their number as by their variety.

With such men as these the greater your greed the greater your wealth ; the wider your acres, the wider your knowledge ; the richer and shrewder, the better and nobler ; a man indeed, famous, glorious, the theme of universal praise.'

Similar invectives are to be found in all Rather's writings, in the *Phrenesis*, in the curious self-portrait ' A guess at some one's character,' in the *Essays*, ' A confession,' ' On discord,' ' On idle talk,' and in the thirteen *Sermons*.   Strife was his natural element, and his re-appointment to the see of Verona was soon followed by a hasty retirement.   He then attached himself to the household of Bruno, brother of Otto of Saxony ; and when his patron became Archbishop of Cologne he was made bishop of his native town of Liége.   Once again, however, his subordinates rebelled, and returning to Italy in 961 he was appointed by Otto, Bishop of Verona for the third time, and soon afterwards for the third time retired.   Henceforth until his death in 974 he seems to have held no office, and perhaps devoted these years to the elaboration of the *Sermons* which are his most characteristic work. Written in an obscure and difficult style they are full of matter, and remind one now of Swift and now of Doune.   To the fourth ' On Lenten duties ' Rather appends this note : ' This prolix discourse was delivered personally by the author, but it seems to have had little effect.'

Gerbert (950–1003)

Last of all we have Gerbert, at the very end of the tenth century.   Gerbert, afterwards Pope Silvester II, was born of poor parents in Auvergne about 950. Educated at the Benedictine monastery of Aurillac under Raimund, he was sent to study mathematics in Spain, and in 970 proceeded to Rome, where his knowledge of music and astronomy led Pope John XIII to recommend him to Otto I as tutor to his sons. Gerbert, however, preferred a wider field than the palace offered, and soon returning to France became head of the cathedral school of Rheims. There he gained a world-wide reputation both as a scholar and as a teacher, and when in 980 he met the Emperor Otto II in Italy he was made by him Abbot of Bobbio and Prince of the Empire. But these dignities proved rather a burden than a benefit to a man whose most ardent desire was for knowledge, and on Otto's death in 983 Gerbert returned to his studies at Rheims. For a short time he was left in quietude, but then he was forced once again into politics to support Adalberon, Archbishop of Rheims, in protecting the interests of the young Emperor Otto III. Gerbert had a considerable share in the elevation of Hugh Capet to the throne of France, and a further complication for him arose in 991, after Adalberon's death, when his own appointment by a synod to the Archbishopric of Rheims was questioned and held in abeyance by the Pope. Finally in 996 he had to journey again to Rome in the hope of gaining a favourable decision, and there met the young Emperor in person. He at once gained an immense influence over him, the pair returned to Germany together in 997, and two years later by Otto's command Gerbert succeeded Gregory V as Pope Silvester II. Now for the first time Pope and Emperor were in perfect harmony and everything seemed possible for them. Their plans were ready, but before they could put them into effect Fate stepped in. Otto died suddenly in 1002 and Gerbert followed his brilliant pupil to the grave in the next year.

Gerbert's fame for learning was so great that in

later ages a whole cycle of legends gathered round his name, and it was generally believed that he was a magician who had sold himself to the devil and owed his miraculous knowledge to infernal agency. His extant writings, however, are not of such extraordinary excellence as to have needed superhuman aid for their composition. One section consists of mathematical works, ' On the use of the abacus,' ' On the division of numbers,' and the ' Geometry ' : another of theological treatises such as ' On the body and blood of Our Lord ' : a third of philosophical essays, chief among them the *De rationali et ratione uti*, an examination of the question whether the use of reason can properly be called an attribute of the reasonable being. Less technical than these and written in a more graceful style are his official reports, especially the *Acta Concilii Remensis*, of which his pupil Richer says that ' it is composed in Ciceronian speech and with a wonderful charm of eloquence.' But the general reader will find Gerbert most interesting in his correspondence. Of his letters we have over two hundred, most of them concerned with affairs of Church and State, but many also of a purely personal character. The earlier of these are written from Aurillac to his masters Gerald and Raimund, the later to various fellow-scholars and to the Emperors Otto II and Otto III. A curious feature is the occasional use of cipher, as in the following (Ep. 125).

' Nature joins many men to us by ties of kinship, many by ties of sympathy. But there is no friendship more fruitful and pleasant than one that rests on the firm foundation of love. Who have I ever found more ready and willing to help me than you ? Therefore in this present political turmoil, when I suffer continually from armed treachery, I turn my eyes continually to you, with the sure hope that I shall not ask for comfort in vain. Unless I were in extreme need I would not have troubled you : so Z.Z.Q.M.B. Remember too that there will be some one else with a strong force on the 30th of September ; and V.Q.O.V.E.X. Then our frightened refugees will be able to return and our enemies will be overawed by our unexpected strength.'

PART IV

MEDIEVAL PROSE
(1002–1321)

MEDIEVAL PROSE

THE word ' medieval ' in this and the next part of our narrative is used in its narrowest sense, and includes only the three centuries 1000–1300, which come between the so-called Dark Ages and the beginning of the Renaissance. Even with these limitations the history of its Latin Literature is a vast subject, and in sheer bulk the writings of this period far outstrip the Classical Latin literature known to us. For throughout most of this epoch thought was active and Latin its normal medium of expression. It is true that, outside Italy, the vernacular tongues were already being written and the foundations of national cultures being laid down. But Latin was still the language of universal culture. M. Manitius in the second volume of his history dealt with the period 950–1100, and even in that century and a half found a hundred and thirty-six authors to discuss at length. We have not attempted such fullness, but have selected the principal writers for especial mention, giving rather a survey than a detailed history. Herein we follow the wise advice of Hugo of St Victor—'Non omnia dicenda sunt quæ dicere possumus, ne minus utiliter dicantur ea quæ dicere debemus.' (*Eruditio Didascalica*, III, 6.)

Richer (c. 950–1010)

One of Gerbert's most brilliant pupils was Richer the historian, a monk of great attainments and wide knowledge, especially of medicine. His father had been a man of eminence and Richer was in constant touch with those from whom he could obtain first-

hand knowledge of contemporary events. In spirit
and in style he belongs to the Carolingian age, but he
lived to see the descendants of Charlemagne driven
for ever from the throne of France. A monk of
St Remy near Rheims he was naturally a supporter of
the Carolingian dynasty against the claims of the
Robertians at Laon. Ever since the death of Louis the
Pious in 840 the throne of the descendants of Charles
had been tottering. Hincmar of Rheims had narrated
the history down to 882. Richer begins with the
minority of Charles the Simple and his elevation to
the throne in 893, and ends with the victory of the
house of Robert under Hugh Capet in 995. His style
and method show the conscious classicism of the
Carolingians. For his model he takes a Classical
historian, Sallust, and his narrative contains many
speeches. He often uses Classical terms (*legio, cohors,
vir consularis* = count) and follows Cæsar in his division
of Gaul now long obsolete. Yet he is at heart a
French nationalist, even though he calls them *Galli*,
and greatly resents the whittling away of Charles'
dominions. His chief authority (for the period 919–946)
is Flodoard's *Historia Remensis Ecclesiæ* ; 'ex quodam
Flodoardi presbyteri Remensis libello me aliqua sumps-
isse non abnuo, at non verba quidem eadem, sed
alia pro aliis longe diverso orationis schemate dis-
posuisse, res ipsa evidentissime demonstrat.' Indeed
Richer is something of an artist, and, if not a first-rate
historian, is certainly no mere annalist. In such a
period wars and sieges bulk largely ; but these greatly
interested this many-sided monk, and especially military
engines. Something between a tank and a testudo is
described as follows (II, 10) :

' Fecit itaque ex vehementissimis lignis compactis machinam, inter
longilateræ domus, duodecim virorum capacem, humani corporis

staturæ in alto æqualem, cuius parietes de ingenti lignorum robore, tectum vero de duris ac intextis cratibus exstruxit. Cui etiam intrinsecus notas quattuor adhibuit, unde machina ab iis qui intrinsecus laterent, usque ad arcem impelleretur. At tectum non æque stratum fuit, verum ab acumine dextra lævaque dependebat, ut iactis lapidibus facilius lapsum præberet. Quæ exstructa, tironibus mox impleta est, ac ad arcem rotis mobilibus impulsa.'

Radulfus Glaber (d. 1050)

Far inferior to Richer as a writer and historian is Radulfus Glaber, Raoul the Bald, a monk of Cluny and author of five books, *Historiarum sui temporis*, from the accession of Hugh Capet to the year 1046. Though valuable in some ways for French history it is a work of little merit, being full of irrelevant matter, such as showers of stones and the virtues of numbers. Errors both chronological and geographical abound. Of greater historical importance are the *Annals* of Lampert of Hersfeld (d. 1077) and the *History of the Hamburg Church* by Adam of Bremen (c. 1075). Both are conscious classicists in style, imitating especially Sallust and Livy.

Ekkehard IV (c. 980–1060)

By far the most interesting writer of the eleventh century is the fourth Ekkehard of St Gall. In that famous monastery he was reared and spent most of his life. Among his teachers was Notker Labeo (Notker the German) for whom he wrote Latin verses. These were afterwards incorporated in his *Liber Benedictionum*, a mixed collection of poems of little merit. After a sojourn as a schoolmaster in Mainz he returned to St Gall, where he was a monk for the rest of his days. Some of the brethren suggested to him that it would be worth while to write an account of the

203

fortunes, good and bad, of the monastery. Ratpert, of whom more below, had already written a history of St Gall down to 883; Ekkehard continues it, with little regard for the order of events, for a further period of about eighty years. So the events related fall before his own lifetime. Judged as history, the *Libri de Casibus Monasterii Sancti Galli* are simply bad, being neither accurate nor truthful. Yet the author is a man of genius of a kind rare in those days. Humour, insight into character, and ability to tell a story are not qualities to be despised. Ekkehard has them all. We cannot fail to visualise the characters that appear in the work, notably the famous trio, *Notker* the Stammerer, 'voce non spiritu balbulus,' easily startled, but not by devils, a veritable vessel of the holy Spirit; *Tuotilo*, a big, strong man with a powerful voice, a skilled workman and musician, full of resource, who should never, said Charles the Fat, have been a monk at all; *Ratpert*, 'doctor planus et benevolus,' a stay-at-home, and more of a student than a priest. Whether these three can really have been close friends and contemporaries we will not ask, any more than inquire into the historicity of Odysseus, Trimalchio, or Till Eulenspiegel. The reality of the characters is enhanced by the reality of the place. The monastery and its neighbourhood seem as it were to afford circumstantial evidence, and we find ourselves believing everything we are told. It is the art not of a historian but of a novelist. Little wonder J. V. Scheffel in the nineteenth century found in Ekkehard IV material for his romantic narrative poem *Ekkehard*. Scheffel's *Ekkehard* is the first of the name, author of Waltharius (see p. 173) who, like Ekkehard II, figures in these memoirs.

Among the misfortunes of the monastery was a great fire in 937. The boys at the school ' who usually

need beating the day after a festival' on one occasion
had obtained indulgence for a second feast-day.

> 'But on the third the overseers, whom we call "prowlers"
> (circatores) report their misdeeds to the master. They are all
> ordered to strip and one of them is sent upstairs to fetch the rods kept
> there. This boy, 'ut se et socios liberaret,' quickly snatched a live
> brand from a stove, thrust it into the dry wooden rods, which were
> just beneath the roof, and blew on them as long as he dared stay.
> When the overseers called up to know what was keeping him, he
> shouted back at the top of his voice that the house was on fire.'

Another sore trial was the duchess Hedwig, who was
far too useful and powerful to be offended. She was
a handsome woman but very hard on her own friends
and a terror to the whole countryside. In her youth
she had been betrothed to a Byzantine prince and
was therefore made to learn Greek. But she did not
wish to marry him. They had never met, so when
a painter was making a likeness of her to be sent to
the prince she opened her mouth and eyes very wide.
Having broken off that engagement she contracted
another : her husband early left her a rich widow.
For the rest of her life she was alternately a benefactress
and a nuisance to the Abbey of St Gall. She insisted
on coming to study Virgil with Ekkehard II (nephew
of Ekkehard I) who often wished she would stay at
home—'moribus tamen illa severis et efferis sæpe
virum exasperans domi interdum quam secum mansisse
multo malle fecerat.'

The invasions of the Hungarians in the early tenth
century caused much distress. The monks of St Gall
were compelled to flee at their approach. But Heribaldus, 'frater simplicissimus et fatuus,' refused to go,
saying that he had not yet had his shoe-leather for the
year, and stayed behind 'strolling about at his ease.'
Most of the treasure had been removed, to the annoy-

ance of the raiders who had expected that in a house
of the gods everything would be made of gold. One
of them espied the weathercock, which looked like
gold, and, making vain attempts to dislodge it with
his spear, fell down and was killed. Another climbed
the eastern tower and, choosing a novel way of expressing his contempt, 'dum ad alvum se parasset
purgandum,' also fell and was killed. But they treated
Heribald well, better, he thought, than his own
brethren. They spared two casks of wine because
they were so amused by the simplicity of his request :
' Sine, inquit, vir bone. Quid vis vero, ut nos, post
quam abieritis, bibamus ? ' But they seem to have
found plenty else both to eat and drink and, eating
enormously themselves, fed liberally both Heribald
and another captive 'clericus' whom they had brought
with them because he knew their language and acted
as interpreter. One day the Hungarians began to
sing horrible songs to their gods and the two were
compelled to join. After this lapse they sang a *Sanctifica
nos* to the great interest of the invaders. The other
captive thought it a good opportunity to appeal to the
mercy of the Hungarians. ' But they, of their savagery,
with terrifying whistles and grunts make signs to their
attendants what they wish done. These eagerly pounce
out, seize the man 'dicto citius,' and call for knives, so
that before killing him they might perform on his
crown the amusing Teutonic practice of pricking—
' ludibrium quod Teutones picchin (Mod. Germ. *picken*)
vocant.' However, thanks to various delays, the two
escaped and remained in hiding till the monastery was
retaken, when the returned monks were astonished to
find Heribald alive and well. ' The brethren, of more
intelligence than he, were amazed that the good God
so loved simplicity that he did not disdain to protect

even the dull and foolish amid the swords and spears of the foe.' They asked Heribald how he liked having such a crowd of guests at St Gall.

'Eia, inquit, quam optime. Numquam ego, credite mihi, hilariores in claustro nostro homines vidisse me memini ; cibi enim potusque datores sunt largissimi. Quod enim ego ante cellararium nostrum tenacissimum vix rogare poteram, ut vel semel sitientem me potaret, ipsi mihi affluenter roganti dabant.'

Ekkehard wrongly makes a Hungarian and Saracen invasion take place at the same time, and so is enabled to make a good story of how King Conrad of Burgundy managed to induce them to fight each other instead of him. Another victim of Hungarian attacks was the princess Wendilgarth, whose husband Ulrich was carried off into captivity. About her Ekkehard tells a story with the familiar plot of the return of the lost husband ; but there is much else besides in Ekkehard's best manner. Wendilgarth, though Ulrich was believed to be dead, would not re-marry, but went to live in retirement with St Wiborada. But she found the constant companionship of the saintly woman a little trying. She liked the good food to which she had always been used, and on this account ' increpata est a Wiborada, quoniam non esset signum pudicitiæ in femina appetere varia cibamina ! ' But the saint had her way. For one day Wendilgarth offered her some choice apples, asking if she had any to match them. To which the saint replied, ' Quibus pauperes utuntur, habeo pulcherrima,' and thrust some sour, wild apples at her. The princess took a bite or two, made a wry face and flung the rest of the apple away. ' Austera es, ait, austera sunt et mala tua. Et, cum esset literata, Si omnia, inquit, mala Factor talia creasset, nunquam Eva malum gustasset.' The allusion to Eve was unfortunate, and the saint had no difficulty in convincing the princess of her sin. Wendilgarth took the veil and devoted herself to good works. One day, when she was bestowing alms, one of the beggars jumped up and kissed her, ' capillisque prolixis in collum manu reiectis, cum etiam aliqui alapas minitassent : Parcite quæso, ait tandem alapis, quas multas pertuli, et Uodalricum vestrum recognoscite.'

But it is not only because they are amusing that these memoirs are worth reading. They throw valuable lights on monastic life of not too strict a kind. Like a modern college the monks of St Gall prided themselves on their regal entertaining no less than their learning. There is interesting information about the school and scholars and how Latin was taught. After the elementary stage the boys learned to speak it rhythmically, then metrically and finally rhetorically. It appears that in their ordinary conversation the monks of St Gall did not always speak Latin, and it was possible for one to attain the position of steward, ' refectorarius,' and not be able to understand it. This is evident from one of the best-known episodes in Ekkehard, that of the enmity of Sindolfus the steward against the three inseparables, Notker, Ratpert and Tuotilo. Sindolfus had wormed his way into the confidence of the abbot Salomon, who was also Bishop of Constance, and had told false tales about the three. He determined to overhear them saying something disrespectful which he could exaggerate and report to the bishop.

' Erat tribus illis inseparabilibus consuetudo, permisso quidem prioris in intervallo laudum nocturno convenire in scriptorio collationesque tali horæ aptissimas de scripturis facere. At Sindolfus, sciens horam et colloquia, quadam nocte fenestræ vitreæ, cui Tuotilo assederat, clandestinus foris appropriat aureque vitro affixa, si quid rapere posset quod depravatum episcopo traderet, auscultabat. Senserat Tuotilo illum, homo pervicax lacertisque confisus, latialiterque [*i.e.* in Latin], quo illum, qui nihil intelligeret, lateret, compares adloquitur : Sed tu, Notker, quia timidulus es, cede in ecclesiam. Ratperte autem mi, rapto flagello fratrum, quod pendet in pyrali, deforis accurre ! Ego enim illum, cum appropinquare te sensero, vitreo citissime redaperto, captum capillis ad meque pertractum violenter tenebo. Tu autem, anime mi, confortare et esto robustus, flagelloque illum totis viribus increpita et Deum in illo ulciscere.'

The plan succeeded. Sindolfus was seized by the hair and soundly flogged. His screams brought the rest of the monks. It was quite dark. Tuotilo was shouting that he had been attacked by the devil and called for a light that he might see what shape he had taken. Ratpert, who had done the flogging, disappeared before the light was brought. Then Tuotilo, still holding Sindolfus by the hair, when he saw who it was, ' Me miserum, ait, in auricularem et intimum episcopi manus misisse.' But confidently asserted that it must have been an angel of the Lord who had thrashed him.

Ekkehard's faults as a historian have been mentioned. He has another serious defect ; his Latin is not always intelligible. The passages cited are mostly favourable examples, though there are grammatical errors. His sentences are often abrupt and not easy to follow. He had learned Latin from Notker, who wrote Middle High German. He does not, like those who recollected the historians of the Carolingian School, take a classical model. Hence his style is at least his own. But Latin had not yet acquired the new lease of life which it took in the next century. Ekkehard wrote Latin as well as he knew, but it was an acquired tongue ; and if he sometimes, like Richer and others, uses especially classical words such as *primipilares*, he has also many Teutonisms, *e.g. sparro* = spear, *wanno* = basket. The mixture of vocabulary is no great fault, rather an aid

to variety and colour ; but Ekkehard was not fully a
master of his medium, if indeed an adequate prose
medium existed at the time, and for all his brilliance
he was not a great enough master of language to
create one of his own.

Peter Damiani (1007–1072)

Meanwhile in Italy far better Latin was being
written and a greater man than Ekkehard was spending
his earlier years as a teacher of Latin letters. This was
Peter Damiani, ascetic, Church reformer, Papal Legate,
poet, and so great a master of vituperative Latin that
he counted it among his worst sins. He gave up his
study of the pagan Cicero and his lucrative secular
teaching and entered the rigidly ascetic community of
Fonte Avellana. But he was destined to serve his
Church more actively. Already fifty years of age he
was compelled by the Pope to leave his cell and become
Cardinal-Bishop of Ostia, so much against his will that
he almost doubted the validity of his consecration.
The much-needed reform of the Church had been
prosecuted by Hildebrand but much remained to be
done both in Italy and abroad. Among the worst was
the church of Milan, which not only kept its own
Ambrosian traditions in preference to the Roman, but
whose whole ecclesiastical system was badly tainted
with simony, and allowed marriage of the clergy.
Here was a task suitable for Peter's powers of denun-
ciation. He reduced the Milan church to submission
by his eloquence, but the difficulties of Rome were
far from ended. The Lombard bishops in 1061 elected
as Pope Cadalus (Honorius II Antipopa), while in
Italy was chosen Alexander II whom Damian, of course,
supported. With the fury of the Old Testament
prophets, whom he frequently cites, he denounces

Cadalus in two long letters (Epist. I, 20, 21). He begins by wishing him not *salus* but the fate he deserved : ' Cadaloo dicto episcopo, Petrus peccator monachus quod dignum et iustum est.' His very name shows that he is destined to be the ruin of the people. ' Cadalous quippe vocaris. Et prima quidem pars huius nominis manifeste denuntiat casum, secunda populum, λαὸς siquidem Græce, Latine populum sonat. Et quid aliud in hoc exprimitur nomine nisi quod scriptura dicit : Quia videlicet ruina populi sunt sacerdotes mali ' (Ezek. 21). As for his election, the Bishops of Placentia and Vercellæ ' thoroughly wanton and low-bred, skilled only to discuss the comeliness of women, how could they have any right judgment in the choice of a pontiff ? ' That some Roman had been present at the election is an idle and vicious argument. ' Sed quispiam fortassis obiiciat, inordinatæ huic ordinationi aliquem interfuisse Romanum. Erubescat ad hæc lingua phrenetica, et quæ nescit esse facunda, discat esse vel muta : nescit aliquid utiliter dicere, sciat saltem sine damno facere.' There cannot be two Popes. ' Porro autem sicut diabolus divino nomini pluralem numerum indidit, ut diceret mulieri : Eritis sicut dii, scientes bonum et malum (Gen. iii.). Ita tu grammaticorum regulis novum aliquid addidisti, ut in declinatione iam pueri dicant papæ, paparum.' The letter received no answer and is followed by another in which Peter attempts to convince him by adducing parallels from Roman History, from Hannibal to Alaric, as well as the usual Scriptural quotations.

Yet however much he may have scourged the evils of simony and clerical concubinage, such was not the work he himself would have preferred. From the little work *De Vita Eremetica* and others it is evident that he regarded the hermit's life as the best. The greater

the mortification of the flesh, the greater the glory.
The self-torturing St Romuald and young Dominicus Loricatus, who held the record for the number
of scourgings in a day, were his heroes, and he wrote
accounts of their lives and of other ascetic forerunners
of the Carthusians. Hence he was glad, after important missions to France (1063) and Germany (1069)
to return again to Fonte Avellana, where he died
in 1072.

Two further examples of his Latinity must suffice,
the former fiery and oratorical, showing the influence
of the Vulgate, the second in a quieter mood.

> 'Pensate diligenter verba veritatis, pensate cum timore quod
> dicitur; alligate fasciculos ad comburendum; zizania quippe
> fasciculis alligantur, quia in illo perpetuæ damnationis incendio
> homicidæ cum homicidis, adulteri cum adulteris, perjuri cum per-
> juris, incestuosi cum incestuosis, non diverso pœnalium tormentorum
> genere constringuntur. Illic eos infinitæ pœnæ patens gehennæ
> barathrum devorat, qui hic se arroganter in superbiæ cornibus
> extollebant; illic eorum carnes atque medullas saginis irriguas
> crepitans flamma depascet, qui hic arsere deliciis, et æstuantis
> explevere illecebras voluptatis.'

In contrast to this blood-curdling sermon (no. 37)
one may read a pagan story in Christian dress, intended
to show the spiritual value of gifts given to the poor
(*De Bono Suffragiorum* VI). A widowed lady, wishing
to have masses said for her husband's soul, used to send
rich gifts of food to the priest. The hungry servant-
girl who used to bring them never received so much
as a blessing from the priest, much less a share of the
good things. At length she could stand it no longer
and one day ate the whole of the food herself, but
added a prayer, 'Deus, inquit, omnipotens, qui das
escam omni carni, sicut caro mea refecta est hoc cibo
corporeo, ita per misericordiam tuam hodie et anima

domini mei satietur in paradiso.' That night the husband appeared to the lady in a dream and in reply to her enquiries after his welfare replied :

'Usque heri mihi male fuit, sed et inter cetera meæ calamitatis incommoda gravius me fames afflixit. Heri vero, te præbente convivium, splendide refeci ; ac funditus fame consumpta, largis alimentorum dapibus abundavi. Et his dictis præsto disparuit. Cumque mulier evigilasset, ac de viri sui verbis sollicite pertractare cœpisset, non mediocriter mirabatur, cur ille dixerit hesternum se tantummodo ab ea percepisse convivium, quandoquidem illa sacerdoti frequentissime direxisset xenium. Igitur altiori pertractans viri verba consilio, intellexit non sine mysterio esse quod dixerat.'

Lanfranc (1005–1089) and Anselm (1033–1109).

Lanfranc and Anselm, successively Archbishops of Canterbury, are men of importance both in English History and Medieval Theology, and each in his way also demands notice as a writer. Both, like Damiani, were Italians to whom Latin came easily. For in Italy, it should be remembered, the vernacular had in the first place not departed so far from Latin as elsewhere in Romania, and secondly, had not made so much headway among the more educated classes. Lanfranc was the elder. He taught Anselm at Pavia and when he removed to Bec in Normandy Anselm followed. Though of one mind in their opposition to Berengarius of Tours, who denied transubstantiation, they are men of different character. Lanfranc is predominantly a vigorous champion of the Church as reformed by Hildebrand and Damiani, submissive entirely to Papal authority. Anselm is also that, but as a thinker and writer he stands superior to Lanfranc. He is the more original, but always careful not to transgress orthodoxy. He faced problems of Christian theology, though not without misgivings about doing so, such as the essential nature of God in the *Monologion*, the existence of God in the *Proslogion*, and why God became man in *Cur Deus Homo*. With the validity of his reasoning we are not concerned, but it should be noted that Anselm's basis of argument was Faith first and Reason after ; you cannot understand what you do not believe ; therefore believe, that you may understand. The following passage from the *Proslogion* (ch. ii.) will illustrate this :

> ' Ergo, Domine, qui das fidei intellectum, da mihi ut, quantum scis expedire, intelligam quia es, sicut credimus ; et hoc es quod credimus. Et quidem credimus te esse aliquid, quo nihil maius cogitari possit. An ergo non est aliqua talis natura, quia dixit insipiens, in corde suo : Non est Deus. Sed certe idem ipse insipiens cum audit hoc ipsum quod dico, aliquid quo maius nihil cogitari potest, intelligit quod audit, et quod intelligit in intellectu eius est, etiamsi non intelligit illud esse.'

If that were Anselm at his best, his literary value would be nil. But his best prose is rhetorical, easy flowing and rhythmical :

> ' Ecce, anima Christiana, hæc est virtus salvationis tuæ, hæc est causa libertatis tuæ, hoc est pretium redemptionis tuæ. Captiva eras ; sed hoc modo es redempta. Ancilla eras, et sic es liberata. Sic es exsul, reducta ; perdita, restituta ; et mortua, resuscitata. . . Ergo, homuncio, illorum crudelitatem dimitte Dei iudicio, et tracta de his quæ debes Salvatori tuo. Considera quid tibi erat, et quid tibi factum sit, et pensa, qui hoc tibi fecit quo amore dignus sit. Intuere necessitatem tuam, et bonitatem eius, et vide quas gratias reddas, et quantum debeas amori eius.'

This is the kind of language which most people have in mind when they use the term Medieval Latin, and not without reason, for the best prose of the next two centuries is marked by the same features. These features, alliteration and assonance, ' modern ' order of words, rhyme and a clearly marked rhythm depending on accent rather than metrical quantity, differentiate it from Augustan, Silver Age and Patristic Latin. Neither the Carolingian nor the Ottonian Renaissance had succeeded in making Latin a living language again. Languages must change to live ; and the remarkable thing is that the earlier attempts to *fix* Latin did not kill it altogether, as the great Renaissance did. What saved it was of course the Church, whose language it was. But not even the Church could have saved it alive, had it not been for men of genius who stamped their own intellect upon their language, and created a Latin adapted to the needs of the time. Anselm was one of these. He thought in Latin and wrote in Latin after the manner of his thought, not after a ' correct ' model. His affectations and peculiarities are not due to imitation, but are marks of this new prose of which he was one of the creators. He is not the only creator ; there is not *one* founder of scholastic Latin any more than of scholastic thought. He is mentioned here because his literary interest is greater than that of the other disputants Berengarius and Roscellinus.

Petrus Abælardus (Abelard) (1079-1142)

Abelard was born near Nantes in 1079. He studied under various masters and quarrelled with them all. But wherever he went he attracted students by his brilliant lectures. In 1110 we find him in Paris, unrivalled in logic and dialectic, studies which afterwards made famous the university of that city. Then occur the liaison with his pupil Heloïse, their elopement and separation. Later he is in a monastery of St Denys and driven thence for his unpleasing researches into its history. His theology is suspect, especially his identification of the Holy Ghost as *anima mundi*. In 1142 he died at Cluny, a broken man. Proud and argumentative, Abelard was born neither to live at peace himself nor to allow others to do so. Though nothing was farther from his mind than to attack his own religion, he made scores of enemies by his fearless discussion of Christian doctrines. Not only was he gifted with a fatal power to see the other side of every question, but he put his opponents' case with no less skill and cogency than the Christian view, notably in the *Dialogue between a Philosopher, a Jew, and a Christian*, and in the *Sic et Non*. This latter work was especially dangerous. Instead of simply stating the Christian propositions in each chapter, as for example, ' Quod sit credendum in Deum solum,' he adds *et contra* or *et non*. Hence the title of the work. To make matters worse, he adduces evidence from the Scriptures and the Fathers for *both* sides of every proposition. This may have delighted his students, but it is not surprising that his fellow-doctors hated him for it, and that St Bernard of Clairvaux, in whose eyes such enquiry was sheer wickedness, called him ' hostis ecclesiæ, fidei persecutor in gremio fidei ' (St Bernard, Ep. 338), and wrote to Pope Innocent II saying ' Habemus in Francia novum de veteri magistro theologum, qui ab ineunte aetate sua in arte dialectica lusit, et nunc in Scripturis sanctis insanit, ponit in cœlum os suum et scrutatur alta Dei, rediensque ad nos refert verba ineffabilia quæ non licet homini loqui ' (Epist. 190). It was this same Bernard who finally crushed him at the Council of Sens in 1141.

But the world remembers not Abelard the scholastic dialectician, ousting his teachers and lecturing to crowded audiences, making enemies no less by his love of truth than his vain and disputatious nature. The world remembers the love of Abelard and Heloïse. The letters that passed between them are among the

flowers of twelfth-century literature. But they are
not love-letters ; they belong to a time long after the
two had separated, she to become nun and abbess, he
to continue his stormy career. They are written in
the most careful and elaborate prose of the period,
with copious illustrations from classical and sacred
literature. For Heloïse, like her lover, was well learned.
Yet none the less are they moving human documents
of perennial interest. Abelard's first epistle, not
addressed to Heloïse but to a friend for his consolation,
is appropriately called *Historia Calamitatum*, for it is
a record of his many woes. In it he tells how in Paris
at the age of thirty-six he met Heloïse, then a girl of
fifteen living with her uncle, a canon. With the help
of friends it was arranged that Abelard, whose character
was in as high repute as his learning, should live in
the house and become the girl's sole tutor, with full
permission, he tells us, to slap her.

'Quid plura ? Primum domo una coniungimur postmodum
animo. Sub occasione itaque disciplinæ amori penitus vacabamus,
et secretos regressus quos amor optabat studium lectionis offerebat.
Apertis itaque libris plura de amore quam de lectione verba se
ingerebant, plura erant oscula quam sententiæ. Sæpius ad sinum
quam ad libros reducebantur manus, crebrius oculos amor in se
reflectebat quam lectionis in scripturam dirigebat.'

Soon every one knew of the affair, her uncle being
the last to find out. Abelard has to leave Paris.

'Non multo autem post puella se concepisse comperit, et cum
summa exsultatione mihi super hoc illico scripsit, consulens quid de
hoc ipse faciendum deliberarem. Quadam itaque nocte avunculo
eius absente, sicut nos condixeramus, eam de domo avunculi furtim
sustuli, et in patriam meam sine mora transmisi. Ubi apud sororem
meam tamdiu conversata est, donec pareret masculum quem Astro-
labium nominavit.'

With Heloïse safe in Brittany Abelard visits the irate
uncle and promises to wed his niece if the canon

will keep the marriage secret. With great difficulty the noble Heloïse is induced to consent. She did not ask for marriage, only for love. She seemed to know that it would leak out. Above all she considered her lover's career in the Church, in which marriage would be a far greater blot than the recollection of a youthful liaison. But Abelard insisted. Leaving the child with his sister, he brought her to Paris, and in the presence of her uncle and a few close friends they were married —only to part. ' Moxque occulte divisim abscessimus, nec nos ulterius nisi raro latenterque vidimus, dissimulantes plurimum quod egeramus.' But the treacherous canon spread abroad the marriage, and when Abelard removed his young wife to a monastery, not yet to take the veil, he and his friends, thinking that Abelard only intended to get rid of her, planned a dastardly vengeance.

> ' Unde vehementer indignati, et adversum me coniurari, nocte quadam quiescentem me atque dormientem in secreta hospitii mei camera, quodam mihi serviente per pecuniam corrupto, crudelissima et pudentissima ultione punierunt, et quam summa admiratione mundus excepit : eis videlicet corporis mei partibus amputatis, quibus id quod plangebant commiseram.'

Finally both enter monastic life. Abelard goes on to narrate how his books were burned and himself persecuted. Ten years after she became a nun Heloïse, now abbess of the nunnery of the Paraclete, reads this *Historia Calamitatum*. For all her vows she is still deeply in love and longs to hear from him again. She writes one of the most tragic letters in history, from which we must forbear to quote. For the whole is a work of art, not simply the outpourings of a broken heart. Yet for all its elaboration and historical allusions it is full of a tenderness and pathos unsurpassed. Abelard's reply is full of brotherly affection but not of

earthly love. He reminds his ' sister', ' in sæculo quondam cara, nunc in Christo carissima ', that their lives
now belong to God, not to the world. Heloïse writes
again. She does not reproach her lover, save for his
suggestion that his enemies may one day kill him. She
blames herself and all women as the cause of Abelard's
distresses. She reproaches even God, who has visited
her husband with heavy punishment, as if he had been
a sinful adulterer. She confesses her undying and
unrepentant human love for him.

> ' In tantum vero illæ quas pariter exercuimus, amantium volup-
> tates dulces mihi fuerunt, ut nec displicere mihi, nec vix a memoria
> labi possint. Quocunque loco me vertam, semper se oculis meis cum
> suis ingerunt desideriis. Nec etiam dormienti suis illusionibus
> parcunt. Inter ipsa missarum solemnia, ubi purior esse debet oratio,
> obscena earum voluptatum phantasmata ita sibi penitus miserrimam
> captivant animam, ut turpitudinibus illis magis quam orationi vacem.
> Quæ cum ingemiscere debeam de commissis, suspiro potius de
> amissis.'

The correspondence goes on but loses human interest,
for Abelard will discuss nothing but the needs of her
nunnery, and she is driven to do the same in order to
have an excuse for writing to him. Abelard appears
to have visited the Paraclete occasionally but only as
spiritual adviser. When he died his body was brought
thither for burial ; twenty-one years later Heloïse was
laid beside him.

William of Malmesbury (c. 1095–1143)

Towards the end of the reign of William Rufus
there was born in England William, monk of Malmesbury, the first English historian worthy of the name
since the Venerable Bede four hundred years before.
He was educated in the monastery at Malmesbury
and became monk and then librarian there. He was of

mixed Norman and Saxon blood and in his history tries to deal fairly with both races. He may have lived for some time at Glastonbury; for in his *Life of St Dunstan* he speaks of himself as following the calling of monk there, 'in quo cælestem profitemur militiam.' He certainly made a close study of Glastonbury and its history, as is evident in his *Liber de Antiquitate Glastoniensis Ecclesiæ*. His most famous works are (1) five books *De Gestis Pontificum Anglorum*, an account, arranged by localities, of the chief bishops and priests among the English, and (2) the better known *De Gestis Regum Anglorum*, also in five books. Both works were revised and re-issued from time to time. The *De Gestis Regum* ends with the year 1121, but there is a continuation called *Historia Novella*, carrying on the history almost until the author's death. Unfortunately the three short books of the *Historia Novella* are little more than ill-arranged notes; and this is just the period when William's work might have had especial value as written by a contemporary historian. But he writes best not on recent events but when he is using older works, such as Bede's *Ecclesiastical History*, Asser's *Life of Alfred*, and the native chronicles. With great insight into character, and the medieval historian's love of stories and episodes, he shows skill in making readable historical narrative. The matter is not always well arranged; for example, in early English history the different kingdoms are dealt with one after the other; but he seems to have aimed at variety and certainly succeeded in making his book interesting. It was widely read and copied from by subsequent writers. He set out to imitate Bede, for whom he had the highest admiration. To tell Bede's praises, he says, 'deficit . . . ingenium, succumbit elogium, nesciens quid plus laudem, librorum numerositatem an sermonum sobrietatem ; infuderat eum procul dubio non indigo haustu divina sapientia, ut angusto vitæ spatiolo tanta elaboraret volumina ' (I, 47). Bede is also the source of much of his information. His other authorities are many and varied, a testimony to his learning. But he is inclined to select from them just those things which will heighten the popularity of his history, as the familiar story of the diminutive lover carried across the snow (p. 142), and legends in which Gerbert, Archbishop and Pope, appears as magician and astrologer (pp. 195 ff.). These last, however, are of some importance, not so much because Gerbert's ingenious inventiveness may lend them some slight basis of truth, as because William is here our main source of knowledge. It is therefore not unfair to take from the digression on Gerbert (II, §§ 167–172) a sample of William's writing—how Gerbert discovered the ' Treasures of Octavian.'

' Erat iuxta Romam in campo Martio statua, ærea an ferrea incertum mihi, dexteræ manus indicem digitum extentum habens, scriptum quoque in capite : Hic percute.'

Others had battered the innocent statue in the hope of finding treasure but Gerbert solved the problem.

' Namque meridie, sole in centro existente, notans quo protenderetur umbra digiti, ibi palum figit ; mox superveniente nocte, solo cubiculario lanternam portante comitatus, eo contendit. Ibi terra solitis artibus dehiscens latum ingredientibus patefecit introitum. Conspicantur ingentem regiam, aureos parietes, aurea lacunaria, aurea omnia ; milites aureos aureis tesseris quasi animum oblectantes ; regem metallicum cum regina discumbentem, apposita opsonia, astantes ministros, pateras multi ponderis et pretii, ubi naturam vincebat opus. In interiori parte domus carbunculus, lapis imprimis nobilis et parvus inventu, tenebras noctis fugabat. In contrario angulo stabat puer, arcum tenens extento nervo et arundine intenta.'

But as soon as anyone dared to touch those treasures, the ghostly figures were seen to attack him.

> ' Quo timore pressus Gerbertus ambitum suum fregit ; sed non abstinuit cubicularius quin mirabilis artificii cultellum, cum mensæ impositum videret, abriperet ; arbitratus scilicet in tanta præda parvum latrocinium posse latere. Verum mox omnibus imaginibus cum fremitu insurgentibus, puer quoque, emissa arundine in carbunculum, tenebras induxit ; et nisi ille monitu domini cultellum reiicere accelerasset, graves ambo pœnas dedissent. Sic insatiata cupiditatis voragine, lanterna gressus ducente, discessum.'

Another important part of the *History of the Kings* is an account of the First Crusade (Bk. IV, §§ 343–389). Here William had more abundant authorities, but the events of the end of the eleventh and early twelfth century were so recent that he may well have had reports from eye-witnesses. So at least he says on one occasion, speaking of Godfrey de Bouillon :

> ' I have heard a truthful witness state that he himself saw the following incident : During the siege the general's servant went out foraging and was attacked by a lion. For a time he avoided destruction by holding his shield in front of him. Godfrey seeing his distress pierced the lion with a spear. The wounded animal, maddened by the pain, rushed at the prince and with the weapon protruding from the wound damaged him on the thigh. Had not he quickly plunged his sword in the lion's belly, that pattern of valour might have perished in a wild animal's maw.'

How this same King of Jerusalem cut a Turk in two with his sword is only vouched for by ' notum est. . . . Et iam palpitabat arvis medietas hominis, cum alteram cornipes volucri cursu asportavit, adeo firme nebulo insederat ; alterum æque congressum, librata in caput spatha a vertice ad inguina diffiderit ' (§ 433).

Yet William of Malmesbury is a careful and intelligent historian and an able Latin writer, and in his avowed intention of filling the gap between Bede's history and the recent work of his contemporary Eadmer he succeeded well. Before passing to Geoffrey of Monmouth it will be of interest to see what the sober William has to say about King Arthur. He has no doubts about Arthur's existence but says little of him and refers contemptuously to Welsh legends and superstitions.

> ' Et iam tunc profecto pessum issent [Britones], nisi Ambrosius, solus Romanorum superstes, qui post Wortigernum monarcha regni fuit, intumescentes barbaros eximia bellicosi Arturis opera pressisset. Hic est Artur de quo Britonum nugæ hodie quoque delirant; dignus plane quem non fallaces somniarent fabulæ, sed veraces prædicarent historiæ, quippe qui labantem patriam diu sustinuerit, infractasque civium mentes ad bellum acuerit ' (§ 8, cp. also § 287).

Geoffrey of Monmouth (c. 1100–1154)

The *Historia Britonum* or *Historia Regum Britanniæ* of the Welsh monk Galfredus Monumetensis is chiefly remembered as the source from which many English and French poets drew rich material for their works. Directly or indirectly it provided the groundwork of Layamon's *Brut*, Shakespeare's *King Lear*, Drayton's *Polyolbion* and others. But in the author's own opinion he was writing sober history, albeit at second hand. He says :

> ' After much and frequent consideration with myself, upon my reading the History of the Kings of Britain, I wondered that in the account that Gildas and Bede in an elegant treatise had given of them, I found nothing said of those kings who lived here before the Incarnation of Christ, nor of Arthur and many others who succeeded after the Incarnation ; when yet their actions both deserved immortal fame, and were also celebrated by many people in a pleasant manner and by heart, as if they had been written. Being often intent upon these and such like thoughts, Walter, Archdeacon of Oxford, a man of great eloquence, and learned in foreign histories, offered me a very ancient book in the British tongue, which in a continued regular story and eloquent style, related the actions of them all, from Brutus the first king of the Britons, down to Cadwallader the son of Cadwallo.

At his request therefore, though I had not made fine language my study by collecting florid expressions from other authors, yet contented with my own homely style, I undertook the translation of that book into Latin ' (Bk. I, ch. 1, tr. A. Thompson, 1718).

This book belonging to Walter Map (on whom see p. 233) has not been identified, and it is usually considered only to have existed in Geoffrey's lively imagination, and to have been introduced by him only to give some authority to his largely incredible history. But it is hard to see why Geoffrey and Walter should have conspired to tell such a lie, and it is just possible that such a book may have then existed, though the known Welsh manuscripts dealing with these legends are all later than Geoffrey. Whether the work be a translation from the Welsh or not, it clearly owes something to Gildas and Bede, and perhaps oral tradition, and still more to a short ninth-century work known as the *Historia Britonum* of ' Nennius,' in which the facts are mostly legendary. The result is a mixture of truth and legend reminiscent of the earlier books of Livy, but of far less historical value; for at times Geoffrey seems to be drawing entirely on his own imagination.

However that may be, the general character of the work will be evident from a glance at the kind of information it contains. He tells, following ' Nennius,' how a certain Brutus, son of Ascanius and grandson of Æneas, having accidentally slain his father, went to Troy and restored the fallen kingdom of his ancestors. With the help of another Trojan Corineus, ' qui, si cum aliquo gigante congressum faceret, illico eum obruebat, ac si cum puero contenderet,' he overruns Aquitaine and invades the island of Albion, at that time uninhabited save for a few giants. The fiercest of those, by name Goemagog, twelve cubits high, was

thrown into the sea by Corineus in the following
manner.

'Initio deinde certamine instat Corineus, instat gigas, et alter
alterum vinculis brachiorum adnectens crebris afflatibus æra vexant.
Nec mora, Goemagog Corineum maximis viribus astringens, fregit
ei tres costas, duas in latere dextro, unam vero in sinistro. Unde
Corineus compulsus in iram revocavit vires suas, et imposuit illum
humeris suis, et quantum velocitas pro pondere sinebat ad proxima
litore cucurrit. Deinde summitatem excelsæ rupis nactus, excussit
se, et prædictum letabile monstrum, quod super humeros suos
ferebat, in mare proiecit. At ille per abrupta saxorum cadens in
mille frusta dilaceratus est, et fluctus sanguine maculavit.'

Corineus, we further learn, gave his name to Cornwall,
while Brutus gave his to make Britannic and Britones.
The language of the people had hitherto been Trojan
or 'crooked Greek' but was henceforth called British.
On the Thames Brutus founded the city New Troy.
These events are contemporary with the capture of
the Ark of the Covenant by the Philistines. Some
two hundred years later, about the time of Isaiah and
Romulus, comes the story of King Lear (Bk. II).
The third book speaks of Brennius the Gaul and his
attack on Rome, while the fourth opens with a surprising pair of letters between Julius Cæsar and Cas-
sivelaunus. Cymbeline was king when Christ was
born. In the account of the Roman invasion of A.D. 43
there is no mention of Caractacus. Christianity is
introduced by a king Lucius before the reign of
Diocletian. The career of Vortigern, who united
Saxon aid against the Picts (Bk. VI, after the departure
of the Romans), is interesting and not entirely legendary.
Book VII is a repetition of an earlier work *De Prophetiis
Merlini*. Vortigern observed a fight between a white
serpent and a red in which the white was victorious;
he appealed to the seer Merlin for an explanation.

P   225

' Mox ille in fletum erumpens spiritum hausit prophetiæ, et ait : Væ rubeo draconi, nam eius exterminatio festinat ; cavernas eius occupavit albus draco, qui Saxones quos invitasti significat. Rubeus vero gentem designat Britanniæ, quæ ab albo opprimetur.' Then follows a long list of woeful prophecies. Vortigern is succeeded by Utherpendragon, and he by his son Arthur, whose exploits in the early sixth century are narrated in Books IX and X. This is not Arthur of the days of chivalry : there is no mention of Knights of the Round Table, as in the French poet Wace. Arthur is here a conquering king. He subdues Ireland, defeats the Picts and Scots at Loch Lomond, conquers Orkney, Iceland, Norway, Gotland and Dacia (!), and all their vassal kings attend his coronation. But his greatest wars are against the Romans, whose leaders are senators and consuls, and have names taken from the history of Republican Rome and mixed together in such combinations as Marius Lepidus and Caius Metellus Cotta. Arthur was slain in battle in the year A.D. 542 (XI, 3), and his kingdom fell a prey to ' Saxons and Africans.' The narrative is carried down to A.D. 689.

> ' But as for the kings that have succeeded them in Wales since that time, I leave the history of them to Caradoc of Lancarvan, my contemporary : as I do also the kings of the Saxons to William of Malmesbury and Henry of Huntingdon. But I advise them to be silent concerning the kings of the Britons, since they have not that book writ in the British tongue, which Walter Archdeacon of Oxford brought out of Britain, and which, being a true history published in honour of those princes, I have thus taken care to translate ' (XII, 20).

Little literary interest attaches to the majority of the twelfth-century chroniclers such as Florence of Worcester, Eadmer, Orderic Vitalis, Simeon of Durham, Henry of Huntingdon, Gervase of Canterbury and

William of Newburgh. The best of them is perhaps
Jocelyn de Brakelonde whose chronicle of the Abbey
at Bury St Edmunds is familiar to us through Carlyle's
Past and Present. It is written in clear and vigorous
Latin though the vocabulary is sometimes a little
puzzling. The central figure is Abbot Samson whose
stern measures restored the fallen fortunes of the
abbey.

> ' Homo supersobrius, nunquam desidiosus, multum valens, et
> volens equitare vel pedes ire, donec senectus prævaluit. . . .
> Murmuratores cibi et potus et præcipe monachos murmuratores
> condemnans, tenorem antiquum conservans quem olim habuit dum
> claustralis fuit. . . . Homo erat eloquens Gallice et Latine, magis
> rationi dicendorum quam ornatui verborum innitens. Scripturam
> Anglice scriptam legere novit elegantissime, et Anglice sermocinari
> solebat populo, sed secundum linguam Norfolchiæ ubi natus et
> nutritus erat ' (p. 244, Arnold).

John of Salisbury (c. 1110–1180)

The purest Latin prose of the twelfth century was
written by John of Salisbury. He was secretary to
Theobald, who preceded Thomas à Becket as Archbishop of Canterbury, then to Becket himself. He
afterwards became Bishop of Chartres. He had been
educated in the cathedral school of that city, the
stronghold of humanism and the study of the *auctores*,
but he far outstripped the average attainments of its
pupils. For his master Bernard and his educational
methods he had the greatest admiration ; too many,
he thinks, are inclined to cut short or shirk sound
training in the Classics which makes an educated man.
This training not only enabled John to quote the
Latin Classics freely, but also to write a Latin not so
widely removed from the classical standard as that of
those medieval writers already discussed. Yet John

does not return to the imitation method of the
Carolingian Age. He writes the living Latin of the
twelfth century, influenced perhaps more than he
knew by the stylistic tendencies which had their origin
not in the study of Latin authors but in the philosophical
and theological work which was soon to dominate
Western thought. At Chartres the Seven Liberal Arts,
Grammar, Rhetoric and Dialectic (the Trivium),
Arithmetic, Geometry, Music, Astronomy (the Quadrivium) were of course studied, but only in the works
of the *auctores*, not as objects or instruments of knowledge. Anselm, Berengarius of Tours and Abelard
were original thinkers, capable of applying logic and
dialectic to philosophical and theological problems ;
but this new study was taken up zealously by other
frequenters of the schools of Paris who lacked the
intellectual equipment and, John would add, classical
training, but found the wordy battles there more
amusing than the scholarship of Chartres. These are
the foes of humanism whom John attacks, calling them
Cornificiani, followers of Cornificius, who disparaged
Virgil.

The *Policraticus* or *Statesman* was completed in 1159
and dedicated to Thomas à Becket, at that time still
Chancellor to Henry II. It is by far the most important
work on political philosophy in the Middle Ages. It is
not, however, a discussion of the relative merits of
different forms of government ; monarchy is assumed
throughout. And although the feudal system was then
at its height, it is not a description of feudal society.
It is a work of political theory, not history. Aristotle's
Politics was as yet unknown, but of Cicero and other
Latin writers John had good knowledge. Yet his
political ideas owe little or nothing to these. His
central theme is Prince and Law, his chief doctrine

that all princes are subject to law and must rule according to it. Otherwise they are tyrants. Tyrants may occur in any walk of life where power is exercised, not least among popes and priests of the Church. The law by which a prince shall rule is the law of God ; that law is to be found in the Bible. ' That he may learn to fear the Lord his God, to keep all the words of this law and these statutes to do them' (Deuteronomy xvii. 19). ' Timeat ergo princeps Dominum, et se promta humilitate mentis et pia exhibitione operis servum profiteatur. Dominus etenim servi dominus est. Servit itaque Domino princeps, dum conservis suis, subditis scilicet sibi, fideliter servit ' (IV, 7). As in Plato's *Republic* the picture of society is ideal and static, every man content with his own station. Of problems of his time, relations between king and baron, Church and State, there is no discussion. The familiar analogy between the human body and the body politic is freely used and elaborated. ' Est autem res publica . . . corpus quoddam quod divini muneris beneficio animatur.' With the size of the ideal state John is not concerned ; the principle of subjection to the Higher Law holds equally good in Empire or county. While John's enunciation of this Higher Law depends directly on the Scriptures, his explanations and illustrations of it are taken from the whole field of history and are largely the fruit of his first-hand knowledge of the Latin Classics : Greek he scarcely knew. Lucan is *poeta doctissimus ;* the Satires of Horace and Juvenal provide many moral maxims. Even Ovid ranks as *ethicus* after the fashion of the Middle Ages ; but the greatest is Virgil who is often simply *poeta* as Rome is *urbs.* In prose his historical illustrations are drawn not so much from Livy, Cæsar and Tacitus, with whom he seems to be unfamiliar, as from Suetonius, Valerius Maximus, Aulus Gellius (whom he miscalls Agellius) and others. Cicero's philosophical works often provide illustrations.

The *Policraticus* has a sub-title, *De Nugis Curialium et Vestigiis Philosophorum*, which the discursive nature of the work certainly justifies. The first three books contain random observations on many subjects, hunting, gambling, mathematics, music, magic, omens, free-will, flattery and the vanity of human wishes. The political philosophy is contained mainly in Books IV, V, VI. The seventh book begins with a sketch of ancient philosophy and discusses such questions as the authority of Reason, Sense-perception, and Religion. The eighth and last book is mainly his own ethical views. John's philosophy is not the hair-splitting discussions of the schoolmen. The aim of the philosopher is to learn Christian charity. ' Qui vero philosophando caritatem adquirit aut dilatat, suum philosophantis assecutus est finem ' (VII, 11). There is really no difference between politics and ethics since all men are subject to the Higher Law and ' the fear of the Lord is the beginning of wisdom.' ' Ante legem, sub lege, sub gratia omnes lex una constringit : Quod tibi non vis fieri, alii ne feceris ; et : Quod tibi vis fieri faciendum, hoc facias alii.' As a Christian he does not attach himself to any pagan school of philosophy, but he has a preference for Plato and the Academy, known of course only indirectly. This gives an added interest to the following passage on the evil effects of seductive music ; but John's views are entirely Christian.

' Ait enim : Sumite psalmum, date tympanum, psalterium iocundum cum cithara. Ad quid, inquis ? Ut laudetis Dominum in tympano et choro, in chordis et organo. Hic est enim usus musicæ aut solus aut præcipuus. Phrygius vero modus et cetera corruptionis lenocinia sanæ institutionis non habent usum, sed produnt malitiam abutentis . . . Ipsum quoque cultum religionis incestat, quod ante conspectum Domini in ipsis penetralibus sanctuarii lascivientis vocis luxu, quadam ostentatione sui, muliebribus modis notularum articulorumque cæsuris, stupentes animulas emollire nituntur. Cum præcinentium et succinentium, canentium et decinentium, intercinentium et occinentium præmolles modulationes audieris, sirenarum concentus credas esse, non hominum ' (I, 6).

But John's philosophy does not end with Ethics and Politics. He was at least the equal of contemporary schoolmen in their own field of dialectic. The *Metalogicus* is a work mainly devoted to logic and to discussion of current philosophical problems ; yet for John scholarship comes first, and of the four books the first is a defence of the study of grammar and the *auctores* against ' Cornificius,' a vain disputer, who would discuss whether a pig being led to market was held by the man or the rope (I, 3), but incapable of understanding a philosopher like Anselm. But John says :

' Excute Virgilium aut Lucanum, et ibi, cuiuscunque philosophiæ professor sis, eiusdem invenies condituram. Ergo pro capacitate discentis, aut docentis industria aut diligentia, constat fructus prælectionis auctorum. Sequebatur hunc morem Bernardus Carnotensis, exundantissimus modernis temporibus fons litterarum in Gallia, et in auctorum lectione quid simplex esset et ad imaginem regulæ positum ostendebat ' (I, 24).

He does not, however, deny the value of dialectic as an aid to other studies, but it is of no use by itself. ' Sicut dialectica alias expedit disciplinas, sic, si sola fuerit, iacet exsanguis et sterilis, nec ad fructum philosophiæ fecundat animam, si aliunde non concipit ' (II, 10). For example added to grammar it has its uses, but it will teach no one how to live aright (II, 11). So John proceeds to discuss substances, numbers, universals and the like but remains a humanist to the

231

end. Philologia, he says, must come before Philosophia or Philokalia (IV, 30).

John's other works include *Letters*, *Lives of St Anselm* and *St Thomas of Canterbury* and a curious poem entitled *Entheticus de Dogmate Philosophorum*. Though by far the most famous of twelfth-century humanists and the best writer of Latin, John is not the only one. His friend Hugo of St Victor the mystic (d. 1141) is no dialectician, but maintains the tradition of studying Latin authors in order to understand the Scriptures. Younger than John is Peter of Blois (d. 1200) who had the same distaste for vain verbal disputes and constantly cites ancient authors. ' Ait namque Seneca : Odibilius nihil est subtilitate ubi est sola subtilitas.' But the religious humanism of Chartres was destined to give way before the logomachic University which grew out of the schools of Paris.

Dictamina

The victory of the Sorbonne was not at once complete. While Chartres declined, Orleans continued to flourish well into the thirteenth century. Here the study of the *auctores* was maintained in opposition to the seven liberal arts as studied and practised in the North. Here the classical tradition in grammar was taught, while in the North Alexander of Ville-Dieu wrote his *Doctrinale*, a versified grammar of twelfth-century Latin. But there was no material gain to be made from the mere study of *auctores*, and the prosperity of the School of Orleans was due to a kind of offshoot of its classical studies, the art of Latin Composition, *ars dictandi*. Here was an accomplishment of saleable value, and many sons of Orleans obtained chancellorships and secretaryships and other posts in which the ability to write official letters in the correct style and language was a necessary qualification. In Italy too the *ars dictandi* was taught. For Law, for which the Universities of Bologna and Pavia were especially famous, not only demanded a knowledge of correct Latin for the understanding of its ancient authorities, but, then as now, required its documents to be drawn up in a particular manner and language needing special training. The books of instruction, whether for legal or other writing, contained numerous specimens, called by the general name *dictamina*. Often, like modern 'letter-writers,' they contained little else, and many collections, *Summæ*, of dictamina were current. The examples were often taken from the work of some recognised master, or, like Berard of Naples, such a master might himself collect and publish his work as specimens for others. In this way numerous medieval letters were copied and re-copied and preserved for us by such writers of *summæ* as Bernard Silvestris and Buoncompagno. But these collections do not contain merely official letters and legal formularies. The *ars dictandi* was turned to good account by every student who wished to write a love-letter or an appeal to his parents for money. He could make an impression with his borrowed eloquence and correct rhythms and strict division of his letter into the correct parts, *salutatio, exordium, narratio, petitio* and *conclusio*, which, says one of the exponents of the art, is 'pars siquidem practica epistolaris ornatus.' In this strange manner some curious and mostly unpublished scraps of medieval prose have come down to us.

Walter Map (c. 1137–c. 1209)

Walter Map (or Mapes) was born somewhere on the Welsh border before the middle of the twelfth century. He studied in Paris and on his return to England received preferment at Court through the influence of his parents. In 1197 he became Archdeacon of Oxford and died early in the next century. He has been credited with the authorship of the various poems on Bishop Golias. Still more doubtfully is he said to have composed the bulk of the Arthurian Romances. But in the midst of a busy life as courtier, itinerant judge and archdeacon he wrote at least one work, and it has made him famous as a raconteur and satirist in prose. The title *De Nugis Curialium*, Trifles of Courtiers, is taken from a sub-title of John of Salisbury's Policraticus. The book consists of five divisions—' distinctiones ' as he calls them. The first contains an account of the rise of the Templars, Carthusians and Cistercians and of various heresies, the second an account of the Welsh people with many of their folk-tales, the third longer tales of devils and fairies and men, some very ancient, the fourth is full of anecdotes and the fifth has some historical value especially for the reign of Henry II. But an analysis is misleading, for there is no real plan or arrangement in the work, which is a random collection of stories and history, criticism and abuse, or whatever occurred to the versatile author, who illustrates his points with equal ease by citations from the Bible, by allusions to the Latin Classics and by scurrilous stories. Few will quarrel with the statement of a seventeenth-century critic, Sir Roger Twysden, who says, ' they say there is many stories of good worth fit to be made publick in it.'

Map is constantly attacking abuses and injustice and is particularly bitter against the Cistercian order for their greed and lack of hospitality. As for their simple clothing, mean fare and hard work, let them come to Wales and see how the poor really live. Moreover it is indecent to wear only one garment; once on a windy day a white monk tripped and fell in the king's presence, and his garment was blown right over his head. King Henry looked the other way and said nothing, but a monk who was with the king made a very rude remark. 'I,' says Map, 'heard the remark and was pained to see holiness thus mocked; but of course you cannot blame the wind for blowing wherever there is room for it!' He is still more bitter against the Jews, 'qui omnem omni studio lucri viam inveniunt et sequuntur, qui omnem avaritiæ portam aperiunt et ingrediuntur.' Some merchants bought a number of sides of bacon from Jews, and while they went to fetch a cart the Jews put the bacon in a press and extracted all the good from it. At the end of the first 'distinction' there is a pleasing account of three hermits told by their last survivor. 'Three of us came into the solitary places to do penance after the manner of our fathers; the first and best of us was a Frenchman, the second, far braver and more steadfast than I, an Englishman, and I a Scot. . . . Anglicus, sed angelicus, catena stringitur ferrea, tam longa ut protendi possit ad pedem septimum.' He always had with him a mallet and a peg by which he made fast the chain to the ground every Sabbath and for the rest of the week within those narrow limits devoted himself to prayer and hymns and rejoicing, never depressed, never complaining. He ate what he found there and next Sabbath moved his camp.

The account of Gillespie, a Scottish hero of great prowess and greater good luck is typical of Map: incidentally it shows us that *Scotus* may now mean a Scot.

'Vidi virum a Scotia cuius laus ibi æternitatem adepta est; nomen ei Gillescop, id est episcopus. [In reality, son of a bishop.]

235

Hic cum omnibus fere ducum principum et regum congressibus illarum partium interfuisset, in singulis sive cum victoribus sive cum victis pretium utriusque tulit agminis, a iuventate in senium felicis homo audaciæ, cui nunquam temeraria præsumptio novercata est, cum in omne periculum quasi cæcus irruerit, et raro vel nunquam tantæ protervitati sint negati successus; episcopus non ex officio dictus, sed a corona calvitiei.'

On one occasion a chieftain from one of the Isles, two miles distant from the mainland, landed before dawn on a Sunday morning and carried off Gillespie's girl. Discovering this Gillespie ' was so savagely angry that, without saying a word to anyone, or looking for or waiting for a boat, unarmed save for his sword, and naked save for his pants which were split at the seat, boldly plunged into the sea; seipso usus clavo, remige et velo, idem navis et rector eius, exercitus in hostem et dux, et, cum in omnia timenda præceps irruat, secure transit et applicat. Pone domum raptoris adit, clamque per foramen modicum introspiciens inter trecentos aut plures convivas amicam suam amplexibus regis hærentem videt. Insilit igitur amenter improvidus, unoque regem ictu consummat et exsilit.' He swam home again safely but seems to have left the girl behind, and lived to perform many other deeds of incredible prowess. The romantic stories of Part III are too long to cite or abridge, but are among the best in the book. In Part IV there is the well-known letter to a friend advising him not to marry. It was copied and annotated by later writers, and its authorship lost sight of, so that it was at one time actually attributed to St Jerome. Though full of examples taken from classical and sacred history it is somewhat disappointing and lacks the wit and originality of Walter's other work.

' Variis et diversis incedunt semitis feminæ; quibuscunque anfractibus errent, quantiscumque devient inviis, unicus est exitus, unica omnium viarum suarum meta, unicum caput et conventus omnium diversitatum suarum, malitia.'

This is a fair sample of the tenor of the whole. There are better things in Part IV, stories of familiar types, compacts with the devil and three warnings before death, a man who could live under the sea and other Christianised folk-lore.

In the fifth and last ' distinction ' we learn that Henry II was an almost perfect king but was unlucky in his mother and in his sons. Indeed all his faults were due to his mother's bad influence. For the rest ' vir hic membrorum habilitate nulli secundus erat, nullius actus impotens quem posset alius, nullius comitatis inscius, litteratus ad omnem decentiam et utilitatem, linguarum omnium quæ sunt a mari Gallico usque ad Iordanem habens scientiam, Latina tantum utens et Gallica.' Giraldus Cambrensis implies that Henry understood English but could not speak it. A somewhat similar mixture of fable and history, but containing more geography and politics than Map's work is the *Otia Imperialia* of his younger contemporary Gervase of Tilbury.

Saxo Grammaticus (late twelfth century)

Somewhat outside the main current of twelfth-century prose style is Saxo Grammaticus, Denmark's oldest historian. His *Gesta Danorum*, which is the ultimate but not the immediate source of Shakespeare's story of Hamlet, was probably written between 1185 and 1215. The writer of a fifteenth-century epitome of it says that it was written by a certain *grammaticus*, literary person, named Saxo, a Zealander : and Grammaticus became attached to his not uncommon name. Of the sixteen books of the *Gesta* the first eight are a mixture of myth and history, folk-lore and ancient custom. But after the time of Charlemagne it becomes of great value for the history of Denmark, England and Scandinavia. His sources are mainly Scandinavian and unwritten but Adam of Bremen was evidently used too. His Latin shows the influence of Valerius Maximus and Martianus Capella, but his style is mainly his own, sometimes vigorous, often heavy and obscure. But Erasmus speaks highly of him, saying, ' I like his keen and vivid intellect, his language which never slackens or falters, his wonderful wealth of vocabulary, his frequent apt sayings . . . so that I cannot adequately express my surprise that such able writing is to be found from the pen of a Dane and at such a time as that. But you could scarcely find a trace of Ciceronian influence in him.' If Erasmus seems to us to exaggerate a little, he does well to remind us of the difficulties by which the earliest Danish writer was faced. To illustrate what Erasmus called his ' sententiæ crebræ ' we may mention the end of his account of how Odin was banished from among the gods, but afterwards was restored (III, 81). ' There are some who say that he (Odin) . . . contrived to return to the high honours which he had long lost by paying an immense sum of money. And if you ask me what price he paid for them, you had better consult those who have found out what price divinity is sold at. For my part I do not think it is worth much.' But Saxo is generally cautious and respectful towards his national traditions. Speaking of giants and magicians, ' Quorum summatim opera perstricturus, ne publicæ existimationi contraria aut veri fidem excedentia fidenter astruere videar, nosse operæ pretium est, triplex quondam mathematicorum genus inauditi generis miracula discretis exercuisse præstigiis.' The three kinds of magic persons are giants, diviners and offspring of the two. . . . 'Hæc idcirco tetigerim, ne, cum præstigia portentave perscripsero, lectoris incredula refragetur opinio' (I, 19, 20, Holder).

Giraldus Cambrensis (1147–1223)

Gerald de Barri or Giraldus Cambrensis was born in Pembrokeshire of Norman father and Welsh mother about 1147. He was a precocious boy and far out-stripped his companions in his lessons. His studies proper were made in Paris, where he acquired a know-ledge and love of Latin literature that is constantly mirrored in his work. Returning to England about 1170, he entered the Church, influenced by his uncle whom he hoped to succeed as Bishop of St David's. But while his Norman blood helped his promotion to be Archdeacon of Brecon, his Welsh connexions were the bar which prevented his election to the see of St David's in 1176. For although Giraldus was no political rebel, he constantly maintained the independ-ence of St David's from Canterbury, and urged that it should be made a metropolitan see. Disappointed, he returned to his studies, but in 1180 we find him vigorously assailing Peter, Bishop of St David's. In 1184 he was appointed a royal chaplain and next year accompanied Prince John to Ireland; soon after he wrote the first draft of the *Topography* and *Conquest* of Ireland, and held a public recital of the former work in Oxford. Preaching a crusade in Wales in 1188 he gathered material for his *Itinerary*. In 1198 the bishopric of St David's again fell vacant and for five years was in dispute between the Chapter, who wished for Gerald, and the Archbishop of Canterbury, who, backed by Richard I, was resolutely opposed to an independent Welsh Church. King John on his accession at first favoured his old companion, but the archbishop persuaded him to change his mind and the struggle went on. Gerald's visit to the Pope failed to produce a solution and on his return to England he found himself deserted even by the Chapter of St David's. Defeated himself he suggested various others, among them Walter Map, but without success. Finally he acquiesced in the Chapter's final choice of the Prior of Llanthony and for nearly twenty years more, till his death about 1223, he lived chiefly among his books, re-reading and revising his many works.

To his earlier years belong his poems, mostly in elegiac metre, which he wrote remarkably well. They will be referred to later. His earliest prose works are the *Topographia Hibernica* and the *Expugnatio Hibernica*, which were published in several revised editions. They are his best known works and, unlike most of his others, are preserved in many manuscripts. For his powers of invective and his stormy life made him many enemies, especially among the monks, for whom, like most of the secular clergy, he had the greatest contempt. But these works on Ireland gave no offence to monks, who copied them more willingly than his other works. The *Topography* shows Gerald to have been a close observer of natural phenomena, such as the salmon-leap, climate, varieties of river and sea-fish, birds, the difference between the Irish and the English hare. But he was vain and credulous, and no doubt, like many subsequent visitors to Ireland, was the victim of some 'leg-pulling.' For such would seem to be the case when he tells how an apparently quite fictitious saint called Nannan collected all the fleas in a village in Connacht where they abounded, and drove them all into one field, and 'there,' says Giraldus, 'there is such a quantity of them that it remains ever unapproachable not only by men but even by beasts.' He has no good opinion of the Irish, or of any nation for that matter, but allows that they are musical, and physically fine fellows ; this last is due to the fact that mothers take no care of their infants and use no cradles or unnecessary baths. For the rest he finds them to be ' gens silvestris, gens inhospita, gens ex bestiis solum et bestialiter vivens,' and again with glaring falsehood ' gens spurcissima, gens vitiis involutissima, gens omnium gentium in fidei rudimentis incultissima . . . nondum matrimonia contrahunt, non incestus vitant, non ecclesiam Dei cum debita reverentia frequentant.' The *Conquest of Ireland* (by Henry II) is historically valuable, but marred by the same prejudices.

The *Gemma Ecclesiastica* was its author's favourite work, and, if we can believe him, was highly prized by Pope Innocent III himself. It was written for the Welsh Clergy who at this time were very ignorant and badly needed this handbook on the Church mysteries and proper conduct for the clergy. For example the Welsh Church had never thoroughly accepted clerical celibacy. As there was no Biblical warrant for enforcing celibacy Giraldus does not stigmatise its breach as a moral crime but ridicules those who keep a woman, he will not say wife or even mistress, ' qui focariam in domo virtutes in ipso suffocantem universas et suggillantem, domumque miseram infantibus et cunis, obstetricibus quoque et nutricibus refertam habuerit.' He has to feed her and buy her a horse, even if it means going on foot himself, and much expensive clothing, ' caudatas in longum tunicas pulverem trahentes et terram verrentes, pretiosasque vestes quibus non illi solum sed multis placeat.' For, he says, not acknowledging his quotation from Ovid, when women go to a fair, ' spectatum veniunt, veniunt spectentur ut ipsæ.' The true cleric will resist temptation even as Aldhelm, ' qui inter duas puellas unam ab uno latere, alteram ab altero, ut ab hominibus diffamaretur, a Deo vero, cui nota fuerit conscientia ipsius et continentia, copiosius in futurum remuneraretur, iacuisse describitur.' Ignorance of Latin among monks and clergy is also ridiculed and some good ' howlers ' are given. ' S. Ioannes ante portam latinam ' was once interpreted ' St John first brought Latin to England.' A still more comprehensive attack on monks, especially Cistercians, is the *Speculum Ecclesiæ*, where further examples of monkish wickedness and rapacity are given ; they range from monks who cut down the king's trees to an abbot who had ' eighteen or more ' illegitimate children.

There is interesting Welsh folk-lore in the *Itinerarium Cambriæ*. A boy once weary of his lessons hid himself from his masters by a river bank. After two days of starvation the little people found him and invited him to visit them. This he did frequently but on one occasion, as a punishment for stealing, he found the usual passage to fairyland barred, and spent the rest of his life on earth and became a priest. But years afterwards he still remembered the fairy tongue which he had learned. ' Erant autem verba. . . . Græco idiomati valde conformia. Cum enim aquam requirebant dicebant "Ydor ydorum " ; quod Latine sonat " aquam offer." ' Similarly ' Halgein ' is salt. ' Hal vero Græce sal dicitur et haleyn Britannice.' Then Giraldus recalls the supposed Trojan origin of the Britons and discusses the word salt in other languages. As for his stories, we may cite his words : ' But if as a careful student you were to ask what I think of this tale, I will answer with Augustine that divine miracles were intended to be wondered at, not critically discussed. I do not by flat denial set limits to the divine power, nor yet by dogmatic affirmation wilfully extend it, that cannot be extended.'

Of the *Letters* (*Symbola Electorum*, I), the *De Rebus a se gestis*, the *Instruction of a Prince*, it is not possible to speak here. Giraldus was a voluminous and widely read writer with a great command of vituperative Latin, but he was vain and impetuous, prone to exaggerate and to believe the worst, never thinking that he could possibly be in the wrong. One thing he believed, that the most able and learned writer of his time was Giraldus Cambrensis, and as far as England is concerned, he was probably right.

Cæsarius of Heisterbach (c. 1180–c. 1245)

Among the writers of miracles of the Middle Ages Cæsarius of Heisterbach holds a high place both for the merit of his stories and his ability to tell them. He needed not to apologise for his *Latini sermonis inopia*, for though not distinguished his Latin is quite readable. He was probably born about 1180 in Cologne. He was educated at the cathedral school there and before 1200 had entered the Cistercian monastery of Heisterbach in the Siebengebirge, where he afterwards became Master of the Novices, then Prior. His reputation as a teacher was very great and his chief works, the Homilies, a Life of Engelbert, Archbishop of Cologne and the *Dialogus Miraculorum* were widely read. Deservedly most famous is the *Dialogue of Miracles* in twelve books or ' *distinctiones.*' The books have different titles, Conversion, Temptation, Visions, etc., and in each a novice is made to ask questions, to which a monk replies not with argument but by a brief statement enforced by numerous examples and stories. Opinions have varied about the educational value of the work, but the general reader cannot fail to be interested both in the tales and in the religious ideas which they illustrate. The medieval mind, not at its best perhaps, but certainly not at its worst, is mirrored in the works of Cæsarius.

From the wealth of stories in the *Dialogus Miraculorum* it is an invidious task to choose. In the first book different kinds of Conversion are illustrated. The regeneration of the soul may proceed from minute causes even as the purgation of the body from a tiny pill. Excellent reading are the accounts of St Hildegund who became a monk, not a nun (I, 40), and Landgraf Ludwig (I, 27 and 34). Some of the best stories are in Book IV, On Temptation. A certain prior did not approve of his monks going about ' propter tentationes diabolicas.' To justify his prohibition he once went riding with a young monk; they met a very pretty girl. 'When the Prior deliberately checked his horse and saluted her with the utmost politeness, she stopped and returned his salute with a bow. When they had gone a little further, the Prior, wishing to try the young man, said, " That girl struck me as being very pretty." " Believe me, master," said the other, " that struck me also." The Prior answered, " She has only one defect, she has but one eye." " Nay, in truth, master, she has both her eyes; for I had a pretty good look at her." Then the Prior was angry and said, " And I'll have a good look at your back. You ought to have been so innocent that you could not have told whether it was a man or a woman." ' It is sufficient to tempt human nature if even the most unpleasant act is prohibited. A certain knight had a wager with his lady that, if she was forbidden to walk barefoot through the filthy muck in the yard, sooner or later she would do it. He won his bet. Lay brothers, priests and even saints may be attacked by the tempter. Once a lay brother ('conversus') sent on a mission was spending the night in a certain house. In the guest-chamber the maid prepared two beds one at the foot of the other. The brother thought nothing of the matter, put out the light and got into bed. ' Illa silenter vestes exuit, in lectum præparatum se reclinavit, nudis pedibus conversi plantas pulsans, et quia ipsa foret tussiendo se prodens.' Then she tried biting and finally spoke. At length understanding, the brother arose, dressed and went to the window, where he remained in prayer. ' Illa diutina exspectatione suspensa, tandem confusa descendit.' Another virtuous man, a tall, handsome English monk with merry eyes, was hotly besieged by an amorous nun, who was so violently tempted that ' throwing modesty aside she declared her passion to him.' At first he tries to remonstrate with her, but

' Dicente illa : si non consenseris mihi, moriar, respondit ille : Ex quo aliter esse non potest, fiat ut vis. In quo ergo loco conveniemus ? Respondit illa : Ubicunque tibi placuerit, ego in hac nocte veniam ad te. Ad quod ille : Oportet ut in die fiat. Ostenditque virgini domum in pomerio, monens et præcipiens, ut nemine sciente, nemine vidente, tali hora illuc veniret. Quæ cum venisset, dixit vir Dei ad eam : Domina, dignum est et vobis expedit, ut corpus meum, quod tam ardenter concupiscitis, prius inspiciatis, et si tunc placuerit, desiderio vestro per illud satisfaciatis. Hoc dicto, illa tacente, vestimenta sua exuit, cilicium asperrimum quo indutus erat ad carnem deposuit, corpusque nudum vermibus corrosum, cilicio attritum, scabiosum atque nigerrimum illi ostendens, ait : En quod amas, exple nunc si placet voluptatem tuam. Videns hæc illa expavit et nunc in pallorem, nunc in ruborem versa, ad pedes eius ruens, veniam postulavit.'

The fifth book, *De Dæmonibus*, is very characteristic of the age. One of the devil's favourite tricks was to assume the shape of a beautiful woman. In the form of a fair nun a demon came among the lay-brethren of a certain monastery while they were taking their midday sleep. ' Veniens ad quendam conversum, ante illum se inclinavit, et bracchiis collum eius stringens tactuque meretricio demulcens, oscula in eius ora defixit.' One of the others saw this in amazement, and when the intruder vanished went to look at the brother ' quem quidem dormientem sed incomposite et impudice nudatumque iacentem invenit.' The victim died in three days. One more example must suffice (VI, 5). Ensfrid, Dean of St Andrew in Cologne, was an eccentric dignitary who would readily steal in order to give to the poor and on one occasion took off his breeches to give to a beggar in the street. ' Tale aliquid non legitur in actis sancti Martini ' ; says the novice, ' plus fuit braccas dare, quam pallium dividere.' Cæsarius also tells with approval the following tale of the Dean. ' One day he had invited to dinner a number of monks (I cannot say whether they were Cistercians or Præmonstratensians). There was none of the proper food for them and he had no fish so he said to his cook : We have no fish, the monks are simple and hungry, so go and make a stew, take out all the bones and put in plenty of seasoning, and when you serve it up, say : Eat of this excellent turbot.' This was done and the monks, ' sicut viri boni et simplices, boni sui hospitis ac simplicis pium dolum non observantes,' asked no questions, but ate the ' fish.' But ' when the dish was nearly empty one of them found a pig's ear and showed it to his neighbour. The Dean saw him and, pretending to be a little annoyed, burst out : For God's sake eat it up. Monks shouldn't be so inquisitive. A turbot has ears too.'

Such tales are typical not only of the *Dialogue* but

also of the *Homilies*, where many of them are repeated. We read them for amusement but they were intended as food for the minds of young novices. And, as Cæsarius says, defending his method in the prologue to another work only partly extant : ' Qui infirmus est olera manducet. Fragmentis pulmentum adiciendum est, quo Christi reficiantur pauperes.'

Matthew Paris (c. 1190–1259)

Matthew of Paris was an English monk, chronicler of St Alban's. It is not clear why he was called Parisiensis, for he was evidently English in his national outlook. He may have been educated in Paris, for he is familiar with French, but that would hardly account for his surname, since many Englishmen were educated there. It may be that he was born in Paris of English parents, but we know little of him before 1217, when he became a monk at St Alban's. Except for two visits to Norway in later life he seems to have spent most of his life in the monastery. There in 1236 he succeeded Roger of Wendover as Chronicler. But Matthew was more than a mere chronicler, and his great work, the *Chronica Maiora*, is held in high esteem by many historians. As it is not divided into books it will be convenient to refer to the Volumes of the Rolls edition. The first volume, really the work of Roger of Wendover, who compiled it from various sources, is a summary of world-history down to 1066. Volume II deals with the period from the Conquest to the accession of Henry III in 1216. In it and in most of Vol. III (1217–1239) the chief authority is Roger's *Flores Historiarum* (1188–1235). The end of Vol. III (1235–1239) and Vols. IV (1240–1247) and V

(1248–1259) are the most important and original part of the *Chronica Maiora*.

Although England is his chief interest Matthew's history deals with affairs over the whole of Europe, such as relations between the Eastern Patriarch and the Roman See, and especially the never-ceasing conflicts between Pope and Emperor, in which England was torn now one way, now the other. He is full of bitterness against the Popes and their constant demands from England, France and Ireland for money with which to wage their wars. But strong nationalist though he is, he does not spare his own king Henry III, least of all when he too oppresses the people with exactions. He voices the laments of harassed Londoners when the king ' began to ponder earnestly how he might drain dry the inexhaustible well of England.' He had already established a new fair at Westminster under the guise of honouring the feast of St Edward and now sought to use it as a means to extort money from the neighbouring Londoners.

' Statim igitur post memoratæ gaudia sollemnitatis, inito studuit consilio cives Londoniarum gravare hoc modo. Suspendit exercitium mercaturæ civitatis, ut prætactum est, per quindenam, novis nundinis apud Westmonasterium in multorum damnum et præiudicium constitutis, et protinus post hoc missis per satellites suos litteris suis argumentosas et imperiosas preces continentibus ut ipsum iuvarent efficaciter auxilio pecuniari.'

There are frequent references to the Tartars, who are described in more embroidered language every time they are mentioned. The following description will serve to illustrate his style :

' Hi quoque capita habentes magna nimis et corporibus nequaquam proportionata, carnibus crudis et etiam humanis vescuntur ; sagittarii incomparabiles, flumina quævis cimbis de corio factis et portabilibus transeuntes, robusti viribus, corporibus propagati, impii, inexorabiles, quorum lingua incognita omnibus, quos nostra attingit notitia ; gregibus, armentis et equitiis abundantes, equos vero habentes velocissimos, potentes iter trium dierum uno conficere ; ante non retro bene armati ne fugam ineant, ducem habentes ferocissimum nomine Caan (the Khan).'

One of their invasions casts an interesting sidelight on England : 'Hence the inhabitants of Gothland and Friesland, fearing an invasion (of Tartars), did not, as is their usual custom, come to Yarmouth (Gernemue) in England at the herring-fishing season to load their ships. That was the reason why that year herring in England were worth practically nothing, so abundant were they. And even in districts far from the sea the finest quality were sold at forty or fifty for a silver penny.' The *Historia Anglorum*, sometimes called *Chronica Minora*, is a history of England after the Conquest abridged from the larger work.

Salimbene of Parma (1221–c. 1289)

Good autobiographies are so rare in any age that it is surprising to find one in the thirteenth century when man's life on earth counted for so little. But no one could deny the liveliness and interest of Salimbene's *Chronica*. It is further surprising that the author of this record of joyous wanderings, amusing and even coarse incidents, was a devout follower of St Francis with a genuine love of piety and mysticism. But it is true and may be proved from the work itself, whence all our information is drawn. He was born in Parma in 1221 of wealthy and distinguished parents, but at the age of seventeen resolved to join the Minorites (Franciscans), then a rapidly growing Order devoted to poverty and itinerant lives. His father was enraged and for many years alternately cursed his son and pled with him to return. But the young man was well armed with Scriptural quotations and fortified by mystic visions, and perhaps attracted by the care-free life of itinerant mendicancy.   Its physical discomforts sometimes came home to him and on one occasion he was met by a stranger who openly reviled him for begging bread of the poor who had none to spare, while the servants in his father's house had plenty.   But he remained true to his vows, and after some years in Tuscany even returned to Parma.   In 1247 at the bidding of the Minister-General of the Order he proceeded to France, where he travelled about enjoying the hospitality of different monasteries, writing down everything interesting that he saw or heard.   And he saw and heard more than most, for his eye and ear were open and his mind alert, receptive and tolerant.   Though not greatly learned himself, except in the Scriptures which he quotes with unnecessary copiousness and frequent ineptitude, he enjoyed listening to the discussions of others, Dominican or Franciscan, especially to the words of Brother Hugo of Montpellier, whose fervent belief in the prophecies of Joachim he shared.   He returned to Italy in 1249, where he seems to have led a less restless life for some forty years more.

No class of person appears more frequently in Salimbene than the scoundrel-monks ' truffatores et deceptores et pessimi seductores, de quibus beatus Ioannes in secunda canonica dixit : Multi seductores exierunt in mundum.'   While disapproving of them Salimbene is often more amused than shocked and sometimes tells the same tale twice for the sheer pleasure of telling it.   And indeed ' false apostle ' is a scarcely appropriate epithet for a half-idiot monk who ' in cunabulis iacuit fasciis involutus et lac et mammas suxit cuiusdam nesciæ mulieris.'   This same Girardinus

one day went up to where the road begins to rise from
the plain into the hills beyond Parma. 'He stood in
the middle of the road and in his extreme simpleness
loudly shouted to passers-by : Go ye also into my
vineyard. Those who knew him thought him crazy,
knowing well that he had no vineyard,' but people
from the hills came and helped themselves, thinking
him to be the owner. In that there is more fatuity
than wickedness ; not so in the following story. Three
of those, 'who say they are apostles and are not,'
were once received into the house of a young man
who had been married that day :

> 'Suaserunt iuveni ne uxorem cognosceret nec cum ea in eodem
> lecto prima nocte dormiret, nisi quando dicerent ei. Hoc autem
> ideo dicebant, quia volebant iuvenem prævenire atque decipere et
> prius cum uxore eius dormire, sicut factum est. Quia omnes tres
> illa nocte iverunt ad lectum eius, unus post alium, facto modico
> intervallo, et cognoverunt eam. Cum autem quarta vice iuvenis
> sponsus eius vellet eam cognoscere, mirata uxor eius dixit ei : Tribus
> vicibus in hac nocte carnaliter mecum fuisti, et adhuc vis agere opus
> istud.'

Salimbene's greatest charm is his unfailing kindliness.
It is delightful to see him, armed with his usual battery
of Biblical quotations, set out to denounce intemperance,
and end by making allowances for everybody. 'Prov.
xx. dicitur "luxuriosa res est vinum et tumultuosa
ebrietas ; quicunque his delectatur non erit sapiens."
Anglici certe talibus delectantur et "student calicibus
epotandis." Accipit enim unus Anglicus unum mag-
num ciphum vini et bibit totum, dicens "Ge bi a vu."
Quod est dicere "Tantum oportebit vobis dicere,
quantum ego bibam."' And the Englishman 'thinks
that to say and do this is the height of politeness,
and takes it very ill, if any refuse to do what he has
asked and demonstrated.' This intemperate habit is

condemned by a string of quotations. Then the true
Salimbene speaks ' Parcendum tamen est Anglicis si
libenter bibunt bonum vinum quando possunt, quia
parum habent de vino in patria sua. Minus parcendum
est Gallicis, quia plus abundant, nisi forte dicatur :
Durum est assueta relinquere.' After all are not God's
gifts given us to enjoy ? And the poet says :

> ' Det vobis piscem Normandia terra marinum,
> Anglia frumentum, lac Scotia, Francia vinum.
> Silva feras, ær volucres, armenta butyrum,
> Ortus delitias, nemus umbram, stagna papirum.'

The Schoolmen of the Thirteenth Century

The thirteenth century saw the climax of Scholastic
Philosophy. It had moved far forward since the days
of Berengar and Anselm. The problem of Universals
was still discussed but the emphasis has shifted. Chief
among the causes of this development is the re-discovery
of the complete Aristotle. Down to the time of
Abelard logicians had only known Aristotle through
Bœthius' commentaries and his translation of the *De
Interpretatione* (part of the *Organon*). During the
twelfth century the rest of the *Organon* of Aristotle
became known in translation, and, by the beginning
of the thirteenth, most of Aristotle's works. This new
acquaintance with Aristotle came in two ways. The
Latin translations which were current in the latter
part of the twelfth century were themselves made
from Arabic versions of a Syriac translation from the
Greek. Moreover translations into Latin were made
of the commentaries on Aristotle of Arabian philosophers
from Avicenne to Averroes. Among the translators
was Michael Scot, more familiar as a magician in the
Lay of the Last Minstrel. But while translations

from the Arabic were being made at Toledo, Latin versions of the original Greek were being made at Constantinople. At first the Church violently opposed this new knowledge, especially as expounded by the Arabians. But the ban on the study of Aristotle was first relaxed, then removed, and the schoolmen of the thirteenth century devoted themselves to the task of interpreting his philosophy in such a way as to conform to Christian doctrine. Chief among these interpreters were Albert the Great of Cologne and his pupil Thomas of Aquino. Albert, the most widely learned man of his time, did not entirely succeed in creating a complete and coherent system of explaining the universe in terms of philosophy. But Thomas with a less wide range of learning and a narrower but more powerful intellect was stimulated by the incompleteness of his master's work to examine Aristotle afresh, to show the errors of Averroes, to make a Christian philosophy that should be not merely good but true, in a word to show that there was no conflict between science and religion. The success of his efforts was immediate and lasting, but the very intellectual freedom which made his work possible was all but slain. For the task appeared to be finished and nothing to remain for good Catholics but to support St Thomas. Now the greatest centre of this new knowledge was Paris, then as now the foremost intellectual meeting-place of Western Europe. But whilst the Sorbonne grew out of the older schools of Paris and its earlier doctors were not monks but secular clergy, the chief scholastics on the other hand belonged to the Dominican or the Franciscan Order, and had to wage a long struggle before their recognition by the secular doctors of the University. These two mendicant Orders, for all their differences and violent quarrels, had this in common that, instead of remaining closely attached to monasteries, they moved about in the world as missionaries. Both Orders, but especially the Dominicans or Preachers, shared in the increased intellectual activity of the century. The greatest Scholastics, Albertus Magnus and Thomas Aquinas, were Dominicans, Alexander of Hales, Roger Bacon, and Duns Scotus were Franciscans. Yet such learning would have found small favour with St Francis, who while he lived shook his head sadly at such pretensions. Soon after his death in 1226 we find Franciscans established at Paris, Oxford and Cambridge; already the Dominicans were preaching at Paris, Oxford and Bologna. Thus while the twelfth century, as we saw, is marked by a literary revival, the chief interest of the thirteenth is in its intellectual activity. In world-history the latter is by far the more important; its effects are evident to this day. But its interest is primarily philosophical and scientific, whereas our present purpose must be rather to consider some of its greatest writers and their place in letters.

Albertus Magnus (1193 (or 1206)–1280)

Albert the Great of Cologne, deservedly called Doctor Universalis, was born in the neighbourhood of Ulm on the Danube, but was educated chiefly at Padua and Paris. He taught in many places, Paris, Freiburg and Ratisbon, where he was for a short time archbishop, but chiefly at Cologne, where he was Provincial of the Dominican Order. Like his great authority Aristotle he took all knowledge, especially the biological sciences, for his field; but sermons, and commentaries on the Psalms, on different books of the New Testament and on the theological ' Sentences ' of Peter Lombard are among his voluminous writings.

His own theological work was largely superseded by
that of St Thomas. He wrote too on Logic, Ethics
and Metaphysics, in that highly technical Latin to
which we shall refer later, but give this short specimen
here :

> ' Ex inductis accipitur quod substantiæ intellectuales, per essentiam
> suam stantes sunt in esse perpetuo, et non per successionem generatæ ;
> stantes enim per essentiam suam fixam sunt in esse perpetuo secundum
> esse et secundum id quod est.'

His knowledge of ancient philosophers other than
Aristotle is hazy ; thus in the *Liber de causis et
processu Universitatis* the doctrines of Anaxagoras are
ascribed to Epicurus. His best works are those dealing
with Science, especially botany and zoology ; in them
he gives us not Aristotle only but often the results of
his own observations and experiments. One of these
consisted in trying to induce an ostrich to eat bits
of iron.

> ' De hoc ave dicitur quod ferrum comedat et digerat : sed ego
> non sum hoc expertus : quia ferrum a me pluribus struthionibus
> obiectum, comedere noluerunt. Sed ossa magna ad breves partes
> truncata et lapides avide comederunt ' (*De Animalibus*, XXIII,
> 1, 104).

But where he could not observe himself he was too
credulous of sailors' and travellers' tales, such as an
account of how tiger cubs may be taken from their
mother, when her attention is distracted by rolling
before her glass balls in which her mirrored reflection
looks like one of her young :

> ' Aliqui etiam venatores sphæras vitreas secum habentes matri
> obiciunt, in quibus natorum similitudines apparent sicut in speculo
> cum mater ad sphæram adspicit : et sic sphæram post sphæram
> obicientes, deludunt matrem, quæ sphæræ motu filium movere
> putat ; sed cum sphæram constringens pedibus filium lactare quærit,
> delusam se deprehendit, et multoties sic delusa venator ad civitates vel
> ad naves evadit, et illa natos perdidit ' (*De Animalibus*, XXII, 2, 101).

He believed, as did everyone at the time, in magic as the work of demons, and his medical advice prescribes both for man and beast the usual unpleasant mixtures containing half-magical and disgusting ingredients. But he is an outstanding figure in the history of science both for the volume of his knowledge and his spirit of enquiry.

Vincent of Beauvais

Before passing to Thomas Aquinas we may mention the Dominican Vincent of Beauvais (d. 1264), compiler of an encyclopædic work entitled *Speculum Maius*, and William of Moerbeke whose translations of Aristotle were used by St Thomas.

Thomas Aquinas (c. 1226–1274)

Saint Thomas, the Angelic Doctor, was born of noble family near Aquino in Campania. He studied first at Monte Cassino and the University of Naples, but when he decided, much against the wishes of his family, to enter the Dominican Order, he removed to Cologne where the great Albert was teaching. He followed Albert to the University of Paris, where he studied some years, but again accompanied his master to Cologne. About 1250, still only twenty-five years old, he returned to Paris to lecture at one of the Dominican Schools there. These schools of the mendicant Orders were not yet fully recognised by the University nor their masters necessarily admitted as masters in the University. But they were attracting more and better students, and in the end the University had to give in, and Thomas became a master in 1257. Two years later he left Paris at the bidding of the Pope and continued his teaching in various parts of

Italy for about eight years. After the death of Clement IV he returned to Paris for three years (1269–1272) and then came back to Naples. Two years later, on his way to a general council at Lyons, he took ill and after seven weeks' suffering he died, his great work, the *Summa Theologica*, not yet quite finished. His early death (at forty-eight) gave rise to suspicion that he was poisoned, but though Dante records it, the story is doubtful. Ecclesiastical preferment, such as the Archbishopric of Naples, he was offered but refused, preferring to devote his life to teaching, for which he had unequalled gifts. Less than fifty years after his death he was canonised, and ranks with St Augustine as the greatest theologian of the Catholic Church.

Of so vast and important a work as the *Summa Theologica* it would be impossible, not to say impertinent, to give an account here. But the student of literature may legitimately enquire into the method and style of the work, which may be demonstrated by an examination of the third article of the hundred and seventh question of first part. The method is always the same in each article—the contrary proposition is stated and its supposed proofs given, a quotation is given to suggest that this view is wrong and proof follows in the ' body of the article '; lastly answers are given to the supposed proofs of the first proposition. In I, 107, 3, the subject of enquiry is ' whether an angel speaks to God.'

' (1) It appears that an Angel does not speak to God. For speech is for the manifestation of something to another. But an Angel can manifest nothing to God, who knows everything. Therefore an Angel does not speak to God. (2) Moreover to speak is to arrange the thoughts of the mind for the benefit of another, as has been said in the first article of this Question. But an Angel is always arranging the thoughts of his mind towards God. If therefore he sometimes speaks to God, he is always speaking to God, which is evidently inconvenient [in the literal sense] for some ; since one Angel some-times speaks to another Angel. It appears therefore that an Angel never speaks to God.' ' Sed contra est quod dicitur Zachar. I, 12 : Respondit Angelus Deo et dixit : Domine exercituum, usquequo non miseraberis Jerusalem ? Loquitur ergo Angelus Deo.'

Then follows the body of the article, where it is pointed out that speech is of various kinds, including praise and interrogation. And lastly in answer to (1) and (2) above :

' Ad primum ergo dicendum quod locutio non semper est ad manifestandum alteri ; sed quandoque ad hoc ordinatur finaliter, ut loquenti aliquid manifestetur, sicut cum discipulus quærit aliquid a magistro. Ad secundum dicendum quod locutione qua Angeli loquuntur Deo, laudantes ipsum et admirantes, semper Angeli Deo loquuntur ; sed locutione qua eius sapientiam consulunt super agendis, tunc ei loquuntur quando aliquod novum per eos agendum occurrit, super quo desiderant illuminari.'

His voluminous minor works and commentaries must be passed over here ; not so the *Summa contra Gentiles*, which as literature is perhaps his most perfect work. Its proper title is *Summa Philosophica seu de veritate Catholicæ Fidei contra Gentiles*. In it we find not the dry precision of the *Summa Theologica* or the Disputed Questions, but a rich and varied philosophical prose. For not only Scholasticism, but the Latin language reaches its final development in the works of St Thomas. In the language of course the final stage is far from being the highest, but there has been no further development in the history of Latin, which accordingly became a dead language. But down to the time of St Thomas Latin was still alive. The great Scholastics were fashioning it anew, to subserve their ends and express new thought. Such a task language cannot undertake unless it change ; and the new and necessary technical terms thus brought into being are wrongly condemned as barbarous. New habits of thought demand new methods of expression and exposition. In the hands of inferior linguists the results are often sorry reading ; but the Angelic Doctor was a sufficient master of language to create both vocabulary and syntax, and the result is a medium of expression exactly adapted to its requirements. Yet Latin died, died after having lived some 1500 years without ceasing to be recognisably that same language. Scholastic Latin died because Scholastic Philosophy died. The Latin language was killed by the Classicists of the Renaissance, and the prose of St Thomas and Dante is the latest living Latin. That it was alive will be evident from the following passage from the *Summa contra Gentiles* (III, 111), where it is shown that men are rational and intellectual beyond all other creatures :

> ' Præcellunt enim alias creaturas et in perfectione naturæ et in dignitate finis. In perfectione quidem naturæ, quia sola creatura rationalis habet dominium sui actus, libere se agens ad operandum ; ceteræ vero creaturæ ad opera propria magis aguntur quam agant, ut ex supradictis patet [ch. 110]. In dignitate autem finis, quia sola creatura intellectualis ad ipsum ultimum finem universi sua operatione pertingit, scilicet cognoscendo et amando Deum ; aliæ vero creaturæ ad finem ultimum pertingere non possunt nisi per aliqualem similitudinis ipsius participationem.'

Apart from the language that passage shows a loftier conception of man's worth in the world than we have been accustomed to meet in medieval literature. Man was at his best reasonable and dignified, for St Thomas saw them as he himself was, and reasonableness and dignity mark his approach to every question. His attitude towards miracles will serve as an example (III, 101) :

> ' These things which through God's working take place outside the generally appointed order of things are wont to be called miracles. For we are astonished at something when we see the effect but do not know the cause. And since one and the same cause may be known

to some and unknown to others, it comes about that of a number of people beholding a certain effect at the same time some are astonished, others are not. For an astronomer is not astonished when he beholds an eclipse of the sun, because he knows the cause ; but one who is ignorant of this science, not knowing the cause is inevitably astonished. A thing may therefore be miraculous to one person and not to another. So only that is absolutely miraculous which has its cause absolutely hidden. . . . Now the absolutely hidden cause for all men is God. For it has been proved above that no man in this state of life can intellectually comprehend His Essence. Therefore these things are to be called absolutely miracles which take place through God's working outside the generally observed order of things.'

The Franciscans

Among Franciscan writers Alexander of Hales, ' doctor irrefragabilis ' (d. 1245) was the earliest to become fully acquainted with Aristotle. He was teaching in Paris at the same time as St Thomas. One of his pupils was John of Fidanza, better known as Bonaventura (d. 1274) ' doctor seraphicus,' who, while not despising Aristotle, leaned like the founder of his Order more towards the Augustinian Platonism of the early Church. A strong mystical element and an easy-flowing Latin style, more like the earlier rhythmical prose, differentiate him from the majority of thirteenth-century Scholastics, and impel us to quote a passage from the close of the Legend of St Francis (ch. XIV, 6) :

' Tandem cunctis in eum completis mysteriis, anima illa sanctissima carne soluta et in abyssum divinæ claritatis absorpta, beatus vir obdormivit in Domino. Unus autem ex fratribus et discipulis eius vidit animam illam beatam sub specie stellæ præfulgidæ a candide subvecta nubecula super aquas multas in cælum recto tramite sursum ferri, tanquam sublimis sanctitatis candore prænitidam et cælestis sapientiæ simul et gratiæ ubertate repletam, quibus vir sanctus promeruit locum introire lucis et pacis, ubi cum Christo sine fine quiescit.'

Robert Grosseteste, who died in 1255, is the first known chancellor of Oxford. His powers as a teacher and his enthusiasm for knowledge, especially of languages. were a powerful influence among the Oxford Franciscans and bore fruit in the work of Adam Marsh and, most famous of all, Roger Bacon.

Roger Bacon (c. 1214–1292)

Roger Bacon was born in England of wealthy parents. He tells us that in his youth he spent large sums of money on books. It was not until 1247 that he took the Franciscan vows. Meanwhile he had studied both at Oxford and Paris. At Oxford under Grosseteste he had become an ardent student of languages and had found it unsafe to rely on the current translations of philosophic works. In Paris he was surprised to find that many of the learned doctors knew only Latin and not a word of Aristotle in the Greek. This ignorance led him to speak contemptuously of Albert and Thomas and other doctors, calling them all 'mere Latins.' At Paris his scientific knowledge was extended under Peter of Marincourt, an experimental scientist of whom he speaks highly, while hitting at the verbal disputations of the schoolmen : 'Non enim cognosco nisi unum, qui laudem potest habere in operibus huius scientiæ ; nam ipse non curat de sermonibus et pugnis verborum, sed persequitur opera sapientiæ et in illis quiescit ' (*Opus Tertium*, ch. 13). After 1250 he is again in Oxford, but in 1257 his scientific work brought him into conflict with his superiors in the Order. Unable to understand his work and methods they looked with suspicion on them, and removed Bacon from Oxford to Paris, where he was kept under supervision. However, in 1266 he received a letter from Pope Clement IV asking him to send copies of his works. Bacon hailed the opportunity with joy, but was obliged to keep the matter secret. He had written little during his confinement to Paris, but at once set to work to finish the *Opus Maius* and other books. Whether Clement ever read them we do not know, for he died in 1271. His successor was a strict Franciscan. But Bacon continued to write, attacking not merely the vices of the clergy, which would probably have brought him little trouble, but the unscientific and obscurantist methods of the other Scholastics. In 1277 he was arraigned before the Chapter of the Franciscan Order and condemned to imprisonment. What the exact charge was we do not know, but the motives for condemning him are not far to seek. He remained a prisoner till his death about the year 1292.

Bacon's writings are numerous, but many of them have only been published within recent years. Best known are the *Opus Maius, Opus Tertium, Compendium Studii Philosophiæ* and a Greek Grammar. The 'Greater Work' consists of seven parts of unequal length. The first deals with the chief Causes of Error. These are : reliance on weak and insufficient authority, persistence of habit, popular prejudice (sensus vulgi) and 'hiding one's own ignorance under a semblance of wisdom.' Of the first three causes none is more potent than popular prejudice, ' Nam auctoritas solum allicit, consuetudo ligat, opinio vulgi obstinatos parit et confirmat ' (ch. 4). The second part treats of philosophy or science in its relation to theology, the third of languages, especially Greek and Hebrew, and the mistakes due to ignorance of them. The long fourth part is devoted to Mathematics, the foundation of science, with Astronomy and Geography and the application of these to sacred subjects. Optics, a favourite subject with Bacon, has the whole of Part V and Experimental

Science Part VI. The seventh part, a Moral Philosophy, completes the whole. For Bacon, for all his enthusiasm for pure science, regarded the science of human conduct, of good and bad actions, as being on a higher level and closely akin to theology, to which all science was subservient. And although much of Part VII is taken from Seneca, Bacon is essentially a Christian moralist.

He is, however, rightly remembered chiefly as a linguist and a scientist. He loved languages for their own sake and ponders long over the likenesses and differences between Greek and Latin. But he valued their study still more as a safeguard against error. Nothing is so important or difficult as good translation, by one who knows both the subject and the language. 'Oportet quod interpres optime sciat scientiam quam vult transferre, et duas linguas a quibus et in quas transferat. Solus Boethius primus interpres novit plenarie potestatim linguarum. Et solus dominus Robertus, dictus Grossum Caput, novit scientias.' (Part III, Bridges, p. 67.) The translations of the Bible were even more faulty than those of Aristotle (p. 77). Indeed no philosopher ought to be ignorant of all those languages whence we obtain all our knowledge. 'Prima igitur est scientia linguarum sapientalium a quibus tota latinorum sapientia translata est ; eiusmodi sunt Græcum, Hebræum, Arabicum et Chaldæum . . .' 'I do not mean however that one should learn these languages like his mother tongue, as we speak English, French and Latin, nor that we should know enough of these tongues to make interpreters, able to translate Latin philosophy from those languages into our mother tongue.' But he does demand 'ut homo sciat legere Græcum, Hebræum, et cetera' (*Compend. Stud.*, ch. 6). It is interesting to note that Bacon goes on to say that teachers of the oriental languages might be found in Paris, while teachers of Greek were numerous in England, France and Italy.

It should not be forgotten that the aim of Bacon's scientific work was as religious as that of the other schoolmen, whose methods and attainments he despised. His aim was the same as theirs, to establish facts of science in order to set Christian theology on a philosophic basis. But his violent methods, his arguments which were not understood and therefore suspect, and his venomous and proud attacks on others brought upon him the same fate that befell Abelard.

Bacon founded no school and his influence was scarcely felt until after the Renaissance. It was otherwise with Duns Scotus (d. 1308) and William of Ockham (d. 1347). We need not, however, pursue Scholastic philosophy into its metaphysical Scotist phase, with its hair-splitting argumentation, its 'hæcceitas' and 'quidditas' and other strange terms. The Thomist position, the union of theology and philosophy, was assailed. The attack did not dislodge St Thomas, but it led to the decay of Scholastic thought. The Scotists lost themselves in the maze of their own strictly logical methods, for his followers lacked the acute philosophical insight of Duns, whose name by a cruel irony has thus become a byword for stupidity (Dunce). Among writers not primarily Scholastics are Ramon Lull (Raymond Lully) (1235–1315), who wrote philosophical works in Latin, but is far better known for his mystical writings in the Catalan language and his zeal for the conversion of the Arabs. Another scientific writer was Peter of Padua or Peter of Abano (1225–1316), interesting in the history of medicine. Of more literary importance is Ægidius Columna, Egidio

Colonna, more often called Gilles de Rome (d. 1316), whose *De Regimine Principum* was the most popular educational work in the thirteenth century. It was written for the benefit of Philippe le Bel to whom Gilles was tutor. When Philip became King of France in 1285, he ordered the book to be translated into French. Soon after it appeared in Italian. Gilles de Rome, who became Archbishop of Bourges in 1294, has often been confounded with an earlier educational writer, Gilles de Paris, Ægidius Parisiensis, whose *Instructio Puerilis* was written about 1200.

Dante Alighieri (1265–1321)

The best known of Dante's Latin works is the *De Monarchia*. It is not certain whether it was written before his exile, to which it contains no reference, or in his later years. It created a storm of indignation among the clergy, not however until after his death. Its main object was to show that the Holy Roman Empire was not a gift to be bestowed or withheld at will by the Roman Pontiff, but itself a divine creation. By Monarchia is meant the Roman Empire, government in all temporal matters by a single Princeps. The subjects of each of the three books of the *De Monarchia* are stated thus (I, 2). ' First, whether it [Universal Monarchy] is necessary for the good of the world. Second, whether the Roman people had a right to claim for themselves the functions of monarchy. Third, whether monarchical authority is derived directly from God, or from some minister or vicar of God.' It will be noticed that the Populus Romanus and the Imperium Romanum are assumed to have persisted throughout the centuries. In the first book after showing that justice and peace, which are essential for the good of the world, can only be obtained under the rule of a single just prince free from cupidity, he crowns his argument by noting that Our Lord waited for the reign of the Divine Augustus before He assumed mortal form. On the question in Book II, whether Rome had a right to empire :

'Dico igitur ad quæstionem quod Romanus populus de iure, non usurpando, Monarchæ officium, quod Imperium dicitur, sibi super mortales omnes adscivit. Quod quidem primo sic probatur. Nobilissimo populo convenit omnibus aliis præferri : Romanus populus fuit nobilissimus ; ergo convenit ei aliis omnibus præferri.'

That the Romans are the most noble race may be proved from their history, from the lives of Æneas, Cincinnatus, Fabricius and many others. Dante, it may be remarked in passing, quotes freely from Virgil and gives Livy and Cicero as his authorities, not merely the popular Orosius. Again it is evident from history that the Roman people were helped by many miracles ; by St Thomas's definition miracles can only take place by the will of God, therefore the Romans obtained their Empire by God's will. Moreover, they were appointed by Nature to rule (ch. 7). And (ch. 9) 'That people which has prevailed when all were striving for world-empire, has prevailed by the divine judgment.' The Assyrian Empire, the Persian and Alexander's all fell.

'Ex quibus omnibus manifestum est quod Romanus populus cunctis athletizantibus pro Imperio mundi prævaluit ; ergo de divino iudicio prævaluit, et per consequens de divino iudicio obtinuit quod est de iure obtinuisse.'

Lastly the Crucifixion itself, had it not been ordered by one having authority from the Emperor Tiberius, would have been a wanton injury not a formal punishment, and God's purpose that Adam's sin should be punished would not have been fulfilled.

It will already be evident that Dante's language and method bear a strong impress of the Scholastics. This is still more evident in the third book. For to prove the direct dependence of the Empire on God and not on His Vicar is a matter requiring theological demonstration rather than historical evidence. Hence we find ourselves faced with such language as :

'Sed ad non nolle alterum duorum sequitur de necessitate, aut velle aut non velle ; sicut ad non odire necessario sequitur aut amare aut non amare : non enim non amare est odire : nec non velle est nolle, ut de se patet. Quæ si falsa non sunt, ista non erit falsa : Deus vult quod non vult ; cuius falsitas non habet superiorem' (III, 2).

The conventional terms of logic are in constant use. For example, when his opponents argue that God's Vicar has temporal power over all things even as He has :

'For they make their syllogism thus : God is Lord of things spiritual and temporal : the chief Pontiff is the vicar of God ; therefore he is lord of things spiritual and temporal. Now both the premisses are true, but there is a difference in the middle term, and the proof rests on four terms: this means that the syllogistic form is last, as is evident from the theory of the simple syllogism. For God, the subject of the major premiss, and the vicar of God, predicated in the minor premiss, are not the same' (ch. 7).

A flaw is also detected in the argument drawn from : 'Whatsoever thou shalt bind on earth shall be bound in heaven, and whatsoever thou shalt loose on earth shall be loosed in heaven.' The notion that the Empire is in the possession of the Church since Constantine surrendered it to her is discounted. Constantine had no authority to alienate his office, nor the Church to receive it. Dante's strongest and most daring argument is that the Empire existed before the Church, and so cannot owe its authority to her.

'Quod autem auctoritas Ecclesiæ non sit causa Imperialis auctoritatis, probatur sic : Illud, quo non existente aut quo non virtuante, aliud habet totam suam virtutem, non est causa illius virtutis ; sed Ecclesia non existente aut non virtuante, Imperium habuit totam suam virtutem : ergo Ecclesia non est causa virtutis Imperii, et per consequens nec auctoritatis, cum idem sit virtus et auctoritas eius ' (ch. 13).

The last chapter (16) summarises the position of Church and Empire, each being shown independently of each other to proceed from God and to answer man's dual need, spiritual and temporal.

'Propter quod opus fuit homini duplici directivo, secundum duplicem finem ; scilicet summo Pontifice, qui secundum revelata humanum genus perduceret ad vitam æternam ; et Imperatore, qui secundum philosophica documenta genus humanum ad temporalem felicitatem dirigeret.'

The unfinished *De Vulgari Eloquentia* was intended both to be a guide to writers, especially poets, using the Italian language and also to vindicate its position in literature. It was written in Latin in order that it might be read by just these people who decried the vernacular. Dante begins by noting the existence of two current idioms, the Vulgar Speech and the literary language, Latin, which is called *Grammatica*. Enquiring into the origin of speech he concludes that, although the first recorded words are those spoken by 'præsumptuosissima Eva ' to the Devil, 'it is absurd to suppose that so important a human act should have been performed first by a woman, not a man.' The oldest language, and the only one before Babel, he finds to be Hebrew. After Babel there was brought to Europe a threefold language ; of those who brought it, those who spoke its northerly form (Teutons, Slavs, etc.) occupied northern Europe. Another section was the Greeks, both in Asia and Europe. The southerly form is that which concerns the present subject. It became divided into (1) those who for 'yes' said 'oc,' that is Spaniards, by which he seems to mean those who spoke Catalan or Provençal, (2) those who said 'oìl,' that is the French, and (3) the Italians who said 'sì.' But since 'omnis nostra loquela . . . nec durabilis nec continua esse potest,' men invented 'grammatica' or Latin, 'quæ quidem grammatica nil aliud est quam quædam inalterabilis locutionis identitas diversis temporibus atque locis.' Of the three vernaculars each has its merits, but the 'sì' idiom is the best and the nearest to Latin. But there are many different varieties of Italian, and it shall be his task to examine them and see if any be the true Vulgar Tongue for which he is seeking. On examination he finds not his native Florentine but the dialect of Bologna to be the best. Yet even that is not the highest form ; the noblest tongue is that which is common to all but native of none—the speech of educated Italians, which we name ' illustre, cardinale, aulicum et curiale vulgare in Latio, quod omnis Latiæ civitatis est et nullius esse videtur.' The second book deals with the use of this ' illustrious, cardinal, courtly and curial tongue,' for what persons and what subjects it is suitable. It is most suitable for poetry, especially for Canzoni (cantiones). He proceeds to describe the structure and proper vocabulary for this kind of poetry. The work breaks off at the fourteenth chapter.

Dante's other Latin works include a number of letters, personal and political, several being of doubtful authenticity ; a curious scientific monograph entitled *Quæstio de Aqua et Terra*, the question being whether the sea is at any point higher than the land ; and lastly two *Eclogæ* in hexameters. They are frankly in imitation of Virgil but they are perfect in execution and have a beauty worthy of the poet of *La Divina Commedia*.

PART V

MEDIEVAL POETRY
(1002–1321)

MEDIEVAL POETRY

THE difference between medieval and classical Latin prose consists in slight changes of vocabulary and construction : the difference between medieval and classical poetry goes much deeper : it is a difference of kind. Medieval poetry in its most characteristic forms is rhythmical, not metrical; the value of the syllables in each line depends upon accent rather than upon quantity; it is meant to be sung, not recited; above all, it has the ornament of rhyme. To trace it to its first beginnings we must go back to such songs in the plays of Plautus as this :

> ' pessuli, heus pessuli,
> vos saluto lubens,
> vos amo, vos volo
> vos peto atque obsecro,
> gerite amanti mihi
> morem, amœnissimi.'—CURCULIO.

And then we have to leap across the centuries, during which Greek metres reigned supreme in Rome and poetry became an artificial product. It is true that the natural trochaic rhythm appears in the soldiers' songs :

> ' urbani, servate uxores, mœchum calvum adducimus.'

> ' disce, miles, militare, Galba est non Gætulicus.'

> ' mille, mille, mille, mille, mille decollavimus,
> unus homo mille, mille, mille decollavimus.'

In one of the Emperor Hadrian's poems also we see both trochaic rhythm and accent overriding quantity :

'Ego nolo Florus esse,
ambulare per tabernas,
latitare per popinas,
culices pati rotundos.'

Finally at the very end of the classical period we have the *Pervigilium Veneris*, where accent and quantity are harmonised in the refrain :

'Cras amet qui nunquam amavit, quique amavit cras amet.'

The triumph of Christianity began a new era. Poetry came to the people and the hymns of Ambrose, '*Æterne rerum conditor*' and the rest, written at a crisis of Church history, were meant to be sung by a congregation. Ambrose, however, kept to the traditional forms and his iambic dimeters strictly observe the rules of quantity. His predecessor Hilary of Poitiers (+ 368) definitely introduces rhyme into his Epiphany hymn :

'Iesus refulsit, omnium
pius redemptor gentium ;
totum genus fidelium
laudes celebret dramatum.'

Augustine goes further, and his 'Psalm against the Donatists' has not only rhyme but also an exact syllabic numbering which is never found in classical verse. Each line has sixteen syllables divided by a cæsura, the accent in each half falling on the penultimate syllable :

'Abundantia peccatorum solet fratres conturbare.
propter hoc dominus noster voluit nos præmonere,
comparans regnum cælorum reticulo misso in mare.'

To the fifth century probably belongs the charming Christian song which begins :

> ' Dormi, fili, dormi ! mater
>   cantat unigenito :
> dormi, puer, dormi ! pater
>   nato clamat parvulo :
> millies tibi laudes canimus,
>   mille, mille, millies.
>
> Lectum stravi tibi soli ;
>   dormi, nate bellule !
> stravi lectum fœno molli ;
>   dormi, mi animule !
> millies tibi laudes canimus,
>   mille, mille, millies.'

Another piece of the same kind is the ' Stella maris,' which was probably sung by many generations before it was written down :

> ' Maris stella est Maria
> Quæ te certa ducet via ;
>   Stellam maris invoca !
>   Inter tribulationum
>   Fluctus et tentationum
>   Hoc celeusma insona ;
>   O Maria,
> Semper dulcis, semper pia ! '

At the end of the sixth century we have the two glorious hymns of Fortunatus, ' *Pange lingua*,' and ' *Vexilla regis*,' written at the greatest moment of his life, when he saw before him a fragment of Our Lord's Cross. The ' *Pange lingua* ' triumphantly captures the rhythm of the Roman legions' march and puts it to the service of the Church militant : the ' *Vexilla regis* ' keeps to iambics but has a wavering assonance, the rhyme in one stanza coming on alternate lines. But much stronger examples of rhyme are to be found in the hymns that were being written in Ireland in Fortunatus' time ; in the ' *Altus prosator*,' for example, commonly attributed to St Columba, who died at Iona in 597 :

275

' Regis regum rectissimi
  Prope est dies domini,
  Dies iræ et vindictæ
  Tenebrarum et nebulæ,
  Diesque mirabilium
  Tonitruorum fortium.'

Even more striking is the piece from the Bangor Antiphonary with its alternate two-syllabled rhymes :

' Navis nunquam turbata,
    Quamvis fluctibus tonsa,
  Nuptiis quoque parata
    Regi domino sponsa.'

The Anglo-Saxon poets of the seventh century and the Carolingian poets of the eighth and ninth contribute little in the way of rhymed verse and preferred laboriously to follow classical models. But Gottschalk (805–869) was a rebel against convention in poetry as in religion, and we have from him not only one of the earliest examples of the leonine hexameter with internal rhyme, but also the long and beautiful rhymed lyric ' *O quid iubes, pusiole.*' Lastly, to the ninth century belongs the curious poem ' *O admirabile Veneris idolum,*' which was once thought to be addressed to a statue of the goddess Venus but is now seen to be the lament of a Veronese clerk deserted by his favourite choir-boy. The first of its three stanzas runs thus :

' O admirabile Veneris idolum,
  Cuius materiæ nihil est frivolum ;
  Archos te protegat, qui stellas et polum
  Fecit, et maria condidit et solum.
  Furis ingenio non sentias dolum :
  Clotho te diligat, quæ baiulat colum.'

' Wonderful, wonderful image of comeliness,
  Substance wherein there is nothing of homeliness ;
  May the Omnipotent guard thee, whom we confess
  Gave sea and land and the heaven its starry dress.
  Never may thievish deceptions thy heart distress,
  But may the distaff of Clotho bring happiness.'

The poet then with considerable ingenuity proceeds to rhyme ' hypothesis ' with ' Lachesis ' and ' Thetis ' and ' Athesis,' the Latin name of the river Adige. In the third and concluding stanza he comes to his real subject : his dear minion has a heart of stone, and has left him for a rival, leaving him ' howling like a deer who cannot find its runaway young.' In the same rhythm, of the same length, and of about the same date is the pilgrims' song, chanted as the travellers came in sight of the eternal city :

> ' O Roma nobilis, orbis et domina,
> Cunctarum urbium excellentissima,
> Roseo martyrum sanguine rubea,
> Albis et virginum filiis candida,
> Salutem dicimus tibi per omnia,
> Te benedicimus ; salve per sæcula.'

> ' Queen of the universe, Rome the victorious,
> Chief among cities, magnificent, glorious,
> Red with the blood of the martyrs who died,
> White with the lilies of virginal pride.
> Lo now with songs of thanksgiving we hail thee ;
> Blessings be thine and may Fortune ne'er fail thee.'

The two poems just quoted are good examples of the last stage in one part of the process whereby medieval Latin poetry originated. In them rhyme is firmly established, although it is still only a monotonous rhyme of one syllable repeated over a number of lines. Accent has definitely superseded quantity and fixes the length of a syllable, so that *Veneris* is scanned as a long and two shorts. Finally, the doctrine that two short syllables are equivalent to one long is abandoned and the number of syllables in all corresponding lines is the same. It remains now to consider the influence of music, and especially of Church music, in creating the new form.

From the very first the Christian ritual was one of song. Whenever two or three gathered together it was occasion for chanting a psalm : as St Cyprian says to his young friend Donatus at the end of their country day : ' Let the sound of psalms be heard at our sober meal ; and as your memory is good and your voice tuneful, do you, as is your wont, undertake that duty. Your friends will relish your good cheer all the more, if we have something spiritual to listen to and the sweetness of religious melody charms our ears.'

So long as Christianity was regarded by the State as a detestable superstition and worshippers met more or less in secret, we may well suppose that these chants were of a very simple character. But with the recognition of Christianity in 331 music, the Cinderella of the arts under Græco-Roman civilisation, was enlisted in the service of the Church, and we begin to get references to a definitely musical liturgy. The Greek church of Antioch became especially famous for its chants, and it was on its example that Ambrose wrote his hymns for antiphonal singing by a congregation, and either composed or borrowed four simple melodies for them. These Ambrosian hymns had a great vogue, and Benedict made them a part of the eight daily services, from matins to compline, which he ordained for his monks. But even more important for our purpose was the development of liturgical music which was proceeding throughout the fifth century and culminated at Rome in the sixth under Gregory the Great. Here too the first steps were taken in the East, and it was probably at Byzantium that plain song was invented. At any rate it was after his return from Byzantium in 585 that Gregory introduced into Western Europe the chants that still bear his name, and established the Schola Cantorum at Rome as a permanent institution. As a result, the music of the Mass became more and more elaborate, and during the seventh century there was a continual importation of fresh melodies from the East which were learned by the professional singers of the school. The responsorial chants, such as the Graduals and Alleluias of the Proprium, in which the choir replies to a solo voice, with a recurring refrain, lent themselves especially to ornate treatment ; and these vocal melodies, unsupported by any instrumental accompaniment, called for considerable skill on the part of the executants. Now while in modern music notation is explicit, in the seventh century it was only implicit, and the proper performance of the Alleluia melodies depended largely on individual training. Accordingly when Charles the Great wished to encourage Church music in his own empire across the Alps he had to send for professionals from Rome. Some of these established themselves at St Gall, others at Metz ; and these two places became the centres from which musical knowledge spread through Germany and France.

But even though the Roman singers did their best, their northern pupils found it difficult to execute the Alleluia Jubilus. It must be remembered that this was not sung to any words in the liturgy—for the words already had their own music—but was a lengthy melodic extension following the final a of the Alleluia, divided into parts each of which was called a Sequence. Therefore as an aid to memory the practice grew up in France and England during the eighth and ninth centuries of adapting words to some of these divisions, this text being called a ' Prosa ' or ' Versus ad sequentias,' and, as an early French example shows, having a very simple form :

Alleluia.

' Qui regis sceptra
Forti dextra
Solus cuncta,

Tu plebi tuam
Ostende magnam
Excitando potentiam,

Præsta dona illi salutaria.

Quem prædixerunt prophetica
Vaticinia,

A clara poli regia
In nostra,
Iesu, veni, domine arva.'

Notker (c. 840–912)

According to the well-known story a French monk
from Jumièges appeared at St Gall one day in 862
after his monastery had been sacked by the Northmen,
bringing with him an antiphonary which contained
examples of these proses. Notker the Stammerer, of
whom we hear so much in Ekkehard's *Casus S. Galli*,
was then living at St Gall, where he studied music
under Ratpert, Iso, and the Irishman Moengal ; and
on reading this antiphonary he determined to improve
upon it by writing a prose where a single syllable
should correspond to each note in the melody. He
also apparently conceived the idea of framing a composition which should include the whole melody of
the Alleluia, and while he kept to the original Jubilus
at the beginning and end, he entirely remodelled the
central portion. One of the first results of his efforts
was the ' *Psallat ecclesia*,' a prose for dedication of a
church :

1. ' Psallat ecclesia,
Mater illibata
Et virgo sine ruga,
Honorem huius ecclesiæ.

280

2. Hæc domus aulæ
Cælestis
Probatur particeps

3. In laude regis
Cælorum
Et ceremoniis

4. Et lumine continuo
Æmulans
Civitatem sine tenebris

5. Et corpora in gremio
Confovens
Animarum, quæ in cælo vivunt ;

6. Quam dextra protegat dei. 7. Ad laudem ipsius diu ! '

It will be seen from this, the first half of the prose, that in style it resembles our ' vers libre ' ; it is rhythmical prose rather than verse as we usually conceive it ; the music is the determining factor and the words are merely added. But the decisive step was taken when the words and melody of the central portion were composed by the same author ; and whether that step was first taken by Notker or by some one else we need not now consider. Henceforth in the Sequences, as in the Tropes of the ' *Gloria* ' and the ' *Kyrie* ' which Notker's friend Tuotilo wrote, the prose became more and more important. Soon to rhythm was added assonance and then rhyme, and finally we have a form that bears a close likeness to the rhymed hymn.

' The Cambridge Songs '

Throughout the tenth century the development of the Sequence went on busily in France, in Germany, and to a less degree in Italy. Notker's sequences were collected—we now possess about forty genuine specimens of his work—and the two first of the four Ekkehards carried on his tradition at St Gall. Tropes also, following the example of Tuotilo, whose famous ' *Hodie cantandus* ' found a place in our Winchester troper, were written by the hundred in Normandy and England and eventually gave rise to the liturgical drama. But while sequences and tropes were religious products and were carefully copied, there was another class of poetry which, as we know now, was being widely written at this time and owes its preservation almost to chance. In the Cambridge University Library there is a manuscript G.g. 5.35, whose last ten pages contain the series of poems which are known as *The Cambridge Songs*. This curious medley, published in facsimile by Dr Breul in 1915, is written on ten leaves of parchment and was apparently copied at the monastery of St Augustine in Canterbury from the song-book of some wandering scholar. It originally contained fifty pieces, thirty of them occasional verse, religious and secular, four passages from Virgil, Horace and Statius, and about a dozen love poems. The first and longest section is chiefly interesting for its series of popular stories, in verse. There is the ' Snow Child,' a Swabian fable of the trick played upon a husband by a wanton wife and the revenge exacted from her ; the ' Swabian and the Hare,' telling how a cunning liar as the result of a wager won a king's daughter in marriage ; ' Elfrida,' the nun whose pet ass was eaten by a wolf ; ' Little John,' the monk who tried to live on herbs but was glad to return to a flesh diet ; and ' Heriger,' a combination of two legends, the man who came back from hell and the man who stole the liver from St Peter in heaven. All these are very well in their way, but their versification is rough when compared with the love poems. Unfortunately, after these latter had been copied on the parchment the authorities seem to have intervened. One leaf of the manuscript apparently has been violently torn out ; three poems, one of them a dialogue between a nun and a clerk, have been very effectively destroyed by erasure and by the use of a tincture of galls ; a fourth, an invitation to supper from a young man to his mistress, has been greatly mutilated. What remains of this last is quite innocent, as some stanzas will prove. The lover speaks and his mistress replies :

' Iam, dulcis amica, venito,
Quam sicut cor meum diligo ;
Intra cubiculum meum
Ornamentis cunctis onustum.

Ego fui sola in silva
Et dilexi loca secreta
Frequenter effugi tumultum
Et vitavi populum multum.

Est ibi mensa apposita
Universis cibis onusta ;
Ibi clarum vinum abundat
Et quicquid te, cara, delectat.

Non me iuvat tantum convivium
Quantum post dulce colloquium,
Nec rerum tantarum ubertas
Ut dilecta familiaritas.'

' Come, darling girl, my sweetest maid,
Dearer than my own heart to me,
For you my chamber waits arrayed
In all its bravery.

" Used to the forests I have grown
And find the woodland quiet sweet.
I hate the clamour of the town
The tumult of the street."

My board with dainty food is set
And golden wine in goblets bright ;
All that a lover's care could get
To furnish you delight.

" I need no feast nor banquet grand,
Such things in me no pleasure move.
Give me sweet converse hand in hand
And the dear joys of love." '

There does not seem to be anything here that calls for serious reproof, and we may suspect that the pieces

which have been erased offered no great insult to
morality. But happily for us the pious censorship of
the Augustine monks had some moments of laxity.
They spared, for example, the Veronese poem ' *O
admirabile Veneris idolum*,' which we have already
quoted ; and they spared the poignant ' Nun's Complaint,' which is the first perfect example of medieval
verse :

> ' Levis exsurgit Zephyrus
> Et sol procedit tepidus ;
> Iam terra sinus aperit
> Dulcore suo diffluit.
>
> Ver purpuratum exiit,
> Ornatus suos induit ;
> Aspergit terram floribus,
> Ligna silvarum frondibus.
>
> Struunt lustra quadrupedes
> Et dulces nidos volucres ;
> Inter ligna florentia
> Sua decantant gaudia.
>
> Quod oculis dum video
> Et auribus dum audio,
> Heu, pro tantis gaudiis
> Tantis inflor suspiriis.
>
> Cum mihi sola sedeo
> Et hæc revolvens palleo,
> Sic forte caput sublevo,
> Nec audio nec video.
>
> Tu saltem, Veris gratia,
> Exaudi et considera
> Frondes, flores, et gramina ;
> Nam mea languet anima.'

> ' Softly now the Zephyr blows,
> Warm the sun in heaven glows,
> Earth unlaces winter's dress
> Diffluent in her loveliness.

Spring comes forth in wanton play,
Dons his coat of colours gay,
Strews the fields with flowery sheen,
Pranks the woods with foliage green.

Beasts dig out their summer lair ;
Little birds their nests prepare,
Singing welcome to the spring
'Neath their leafy covering.

All I hear and all I see
Breathes enchantment : but—ah me !
While the world is full of gladness
I am full of tears and sadness.

Sitting in my lonely cell,
Pale with the thoughts I dare not tell,
If perchance I lift my head
Eyes and ears in trance are dead.

Hearken, hearken, gracious Spring,
And some comfort to me bring.
Bright each flower and fresh each leaf :
But my soul is faint with grief.'

Until we come to the great outburst of song in the twelfth century the 'Nun's Complaint' is almost unique in its appeal to modern sentiment. Nearest to it perhaps is the ' *Lydia*,' a poem of very uncertain date, which does not come in the *Cambridge Songs* but may possibly belong to the tenth century :

' Lydia, bella puella candida,
Quæ bene superas lac et lilium
Album, quæ simul rosam rubidam
Aut expolitum ebur Indicum,
Pande, puella, pande capillulos
Flavos, lucentes ut aurum nitidum ;
Pande, puella, collum candidum
Productum bene candidis humeris ;
Pande, puella, stellatos oculos
Flexaque supra nigra cilia ;
Pande, puella, genas roseas
Perfusas rubro purpuræ Tyriæ ;

285

Porrige labia, labra corallina ;
Da columbarum mitia basia :
Sugis amantis partem animi ;
Cor mi penetrant hæc tua basia :
Quid mi sugis vivum sanguinem ?
Conde papillas, conde semipomas,
Compresso lacte quæ modo pullulant—
Sinus expansus profert cinnama,
Undique surgunt ex te deliciæ—
Conde papillas, quæ me saucias
Candore et luxu nivei pectoris.
Sæva, non cernis quod ego langueo ?
Sic me destituis iam semimortuum ? '

My pretty snow-white maid, that shows
A red more ruddy than the rose,
Yet can with milk and lilies vie
Or polished Indian ivory ;
O let me now those locks behold
Shining with gleams of burnished gold ;
O, let me see that neck of snow
With snow-white shoulders set below
Wherefrom its slender tower doth rise ;
O, let me see those starry eyes
With curving lashes dark as night,
Those vermeil cheeks as roses bright,
Such red a Tyrian dyer dips ;
O press to mine those coral lips,
And let me like some turtle-dove
With tender kisses seal our love.
But no ! You drain my life away ;
I cannot bear your kisses ; stay !
You suck the life blood from my heart,
Your kisses thrill my every part.
Hide, hide the apples of your breast
Swollen with milk in their soft nest ;
Hide, hide your bosom ; left unbound
Its wanton fragrance shed around
Pierces me with delicious pain
And scarce I dare to breathe again.
Ah, cruel, see ! I languid lie !
And would you leave me thus to die ? '

Fulbert (c. 970–1028)

The pieces in the *Cambridge Songs* are mostly anonymous and their date cannot be exactly fixed; but with Fulbert, who is commonly reputed to be the author of *Little John*, we may return to chronological history. Fulbert was born of poor parents, either in Italy or in Aquitaine, about 970, and so forms a link between the tenth and eleventh centuries. He studied under Gerbert at Rheims, and there made the acquaintance of Robert, afterwards King of France, who was a fellow-pupil and later, as a composer of sequences, a fellow-poet with him. It was probably in his early youth that Fulbert wrote the somewhat unclerical *Little John*; for his fame as a scholar was established in early manhood and he was only twenty-seven when he was appointed head of the cathedral school at Chartres. There, first as master, then as chancellor, and finally as bishop, he lived for the rest of his life, making Chartres an educational centre equal to the famous schools of Tours, Fulda, and Rheims in the past. Theology was, of course, the main subject of study; but the humanities were also taught and much attention was paid both to prose and verse composition. In the latter the old metrical and the new accentual system were practised side by side; and Fulbert himself in his monorhymed ' Ode to the Nightingale ' produced a piece which is one of the landmarks in the progress of poetry :

> ' Cum telluris vere novo producuntur germina,
> Nemorosa circumcirca frondescunt et brachia :
> Fragrat odor cum suavis florida per gramina
> Hilarescit Philomela, dulcis sonus conscia,
> Et extendens modulando gutturis spiramina,
> Reddit veris et æstivi temporis præconia.'

The single rhyme continued for twenty-two lines produces to us an effect of monotony, but as an example of that genuine feeling for Nature which was later to be such a feature of medieval verse this poem is of the highest importance.

Fulbert, however, was even greater as a man and a teacher than as a poet. His character won him the respect of all, and in defence of his bishopric he stood up boldly for the rights of the Church whenever they were threatened by the political disturbances of the age. His pupils regarded him with an equal measure of reverence and affection, and one of them, Adelmann of Liége, gives us a vivid picture of his master. ' Do you remember,' he says, ' the evening talks our venerable Socrates used to have with us in the cathedral garden, when he would beg us, with tears that sometimes interrupted speech, not to be led astray into new paths ? ' So another writes : ' At Fulbert's death the study of philosophy in France died with him, and the glory of the Church was extinguished.' But as a matter of fact, his pupils carried on Fulbert's work. Rainald made the school of Angers a resort for scholars of every land. Berengar revived the fame of the school of Tours and handed on the torch to Hildebert. Chartres itself remained for centuries a home of learning, and even to-day cherishes the memory of Fulbert as one of its chief glories.

Alphanus (c. 1020–1086)

What Chartres was to France, the monastery of Monte Cassino was to Italy in the middle of the eleventh century. When Desiderius became abbot there in 1058 the Normans had not yet conquered Southern Italy ; Lombard princes were living in splendour at Benevento, Capua and Salerno ; and under the energetic rule of its new head Monte Cassino, the ancient home of Lombard learning, reached its highest pitch of magnificence. The Basilica was rebuilt, the library enriched with ancient manuscripts, and scholars flocked in from every part of Italy ; among them two poets of remarkable quality, Alphanus and Peter Damiani.

Alphanus was descended from a noble Lombard family and in early manhood studied medicine at the famous school of Salerno. Desiderius met him there, and the two friends after many adventures together both entered Monte Cassino in 1056. In 1058 Alphanus became Bishop of Salerno, and going with the Lombard Prince Gisulf to Byzantium to get help against the Normans was left behind for some years as a hostage. In 1077, however, he had returned to Italy and was in time to intercede with Robert Guiscard who was then besieging Salerno. With Robert's help in his later years he built the church of St Matthew in his cathedral city to hold the bones of the apostle, and when he died in 1086 he with Pope Gregory VII was there buried.

To Ernest Renan the poems of Alphanus seemed ' un dernier souffle de l'antiquité,' and they are indeed an excellent example of the influence for good of classical models on a man imbued with the spirit of humanism. The best of them are the historical odes, such as those in honour of St Matthew and of St Benedict, founder of Monte Cassino. There is also a long hexameter poem on the twelve martyrs of Beneventum, a long ' confession ' in elegiacs, and a fine letter in verse addressed to Hildebrand, in which a lesson for the present is drawn from the past glories of Rome. All these poems, like the sapphics on St Maur, are in classical metres written very carefully

T   289

with due regard to scansion and quantity; and even in his hymns Alphanus seems to keep Horace in mind. This is his description of Paradise:

> ' Illic purpureus rosæ
> Flos et nardus adest, vernat amaracus,
> Floret cum violis crocus,
> Spirant thura thymus, lilia balsamum.
>
> Hymnos angelici chori,
> Condignum resonant carmen apostoli,
> Psallant quem pie martyres,
> Et plectro feriunt tympana virgines.'

Peter Damiani (1007–1072)

Of Damiani's life we have spoken elsewhere, and here we need only consider him as a poet. His verse, like his prose, exhibits medieval religion in its gloomiest and most forbidding aspect. For Damiani life is but a toilsome preparation for death and the world is a place where the devil roams abroad seeking whom he may devour. Terror of the Last Judgment haunts him continually, and in two great poems, written in accentual trochaics, he imagines with the utmost vividness the terrors of that awful day and draws a tremendous picture of the torments that will then await sinners:

> ' Illic dolor, cruciatus, fletus, stridor dentium,
> Adsunt fremitus leonum, sibili serpentium,
> Quibus mixti confunduntur ululatus flentium.'

And yet Damiani's feverish spirit sometimes finds relief. In a beautiful hymn, which was formerly attributed to St Augustine, he sings happily of the glories of Paradise:

> ' Ad perennis vitæ fontem mens sitivit arida,
> Claustra carnis præsto frangi clausa quærit anima,
> Gliscit, ambit, eluctatur exul frui patria.'

' To the fount of life eternal parched with thirst my spirit strains,
  Pent in prison fetters struggles to break loose the body's chains,
  Strives to reach the land whence banished now in exile it remains.'

Of even sweeter music is the mystical commentary
on the *Song of Songs :*

' Quis est hic qui pulsat ad ostium,
  Noctis rumpens somnium ?
  Me vocat : " O virginum pulcherrima,
  Soror, coniunx, gemma splendidissima !
  Cito surgens aperi, dulcissima." '

' Who is it, who, that knocks upon the door
  And breaks my slumber ere the night is o'er ?
  " O fairest, fairest maid, behold ! " he cries,
  " Sister and wife, the jewel that I prize
  Beyond all else, my sweetest, swift arise

And open to me. Lo, I am the Son
First born and last born of the Highest One ;
Who came from heaven to this land of night
And suffered death and many a foul despite,
To free men's captive souls and give them light."

Swiftly I left my bed and ran to meet him,
Drew back the bolt, and stood prepared to greet him.
For my beloved I flung the portal wide
That nothing from my eager heart should hide
Him whom I longed for more than all beside.

Quick did I run : but ah ! I was too late.
None could I see.   He had passed by the gate.
What could I do but follow sad behind,
If so I might the youthful monarch find
Who from the primal clay composed mankind ?

The watchmen stripped me of my purple dress,
And threw a cloak above my nakedness
When in the darkness of the night they caught me,
And then a prisoner to the king's house brought me,
That I should sing the new songs they had taught me.'

Hildebert (1056–1133)

From Italy towards the end of the eleventh century we return to France and to the three chief poets of their time, Hildebert of Lavardin, Marbod of Rennes, and Baudry of Bourgueil. Hildebert was born in 1056, and after studying under Berengar at Tours became in 1091 Archdeacon of Le Mans. William Rufus refused to recognise his election to the bishopric there in 1096, and carried him off as a prisoner to England ; but fortunately his early death saved Hildebert from further persecution and Henry I proved to be a friend. By that time, however, Hildebert was weary of his bishopric and made an ineffectual journey to Rome to ask permission from the Pope to retire. The sight of the eternal city, which in 1084 had been besieged by Henry IV of Germany and then pillaged by the Normans and Saracens under Robert Guiscard, inspired Hildebert to his noble elegy :

> ' Par tibi, Roma, nihil, cum sis prope tota ruina ;
> Quam magni fueris integra fracta doces.'

If Hildebert had written nothing but this one poem his fame would still be secure, for it is so perfect in execution and so thoroughly classical in manner that before its authorship was established it found its way into anthologies of ancient Latin verse. But the *Roman Elegy* is at least almost equalled by the long poem *De Exsilio Suo* in elegiacs, and perhaps even surpassed by the accentual hymn which was so beautifully translated by Crashaw :

> ' Me receptet Sion illa,
> Sion David urbs tranquilla,
> Cuius faber auctor lucis,
> Cuius portæ lignum crucis,

Cuius claves lingua Petri
Cuius cives semper læti,
Cuius muri lapis vivus,
Cuius custos rex festivus :
In hac urbe lux solennis,
Ver æternum, pax perennis :
In hac odor implens cælos,
In hac semper festum melos ;
Non est ibi corruptela,
Non defectus, non querela ;
Non minuti, non deformes,
Omnes Christo sunt conformes.'

' In Sion lodge me, Lord, for pity—
Sion, David's kingly city,
Built by Him that's only good,
Whose gates be of the Cross's wood,
Whose keys are Christ's undoubted word,
Whose dwellers fear none but the Lord,
Whose walls are stone, strong, quick, and bright,
Whose keeper is the Lord of Light :
Here the light doth never cease,
Endless Spring and endless peace ;
Here is music, heaven filling,
Sweetness evermore distilling ;
Here is neither spot nor taint
No defect, nor no complaint ;
No man crooked, great nor small,
But to Christ conformèd all.'

Marbod (1035–1123)

Marbod, Scholasticus of Angers and Bishop of Rennes, was an elder contemporary of Hildebert, and in his own time of almost equal fame with him. But the didactic poems which commended him to his people seem to us slightly tedious. His *Liber Lapidum*, an account of the precious stones in verse, is one of the best of the many lapidaries and bestiaries which were so popular in medieval times, but it has little literary merit. Nor are his leonine hexameters on St Lawrence, the Passion of St Victor, and the Annunciation deserving of much praise. Far more interesting than these to us are the love poems of his youth, for which he afterwards apologised, and the fierce verses on women which he wrote in the sourness of old age. 'Among the countless snares which the crafty foe has spread over all the hills and plains of the world the greatest is woman,' he says in the *De Meretrice*, and in another epigram he cries :

> 'Whoever you are who believe
> In the faith of a woman, take care :
> Believe me, she lives to deceive ;
> She's a woman, as false as she's fair.'

How far these pieces are mere rhetorical declamation is a curious question : but it may be noted that Hildebert, who was rebuked by stern Bishop Iso for his fondness for female society, is also guilty of similar attacks, and writes :

> 'Femina res fragilis, nunquam sine crimine constans,
>   Nunquam sponte sua desinit esse nocens.'
> 'Frail woman, never constant save in crime,
>   Is fain in mischief to pass all her time.'

A better field, however, for Marbod's powers of satire was afforded him by the luxury of his fellow clergy, and on one of them Geoffrey of Vendôme, a minor poet and a most presumptuous abbot, he wrote these stinging lines :

> 'The abbot who tries as a bishop to shine,
> With ring, gloves, and sandals and mitre so fine,
> Can neither as abbot nor bishop be reckoned :
> He's too big for the first and too small for the second.'

Baudry (1046–1130)

The three Frenchmen with whom we are now concerned—and other minor poets also like Guibert of

Nogent and Sigebert of Liége—were all of them
church dignitaries ; but they wore their religion much
more lightly than did Damiani. Baudry in particular,
has none of the Italian's fierce ardour and conviction
of sin, and his poems are of the lightest and most
placid character. Born near Orleans in 1046, Baudry
migrated to Angers and thence to the monastery of
Bourgueil where he became Abbot in 1089. In 1107
he was elected Bishop of Dol in Brittany, but he liked
neither the country nor the people, and spent much
of his later life visiting the Benedictine monasteries in
England and Normandy, until in 1130, old and famous,
he died.

Baudry is important as being a new type of medieval
churchman. By profession a cleric, he was by choice
a man of letters, one of the first of those humanists
who were to give so different an aspect to life. In
original genius he is quite lacking but it is plain from
his writings that such poetical talent as he had was
his dearest possession, and that he considered literature
the greatest treasure in existence. His own poems,
chiefly in elegiacs, are all inspired by this love of art,
and like a minor poet to-day he took care to have
them handsomely produced on fine parchment with
initial letters in gold or colour. His longest poem,
addressed to Adela, daughter of William the Conqueror, is in the form of a vision where he describes at
prodigious length the tapestries that adorn Adela's
bedroom. One of these pictures represents the battle
of Hastings, and it is possible that the poem may have
been suggested by the Bayeux tapestry. Its purpose,
however, is quite practical : Baudry wanted Adela's
protection and he wanted her to give him a cope.
In such gifts the poet took a particular delight and one
of his most charming pieces is a letter of thanks in

verse to the Abbot of Séez who had sent him some tablets of green wax and a fine stilus. In another set of verses he tells us, as Martial did before him, what are the things he most desires ; a country life with friends, a garden, books, and wine. Under these conditions his poetry was composed : when he was transferred to the bleak rocks of Brittany he abandoned verse for prose and wrote the *History of Jerusalem* by which until lately he was chiefly known. Of the Latin poets Ovid was his favourite, but he has nothing of Ovid's naughtiness or narrative skill : in his character as in his writings he is more like a mild copy of Ausonius.

Abelard (1079–1142)

The great writer who ushers in the glories of the twelfth century is of a very different type from Baudry. Abelard, whose life has been narrated elsewhere, was a scholar, a philosopher, a theologian, an orator, and above all a poet. In his early manhood he composed for Heloïse songs which, as she says, were heard in every house and in every street ; but though some of these may have been preserved in the ' Carmina Burana,' that is only a matter of uncertain conjecture, and of his acknowledged verse we now only possess, his hymns, sequences and six *Complaints*. It may be, however, that it was because of these love poems that Bernard of Clairvaux gave him the name of ' Goliath,' for this kind of verse is the antithesis of David's pious minstrelsy ; and if so, it is just possible that Abelard was the original ' Bishop Golias,' father of the ' Goliardi,' whose personality has been such a puzzle to literary historians.

In any case, the hymns, like the songs, were composed for Heloïse who wished to have something that her nuns at the Paraclete might sing ' during the whole cycle of the year.' At her request Abelard wrote three books of hymns, the first for the canonical hours from matins to compline, the second for festivals, the third for Saints' days. All are beautiful, but perhaps the best is the Sabbath Vespers :

> ' O quanta, qualia sunt illa sabbata,
> Quæ semper celebrat superna curia !
> Quæ fessis requies, quæ merces fortibus,
> Cum erit omnia deus in omnibus ! '

More simple in its rhythm but equally melodious is the hymn for the feast of the Holy Innocents :

> ' Est in Rama
> Vox audita
> Rachel flentis,
> Super natos
> Interfectos
> Eiulantis.'

Of the sequences the best known is that on the Annunciation, which begins :

> ' Mittit ad virginem
> Non quemvis angelum,
> Sed fortitudinem
> Suam, archangelum
> Amator hominis.'

The six *Complaints* on subjects taken from the early books of the Old Testament, display an equal variety of verse forms, and have by some critics been considered as expressing Abelard's own personal sorrows. In Samson we are to see Abelard himself after his disgrace ; in Dinah Heloïse victim of an unhallowed passion ; in the virgins of Israel weeping for the daughter of Jephthah the nuns of the Paraclete gathered round the altar :

297

' Ad festas choreas cælibes
  Ex more venite virgines !
    Ex more sint odæ flebiles
    Et planctus ut cantus celebres !
Incultæ sint mæstæ facies
  Plangentium et flentum similes !
    Auratæ sint longe cyclades
    Et cultus sint procul divites.'

Bernard of Clairvaux (1090–1153)

Abelard's great opponent, Bernard Abbot of Clairvaux, wrote poetry but his fame is not based upon his verse. It was as a spiritual director that Bernard, *doctor mellifluus*, wielded his immense influence on the men of his age. From the time when he founded Clairvaux in 1115, until his death in 1153, he ruled the destinies of Christendom, and when one of his pupils was elected Pope as Eugenius III his authority became paramount. Bernard was a pure mystic, the enemy alike of theological subtlety and philosophic reason, and his prose writings express in the most glowing language the emotions that his conception of Jesus as a personal friend evoked in his heart. But in the hymns that are certainly from his pen there is little trace of this poetical fervour, and although the beautiful ' *Iubilus rhythmicus de nomine Iesu* ' has been attributed to him, it is of such different character from his known verse that it seems unlikely that he was the author. Still, the poem is plainly inspired by his mysticism, and some lines from it will give an idea of Bernard's mode of thought :

' Iesu dulcis memoria,
  Dans vera cordi gaudia,
  Sed super mel et omnia
  Eius dulcis præsentia.'

298

> ' Nil canitur suavius,
> Auditur nil iucundius,
> Nil cogitatur dulcius
> Quam Iesu dei filius.'

Bernard of Morlas (born c. 1200)

At Cluny, Peter the Venerable, himself a minor poet but a very great man, gave Abelard refuge ; and at Cluny under Peter's rule lived Bernard of Morlas who dedicated to his abbot the ' *De contemptu mundi*,' one of the most remarkable poems of the twelfth century. It extends to close on three thousand lines, dactylic hexameters with both internal and end rhymes, and it is an astonishing piece of craftsmanship, only rendered possible, as the author tells us, by the help of divine inspiration. The first of its three books begins :

> ' Hora novissima, tempora pessima sunt, vigilemus :
> Ecce minaciter imminet arbiter ille supremus.'

> ' The world is very evil,
> The times are waxing late :
> Be sober and keep vigil ;
> The Judge is at the gate.'

Therefore, says Bernard, let men avoid evil and choose good, and by labour they shall win at last the joys of heaven. Then follows the best known passage in the poem, the ecstatic description of Paradise, from which Dr Neale drew his hymn ' Jerusalem the golden, with milk and honey blessed.'

> ' Urbs Syon aurea, patria lactea, cive decora,
> Omne cor obruis, omnibus obstruis et cor et ora.'

Even here, however, Bernard cannot forget the sins of this world, and he breaks out into self-reproach :

' O land without guilt, strong city safe built in a marvellous place,
   I cling to thee, ache for thee, sing to thee, wake for thee, watch
     for thy face.
Full of cursing and strife are the days of my life, with their sins
   they are fed,
Out of sin is the root, unto sin is the fruit, in their sins they
   are dead.
No deserving of mine can make answer to thine, neither I unto
   thee ;
I a child of God's wrath, made subject to death, what good
   thing is in me ?
Yet through faith I require thee, through hope I desire thee, in
   hope I hold fast,
Crying out day and night that my soul may have sight of thy joy
   at the last.'—Tr. A. C. SWINBURNE.

The picture of Paradise is but a short interlude, and
the tremendous recital of the punishments that await
the wicked, ' Weep, ye guilty. God is preparing for
you a fiery furnace,' continues with an accumulation
of horror for the rest of Book I. Book II begins with
an account of the Golden Age now unfortunately past,
and then comes to the writer's own generation, ' which
lives in sin, praises sin, and is wholly given over to
rivalry in sin.' Every order of society, clerical and
secular alike, according to Bernard, is tainted with
crime, ' a race of asses, revelling in drunkenness and
vice.' The word ' vice ' leads at once to ' woman ' ;
and the rest of the second book is an attack on the
female sex which for coarseness of detail and ferocity
of invective puts even Juvenal into the shade :

   ' Femina res rea, res male carnea, vel caro tota,
     Strenua perdere, nataque fallere, fallere docta.
     Fossa novissima, vipera pessima, pulchra putredo,
     Semita lubrica, res male publica, prædaque prædo.'

'A creature of crime, a thing for all time fleshly evil, just flesh
   without mind,
Ever busy to harm, taught to use nature's charm for mischief, in woman we find ;

> The foulest of jakes, the most deadly of snakes, fair outside
> and corruption within,
> A path where you trip, she strips those who strip her, a public
> incentive to sin.'

The third book continues in the same strain, although it now deals with the sins of Sodom and Gomorrha. Then follows an attack on the luxury and ostentation of rich prelates ; and so we come to the familiar subject of the venality of the Papal Curia and the general corruption of Rome. At last Bernard says that he can write no more of these evils and ends with a prayer to Christ :

> ' Respice, respice nos, patris unice origine nate ;
> Da mala plangere, da bona sumere, da tua, da te.
> Aurea tempora primaque robora redde, rogamus ;
> Nos modo dirige, postmodo collige, ne pereamus.'

Alan of Lille (1128–1202)

About the same time that Bernard was writing at Cluny, Alanus de Insulis, otherwise Alan of Lille, *doctor universalis* and pupil of Bernard Silvestris, author of the *De mundi universitate*, was composing his long allegorical poems the *Anticlaudianus* and the *De planctu naturæ*. Of these two the latter may well be left unread, for it treats of those unnatural vices which were the curse of monastic life. Written in a mixture of prose and verse it is in the form of a dialogue between Nature and the poet, who addresses to the world mother a long sapphic ode :

> ' O dei proles, genetrixque rerum,
> Vinculum mundi stabilisque nexus,
> Gemma terrenis, speculum caducis,
> Lucifer orbis.'

Far more worthy of study is the ' *Anticlaudianus*,' which derives its name from a statement made by Claudianus Mamertus that the soul had its origin

' out of something.' Alan believed that Nature formed man's body from the four elements, but the soul was created from nothing by God's will ; and in his poem he traces the operations of God, Nature, Fortune, and Vice. Nature, dissatisfied with her works, desires to make a perfect man and calls her sisters, the Virtues, to a council in her garden. To them she explains her wish to create a being who ' on earth shall be human and among the stars divine.' Prudence reminds her that only God can provide this being with a soul, and on the motion of Reason, seconded by Concord, the council dispatches Prudence to present Nature's petition to the court of heaven. For the journey a splendid chariot is made by the Seven Arts, daughters of Prudence ; the five senses are its horses and Reason holds the reins. On her way to heaven Prudence learns all the mysteries of nature ; she sees the demons who have been cast down from the sky ; she passes beyond the planets and the fixed stars ; and at last she reaches the limits of the world of sense where Reason can no longer guide her. At this point a maiden appears at heaven's summit, the goddess Theology, who takes Reason's place, and, the poet, dismissing ' earthly Apollo,' invokes new inspiration from the ' heavenly Muse.' A long description of the Christian heaven follows, with its orders of angels, saints, martyrs, and doctors. But first above all in honour is the Virgin :

> ' Hæc est stella maris, vitæ via, porta salutis,
> Regula iustitiæ, limes pietatis, origo
> Virtutis, veniæ mater, thalamusque pudoris,
> Hortus conclusus, fons consignatus, oliva
> Fructificans, cedrus redolens, paradisus amœnans.'

Prudence is dazzled by the glories she beholds, and Faith has to come to her aid when she enters the presence of the Trinity. Here her request is granted : God creates a soul, Nature fashions a body, Concord unites the two, the Virtues and the Arts bestow their gifts. Then the palace of Fortune with her famous wheel is visited and Man is ready to return to earth. But the powers of evil have heard of the new creation, and a fierce conflict for man's soul ensues in which Virtue triumphs ; and the poem ends.

The English Satirists

The first purely secular English poet is Serlon of Wilton (fl. 1160), of whom two striking tales are told. When he was a student at Paris, Serlon was a loose liver and wrote licentious verse. One day he visited a friend on his death-bed and asked him to return from purgatory to tell his experiences. Next night the dead man appeared, wearing a parchment gown on which was written a mass of scholastic arguments. ' This gown,' he said, ' weighs heavier on me than a church tower ' : and when he stretched out his hand and touched Serlon his fingers burned the flesh to the bone. Thus it was that Serlon abandoned the world and became a Cistercian monk. The other story, which comes from Giraldus Cambrensis, concerns his later life. Gerald went to see Bishop Baldwin of Worcester and found with him an old man in the white robes of a Cistercian abbot. The old man was Serlon, and as Gerald entered he looked intently at him and murmured ' Can youth so fair ever die ? '

Serlon's extant poems, as might be expected, are of two kinds. Those of his old age, such as his ' Farewell to the world,' with its elegiac refrain ' *mundus abit*,' are deeply religious and somewhat lacking in vigour. Those of his youth, though far less edifying, are surprisingly original and deserve to be better known.

303

Some of them are in leonine hexameters, such as the complaint to a venal beauty :

> ' Te voco Näida, sentio Thäida, scireque nolo ;
> Et prece nequeo, te mihi mulceo munere solo.'

> ' I call you a maid, but I feel you're a jade
> Though I wish not to know it.
> When I ask for a kiss, your reply is just this
> " Money down ! You can't owe it." '

But most of Serlon's youthful verse is in the elegiac metre and is concerned with light amours :

> ' Pronus erat Veneri Naso, sed ego mage pronus.
> Pronus erat Gallus, sed mage pronus ego.'

As we have said, the morality of these poems is of a very loose kind, but their technical skill is remarkable, and Ovid himself might have written the piece that begins :

> ' Quadam nocte loco quodam cum virgine quadam
> Solus eram : soli sola maligna fuit.'

In England the nearest equivalent to the French centres of learning in the twelfth century is to be found in the household of the Archbishop of Canterbury. There under Theobald (1139–1162), and later under Thomas à Becket was gathered a group of men of really remarkable talent, a group which included John of Salisbury, Roger of Pont-l'Évêque, Walter Map, and Gerald de Barri. Of these John of Salisbury is, of course, chiefly known for his prose ; but he is also the author of the long didactic and satirical poem *Entheticus de dogmate philosophorum*, written at Becket's request, in which he summarises the opinions of the various schools of philosophy. Like Lactantius before him, he lays stress on the truth that philosophy and religion are identical :

> ' Si verus deus est hominum sapientia vera
> Tunc amor est veri philosophia dei.'

Then, after classifying the chief philosophies, John turns to satire and bitterly attacks the corruption of his own time, ending finally with praise of the society of Canterbury, but pointing out that even there fools and knaves abound and that it is not the monk's garb, black or white, which will save him at the last but only the divine grace :

> ' Excipit infernus pereuntes veste remota,
> Nec minuit pœnam tetra vel alba suam.'

Gerald de Barri, otherwise Giraldus Cambrensis, and Walter Map are also two prose writers who only occasionally used verse. Here it will suffice to quote the couplet which Gerald had inscribed over his stall at St David's :

> ' Vive deo, tibi mors requies, tibi vita labori,
> Vive deo ; mors est vivere, vita mori.'

To Walter Map, however, a large number of the Goliardic poems in the *Carmina Burana*, to which we shall refer later, were once attributed. They certainly are not his, but many of the anonymous satirical pieces in that and other collections may well be the work of English poets of Map's day. The best of them is the ' Apocalypse of Golias,' a poem of 440 lines. The poet lying under an oak tree falls asleep and dreams that he meets Pythagoras, and with him passes into another world where he finds Aristotle, Cicero, Lucan and most of the great Roman poets. Then an angel appears with seven candles, and the rest of the piece is a fierce attack on the seven orders of the clergy from the Pope down to the monk :

> ' Est nullum monacho maius dæmonium,
> Nihil avarius, nil magis varium ;
> Qui, si quid datur, est possessor omnium ;
> Si quicquam petitur, nil habet proprium.'

Of the same character are the various sermons and verse discourses supposed to be delivered by Bishop Golias. The duplicity of monks and the arrogance of the higher clergy are their favourite themes; and above all the venality of the Papal Curia. This last is the especial subject of the well-known piece in 180 lines which begins:

> ' Propter Syon non tacebo
> Sed ruinam Romæ flebo,
>   Quousque iustitia
> Rursus nobis oriatur
> Et ut lampas accendatur
>   Iustus in ecclesia.'

We still have to mention the three dialogues, ' Wine against Water,' ' The heart and the eye,' and ' The body and the soul '; and also the amusing *De conjuge non ducenda*, a discourse against marriage based on the wise advice of Ss. Peter, John, and Lawrence:

> ' Qui ducit coniugem se nimis onerat
> A cuius onere mors sola liberat.
> Vir servit coniugi et uxor imperat,
> Et servus factus est qui liber fuerat.'

Whether these poems were written by Englishmen can scarcely be proved, but England during the twelfth century was certainly the chief home of Latin satirical and didactic poetry. Godfrey of St Swithins and Henry of Huntingdon both wrote epigrams in the manner of Martial; Reginald of Canterbury a verse life of the hermit Malchus; Hilary, a pupil of Abelard, three verse plays; Geoffrey de Vinsauf a *Poetria Nova*, a kind of *Ars Poetica* with examples by himself; and Joseph of Exeter an epic poem on the Trojan War. More definitely satirical than any of these is the

Architrenius or 'Arch-mourner' of John de Hanville (fl. 1184), an ambitious but rather tiresome piece in hexameters. The hero is a young man who, lamenting his wasted life, determines to ask Mother Nature for a remedy. On his way to her he visits the palace of Venus and the hall of Gluttony, and so comes to Paris, where he notes the hardships of the students' lives and the fruitlessness of their studies. Proceeding further he reaches the mount of Ambition, where kings and their courtiers waste their time in vain show, and then the hill of Presumption, a haunt of monks, clergy, and scholastic professors. Finally the pilgrim comes to Nature herself, who remedies all his troubles by the gift of a fair bride—Moderation.

More amusing than the 'Arch-mourner,' and much more caustic in its wit, is the *Speculum Stultorum* of Nigel Wireker, precentor of Christchurch, Canterbury († 1200). The 'Mirror of Fools' is a long elegiac account of the adventures of the ass Brunellus— 'brunellus' diminutive of 'brown' as 'donkey' is diminutive of 'dun'—and under the figure of the ass who wants a longer tail Nigel satirises the monk who desires to become prior or abbot. Brunellus first consults Galen and is sent off to Salerno with a prescription, which he is to bring back in a glass bottle. On his way, however, he is stripped bare by robbers and loses half the small tail he had. Ashamed to return home, he joins the English 'nation' at the University of Paris, and after studying the liberal arts for seven years finds that he still knows nothing. He therefore turns from the arts to theology, and tries all the monastic orders. Then he meets Galen once more, and discusses with him the general corruption of society, the ambition of kings, the pride of bishops, and the venality of the Papal Curia at Rome. Finally his old master Bernard appears and Brunellus returns to the cloister as a simple monk.

The last two English didactic poets of this period are John Garland and Alexander Neckham. John Garland, born 1180, took part in the Albigensian crusade and was for a time professor at Toulouse. He wrote various educational treatises in verse, one of them an *Accentuarium*, another *Exempla honestæ vitæ*, and also a long historical poem *De triumphis ecclesiæ*: but as literature none of these has any great merit. A much more skilful writer is Alexander Neckham, born 1157, foster-brother of King Richard. Neckham was a polymath and produced a *Physiologus*, a Bestiary, and a very curious book *De Naturis Rerum*, which is partly an encyclopædia of natural science and partly a commentary on Ecclesiastes. This treatise in his later years Neckham put into verse with the title *De laudibus divinæ sapientiæ*, and it was probably in his old age that he composed the *De vita monachorum*, if indeed that satire is his. Whether by Neckham or not, it is a very striking poem, and one of the best examples of medieval misogyny. To the author Woman is Satan's flaming torch, and he cries :

> ‘ A woman has a thousand ways to work her will upon us,
> She prides herself the more, the more of evil she has done us.
> Most mischievous of all created things the devil in her
> Beholds his perfect instrument, the true predestined sinner.’

Adam of St Victor (born c. 1110)

The satirists, as might be expected, deal with the darker side of church life : we must now return to France and to the religious poems in which the faith of the Middle Ages finds its highest expression. The first famous name is that of the Breton poet Adam, who entered the Augustinian monastery of St Victor about 1130 and lived there in peaceful seclusion for the greater part of the twelfth century. We are told that his favourite retreat was the Virgin's chapel in the abbey crypt and that there one day when he was repeating some verses he had composed in Mary's honour her image greeted him and gave him thanks. At St Victor he died, and the following epitaph was placed upon his tomb :

> ' Post hominem vermis, post vermem fit cinis, heu, heu !
> Sic redit ad cinerem gloria nostra suum.
> Hic ego qui iaceo miser et miserabilis Adam
> Unam pro summo munere posco precem :
> Peccavi, fateor, veniam peto ; parce fatenti :
> Parce pater, fratres parcite, parce deus.'

The exact number of sequences that can be attributed to Adam is a matter of doubt, but probably we have now about forty that are certainly from his hand. His poetry is essentially dogmatic and he is continually setting forth those symbolical interpretations of Scripture and the world around us which were the special delight of the theological school of St Victor. Of lyrical beauty he has little, for he keeps strictly to his subject, which is usually the feast of an apostle or martyr, and there is some justice in Remy de Gourmont's criticism :

> ' Il lui manque de joindre à son génie d'artiste un peu de la folie de l'amour, un peu de l'envol du mysticisme ; il lui manque encore une originalité réelle de pensée.'

The greatness of Adam as a poet consists not in loftiness of thought or fervour of feeling but in perfect mastery of form. Even Abelard is inferior to him in skill of versification and in smoothness of rhythm ; and for one great change Adam alone is chiefly responsible. He may indeed be considered the father of modern poetry, for he is the first writer who uses with any real art the two-syllabled rhyme on which most of our effects depend. The first third of his sequence in honour of St Stephen will give an example of the new beauty that he brings into verse ·

> ' Heri mundus exsultavit
> Et exsultans celebravit
> Christi natalitia ;
> Heri chorus angelorum
> Prosecutus est cælorum
> Regem cum lætitia
>
> Protomartyr et levita,
> Clarus fide, clarus vita,
> Clarus et miraculis,
> Sub hac luce triumphavit
> Et triumphans insultavit
> Stephanus incredulis
>
> Fremunt ergo tanquam feræ,
> Quia victi defecere,
> Lucis adversarii ;
> Falsos testes statuunt
> Et linguas exacuunt
> Viperarum filii.
>
> Agonista, nulli cede,
> Certa certus de mercede,
> Persevera, Stephane !
> Insta falsis testibus
> Confuta sermonibus
> Synagogam Satanæ.'

Philip de Grève (c. 1180–1236)

Adam of St Victor was followed in the thirteenth century by a whole school of sequence writers who took pattern by him as far as the outward form of their verse was concerned. In France the most interesting of them is Philip de Grève. Philip was born in Paris about 1180, and after receiving there the best education

that his age could give he was appointed in 1218
Chancellor of the Paris Church. His fierce quarrels
with the University and with the Popes who failed to
support him were the chief episodes in his life ; but
for us he is more important as a poet than as a man of
affairs, and in poetry it is his hymns rather than his
satirical verse which form his true title to fame. Philip
could certainly be very bitter, as he shows in *Bulla
fulminante*, a verse attack on the corruption and
venality of the Roman Curia :

> ' Papæ ianitores
> Cerbero surdiores
> In spe vana plores,
> Nam etiamsi fores
> Orpheus quem audiit
> Pluton, deus
> Tartareus,
> Non ideo perores,
> Malleus argenteus
> Ni feriat ad fores
> Ubi Protheus
> Variat mille colores.'

Equally provocative is his prose Advent sermon in
which he compares the doctors of Paris University to
cocks who should wake men from sleep but prefer to
fight among themselves. But Philip could also write
hymns full of tender sweetness, such as the lines for
St Mary Magdalene :

> ' Pange, lingua, Magdalenæ
> Lacrimas et gaudium,
> Sonent voces laude plenæ
> De concentu cordium,
> Ut concordet philomenæ
> Turturis suspirium.'

And for mystical grace his verses on the Virgin can
hardly be surpassed :

'O Maria, virginei
        Flos honoris,
Vitæ via, lux fidei,
        Pax amoris.
O regina, tu laquei,
        Tu doloris
Medicina, fons olei,
        Vas odoris.'

Stephen Langton (d. 1228)

From France we come to England and to Stephen
Langton, Archbishop of Canterbury, who is almost
certainly the author of the 'Golden Sequence,' 'Veni
sancte spiritus.' It is true that this has been attributed
to King Robert the Pious († 1031), to Hermann the
Lame († 1054), and to Pope Innocent III; but
Langton has much the most substantial claims. At
what time in his life Langton composed the masterpiece is quite uncertain; it may have been before
1206 when he was appointed Archbishop of Canterbury;
it may have been after 1215 when he was the directing
force behind the barons in wresting Magna Carta
from King John; but in any case the date is unimportant compared with the sequence itself.

'Veni, sancte spiritus,
    Et emitte cælitus
        Lucis tuæ radium ;

Veni, pater pauperum,
Veni, dator munerum,
    Veni lumen cordium.

Consolator optime,
Dulcis hospes animæ,
    Dulce refrigerium ;

In labore requies,
In æstu temperies,
        In fletu solacium.'

Thomas Aquinas (c. 1226–1274)

From England we pass to Italy, where Thomas
Aquinas was born about 1226. His father was Count
of Aquinum, but Thomas from his early youth was
drawn to the Church and in his twentieth year joined
the Order of the Dominicans who were then introducing Aristotle to the Catholic world. Upon the
young Italian the Greek thinker made the most profound impression ; indeed the influence of Aristotle is
seen as plainly in his poetry as in his prose, and his
great sequence *Lauda Sion* is as severely logical as
the *Summa Theologica*. This sequence was composed
in 1264 when Urban IV instituted the new festival of
Corpus Christi. Until then there had been no special
celebration of the central mystery of the Catholic
faith. But in the early years of the thirteenth century
a certain Belgian nun named Juliana saw in a vision a
full moon sullied by one black spot. The moon was
the Church, the black spot was the omission of a feast
in honour of Christ's Body, an omission which Urban
rectified when he established the festival and commissioned Thomas to write the office for the day.
As a result we have not only the Vespers hymn *Pange
lingua gloriosi corporis mysterium*, but the magnificent
sequence whose first strophes run thus :

> ' Lauda Sion salvatorem,
> Lauda ducem et pastorem
>   In hymnis et canticis.
> Quantum potes tantum aude,
> Quia maior omni laude,
>   Nec laudare sufficis.
>
> Laudis thema specialis
> Panis vivus et vitalis
>   Hodie proponitur,

313

Quem in sacræ mensa cenæ
Turbæ fratrum duodenæ
   Datum non ambigitur.

Sit laus plena, sit sonora,
Sit iucunda, sit decora
   Mentis iubilatio :
Dies enim sollemnis agitur
In qua mensæ prima recolitur
   Huius institutio.'

The sequence extends to eighty lines, and while it is a clear dogmatic exposition of the true faith it is also a poem of the most austere grandeur, superior in elevation of thought to any of Adam's and at least equalling him in artistry.

John Pecham (c. 1230–1292)

From Italy we return to our own country, for the next great religious poet is an Englishman, John Pecham, Archbishop of Canterbury. Pecham was born near Lewes about 1230, and after studying at Oxford migrated to Paris, where he listened to Bonaventura and himself gave lectures in Theology. Returning to England about 1270 he became Provincial of the English Franciscans, and some years later ' lector sacri palati,' lecturer in divinity at the papal school in Rome. In 1279 Pope Nicholas III appointed him Archbishop of Canterbury, and that post he held until his death in 1292.

Pecham in his poems is one of the best representatives of the new spirit introduced into the Church by Francis of Assisi—' mihi absit gloriari nisi in cruce Domini.' In Pecham, even better than in Bonaventura or in his English predecessor John of Hoveden, we find that note of personal grief, that brooding over Christ's sufferings and passion, which appears in all the literature and all the art which draws its inspiration from

Franciscan Christianity; and in the *Philomena*, his greatest work, this devotional fervour is accompanied by a consummate poetical skill. Of the Philomena Mr Raby gives an admirable analysis in his *Christian Latin Poetry*, p. 426.

'The subject of the poem is the nightingale, the forerunner of the spring, the bird who, "in her saddest, sweetest plight," sings a song which typifies the crying out of the soul for the heavenly country. For the nightingale, when she perceives that she is near to death, flies to a tree top, and at dawn pours forth her song. When the day begins to break, she sings without pause ever louder at the hour of prime, and at tierce the joy and passion of her song increase, until it seems as if her throat must burst with the torrent of melody. Then at last, when noon arrives, her body can endure no longer; Oci, Oci, she cries, and in the anguish of her song she sinks and fails. At none she dies, her tiny body shattered and broken. The nightingale is the type of the pious soul, which longs for the heavenly country, and, longing, beguiles itself with song. So it lives, as it were, through a mystical day, the hours of which correspond to the stages of its redemption. Dawn is the stage of man's creation; Prime the season of the incarnation of Christ; Tierce is the period of His life on earth. Sext represents the hour of His betrayal, scourging, and crucifixion, None of His death, and Vespers of His burial. Stage by stage the soul follows in meditation, and out of its meditation fashions a song. The sweetness and sadness of the meditation increase as the hour of the Passion approaches, and the soul remembers the sufferings of the Redeemer, in which it longs to share, until, at the hour of the *Consummatum est*, it fails and dies in the ecstasy of love and compassion.'

The poem is written in stanzas of four lines, each line containing thirteen syllables, and it is mono-rhymed. As a specimen of its rhythm we may take the lines where the poet wishes that he might have ministered to the Infant Jesus:

'Heu me, cur non licuit mihi demulcere
Vagientem parvulum, dulciter tenere,
Illos artus teneros sinu refovere,
Eiusque cunabulis semper assidere!'

315

Jacopone da Todi (c. 1230–1306)

According to the story Jacopone until he was forty years old was a rich and successful lawyer. Then his young and beautiful wife was killed in an accident, and when they took the clothes from her body they found a hair shirt next to her skin. Overcome with grief and remorse Jacopone sold his goods, gave the money to the poor, and took to the road as a religious vagrant, bearing shame and indignity ' for the love of Jesus Christ who bore such shame for the human race.' For ten years he followed this life, composing meanwhile in the Umbrian dialect innumerable *laude*, short dramatic poems on the miracles of the Virgin, the gospel of St Francis, the joys of divine love and paradise. Finally, about the year 1280, he was admitted to the Franciscan Order as a Brother Minor, his election, if we may believe the legend, being secured by his Latin poem *De Contemptu Mundi* :

> ' Cur mundus militat sub vana gloria,
> Cuius prosperitas est transitoria ?
> Tam cito labitur eius potentia
> Quam vasa figuli, quæ sunt fragilia.'

Once within the Order Jacopone threw himself fiercely into ecclesiastical politics. Money he hated, knowledge he despised : ' Paris has destroyed Assisi,' he said ; and his one desire was that every Franciscan should follow the example of their great founder. In 1295 he attacked Pope Boniface VIII in scurrilous verses, and by him was thrown into an underground prison from which he did not escape until the death of Boniface in 1303. Three years later Jacopone himself passed away, and on his tomb at Todi to-day the following sixteenth-century inscription may be read :

> ' Ossa beati Jacoponi de Benedictis, Tudertini, fratris ordinis minorum, qui stultus propter Christum nova mundum arte delusit, et cælum rapuit.'

The circumstances of Jacopone's life supply the only argument against his authorship of the ' Stabat mater ' ; but as that sublime sequence is definitely assigned to him by three early manuscripts and all other attributions lack any real evidence, we may reasonably give it to him. It is in form a strict sequence, and of its ten stanzas the first two are here given :

> ' Stabat mater dolorosa
> Iuxta crucem lacrimosa,
>   Dum pendebat filius ;
> Cuius animam gementem
> Contristantem et dolentem
>   Pertransivit gladius.
>
> O quam tristis et afflicta
> Fuit illa benedicta,
>   Mater unigeniti.
> Quæ mœrebat et dolebat
> Et tremebat cum videbat
>   Nati pœnas incliti.'

Thomas of Celano (fl. 1225)

> ' Dies iræ, dies illa,
> Solvet sæclum in favilla,
> Teste David cum Sibylla.
>
> Quantus tremor est futurus,
> Quando index est venturus,
> Cuncta stricte discussurus !
>
> Tuba mirum sparget sonum
> Per sepulcra regionum,
> Coget omnes ante thronum.

317

Mors stupebit et natura,
Cum resurget creatura
Indicanti responsura.'

' O day of wrath, O dreadful day—
Hear David and the Sibyl say—
When earth in fire shall pass away.

How all the world will shake in fear
To see the Almighty Judge appear
And know that vengeance draweth near !

Then shall the awful trump be blown,
Each grave its wondrous power shall own,
The dead must come before the throne.

Nature and Death shall stricken fall
When God's creations one and all
Rise in obedience to His call.'

So begins the greatest of medieval religious poems, the *Dies Iræ*, commonly attributed to Thomas of Celano, a Brother Minor and the biographer of St Francis. In form it is not a sequence but a ' pia meditatio,' and it is not without significance that the piece in which the medieval mind finds its best expression should have been written by a comparatively unknown man. There are reminiscences in it of very many previous writers, of Jerome, of Damiani, of Radewin, and of the ' *Responsorium* ' in the Mass for the dead ; but none of these detract from the perfect art of its composition. As Prof. Saintsbury well says :

' In the five stanzas that begin " *Judex ergo cum censebit* " not a word could be displaced without loss and the climax of verbal harmony is reached in the final

" Quærens me sedisti lassus,
Redemisti crucem passus ;
Tantus labor non sit cassus."

After the " *Dies Iræ* " no poet could say that any effect of poetry was, as far as sound goes, unattainable, though few could have hoped to equal it, and perhaps no one except Dante and Shakespeare has fully done so.'

318

Throughout the twelfth century and during the first quarter of the thirteenth—the period that saw the great series of religious sequences which begins with the ' *Heri mundus exsultavit* '—a mass of poetry very different in spirit was being written all over Europe. This second kind was indeed modelled in rhythm on the double rhymed sequences, and it often parodied the language of the Church; but its theme is not the fervour of religious passion but the worldly joys of wine, women, and song. Its authors were the wandering scholars, *vagi clerici*, who were then roaming from university to university in search of knowledge, undisciplined sons of the Church, who enjoyed the privileges of the clergy but set themselves to escape from all clerical restraints. Poor, young and careless they trudged the roads, lodging sometimes in a tavern, sometimes in a monastery, sometimes in the back streets of a university town, and everywhere turning their joys and sorrows into verse. The type is eternal and continually reappears in literature, now under the name of Archilochus, now of Villon, and now of Verlaine ; but in the twelfth century there seems to have been not one but dozens of these rebels against convention. Their verse was usually anonymous and much of it has disappeared, although fragments are to be found hidden away in most of the great European libraries. By far the largest collection is contained in the celebrated manuscript for many years preserved at the monastery of Benedictbeuern in Bavaria and now at Munich. Written in the thirteenth century it was first edited by Andreas Schmeller in 1847 under the title of Carmina Burana, and to his second edition (1883) the references in the following pages are made.

The strongest impression given by reading the *Carmina Burana* is one of youth and spring and love.

The spring poems are as numerous as those in the Greek Anthology and are even fresher in their youthful fervour.

> ' Tempus est iucundum,
>   O virgines,
>   Modo congaudete,
>   Vos iuvenes
>
>   O. o. totus floreo,
>   Iam amore virginali
>   Totus ardeo,
>   Novus, novus amor
>   Est, quo pereo.'—C.B. 140.

> ' Jocund Spring is with us,
>   Come, virgins all ;
>   Come, lads, join the revel
>   Answer Spring's call.

(Chorus)
>   Hurray, hurray ! O happy day
>   With love I'm all on fire.
>   To have a maid beside me laid
>   Is now my one desire.'

The next impression is one of surprise at the extreme technical skill displayed in the versification and the ease with which the most elaborate and difficult system of rhyme is sustained. Latin in the hands of these twelfth-century poets seems suddenly to have gained a lyrical quality which those who are only familiar with the Augustans would scarcely suspect, while the rhyme to English ears gives an additional attraction :

> ' Sic mea fata canendo solor,
>   Ut nece proxima facit olor ;
>   Blandus hæret meo corde dolor,
>   Roseus effugit ore color,
>   Cura crescente,
>   Mærore vigente
>   Vigore labente,
>   Miser morior,
>   Tam male pectora multat amor ;
>   Ah morior ; ah morior ; ah morior
>   Dum quod amem cogor et non amor.'—C.B. 167.

' Come, let me solace my grief with a ditty,
As when his death hour draws nigh sings the swan ;
Love's subtle pain racks my heart without pity,
Sad is my face and my cheeks pale and wan.

> My vigour decreases,
> My sorrow increases,
> My pain never ceases,
> Nor lets me go free ;
> I ever am sighing,
> I'm dying, I'm dying,

I'm in love and my lady love will not love me.

If she whom I love would but deign now to love me,
If I might taste of the dew on her lips,
Jupiter throned in the heaven above me
I in felicity far should eclipse.

> If I could wed her,
> I'd take her and bed her
> When home I had led her,
> And gladly would pay
> My life to enfold her
> And in my arms hold her

And then from such joys pass to death straightaway.'

Love and springtime are the favourite subjects, but
the joys of wine come closely after. Of the drinking
songs the best known is a wicked parody on the
Lauda Sion of Aquinas :

> ' In taberna quando sumus
> Non curamus quid sit humus
> Sed ad ludum properamus
> Cui semper insudamus. . . .
>
> Bibit hera, bibit herus,
> Bibit miles, bibit clerus,
> Bibit ille, bibit illa
> Bibit servus cum ancilla.'—C.B. 175.

Almost equally famous is that other parody :

> ' Vinum bonum et suäve,
> Bonis bonum, pravis prave,
> Cunctis dulcis sapor, ave,
> Mundana lætitia.

X   321

> Ave, felix creatura
> Quam produxit vitis pura ;
> Omnis mensa fit secura
> In tua præsentia.'

While the majority of the pieces are short, there is one long and charming tale in verse, the *Phyllis and Flora*. This extends to over six hundred short lines and begins thus :

> ' Anni parte florida
> Cælo puriore
> Picto terræ gremio
> Vario colore,
> Dum fugaret sidera
> Nuntius Auroræ,
> Liquit somnus oculos
> Phyllidis et Floræ.'—C.B. 65.

> ' 'Twas the flowery time of spring
> When the sky grows clearer,
> And the earth with bosom gay
> Feels the summer nearer ;
> All the stars of night had gone
> Flying from Aurora
> When soft slumber left the eyes
> Of Phyllis and of Flora.'

Neither of the maidens can sleep, the poet tells us, for Phyllis is in love with a soldier, Flora with a cleric ; and so they decide to go for a country walk. They come to a meadow, where :

> ' Whispering zephyrs in the trees
> Overhead were blowing ;
> Through the grass a little brook
> At their feet was flowing,
> Running now with merry note
> Past the hazel bushes,
> Staying now awhile to sport
> With the swaying rushes.'

322

But even this pleasant scene cannot prevent the girls from sighing, Phyllis for her Paris, Flora for her Aristotle, and after a while they begin to compare the merits of soldiers and clerics as lovers. The debate grows warm, and finally they determine to refer the question to Cupid; so mounting upon a mule and a horse, both wonderful animals minutely described, they set out for the Garden of Love. The delights of that Paradise form the subject of the latter part of the poem, the fragrance of its flowers and fruits, the songs of its countless birds, and the music of its harps and viols to which bands of youths and maidens gaily dance. The girls at first are almost afraid to enter, but when they see young Cupid, surrounded by laughing fauns and satyrs, they timidly approach and ask him to give judgment. Cupid refers the question to his two assessors, ' Usus ' and ' Natura,' and the poem ends with their verdict in the cleric's favour.

Hugh of Orleans (born c. 1090)

It has been said that the authors of most of the students' songs are unknown, but the patient research of German scholars has revealed to us two shadowy figures in the crowd. In 1907 Wilhelm Meyer published twenty-three poems from a manuscript which he discovered in Oxford which are the work of a certain Hugh who lived in Orleans in Abelard's time and was, as he tells us, Primate of the Order of Wandering Scholars. Side by side with this may be put the Arundel MS., edited by Thomas Wright in 1838 and re-edited by Meyer in 1908; for even if Hugh cannot be proved responsible for the verses in the Arundel MS., they are in their frank animalism so akin to his spirit that they may be provisionally attributed to him without much injustice. The fifty-one poems united give us a vivid, almost too vivid, picture of purely sensual passion, and the three pieces on the light o' love Flora in the Oxford MS. correspond very closely with the licentious freedom of the Arundel *Præclusi viam floris, Sævit auræ spiritus,* and *Grates ago Veneri.* Translation of any one of these six is impossible, and the Latin of the last two, when transferred to other collections, only appears in a castrated form. Still, if they are considered only as literature, they are wonderful productions, and the longest poem, where Hugo, *magnus trutannus et maximus truffator,* tells the story of his downfall, has even a certain moral value.

> ' Dives eram et dilectus
> Inter pares præelectus ;
> Modo curvat me senectus
> Et ætate sum confectus.'

> ' Years ago I used to be
> The pride of all my company ;
> But now I'm poor and bent and gray
> And youth, alas, has passed away.'

The Archipoeta (born c. 1130)

Hugh of Orleans was a licentious rogue whose only merit was his gift for poetry. A more sympathetic figure is the Archpoet of Cologne, whose history has been traced by Max Manitius. The Archpoet flourished —as far as poverty, ill-health and the artistic temperament allowed—about a generation after Hugo, in the reign of Frederick Barbarossa and was a needy dependant of the Emperor's great Chancellor, Reginald von Dassel, Archbishop-elect of Cologne. The first poem which is certainly his can be dated about 1161, when Reginald was in Italy on an embassy to the Pope. It is in hexameters and asks for the gift of a cloak.

' Continuam tussim patior, tanquam tisicus sim.
Sentio per pulsum quod non a morte procul sum.'

The next is a reply to Reginald, who had demanded
an epic on Barbarossa's Italian campaign :

' Archicancellarie, vir discretæ mentis.'

Such a poem, says the poor bard, cannot be written
to order in a week, and soon afterwards we find him in
disgrace trudging the roads :

' Nunc vesanus plus Oreste
Male vivens et moleste,
Trutannizans inhoneste.'

Further reproofs from his patron followed, and at
last we have the *Confessio*, an expression of youth's
rebellion against restraint and the artist's rebellion
against society which has rarely been surpassed.

' Æstuans intrinsecus
Ira vehementi
In amaritudine
Loquor meæ menti.
Factus de materia
Levis elementi
Similis sum folio
De quo ludunt venti.'

So the ' Confession' begins, and so for some two
hundred lines it continues. You must not expect
young men to be serious, says the poet ; nature forbids
it, and when one is on fire one must burn. Some
people, it is true, can work fasting, but personally

' Sitim et ieiunium
odi tanquam funus.'

Love, gaming, and wine are the joys of life, and a
tavern is the best place in which to end one's days :

' Meum est propositum
In taberna mori,
Ut sint vina proxima
Morientis ori :
Tunc cantabunt laetius
Angelorum chori :
" Sit deus propitius
Hüic potatori." '

' Well I know my end will come
In a tavern lying
With a tankard to my lips,
While the angels flying
Up to heaven blithely sing,—
I shall hear them crying—
" Mercy, Lord : a toper stout
Begs for grace a-dying." '

So much for Hugh of Orleans and the Archpoet :
we have still not mentioned the crowning glory of the
Carmina Burana, the *Dum Dianæ Vitrea*, which is to
this secular verse what the *Dies iræ* is to religious
poetry. So pre-eminent is it in beauty, both of thought
and diction, that it may possibly have been written
by Abelard. Three questions have to be faced in
making the attribution. Firstly, is there any other
poem in the collection which is by Abelard ? To this
it may be answered that No. 131, *Hebet sidus læti
visus*, is by him, if we allow the conjecture that Heloïse,
' daughter of Helios,' is referred to in the lines :

' In amoris hæc chorea
Cunctis prænitet
Cuius nomen a Phœbea
Luce renitet,
Et pro speculo
Servit polo : illam colo,
Eam volo nutu solo
In hoc sæculo.'

Secondly, is there any resemblance between Abelard's
known verse and this poem ? To this the reply would

be that there is a curious likeness in rhythm between
the six lines in the *Dum Dianæ* which begin ‘ Nubes
tollit ’ and these six lines, which come from one of
Abelard’s hymns :

> ‘ Instrumenta
> Sunt his tua
> Per quos mira peragis,
> Et humana
> Moves corda
> Signis et prodigiis.’

Thirdly, if this resemblance be granted, would not
the piece be rather a parody of Abelard than his own
work ? To that we can say that there is already an
elaborate parody of the poem in the *Carmina*, No. 176,
Dum domus lapidea, which would suggest that the
original was the work of an early and famous writer.
But even when these objections have been answered,
our positive evidence is slight, and it may suffice here
to say that whoever the author was, he was a consummate artist.

I

> ‘ Dum Dianæ vitrea
> Sero lampas oritur
> Et a fratris rosea
> Luce dum succenditur,
> Dulcis aura zephyri
> Spirans omnes ætheri
> Nubes tollit ;
> Sic emollit
> Vi chordarum pectora,
> Et immutat
> Cor, quod nutat
> Ad amoris pignora.
> Lætum iubar hesperi
> Gratiorem
> Dat humorem
> Roris soporiferi
> Mortalium generi.

327

2

O quam felix est
Antidotum soporis,
Quot curarum tempestates
Sedat et doloris !
Dum surrepit clausis
Oculorum poris,
Gaudio æquiparat
Dulcedini amoris.

3

Morpheus in mentem
Trahit impellentem
Ventum lenem,
Segetes maturas,
Murmura rivorum
Per arenas puras,
Circulares ambitus
Molendinorum,
Qui furantur somno
Lumen oculorum.

4

Post blanda Veneris
Commercia
Lassatur cerebri
Substantia.
Hinc caligantes
Mira novitate
Oculi nantes
In palpebrarum rate !
Hei, quam felix transitus
Amoris ad soporem,
Sed suavior regressus
Soporis ad amorem ! '

' Dian's crystal lamp is shining
Kindled from her brother's beam,
As declining
Westward sank his rosy flame.

Softly now the zephyrs sigh ;
Clouds are driven
From the heaven
By their melody.
Soft it is and strong,
And that vernal song
Knows the hearts of men to move,
Turns men's hearts to love.

Pleasant is the evening light ;
For it brings
On its wings
Gift of dewy sleep by night,
Rest from troublings.
Magic balm that can appease
Care and make all anguish cease,
Antidote to grief,
Stealing over weary eyes
And to all our miseries
Bringing swift relief.
Sleep all other joys above,
Save the joy of love.

Wind amid the corn
On a summer's morn ;
Murmuring rivulet
Whose clear waters fret
O'er silver sand ; the sound
Of mill wheels turning
Round and round ;
Such spells as these the drowsy god
Uses upon you till you fall
Beneath his thrall.

Love's traffick over,
When the prize we gain,
A melting faintness
Falls upon the brain.
Strange and wondrous,
Eyes grow dim,
'Neath the sheltering lids
Languid swim.

Ah, how sweet the passage seems
From tender love to tender dreams !
And yet more sweet 'twill prove
To pass from dreams to love.'

Of the poems in *Carmina Burana* none can be dated later than 1225, and during the second half of the thirteenth century three causes were working together which prevented any further development of this sort of verse. To begin with, the Church grew impatient of the licence of the wandering scholars, and a whole series of decrees was launched against them between 1227 and 1291. Sometimes they are called ' Goliardi,' sometimes ' Eberhardini,' sometimes ' clerici ribaldi ' or ' vagi scholares '; but in all cases they are treated with extreme severity. Ecclesiastics were forbidden to entertain them or give them shelter ; they were deprived of their clerical tonsure ; any benefices they might hold were taken from them ; and they were not allowed to celebrate mass. As a result the ' *ordo vagorum* ' came to an end and their poetry with them. It might be wondered why secular poetry did not use the forms that the scholars had created, but here the other two causes come in. By the end of the thirteenth century the four chief languages of Europe, English, French, German, and Italian, had all emerged from their primitive roughness, and becoming suitable for literature were the natural medium for popular verse. As for professional writers, with them the influence of the Renaissance was already at work, and if they wrote in Latin they followed classical models and returned once more to hexameters and elegiacs. So the *Carmina Burana* are the last flowers of Latin as a spoken language, coming at the end as the Plautine songs came at the beginning. It is as though upon the original Latin briar the cultivated Greek rose had been grafted; for centuries the tree brought forth a wealth of luxuriant blooms; but at length it died, and then for one brief spell in the twelfth century the wild stock came again to life.

PART VI

THE RENAISSANCE LATINISTS
(1321–1674)

THE RENAISSANCE LATINISTS

WITH the beginning of the Italian Renaissance in the early years of the fourteenth century Latin literature enters upon its final phase, a phase which lasted for some three hundred years, and starting in Italy spread gradually northwards until it comes to a stop in England about the end of the seventeenth century. Into the extremely controversial question as to whether the Renaissance was a benefit to all the arts, and whether socially the new doctrine of individual freedom of action was an improvement on the medieval idea of disciplined submission to authority, we need not now enter. Here we are only concerned with Renaissance literature, and with that portion of it which was written in Latin. In that department at least, as perhaps in most others, the Renaissance did both harm and good. It brought an end to the development of Latin poetry which seemed in the twelfth century to be so full of promise, and banishing rhyme and free rhythm it again enforced a slavish imitation of Græco-Roman metre. On the other hand it revived the study of the classics, which had been falling into abeyance, and by making men once more familiar with models of excellence it raised the whole standard of European literature.

When this history begins, in the fourth century, the Roman municipal schools were in existence, and a knowledge of Virgil and Cicero formed part of every boy's training. These schools were swept away by the barbarian invasions of the fifth century and during the next three hundred years the general level of learning in Europe sunk to its lowest point. After the year 800, as the result of Charles the Great's reforms, the task of education was taken up by the monastery and cathedral schools; and when we come to the twelfth century we find that in them a fairly liberal course of Latin reading was pursued. The improvement in style which resulted from this was checked, however, by the influence of the medieval universities, which from the end of the twelfth century became the chief centres of instruction. At the universities dialectic and theology reigned supreme, and their professors, most of them followers of Aristotle, intent on subtleties of metaphysic, were totally indifferent to literary form. In England, France, and Germany during the thirteenth century barbarous Latin became common, and it was reserved for Italy to revive the study of '*Litteræ humaniores*,' the literature that is distinctively humane.

In Italy that study was pursued in a very different spirit from that which had inspired Gerbert, Baudry, and John of Salisbury; and to this new spirit the name 'humanism' is usually given. Humanism is in many ways the opposite of medievalism. To the medieval man the state of his soul in a future world was the only thing of absolute importance; to the humanist the goodliness of this world and man's power to enjoy it had far more reality. The medieval man valued Latin as being the language of God's word, and all pagan writers, except in so far as they could be taken in an allegorical sense, were regarded with suspicion; the humanist found in Latin the key to a new mode of life, and substituting the word ' classic ' for ' pagan,' followed the great writers of ancient Rome as his guides. Of humanism in this sense Petrarch, ' the first modern man,' is an excellent example; and with Petrarch we may begin.

Petrarch (1304–1374)

At the time of Dante's death in 1321 the man who was to be the morning star of the new era was a youth of seventeen, studying law at the University of Montpellier. Francesco di Petracco, or, as he preferred to call himself, Franciscus Petrarca, was the son of a notary of Florence who on being banished from his native city had taken up his home at Arezzo. There Petrarch was born, but in 1313 his father migrated to Avignon and for the next ten years Petrarch lived in France. His father destined him for the law, and, according to the story, finding him one day poring over his Latin classics threw them all into the fire except a Virgil and a Cicero. For seven years, first at Montpellier and then at Bologna, Petrarch wasted his time on legal studies ; but his father's death in 1326 made him his own master, and giving up the law he entered the fashionable world under the patronage of the great Colonna family.

In 1327 at Avignon Petrarch met Laura, wife of Hugo de Sade, and began his career as poet by the series of sonnets which extend in composition over twenty years and have made his name famous. But these ' canzone ' are in Italian and Petrarch affected to regard them as youthful follies. In his own opinion his really important works were in Latin ; and it may be well to give a list of them here. First come the *Letters*, divided into forty-three books, twenty-four *De rebus familiaribus*, seventeen *Letters of Old Age*, and two *Various*. The collection was made by Petrarch himself, who tells us that he destroyed over one thousand letters which he thought unworthy. But for most readers the number we have now is quite sufficient. Next follow the twelve philosophical works written between 1342 and 1370, the most important being the *Of the remedies of either fortune*, the *Of ignorance, his own and that of others*, and the *Epistle to Posterity*. Last, but in Petrarch's eyes not least, the Latin poems the *Eclogues*, the *Metrical Epistles*, the *Penitential Psalms*, and above all the *Africa*.

How Petrarch found the means to live his life of leisure, study, and foreign travel is a mystery into which we need not inquire. In 1330 we find him at Avignon, where he met the Englishman Richard de Bury, author of the *Philobiblon*, as keen a collector of manuscripts as he was himself, and as ardent a lover of the classics. But nothing very much came of the meeting of these two kindred spirits. Petrarch was anxious to learn the exact position of the 'Ultima Thule' of the ancients, but to his surprise De Bury refused to take any interest in the subject. It was soon after this that Petrarch took up his home at Vaucluse near Avignon, close by the source of the river Sorgue, and added to his love of literature an enthusiasm for the charms of nature. His manner of life there he describes in one of his most interesting letters (XIII, 8).

> 'Ad fontem Sorgiæ æstatem ago : iam quod sequitur, tacito me licet, intelligis ; sed si loqui iubes, brevibus expediam. Corpori meo bellum indixi. Ita me ille adiuvet, sine cuius ope succumberem, ut gula, ut venter, ut lingua, ut aures, oculique mei sæpe mihi non artus proprii sed hostes impii videntur. Multa quidem hinc mihi mala provenisse memini, præsertim ab oculis, qui ad omne præcipitium mei fuerunt duces. Hos ita conclusi ut præter cœlum, montes ac fontes, fere nihil videant.'

The account of his 'transalpine Helicon' which follows may be compared with his narrative of a visit to Vesuvius and of an ascent of Mount Ventoux in other letters; all three reveal that appreciation of natural beauty which is one of Petrarch's chief contributions to the modern spirit. The enjoyment of the charms of Vaucluse, however, was frequently interrupted by foreign journeys in search of manuscripts to Rome, N. France and Germany, and in 1333, to his great delight, he discovered Cicero's *Pro Archia* at Liége. Returning to Vaucluse he began a serious study of Roman history and started the great Latin epic, which was, he hoped, to bring him eternal glory. Soon the first drafts of the *Africa* began to circulate in manuscript. The line of Propertius ' *nescio quid maius nascitur Iliade* ' was on every one's lips, and after Petrarch had paid a visit to one of his most distinguished patrons, King Robert of Naples, he was in April 1341 solemnly crowned as poet-laureate upon the Capitol at Rome.

The *Africa* might more properly have been called the *Scipiad*, for such interest as it possesses (and it possesses very little) centres in the character of its hero, Scipio Africanus, the conqueror of Zama, to whom the far more romantic figure of Hannibal is made to serve as a mere foil. The poem itself is a weak dilution of Livy and Virgil, the subject-matter taken from the first, the treatment of that matter from the second. Scipio is a very inadequate Æneas ; Lavinia and Dido are combined in the fair Sophonisba :

> ' Candida purpureis imitantur floribus almæ
> Lilia mixta genæ, roseis tectumque labellis
> Splendet ebur serie mira, tum pectus apertum
> Lene tumens blandoque trahens suspiria pulsu . . .
> Hinc leves longæque manus, teretesque sequaci
> Ordine sunt digiti, propriumque ebur exprimit ungues.
> Tum laterum convexa decent, et quidquid ad imos
> Membrorum iacet usque pedes.'

If the *Africa* had never been published all would have been well, and it seems that Petrarch himself felt some qualms as to its real merit ; for there is a yawning gap between the fourth and fifth books which he never filled up, and of the twelve books he originally contemplated we now luckily only have nine. Historical epics are notoriously hazardous : they are apt to be too historical for poetry and too poetical for history : moreover, Petrarch's genius was so essentially lyrical that he was quite unfitted for the part of epic poet. Nothing to him seemed quite so interesting as his own existence, and perhaps the most vivid passage in the *Africa* is the prophecy, put into the mouths of Homer and Ennius, of the birth in Italy sixteen centuries after Zama of a great bard who should revive the glories of Latin verse.

After 1341 Petrarch was without dispute arbiter of letters over all Europe and one of the most important persons in Italy. He mixed as an equal with the greatest, and several times refused the offer of a papal secretary-ship which might have led to the highest positions in the Church. But although Petrarch was an ecclesiastic, he always preferred literature to Church politics ; and although he was the friend of most of the Italian tyrants, he was in theory and in his writings an ardent supporter of liberty. A far richer prize to him than any Church preferment was the discovery of Cicero's *Letters to Atticus*, which he made at Florence in 1345 ; and when Rienzi proclaimed himself tribune at Rome in 1347 Petrarch sacrificed his old and generous friends the Colonnas to join the cause of freedom. His conduct in the Rienzi affair revealed, perhaps even to himself, the ineffectiveness of idealism in politics ; and for the rest of his life he devoted himself more sedulously than ever to his books. Laura and many of his friends died in the plague of 1348, but Boccaccio, his closest associate and fellow-Latinist, remained, and a new interest was given to life by the rediscovery of Greek manuscripts. Boccaccio had learned some Greek from a certain Leontius Pilatus whom he had met at Naples and kept for three years in his house at Florence, ' an animal,' as Petrarch describes him, ' morose in his temper and disgusting in his habits, who concealed a bovine ignorance beneath a lion's hide of ostentation.' At this teacher's dictation Boccaccio made the first Latin translation of Homer for modern readers ; and although Petrarch only knew the Greek alphabet, with this translation at his side it was his greatest pleasure to pore over the manuscript of the *Iliad* and *Odyssey* which reached him from the East in 1354 and was placed in his library side by side with his Plato.

Between 1354 and 1369 Petrarch was living chiefly at Mantua and Padua, busy with his books and with the letters which he addressed now to his contemporaries and now to the great authors of the past, for to him the ancients were as real as living men. To Livy he writes lamenting the loss of so much of the *History* : 'O si mihi totus contingeres.' To Cicero he cries : ' Tu quidem, Cicero, quod pace tua dixerim, ut homo vixisti, ut orator dixisti, ut philosophus scripsisti.' At last he grew weary of the courts of princes and about 1370 retired to the little village of Arquà among the Euganean hills. There, according to the story, in 1374, as he was annotating the translation of the *Odyssey* in his library, he died.

Petrarch's importance in Latin literature lies not so much in his writings as in his influence. His epic the *Africa* was, as we have said, a failure ; and his letters and philosophical treatises, in spite of his love for Cicero, are based rather on the style of Seneca and

341

Augustine in their weaker moments. But by his recognition of the true features of Latin prose, by his appreciation of Cicero as its supreme master, by his passion for collecting manuscripts and inscriptions, and by his perception that the future of scholarship depended upon Greek, Petrarch is responsible for the four chief features of Renaissance Latin. Moreover, by his personal influence he gained supporters for humanism among the rich and powerful whose favour was indispensable for its success. The Church at first looked askance at the new movement, the Universities were indifferent or actively hostile, popular enthusiasm was hardly to be expected. Petrarch almost alone prepared the way for the revival of classical Latin. Rightly has he been called the father of humanism, for not only was he himself the first humanist, but he also inspired others, who spread his ideas throughout the world.

The chief link between Petrarch and the next generation was his vagrant secretary John of Ravenna, who left his copying duties in search of fresh knowledge, returned starving and penniless, and then once more set off on a new quest. After Petrarch's death John appears as an itinerant lecturer at Florence, Padua, and Venice, spreading everywhere the enthusiasm for Ciceronian Latin which he had imbibed from his master, and counting among his pupils Filelfo, Bruni, Guarino, Vittorino, and Poggio. Many of John's auditors also attended the Greek lectures given by Manuel Chrysoloras, who was appointed professor at Florence in 1396; and by the beginning of the fifteenth century a real knowledge both of the Latin and the Greek classics was quickly extending over the whole of Italy. Florence was the great centre; but Naples, Rome, Mantua, and Ferrara had also each its special quality of distinction.

Ferrara and Mantua were famous for their schools. At Ferrara Guarino (1374–1460) was teaching from 1436 until his death, and in the intervals wrote Latin and Greek grammars, a translation of Plutarch on education, and six hundred letters which still await publication, one among his many pupils being the Hungarian Janus Pannonius, who sang his master's praise in many eloquent poems. Mantua had an even greater instructor in Vittorino (1378–1446), who under the patronage of Gonzaga established the first 'school of the humanities' where in the 'Pleasant House' by the Mincio seventy scholars of all ranks worked and played together, reading Homer, Demosthenes, Virgil, and Cicero, riding, wrestling, and fencing in the spacious park around the school, and joining every day in common religious worship.

The strict rules of morality and religion observed at Mantua were not so closely followed elsewhere. At the court of King Alfonso of Naples the favourite poet was Beccadelli, and his *Hermaphroditus*, a collection of short pieces in verse, contains some of the most obscene stuff imaginable. Valla (1407–1457), also, the chief prose writer in Alfonso's circle, although a man of much higher character than Beccadelli, was an opponent rather than an upholder of Church doctrine. In his first essay, *De voluptate*, he supported the epicurean against the stoic theory of life, and roundly declared that virginity, the virtue so dear to medieval saints, is an offence against nature. In the next he critically examined the *Donation of Constantine*, the document on which the Popes based their claim to be the lawful rulers of Italy, and proved that it was a forgery. In his third book, 'On the elegancies of the Latin language,' he applied the same methods of scientific investigation to literature, accused Jerome, Priscian, and Isidore of gross inaccuracy, and laid down precepts of grammar and style which even to-day are by no means out of date.

For all this Valla was charged with heresy, but Alfonso promptly quashed the proceedings; and in 1450 he was called to Rome by Pope Nicholas V, who had just established the Vatican library and was a humanist before he was a cleric. For Nicholas Valla translated Thucydides, Herodotus, and Demosthenes into Latin, and finally he became one of the papal secretaries. In that office he had as colleague his former teacher, the Florentine Leonardo Bruni (1369–1444), who was himself a very competent Greek scholar. Bruni translated Aristotle's *Ethics* and *Politics*, which he dedicated first to Humphrey Duke of Gloucester and then to Pope Eugenius IV. He was also famed for the excellent Latinity of his letters; but his chief works were two histories, one of the First Punic War to take the place of Livy's lost decade and the other a *History of Florence* in twelve books. His funeral oration in Latin was pronounced by his fellow-citizen and scholar Manetti, and the following epitaph, modelled upon that of Plautus, may be read on his tomb in Santa Croce :

' Postquam Leonardus e vita migravit, Historia luget, Eloquentia muta est, ferturque Musas tum Graecas tum Latinas lacrimas tenere non potuisse.'

Poggio (1380–1459)

Guarino, Vittorino, Valla, and Bruni were men of remarkable talent, and Biondo (1388–1463), author of four great works on the history and antiquities of Rome is also worthy of mention. But the most striking figure in Latin literature during the first half of the fifteenth century is Poggio Bracciolini. Poggio was born near Arezzo in 1380 and was educated in Florence. In his youth he supported himself by copying manuscripts, and in 1403 by the influence of Salutati he obtained a post in the Papal Chancery. In that service he remained for fifty years, but he never took orders, and although he was careful to keep on good terms with the high dignitaries of the Church, he delighted in his writings to expose the vices of the secular clergy and to ridicule the follies of the monks. In 1413 he attended the Council of Constance as one of the papal secretaries, and two years later, as the Apostolic See was for the time vacant and he had no official duties to perform, he used the opportunity to travel through France and Germany in search of ancient manuscripts. The successes which he gained in this journey established his reputation as a scholar in Italy, and when in 1434 Cosimo de' Medici secured control of affairs in Florence, Poggio became one of the leading figures in the learned society which Cosimo gathered round him. On the ground of his literary skill he was admitted to the burghership of Florence, exempted from all taxes, married a rich young wife at the age of fifty-five, and built himself an elegant country-house, the Valdarniana, which he ornamented with ancient sculptures collected from Rome and from Greece. In 1483 he reached the summit of honour and was made Chancellor to the Republic, and when he died in 1459 his statue was set up in Florence.

Poggio was a person of manifold activities and won fame in three separate branches of learning. He was one of the keenest and most successful discoverers of lost manuscripts ; he was a sound archæologist who pursued his researches in a thoroughly practical spirit ;

he was an author equally skilful in serious and frivolous subjects, a vivid letter-writer, a dangerous controversialist, an eloquent historian, and a witty narrator of humorous anecdotes. If he had confined his energies to any one of the three arts he practised, he would still have been remarkable. His great achievements in all alike render him a typical Renaissance figure.

Petrarch was a fortunate treasure hunter in monasteries, but Poggio far surpassed him. At Cluny in 1415 he found the *Pro Murena* and the *Pro Sextio Roscio* of Cicero; at St Gall in 1416 and 1417 Quintilian, Valerius Flaccus, Columella, Vitruvius, Manilius, Ammianus, Silius Italicus, and Lucretius; at Langres in the summer of 1417 Cicero's two speeches for Rabirius and the *Pro Roscio Comœdo*. Of his visit to St Gall and his discovery of Quintilian there he tells us in one of his letters:

> ' In the middle of the library we came upon Quintilian, safe as yet and sound, though covered with dust and filthy with time and neglect. The books, I must tell you, were not housed according to their worth, but were lying in a foul dark dungeon at the very bottom of a tower, a place into which condemned criminals would hardly have been thrust. . . . Indeed I believe that if we had not come to the rescue our Quintilian must soon have perished; for it cannot be imagined that a man so magnificent, elegant, urbane, and witty could much longer have endured the squalor of the prison house in which I found him, the savagery of his jailers, the filthy solitude of the place. He was truly a sad sight to behold, ragged like a convicted malefactor, with rough beard and matted hair, protesting by his looks and dress against the injustice of his punishment. He seemed to be stretching out his hands, calling upon the Romans and asking to be saved from so unmerited a doom.'

As an archæologist Poggio rendered equal services to posterity, and the first book of his treatise *De Varietate Fortunæ* is the best account we possess of the state of Rome and its ancient monuments in the fifteenth century. This first book is often quoted as *Urbis Romæ Descriptio,* and it is in fact an accurate description of Rome in Poggio's time. We learn from it that the Baths of Caracalla were then still adorned with marble, and that it was only recently that the tomb of Cæcilia and the Temple of Concord had been pillaged and their marble burned for lime. We have descriptions also of the Coliseum, the Arches of Titus and Constantine, the theatres of Pompey and Marcellus, the columns of Trajan and Antonine, and of many ancient statues in marble and bronze. Indeed our only regret is that this first book was meant to be merely an introduction to the essay's main subject of the mutability of Fortune, and that Poggio does not give us fuller details of what he knew so well.

It is however as a writer that we are chiefly here concerned with Poggio. Of his letters we have already given a specimen : as a controversialist he is seen at his best—or at his worst—in his long and fierce feud with Filelfo, the most brilliant, but by no means the most estimable, of the professors of his day. Filelfo (1398–1481) who has been described as having the accomplishments of a scholar with the insidiousness and brutality of a brigand, had attacked both Cosimo and the whole society of Florence. Poggio replied in prose to his opponent's hexameters and poured out insults upon Filelfo himself, upon his mother, and upon his wife, the daughter of Chrysoloras. Neither Poggio nor Filelfo come out from the dispute with much credit, and it is as an example of extravagant abuse that Poggio's contribution to it is chiefly interesting. A more valuable work is the *History of Florence,* written as a continuation of Bruni; but the best known of Poggio's writings is the *Liber Facetiarum,* which in its own day was as popular

347

as the *Epistolæ obscurorum virorum* was in the next century.

The *Facetiæ*, however, is not for modern readers very amusing ; many of its anecdotes are scurrilous, many are indecent, few are really humorous. Most of them are concerned with the clergy, of whom Poggio has a very low opinion. The typical parish priest for him is the ignoramus who told his congregation that on the morrow they would celebrate the feast of Epiphany : ' whether Epiphany was a man or a woman I do not know ; but it is a solemn feast and we shall observe it strictly.' The typical friar is the lascivious rogue of the story of the friar's breeches, who uses his opportunities at the confessional to take advantage of women. The typical bishop is the prelate who sent his man to buy fish on a Friday, and when he returned with two partridges, declared that as he could turn bread into the body of Our Lord he could also turn partridges into fish ; and doing so ate the brace. As for the laity, all wives are wanton, all husbands are cuckolds, all countrymen are simpletons made to be cheated. For example, some peasants were sent to town to buy a crucifix, and when the vendor asked them if they would have it dead or alive, they said they would prefer it alive : ' for then our people can kill it if they do not like it.' Such facetiousness as this is somewhat depressing ; and the chief merit of Poggio's anecdotes is that they are brief. A fair specimen runs as follows : ' When Luigi Marsili was asked by a friend what the two points on a bishop's mitre meant, he replied that the front one signified the New Testament, the one behind the Old Testament. "Well," said the other, "what is the meaning of the two velvet ribbons that hang down over the two points ? " " They mean," answered Marsili,

" that the bishops know nothing about either of them." '

Politian (1454–1494)

Petrarch represents the first stage of humanism, Poggio the second : with Politian we pass to the third period, when after the capture of Constantinople in 1453 Florence under the rule of Lorenzo de' Medici became the Athens of Italy. Angelo Poliziano, better known to us as Politian, was born in 1454 at Monte Pulciano, near Florence, where his father, Benedetto Ambrogini, was so ardent a supporter of the Medicean faction that he was murdered by their enemies. Accordingly, when Lorenzo gained control of Florence, the young Pulcianus was received into his household and became one of the most brilliant stars in the galaxy of talent there gathered. As Marchese says : ' The Magnifico called to him from every part of Italy men of genius, as Pericles and Augustus had done before. Poets of every kind, gentle and simple, with golden cithern and with rustic lute, came to animate his suppers. Whoever sang of arms, of love, of saints, of fools, was welcome : and first among them all was Poliziano.' At Lorenzo's table Politian as a poet began his literary career, and many of the pieces he composed for these gatherings are very pretty specimens of youthful verse. There is, for example, the humorous apology, in which the poet, having asked Lorenzo for a suit of court dress, pretends to be abashed at its magnificence.

> ' Lorenzo, chiefest glory of thy time,
> When I essayed to render thanks in rhyme
> The muse whom long I summoned to my aid
> Came and her fingers on my harp strings laid.
> She came ; but when she saw my robes of gold
> She turned away nor knew her bard of old.

If then I cannot sing thy praise aright
It is because I am stranded by her flight :
When she is used to pomp and grown more tame
I will take my lyre and glorify thy name.'

There is the epigram on sleep :

' O mihi quanta datis fallacia gaudia somni !
Invideo, Endymion, Latmia saxa tibi.
Iam si nil sopor est gelidæ nisi mortis imago,
Omnia mors superat gaudia : vita, vale.'

' Of what delights in sleep am I possessed !
Be mine Endymion's eternal rest.
If sleep is but death's image, life good-bye.
Death has more joy to offer : let me die.'

Equally graceful is the little poem in which he
thanks his mistress for a gift of flowers :

' Felices nimium violæ, quas carpserit illa
    Dextera, quæ miserum me mihi surripuit,
Quas roseis digitis formoso admoverit ori
    Illi, unde in me spicula torquet Amor.
Forsitan et vobis hæc illinc gratia venit,
    Tantus honor dominæ spirat ab ore meæ.
Aspice lacteolo blanditur ut illa colore,
    Aspice purpureis ut rubet hæc foliis.
Hic color est dominæ, roseo cum dulce pudore
    Pingit lacteolas purpura grata genas.'

' O happy flowers, plucked by the rosy hand
That now has robbed me of my soul's command,
And kissed by those red lips whereon do lie
The sharpest darts of all Love's armoury.
It is from her your fragrance you derive,
Such charms upon her radiant visage live.
Look how this bud its milky whiteness shows,
And how this other with faint crimson glows :
Such is my lady's hue when tender shame
Kindles her cheeks and sets her face aflame.'

These imitative verses, however, only show us one
side of Politian's genius. Before he was twenty he had

written his tragedy *Orfeo*, in Italian, with a song in
Latin Sapphics to be sung by Orpheus, a play from
which the libretto of Gluck's opera was ultimately
derived. In his early youth also he composed Greek
epigrams and published a verse translation of four
books of the *Iliad*, which gained him the title of
Homericus iuvenis. Before he was thirty he was giving
public lectures in Greek and Latin at Florence and
acting as tutor to Lorenzo's children, and in the last
decade of his short life his fame eclipsed that of all his
contemporaries. During those ten years he poured
forth an immense amount of occasional writing both
in verse and prose. ' If a man wants a motto for his
sword,' he writes to a friend, ' or a posy for a ring,
an inscription for a bedroom, or a device for his silver,
it is to Politian that he runs. One teases me for a
drinking song, another for a serious poem, a third for
a serenade, and a fourth for a carnival squib.' Of his
fugitive prose the most important pieces appeared in
the *Miscellanea* published in 1489, a book which
excited lively interest, as a passage in a letter from one
of Politian's friends testifies : ' When I went the other
day into one of our public offices I found the clerks
quite neglecting their proper business, engrossed in
reading a book which had been distributed in sheets
among them. I asked what new book it was, and they
said " Politian's Miscellanies." So I too climbed up
to their desk, sat down among them, and began eagerly
to read.'

But great as are Politian's merits as a writer, it was
as a lecturer that he made the strongest impression
upon the men of his time. His appearance was not in
his favour, for he squinted slightly and his nose was
very large ; but he had a singularly beautiful voice,
and as soon as he began to speak his listeners sat spell-

bound. Among his pupils were some of the chief
scholars of Europe, Reuchlin from Germany, Grocyn
and Linacre from England, Tessiras from Portugal, and
it was to his lecture-room audience that he recited
the four long hexameter poems, known as the *Silvæ*,
which are his most permanent memorial. Of these
the *Nutricia* is a general introduction to the history
of poetry, the *Rusticus* an account of the bucolic poets,
the *Ambra* a panegyric on Homer, and the *Manto* an
equally eulogistic description of Virgil's life and poems,
concluding thus :

> ' At manet æternum et seros excurrit in annos
> Vatis opus, dumque in tacito vaga sidera mundo
> Fulgebunt, dum sol nigris orietur ab Indis,
> Prævia luciferis aderit dum curribus Eos,
> Dum ver tristis hiems, autumnum proferet æstas,
> Dumque fluet spirans refluetque reciproca Tethys,
> Dum mixta alternas capient elementa figuras,
> Semper erit magni decus immortale Maronis,
> Semper inexhaustis ibunt hæc flumina venis,
> Semper ab his docti ducentur fontibus haustus,
> Semper odoratos fundent hæc gramina flores,
> Unde piæ libetis apes, unde inclita nectat
> Serta comis triplici iuvenalis Gratia dextra.'

Most of the Renaissance scholars lived to an advanced
old age : Politian died when he was only forty. Paolo
Giovio, otherwise Paulus Jovius (1483–1552), who
wrote ' Eulogies ' of his contemporaries says that he
died of a mad passion for a beautiful youth. But
Jovius is apt to dip his pen in vinegar, and if we want a
reason it is more charitable to suppose that Politian's
end was hastened by his grief for the premature death
of Lorenzo in 1492. At any rate, the Elegy he wrote
for Lorenzo, in which he follows the Latin of Jerome
in free rhythm, testifies to the sincerity and to the
intensity of his sorrow :

' Quis dabit capiti meo
Aquam ? Quis oculis meis
Fontem lacrimarum dabit ?
Ut nocte fleam
Ut luce fleam.
Sic turtur viduus solet,
Sic cygnus moriens solet,
Sic luscinia conqueri.'

' O that the waters deep
My head might borrow.
O that my eyes might weep
Fountains of sorrow.
As the swan sings his fate,
As the dove mourns his mate,
As grieves the nightingale,
So would I never fail
But weep the long day through until the morrow.'

The Academy of Florence which met to do honour
to Plato at Lorenzo's villa near Fiesole contained
many illustrious members beside Politian. Of one of
them Politian himself writes : ' Nature seemed to have
showered on this man, or rather on this demi-god, all
her gifts. He was tall and finely shaped, and from his
face something of divinity shone forth. Acute and
gifted with a prodigious memory, he was unwearied in
study, perspicuous and eloquent in speech. You could
not say whether his talents or his virtues shed upon
him the greater lustre.' This paragon was Pico della
Mirandola whose early death robbed Florence of one
of her brightest stars. Another great scholar was
Landino who translated Plato, Plotinus, and Dionysius
into Latin ; and almost equal to him Landino, whose
Disputationes Camaldulenses, a dialogue modelled on
Cicero's *Tusculans*, gives us a vivid picture of a
typical Academy meeting. Lastly we must mention
Alberti, for his comedy *Philodoxius* so exactly repro-

duced the idiom of Terence that it was published and received as the work of an ancient comedian Lepidus.

With Politian Renaissance Latin in Italy reached its highest point of excellence : after him comes the decadence. In the forty years between 1480 and 1520 there was in Italy an immense production of Latin literature, and especially of Latin verse of which a selection may be read in the four thousand pages of the *Carmina Illustrium Poetarum Italorum* (Florence, 1719) or the three thousand pages of Gruter's *Deliciæ Poetarum Italorum* (Leyden, 1608). Most of this now has passed into oblivion, and brief notice of the best among this host of poets will suffice. Pontano (1426–1503) wrote love poems which somewhat transgress the laws of propriety as now established, although they may be excused both on the ground of conjugal affection—at the age of sixty-five Pontano married a young wife—and of his warm Neapolitan temperament. Sannazaro (1458–1530), his fellow townsman, was famous in his day for the *De Partu Virginis*, a strange mixture of Christian and pagan allusions, and for his graceful verses on Cumæ, Venice, and the Bay of Naples. Castiglione (1468–1529), author of ' The Courtier,' is more attractive ; his elegy on the ghost of Pico seen outside the walls of Mirandula is a piece of truly imaginative work, and his lament for Alcon had some influence on Milton's Lycidas :

> ' Alcon deliciæ Musarum et Apollinis, Alcon
> Pars animæ, cordis pars Alcon maxima nostri,
> Et dolor, his lacrimas oculis habiture perennes,
> Quis deus, aut quis te casus, miser, abstulit ? '

Molsa (b. 1489), ' who worshipped Venus more fervently than Minerva,' wrote poems which exactly suited the taste of his patron, Cardinal Alexander

Farnese ; but his contemporaries Flaminio and Navigero were men of a more serious character. Flaminio (b. 1498), ' a name no less dear to Virtue than to the Muses,' lived in peaceful seclusion on Lake Garda and his many occasional poems to his friends are marked by purity both of style and of sentiment. Navigero (b. 1483), a patrician of Venice and author of much elegiac verse, for his part used once a year solemnly to burn a copy of Martial in order to show his detestation of that poet's immorality. Another highly respectable bard was Battista Spagnuoli, often known as the Mantuan (1436–1516), whose pastoral eclogues were prodigiously esteemed by contemporary critics and seriously placed on a level with Virgil. Fracastoro (b. 1483), Navigero's life-long friend, wrote *Syphilis*, a poem which in spite of its theme is quite inoffensive and describes the ' French malady,' which had just made its first appearance in Europe, with scientific precision, the story of the shepherd Syphilus, who incurred the disease by offending the sun god, being brought in as a poetical ornament. Vida (1490–1566) is like Fracastoro, didactic, and takes for his themes ' The management of silkworms,' ' The game of chess,' and the ' Art of poetry.' This last, which contains much original criticism, had a great vogue for many years, and its author is apostrophised by Pope :

> ' Immortal Vida : on whose honour'd brow
> The Poet's bays and Critic's ivy grow ;
> Cremona now shall ever boast thy name,
> As next in place to Mantua, next in fame.'

Bembo (1470–1547)

Most of the men we have just mentioned flourished in the period when Giovanni de' Medici sat in the chair of Peter as Pope Leo X. Leo had been preceded by two enthusiastic patrons of literature in Nicholas V and Pius II (Æneas Sylvius Piccolimini), of whom the latter was himself an author in many different kinds of Latin prose and verse. But Leo far surpassed them both, and under his rule the ability to turn an elegant couplet was the surest road to high preferment in the Church. Of this the last stage of humanism in Italy, Pietro Bembo is the typical representative. Bembo, the son of a Venetian noble, was born and bred at Florence and after studying Greek under Lascaris at Messina joined his father at the court of Ferrara. There he won the favour of Lucrezia Borgia, to whom he writes :

> ' Quicquid agis, quicquid loqueris, delectat ; et omnes
>   Præcedunt Charites subsequiturque decor.'

From Ferrara Bembo passed to Urbino, where he was one of the most brilliant figures in the society pictured in Castiglione's ' Courtier,' and when Leo X became Pope in 1513 he was appointed one of the papal secretaries. In that capacity his skill as a writer of Ciceronian Latin had full scope, and for many years he was the arbiter of letters in Italy. He was a most fastidious stylist, and writing to his colleague Sadoleto, author of the *Laocoön*, he advises him to avoid reading St Paul's Epistles, lest their barbarous language should corrupt his taste : ' *Omitte has nugas, non enim decent gravem virum tales ineptiæ.*' In verse he was equally careful to follow classical models, and although his best known poem *Benacus* with its monotonous refrain

> ' Volvite maiores, vaga flumina, volvite lymphas '

is but a feeble imitation of Catullus, some of his elegiacs are very graceful. His epitaph on Politian is well known.

> ' Heu sic tu raptus, sic te mala fata tulerunt,
>   Arbiter Ausoniæ, Politiane, lyræ.'

His masterpiece in verse, however, is the *De Galeso et Maximo*, from which the following lines are taken. The boy Galesus, when reproved by his noble master, offers no excuses and sheds no tears :

'Nil horum aggreditur ; sed tantum ingrata loquentis
    Implicitus collo dulce pependit onus.
Nec mora, cunctanti roseis tot pressa labellis
    Oscula cælitibus invidiosa dedit,
Arida quot levibus florescit messis aristis,
    Excita quot vernis floribus halat humus.
Maxime, quid dubitas. Si te piget, ipse tuo me
    Pone loco : hæc dubitem non ego ferre mala.'

In 1527 Rome was sacked by the Spanish and German soldiers of Charles V, and after that disaster the glories of Latin literature in Italy came to an end. But fortunately the countries north of the Alps were by that time ready to receive the new knowledge, and more fortunately still there was a northerner able to play the part of Petrarch in spreading that knowledge abroad. Before we come, however, to the life and work of Erasmus, we must go back for more than a century and consider the Dutch mystics and the Dutch reformers, who carried on the work that our Wycliffe (1320–1384) initiated in his *Trialogus, De ecclesia,* and *De civili dominio.*

We may begin with Jan van Ruysbroek (1293–1381), the ' Ecstatic Teacher,' for though he wrote in Flemish, the Latin translations of his works by Sirius, in which he was commonly read, give him a place in this history. Ruysbroek was born near Brussels in 1293 and became vicar of St Gudule in 1317. For a time he laboured as a parish priest, but in his sixtieth year, disgusted at the ignoble sloth into which so many of the clergy were then sinking, he retired with a few companions to the monastery of Groenendael and devoted the rest of his life to the service of his little community, to meditation, and to mystical writing. The Latin titles of his chief books are *De Ornatu Spiritalium Nuptiarum libri tres ; De Septem Gradibus Amoris libellus ; Speculum Salutis Æternæ ; Summa totius Vitæ Spiritalis.* Ruysbroek insisted that the soul finds God in its own depths, and it was this doctrine that especially appealed to Groot, who gave to Ruysbroek's theories a practical application.

Gerhard Groot (1340–1384) was born at Deventer near Utrecht where there was a famous Latin school, and after studying at Paris under Occam, at Cologne, and at Prague, he was appointed to a canonry in Utrecht. In 1366 he visited the papal court at Avignon, but a few years later a spiritual change came over him which resulted in a renunciation of all worldly honours. For three years he lived in a Carthusian monastery and in 1379 became a missionary preacher, inveighing both against the sins of the laity and also against the corruption of the Church. As a result, in spite of his *Publica Protestatio*, he was prohibited from preaching, and retiring to Deventer gathered round him his most earnest converts and established at the house of Florentius Radewyn the first community of the 'Brothers of the Common Life,' a circle of young men, laymen for the most part who gave themselves to pious and charitable work, and especially to the work of education. The Brethren were in close touch with the town school, and under their influence Deventer in the fifteenth century became what Chartres had been in the twelfth, the training ground from which came such men as Rudolphus Agricola, Beatus Rhenanus, Conrad Celtes, Mutianus, and Erasmus himself. All these five were brilliant scholars, but there was one pupil of Deventer who though he was not brilliant produced a book which has had far more readers than any of theirs.

Thomas à Kempis (1380–1471)

Thomas Hammerken, more commonly known from the name of his birthplace as Thomas à Kempis, was born at Kempen near Düsseldorf. His father was a peasant, his mother kept a dame's school, and of her Thomas in later days wrote that she was ' ad custodiam rei domesticæ attenta, in opere alacris, in victu sobria, in potu abstemia, in verbo pauca, in factis pudica.' Gertrude Hammerken had a just perception of the value of learning and saw to it that her little son should go to Deventer ; and after a short time under a dame there Thomas was admitted to the great school and soon reached the class that was taught by Radewyn. This was in 1392, and until 1399 Thomas stayed at Deventer enjoying to the full its atmosphere of mystical theology and practical benevolence. Then as he reached manhood it became necessary for him to decide upon his career, and Radewyn, who was as good a judge of character as he was a teacher, saw in him the predestined monk. On Radewyn's advice he left the Brotherhood and entered the monastery of Mount St Agnes, and there he remained content until his death at the age of ninety-one in 1471.

St Agnes was a poor monastery, and the monks had to earn their living in various ways. The copying of manuscripts was one of their chief employments, and Thomas, who from the first had been a great book lover, was one of the most assiduous of scribes. Of business capacity he had little and as bursar he was hardly a success, but in 1425 he was made sub-prior and so continued till the end. Of his personal appearance we can gather some idea from contemporary

359

writings. He was a little brown mouse of a man with apple cheeks, who usually kept his eyes upon the ground but when he was singing the psalms would rise on tip-toe and turn his face to heaven. He was fond of a quiet joke, but when the conversation became too lively he would get up and retire to his cell and his dear books. In that retreat he wrote the many works that we possess, the lives of Groot and of Radewyn; the history of the monastery of St Agnes; the monastic tracts such as the 'Monk's Manual' and the 'Monk's Epitaph'; the educational 'Manual for children' and 'Dialogue of Novices'; the mystical 'Garden of Roses,' 'Valley of Lilies' and 'Soliloquy of the Soul'; and above all the 'Imitation of Christ.'

It has sometimes been doubted whether the *Imitation* was really written by Thomas, so far does it stand above his other works: but the doubt is probably unfounded, for there is something in the theory of inspiration and the *Imitation* is plainly an inspired book. John Wesley translated it into English, and most of the great religious revivals since its day have owed something to its influence. No one indeed can read it without benefit, for Thomas, unlike some mystics, is perfectly simple and easy to understand: his simplicity is his strength. The *Imitation* has probably had more effect on Christendom than any book except the Bible: we have 400 MSS., a quarter of them from the Netherlands; it has been translated into fifty languages, and it is said that it has run to six thousand editions.

The *Imitatio*, therefore, should be too well known to need a long description. It is divided into four books, the first called 'Of Imitating Christ and Scorning all the World's Vanities.' In the ninth chapter Thomas reveals himself:

'Surely it is a great thing to stand and live obedient
Under superiors,
And not to be a law unto oneself.
Far safer is it to stand in a lowly place
Than in a bishopric.
Many there are that live obedient lives
But love not obedience.
They have their punishment; they murmur always,
And never will know freedom of soul.
Until for God's sake they willingly abase themselves.
You may run here, you may run there,
But you will find no rest save in humility
Beneath the rule of him that is set over you;
And dreams of place and power and change of station
Have been false guides to more than one.'

There we have the man under whose portrait are inscribed the words: 'In omnibus requiem quæsivi, sed non inveni nisi in hœxkens ende bœxkens,' 'I have sought everywhere for peace, but I have found it not save in a little nook and in a little book.'

The second book contains 'Warnings to draw us to the Inward Life'; the third 'Pious Encouragement to the Holy Communion'; and the fourth, which is much the longest and is in the form of a dialogue between God, the author, and the soul, is the 'Book of Inward Consolation.' Its first lines contain the essence of the mysticism which Goethe described as 'the logic of the heart, the dialectic of the emotions:

'I will hear what the Lord God may say in me.
Blest is the soul that hears its Lord's voice speaking within,
And takes the word of comfort from His lips.
Blest are the ears that catch the soft whisper of God,
And turn not to the murmurings of the passing world;
That listen not to voices from without,
But to the truth that teaches from within.'

It will be seen that the *Imitatio* is written in rhythmical prose, and in the edition of C. Hirsche

(Berlin, 1874) it is so printed. In form it often approaches verse, as in the following lines :

' Quod idcirco cum electis tuis dispensanter agis : ut
      Veraciter agnoscant
      Et patenter experiantur
      Quantum infirmitatis ex se ipsis habeant
      Et quid bonitatis et gratiæ ex te consequantur ;
Quia ex semet ipsis duri frigidi et indevoti :
Ex te autem ferventes alacres et devoti
      Esse merentur.'

Erasmus (1466–1536)

In Ruysbroek and Thomas à Kempis we have the fine flower of medieval mysticism, a plant which flourished in the congenial shelter of monasteries but was scarcely able to stand the rough breezes of ordinary life. Such men as these two justify the monastic system ; and if all monks had had their real vocation to the life of inward communion with God, that system could not reasonably have fallen into discredit. But unfortunately many people entered monasteries who had neither desire nor aptitude for mystic contemplation, and of this class Erasmus is a striking example. Desiderius Erasmus, the love child—both names mean the same thing and both are improper forms—was born out of wedlock in 1466. His mother was Margaret of Zevenberge, his father Gerard of Gouda, a priest who had divided his allegiance between the cloister and the hearth and at the time of his son's birth was away in Italy. The child was sent to school at Gouda and was for a time a choir boy in the Cathedral of Utrecht. At the age of nine his mother took him to Deventer, where Hegius and Rudolphus Agricola were then teaching, but when he had been four years there his mother and father both died, and after a period at Bois-le-Duc his guardians persuaded him against his will to enter the monastery of the Augustinian Canons at Steyn. He describes himself as having been kidnapped, and the ten years that he spent at Steyn gave him a distaste for monasteries which remained with him for the rest of his days. He was ordained priest in 1492, but he had no religious vocation, and his temperament, which valued freedom above all things, was entirely unsuited to the restrictions of monastic life. Still, he made good use of the opportunities for study which his leisure allowed, and when in 1493 the Bishop of Cambrai required a Latin secretary, his prior recommended Erasmus for the post, and the young man made his escape into the outer world. For two years he worked with the bishop, and then he induced his patron to send him to the University of Paris, and his real career began.

At Paris Erasmus was a poor student of the Collège Montaigu, and he had to bear a considerable amount of hardship, bad food, insanitary lodgings, and bitter cold in winter. He maintained himself partly on a stipend from the bishop, partly by taking private pupils, one of these being the young Lord Mountjoy, who in 1499 brought him over to England. In London he met More and the Ropers, and at Oxford, where he stayed at St Mary's College, the house of his Order, he made the acquaintance of Grocyn, Linacre founder of the College of Physicians, and Colet who was then beginning to plan his great school. These friends gave him the money for a journey to Italy which he desired to make; but his gold was taken from him by the customs officers at Dover and he returned to France as poor as when he started. To relieve the situation he set to work in haste and wrote the *Adagia*, which he dedicated to Mountjoy, and then leaving Paris, where the plague was raging, he set out on travels through France, the Netherlands and Germany which lasted for five years. During all this period he was intensely busy, reading the classics, studying Greek, and occasionally producing a short book, such as the *Enchiridion Militis Christiani*, 'The Christian Soldier's Dagger,' written at the request of a pious lady of Tournehens to show her dissolute husband the error of his ways, in which he pleads earnestly for a return to the primitive simplicity of the early Christians. In 1506, again by the help of his English friends, he was at last able to visit Italy, and after spending a year at Bologna reached Venice towards the end of 1507. There for some ten months he stayed in the house of the great printer Aldus Manutius, helping him to pass an enlarged edition of the *Adagia* through the press, and studying Greek with Musurus, so that it was not until early in 1509 that he reached Rome. Cardinal Grimani, to whom Bembo had given him an introduction, received him, he tells us, as a colleague ; but before he had been long in the Holy City, an urgent summons came from Mountjoy in England, where the accession of Henry VIII had filled all friends of the new learning with the brightest hopes. Travelling in haste Erasmus reached London in July, wrote the *Praise of Folly* in More's house, and was soon after appointed Lady Margaret Professor of Divinity at Cambridge. In England he remained till 1514 working at his great edition of the New Testament, the Greek text with a Latin translation, which for the first time applied the principles of sound criticism to the Bible, and so prepared for the Reformation : ' Erasmus laid the egg which Luther hatched.'

In 1514, having previously written for Colet the educational *De Ratione Studii* and *De Copia Rerum et*

Verborum, Erasmus left England, and joined forces at Basel with the printing firm of the Frobens. In that mill, as he says, he ground for eight years, passing his New Testament, dedicated to Pope Leo X, through the press, and editing his great series of the Latin Fathers of the Church. By this time he had become for all Europe what Petrarch had been for Italy, and was recognised as the chief living man of letters. It is true that in the realm of Greek studies he had to share the throne with the Frenchman Guillaume Budé (1467–1540) ; but Budé was too deeply absorbed in pure scholarship to concern himself much with the outer world, and even when his own house was on fire he merely lifted his eyes from his book and told his wife that domestic affairs were not his business.

In the year 1517 Martin Luther nailed his Theses on the church door at Wittenberg, and Erasmus was involved in the fierce disputes that followed. But he also was first and foremost a scholar and though he was in sympathy with most of Luther's views, he thought his methods a danger to order and to literature, and refused to break with Rome. His attitude exposed him to bitter criticism from the reformers and his dialogue *Ciceronianus* (1528), in which he satirised the 'apes of Cicero' provoked fierce attacks from the French school. But he laboured on, living now at Louvain, now at Freiburg, and now again at Basel ; and there death, which for twelve years had threatened, overtook him on 12th July 1536. No priest was present at his death-bed, and he left none of the usual legacies to the Church.

It has been necessary to relate the life of Erasmus at some length, for what he did was as important as what he wrote, and his personal influence as a man was at least equal to the influence which he exercised as an author. The list of the books which he wrote and the books which he edited is a very long one, and here we must be content to give a brief account of his four chief works, the *Praise of Folly*, the *Colloquies*, the *Adages*, and the *Letters*. The 'Praise of Folly,' *Encomium Moriæ*, is the best known of them, although Erasmus himself attached no great importance to it. It is a satire, which begins by being light and ends by being serious, in the form of a speech made by Folly, a female dressed in cap and bells, the child of Wealth and Youth, born in the Fortunate Isles, and nursed by the nymphs Drunkenness and Ignorance. Folly, as she declares, is indispensable to the human race : were it not for her men would not marry, women would not bear children, friendship would not exist. Self-confidence and courage are her children and make the world go round : modesty and caution are only obstacles to action. The wise man is an unnatural creature, and by his very qualities is unable to live in harmony with his fellow-men who find in foolish hobbies the greatest pleasures of life. Some delight in hunting, some in gambling, some in the superstitions of religion. At this point the satire takes a graver tone, and Erasmus after castigating the grammarians, the philosophers, and the scholastic theologians, turns to the various orders of the clergy. Those religious who call themselves monks, he says, are neither the one nor the other, for they live far from true religion and there is no sort of man who more frequents public places. Bishops and Cardinals, who should be shepherds caring only for their flocks, much prefer to feed themselves first ; and finally the Pope himself, in the person of Julius II, who had besieged Bologna when Erasmus was living there, is faithfully dealt with :

' Nay, further, whereas the Church of Christ was founded in blood, confirm'd by blood, and augmented by blood, now, as if Christ, who after his wonted manner defends his people, were lost, all government is by the sword. And whereas War is so savage a thing that it rather befits Beasts than Men, so outragious that the very Poets feign'd it came from the Furies, so pestilent that it corrupts all men's manners, so unjust that it is best executed by the worst of men, so wicked that it has no agreement with Christ ; and yet, omitting all the other, they make this their onely business. Here you'll see decrepit old fellows acting the parts of young men, neither troubled at their costs nor weari'd with their labours, nor discourag'd at any thing, so they may have the liberty of turning Laws, Religion, Peace and all things else quite topsie turvie.'—Tr. J. WILSON, 1668.

The *Adagia* in its first form was a ' pot-boiler,' a collection of scattered sayings from the classics, jotted down with a brief explanation of their origin, and then, if the occasion warranted, a short essay on their significance. The first edition, printed at Paris in 1500, contained about eight hundred proverbs ; the edition published by Aldus at Venice in 1508 was enlarged to three thousand and received its final shape in the Froben edition at Basel, 1523. It was very popular in its day, but it is now seldom read, although it contains some pieces of excellent writing, such as the description of the young Alexander, natural son of James IV of Scotland, who was Erasmus' pupil in Italy :

' Deum immortalem, quam velox, quam felix, quam ad quidvis sequax ingenium, quam multa simul complecti poterat. Eodem tempore discebat iureconsultorum literas, nec eas admodum gratas, ob admixtam barbariem et odiosam interpretum verbositatem. Audiebat dicendi præcepta, et præscripto themate declamabat, pariter et calamum exercens et linguam. Discebat Græce, et quotidie quod traditum fuerat stato reddebat tempore. Horis pomeridianis, musicis operam dabat, monochordiis, tibiis, testudini. Modulabatur et voce nonnunquam. Ne ipsum quidem convivii tempus studiorum vacabat fructu. Sacrificus perpetuo salutarem aliquem librum recitabat: puta decreta Pontificum, aut divum

Hieronymum, aut Ambrosium. Nec unquam recitantis vox inter-
rumpebatur, nisi si quid alteruter doctorum, inter quos medius
accumbebat, admonuisset, aut ipse, parum assequens quod legebatur,
sciscitatus esset aliquid. Rursum a convivio fabulæ, sed breves, et
hae quoque literis conditæ. Proinde nulla omnino vitæ pars vacabat
studio, nisi quæ rei divinæ somnoque daretur.—*Adagia.* ' Servire
tempori.'

The *Colloquies* are more interesting than the
Adages, but like them passed through many changes
of form. The first draft, written as early as 1496, was
little more than a school-book; and some of the
dialogues, such as that on early rising, still keep something of a scholastic flavour. But most of them are
quite lively reading and several, the *Procus et Puella*,
the *Adolescens et Scortum*, the *Virgo Misogamos*, and
the *Peregrinatio Religionis ergo*, in the vividness of their
descriptions and the dramatic quality of their dialogue
show that Erasmus possessed all the essentials of a
successful novelist. One of the best perhaps is the
Ichthyophagia, ' The Eating of Fish,' a thing for which
Erasmus had a profound dislike, which contains not
only a bold criticism of those churchmen who would
abstain from eating meat on condition that they
abstained from nothing else, but also a lively account
of the hardships which Erasmus endured in his early
days at the Collège Montaigu. Another excellent
piece is the *Deversoria*, a dialogue on inns, in which
the hostelries of France and Germany are compared
by two friends William and Bertulph. In France,
says William, the lady of the house comes forward at
once to make you welcome, and is followed by her
daughter, a person so gay in speech and manner that
she would make Cato himself lively. In Germany,
replies Bertulph, innkeepers never seem to want guests :
you have to ask your host if you may stay, and if he
does not say ' no ' you are fortunate.

The *Colloquies* are amusing and give us many glimpses of Erasmus in all stages of his career, but the best picture of his life and character is to be found in his *Letters*, of which he prepared some two thousand for publication in 1520. Luther, it is true, said : ' You will find nothing of any account in Erasmus' letters, except praise for his friends and abuse for his enemies ' ; but Luther here is unjust, and as a letter-writer Erasmus comes close after Cicero and Jerome. Here is an extract from the ' Apology ' which he wrote to the Prior of Steyn in 1514 :

' Quoties autem cogitabam de repetendo vestro contubernio succurrebat invidia multorum, contemptus omnium, colloquia quam frigida, quam inepta, quam non sapientia Christum, convivia quam laica ; denique tota vitæ ratio, cui si detraxeris cærimonias, non video quid relinquas expetendum. Postremo succurrebat corporis imbecillitas, quæ iam ætate et morbis ac laboribus aucta est ; quæ facit ut nec vobis satisfacturus essem et me ipsum occiderem. Iam annis aliquot obnoxius sum calculo, gravi sane malo et capitali. Iam annis aliquot nihil bibo nisi vinum, neque quodvis vinum, idque cogente morbo. Non fero quemvis cibum, nec cœlum quidem quodlibet. Nam morbus hic facile recurrens maximam postulat vitæ moderationem ; et novi cœlum Hollandicum, novi victus vestri rationem, ut de moribus nihil dicam. Itaque si redissem, nihil aliud fuissem assecutus nisi quod vobis molestiam attulissem et mihi mortem.'

Erasmus had many faults ; he was neither frank nor brave, neither generous nor forgiving, but he possessed qualities which more than compensated for these defects. He was tolerant, broad-minded, clear-sighted, and his charm of manner made him a most delightful companion. Moreover, he was a humanist in the best sense of the word. He had a profound belief in the value of knowledge and he thought that if knowledge could be spread abroad among all men, most of the miseries of this world would disappear. He realised that, if this happy result was to be achieved, a vigorous effort was necessary, and he devoted the whole of his laborious life first to acquiring knowledge himself, and then to imparting knowledge to others. Moral earnestness, which the Italian Renaissance signally lacked, was the keynote of his work, and all his writings have for their chief object the improvement of his fellow-men.

More (1478–1535)

Before leaving Erasmus mention should be made of two books with which he was connected. One of these is More's *Utopia*, published in 1516 under the title of *De Optimo Reipublicæ Statu deque Nova Insula Utopia Libellus*. Sir Thomas More, scholar, statesman, and martyr, was born in London, educated at St Anthony's school and at Oxford, and after wavering for a time between the priesthood and the law, chose the latter. Of More's English works, his controversial books and his *History of Richard III*, this is not the place to speak, nor is it necessary to tell the story of his life. Here we are only concerned with his Latin writings, of which the first was a translation into Latin of some dialogues of Lucian, done in conjunction with Erasmus and published in Paris 1506. The *Utopia* appeared in 1516, and a collection of Latin epigrams, many of them translations from the Greek Anthology, in 1518. He also wrote between 1520 and 1530 several Latin tracts which now have no great interest.

The *Utopia*, More's chief literary production, is in two books, the second composed in the Netherlands in 1515, the first after his return to London in 1516. It was completed in October and sent to Erasmus who was enthusiastic in its praise: he described it as ' libellus vere aureus nec minus salutaris,' a revelation of the true source of all political evils, and arranged for its publication at the Louvain press, with commendatory letters and poems from several of his friends. In one of the three English translations by Ralphe Robinson (1551), Gilbert Burnet (1684), and Arthur Cayley (1808), the *Utopia* is familiar to most readers, but a short specimen of More's Latin style may be interesting. His introduction to Hythlodaye by Peter Ægidius he describes thus :

'At Petrus ubi me conspexit, adit ac salutat. Respondere conantem seducit paululum, et : " Vides," inquit " hunc ? " (simul designabat eum cum quo loquentem videram). " Eum," inquit, " iam hinc ad te recta parabam ducere." " Venisset," inquam, " pergratus mihi tua causa." " Immo," inquit ille, " si nosses hominem, sua. Nam nemo vivit hodie mortalium omnium qui tantam tibi hominum terrarumque incognitarum narrare possit historiam. Quarum rerum audiendarum scio avidissimum esse te." " Ergo," inquam, " non pessime coniectavi. Nam primo aspectu sensi hominem esse nauclerum." " Atqui," inquit, " aberrasti longissime : navigavit quidem non ut Palinurus, sed ut Ulysses ; immo, velut Plato. Nempe Raphael iste, sic enim vocatur, gentilicio nomine Hythlodæus, orbis terrarum contemplandi studio Americo Vespucio se adiunxit, atque in tribus posterioribus illarum quattuor navigationum perpetuus eius comes fuit." '

Epistolæ Obscurorum Virorum (1515)

The second book which is connected with Erasmus is the *Epistolæ Obscurorum Virorum*, a satire, like the *Praise of Folly* and the *Utopia*, but of a much more pungent character than either of those mildly amusing and instructive works. The *Epistolæ* is in places coarse, in places scurrilous, in places irreverent ; but it is always uproariously funny : it is Aristophanic in the freedom and audacity of its humour and is one of the most entertaining books in Latin literature. Its production was the brightest episode in the long conflict waged in Germany between the New and the Old Learning, between the humanists who wished to advance

371

and the scholastic theologians who wished to stay where they were; and the circumstances of its publication were as follows: A converted Jew named Pfefferkorn had declared that all Hebrew writings except the Bible were heretical. The great scholar Reuchlin, supported by Erasmus, entered the lists against him; the Faculty of Theology at Cologne, under Ortuinus Gratius of Deventer, took his side; and the dispute was finally carried to Rome for decision. In 1514 Reuchlin had published a volume of opinions from eminent men in his favour, *Epistolæ Clarorum Virorum*; in the next year his young supporters at the University of Erfurt put out the *Epistolæ Obscurorum Virorum*, which purports to be a counterblast from the other party. The first book, which contains forty-eight letters, is mostly by Crotus Rubianus; the second book, which has seventy letters and is slightly fiercer in tone, is by Ulrich von Hutten, both of them being members of the circle at Erfurt who gathered round Mutianus Rufus.

The obscure men all address their letters to Ortwin, and in their letters they are made to reveal themselves. Master Conrad of Zwickau in several epistles betrays both his weakness for women and his strength as a poet, in such couplets as

' O pulchra Dorothea, quam ego elegi amicam,
　　Fac mihi etiam sic qualiter ego tibi.'

Lupold Federfuscher, Licentiate—very shortly—writes to enquire whether Pfefferkorn, being now a baptised Christian, has also gained preputial regeneration. Master Mammotrectus Buntemantellus begs his revered teacher for a love charm out of his little book to use upon his fair Margaret. Antonius—almost Doctor and soon to be graduated—explains how he proved to Erasmus himself that Cæsar could not have written the *Commentaries*, for he was far too busy to have learned Latin. Nearly all the letters are scandalously funny, but perhaps the most scandalous of all is one where the authors do not rely on their own invention but quote from the other side. Friar Dollenkopf (Bk. I, Ep. 28) sends Ortwin some extracts from a book by ' Doctor Thomas of Wales,' in which the *Metamorphoses* of Ovid receive allegorical interpretation with a profundity that passeth belief :

' Concerning *Jupiter*, who after the defloration of *Callisto* returned to heaven, it is written, Matt. xii., " I will return to my house from whence I came out."

Of the lapidification of the maiden *Aglauros*, whom *Mercury* turned into a stone, Job hinteth, " Whose heart is as firm as a stone."

Concerning *Actæon*, who beheld *Diana* naked, *Ezekiel* prophesied, saying, " Thou wast bare and full of confusion, and I passed by thee and saw thee." '

And so on and so on. ' All this, and much more, I have learnt out of that book.'

In Latin literature the sixteenth century is an age of prose scholarship, rendered illustrious by the names of Lambinus, Dorat, Casaubon, the two Scaligers, Nebrissensis, Lepsius, and Janus Dousa the ' Batavian Varro,' founder and first Rector of Leyden University. But most of these scholars indulged in Latin poetry, and those who wish may read their verse in the copious collections of Gruter, who gives four volumes to the Netherlands and seven to Germany. To read through Gruter, however, costs time and energy, and the student may well be content with a shorter and more modern anthology, Ellinger's *Deutsche Lyriker des Sechzehnten Jahrhunderts* (Berlin, 1893). Not that Ellinger is exciting. The Germans are good craftsmen, but they have very little to say. Invitations to dinner, pictures of gardens, and descriptions of places, such as the series on Nuremberg by Eobanus Hessus, form the staple of their verse. The religious poets Melanchthon, Jakob Balde and Bergius, have the most substance in them : Fabricius, Melissus, and Stigelius represent best the general level. Sebastian Scheffer, author of the ' Nine Skins of Women,' is more amusing than the rest, and a version of one of his shorter pieces will give some idea of Germanic humour :

> ' A youth rebuked a blushing maid
>   Who looked him in the face.
> " Cast down your eyes," he sternly said,
> " The ground's their proper place."
>
> " Nay," cried the nymph, " yourself look down ;
>   You men were made from earth.
> Girls must observe, you'll surely own,
>   The rib whence Eve had birth."

Joannes Secundus (1511–1536)

Of much greater value than these lyrics are two plays in Latin verse written by Germans in this century, the *Acolastus* of Willem Volder and the *Pammachius* of Kirchmayer. But the most attractive by far of the Northern Latin poets is Joannes Secundus. Jan Everaerts—to call him for once by his real Dutch name instead of the more familiar Latin form—was born at The Hague, 29th November 1511, one of a family of eighteen children, of whom nine reached manhood. His father, Nicholaus Everaerts, was a jurist of repute and a zealous supporter of Charles V, by whom he was made President of the States of Holland and Zealand, and finally President of the Council at Mechlin, one of the most important posts in the Netherlands. The imperial favour was extended to the whole family, and five of the six brothers had distinguished careers. Peter became Head of the Premonstratensian Order, Everard President at Mechlin after his father, Gruding an Imperial Counsellor and Knight of the Golden Fleece, Marius Chancellor of Zutphen. These two last were, like Joannes, poets as well as men of affairs, and their Latin verses with some of his were published in 1612 at Leyden under the title *Poemata et effigies trium fratrum Belgarum.* Joannes was the youngest of the six, and perhaps took his name Secundus from the fact that he was the second Jan in the family, the first dying in infancy. On his father's death in 1532, Joannes, who had been studying under the lawyer poet Alciati at Bourges, was given the place of secretary to the Archbishop of Toledo. He there established such a reputation that the Emperor decided he should accompany him, like another Ennius, on his African expedition. Joannes, however, fell ill, and was compelled to return to Holland, where he became secretary to the Bishop of Utrecht. In that capacity he was staying at Tournay in 1536 when his malady returned, and he died of malignant fever, 8th October.

That a young Dutchman who died before he was twenty-five, who wrote in a foreign language, and was during the few years of his brief manhood engrossed in high affairs of Church and State ; that he, in spite of all the disadvantages of age, country, and profession, should be one of the half-dozen greatest Latin love lyrists may at first sight seem to be a highly contestable statement. Yet few who have read the *Basia* of Joannes in the original would care to deny its accuracy ; and the *Basia* form but a small part of his writings, which fill more than six hundred pages in the monumental edition of Burmann-Boscha, published in 1821

Of his prose writings the most entertaining are the travel diaries of his three journeys to Bourges and Spain. With Joannes, of course, these were sentimental journeys, and his adventures chiefly adventures of the heart. He gives a humorous picture, for example, of the convent at Mons, where the nuns devoted themselves to their religious duties in the morning but after lunch arrayed themselves gaily and were quite prepared to entertain the young traveller with dancing and even less innocent diversions. Nothing more exciting than bad roads and bad weather seems to have happened to Joannes; but he has a lively pen and his descriptions of Paris, Dijon, Lyons and the many other places he visited on his way from Flanders to Spain, make his itineraries a valuable record of travel in the sixteenth century.

The letters in prose and the two books of verse epistles addressed to his brothers, his learned sister Isabella, and his friends, suffer from a certain diffuseness; but *Funera*, a collection of obituary poems, contains several pieces of considerable interest. The first is a beautiful eulogy of the poet's father; and this is followed by a series of short epitaphs which includes one on Erasmus, one on Margaret of Austria, and one on Katharine of Aragon : 'My beauty, my chastity, and my royal birth might well have won me favour with my husband the King. But a wanton drove me from the bed that was rightfully mine; and now, as my death alone can please my lord, to my death I go.' Then come two long poems on the death of Nicholas Hacquin, Henry the Eighth's envoy to the Emperor, which give a lifelike picture of our Tudor King, 'the monster whose loves reek with blood,' of Anne Boleyn, 'the cheap concubine, without a dowry and without rank,' and above all of Sir Thomas More, whose execution is most vividly described.

After the *Funera* follow twelve Odes, of which the best are the 'Dancers,' Horatian in metre but very modern in feeling, and the curious 'To God the great and good, disturbed by the tumults of the Anabaptists'; and then two books of Epigrams, the second book mainly translations from the Greek Anthology, which show the author to be a dexterous satirist of considerable wit. All these sections, however, of Joannes' work may fairly be called minor verse, and Beza's Latin epigram strikes a note of exaggerated praise :

> 'Now with great Virgil soaring high
>   He strikes the epic lyre,
> And now with Ovid loves to vie
>   In elegiac fire.
> His odes the victory have won
>   And Pindar leaves the field,
> While Bilbilis allows her son
>   In epigram must yield.
> One against four he strives ; and in each race
> Secundus never takes the second place.'

Joannes, for all his skill, cannot be put on the same line as Virgil and Pindar ; but when he is at his best he can justly be compared with the minor Latin classics, and in the elegiac *Amores* he partly reveals his true powers as a love poet. The first book, *Julia Monobiblos*, is concerned with his first great passion, a passion that came to an untimely end when the placid Julia had the bad taste, or perhaps the good fortune, to choose another man than her fiery lover for husband. In the second book Julia is replaced by Lydia and Venerilla, and the tone of the verse is somewhat lighter, in the style of Ovid rather than of Propertius. But good as the *Amores* are, they seem insignificant beside the nineteen pieces addressed to Neæra, known as *Basia*, 'The Kisses,' where Joannes challenges Catullus on his own ground. Here only quotation can give an idea of the gay music of Joannes' verse, and perhaps the fifth and the eighth Kisses are as good examples as any. The fifth runs thus:

> ' Dum me mollibus hinc et hinc lacertis
> Adstrictum premis imminensque toto
> Collo, pectore lubricoque vultu
> Dependes umeris, Neæra, nostris
> Componensque meis labella labris
> Et morsu petis et gemis remorsa
> Et linguam tremulam hinc et inde vibras
> Et linguam querulam hinc et inde sugis,
> Adspirans animæ suävis auram
> Mollem, dulcisonam, humidam meæque
> Altricem miseræ, Neæra, vitæ ;
> Hauriens animam meam caducam,
> Flagrantem, nimio vapore coctam,
> Coctam pectoris impotentis æstu,
> Eludisque meas, Neæra, flammas
> Flabro pectoris haurientis æstum—
> O iucunda mei caloris aura !
> Tunc dico : " Deus est Amor deorum,
> Et nullus deus est Amore maior.
> Si quisquam tamen est Amore maior,
> Tu, tu sola mihi es, Neæra, maior ! "

> ' When in your tender arms you hold me,
>   Clipped to your neck in love's embrace,
> And on your bosom close enfold me,
>   While you look down with smiling face.

> When on my shoulder you are lying
>   And on my lips your lips are laid,
> Now with a bite my courage trying,
>   Now of my teeth yourself afraid.

> When your swift tongue my swift tongue captures,
>   Drawing my life your life to meet.
> And with its fragrant touch enraptures
>   My hapless soul, so soft, so sweet.

When in fierce flame my heart is burning
    And I can scarce the fire contain,
As from my arms Neæra turning
    Bids me my passion still refrain.

Then do I cry : " O Love victorious,
    Greatest of all the powers that be ;
If there be any god more glorious,
    That god, Neæra, is for me." '

The eighth is addressed to Neæra, who in kissing her
lover had bitten his tongue :

' What frenzy was it, void of skill,
Bade you, Neæra, work your will
Of mischief on my hapless tongue,
And do to it this grievous wrong ?
You knew that you had pierced my heart
With shafts of love in every part :
And were you still unsatisfied
Until you had your sharp teeth tried
Upon that other member too
Who only lives to sing of you ?
From early morn to eve's decline,
Through nights of grief and day's sunshine
This faithful tongue, you know it well,
Has only but one tale to tell.
" Behold Neæra's sparkling eyes.
Behold her braided locks," it cries ;
" Behold her bosom white as milk,
Behold her neck more soft than silk."
Neæra's charms in wanton verses
Among the stars it still rehearses
Beyond Jove's flame, and is so zealous
It makes the very heavens jealous.
" Flower of my soul "—they hear it call—
" My dearest life, my all in all,
My sweetest sweetling, in whose arms
I find escape from all alarms.
My milk-white pigeon, queen of love "—
See Venus frown—" my turtle-dove."

How was it then you had the whim,
Proud beauty, thus to injure him
Who dares to exalt above the skies
The beauty of your lips and eyes ?
It was, forsooth, because you know
I never should so angry grow
As not to make that tongue proclaim,
Albeit in broken words, your fame,
And of your teeth the praises sound
Which dealt it this so cruel wound,
And bleeding still your charm confess.
O tyranny of loveliness ! '

In Joannes there is no doubt we have a very remarkable poet. He is almost forgotten to-day, but his
influence on our literature in the seventeenth century
was very great. Most of the minor Carolines and
most of the Restoration poets—Suckling, Sedley, Carew,
and the rest—are in his debt, and perhaps it is from
him rather than from any classical Latin writer that
they derive the peculiar blend of raillery and passion
which is the distinguishing mark of their verse. Moreover, there is another English poet, one far greater
than any of these men, who in the days when he was
living in Italy and surrendering for a brief space to the
joys of life, must often have read Joannes with sympathetic delight. The stern Milton of *Paradise
Regained*, the old man lonely and blind who still
would eat a few olives at supper to remind him of his
Italian pilgrimage, may seem a very different figure
from Neæra's passionate lover ; but Milton in his
grave youth felt for a time at least the charm of loving
dalliance and, although he put it from him, he could
write :

' Were it not better done as others use
To sport with Amaryllis in the shade
Or with the tangles of Neæra's hair ? '

To whom more probably than to Joannes do these lines refer ? And of whom more probably than of Joannes was the great Puritan thinking when he said that as compared with rhetoric poetry is simple, sensuous, and passionate ?

French Sixteenth-century Poets

Joannes' poems, which are rather Gallic than Batavian in style, soon won favour in France, and of the hundred Frenchmen collected in Gruter's *Deliciæ poetarum Gallorum* many take him as their model. One of them indeed, Jean Bonefons, pays him the doubtful compliment of the closest imitation in his *Pancharis*, but others are Joannes with a difference. Joachim du Bellay, for example, is almost as good in Latin as he is in French, and his love poems to Faustina are delightful :

> ' Tu Veneri veneres, cæco tu spicula Amori,
> Mercurio linguæ munera surpueras.
> At qui te, mea lux, mea spes, mea vita, meum cor,
> Invidus ah nostris abstulit ex oculis,
> Ille oculos sensusque omnes mentemque animumque
> Atque adeo totum me mihi surripuit.'

Of the rest Dolet, Beza, and Muretus were men of great literary talent, who doubtless would have won fame as Latin poets if Latin verse had been their only medium. But all three gave their best energies elsewhere, and a very brief account of their Latin writings will suffice. Étienne Dolet (1509–1546), ' martyr to the Renaissance,' executed on a charge of atheism in the Place Maubert at Paris, wrote two learned works in prose, the *Commentarii* and the *Formulæ*, and also a few poems. Theodore Beza, best known like Dolet for his theological studies, was in his youth a poet of rather daring wit, as may be seen from the selection of his verse in the *Amœnitates Poeticæ*, Paris, 1779. One piece will serve as an example :

> ' Nuper Candidulam meam salutans
> " Salve," inquam, " mea mens, mei et lepores,
> Corculumque meum." Illa tunc, disertam
> Cum sese cuperet mihi probare,
> " Salve," inquit," mea mentula." O disertam
> Et docto bene feminam cerebro !
> Nam si dicere corculum solemus,
> Cur non dicere mentulam licebit ? '

Muretus (1526–1585) for his part was during most of his life absorbed in the teaching of the classics, and his most important work *Variæ Lectiones* is one of pure scholarship ; but he also is well represented in the *Amœnitates* and among his *Juvenilia* there is at least one fine poem :

> ' Pande oculos, pande stellatæ frontis honorem,
> Queis doleat visis invideatque Venus.
> Pande agedum lasciva. O quidnam occulis illud
> Quo mea versantur corda supercilium ?
> Saltem ebur hoc manuum interea spectare licebit :
> Ah Etiamne manus ? Sæva, Etiamne manus ? '

George Buchanan (1506–1582)

Dorat, the two Scaligers, and Casaubon were all distinguished Latinists ; but a greater writer than any of these Frenchmen was the Franco-Scot Buchanan, to whom Scotch, French, and Latin were nearly equally mother-tongues. George Buchanan was born in Stirlingshire, 1506, and lived till 1582. At the age of fourteen he was sent by his uncle to study Latin in Paris, and thence after two years' stay proceeded to the University of St Andrews. In 1526 he came back again to Paris, and in his early Latin poems describes with the greatest vigour the hardships and privations of a foreign student's life. A second return to his native land involved him in the political schemes of James V, for whom he wrote the satire *Franciscanus*, and in 1539 he was compelled once more to cross to France, where he eventually settled down as a teacher at Bordeaux, with Montaigne as one of his pupils. These three years were probably the happiest in his stormy life, and during this breathing space he wrote his four Latin verse plays, *Medea*, *Alcestis*, *Baptistes*, and *Jephthes*. In 1544 we find him again in Paris, where he formed one of the brilliant circle of scholars that included Scaliger, Turnebus, and Stephanus. An enforced sojourn in a Portuguese monastery gave him time to write his longest and greatest work, the metrical Latin version of the Psalms, and in 1562 he returned finally to Scotland. For Mary Stuart he wrote two Latin *Epithalamia*, one on her marriage with the Dauphin, and the second on her marriage with Darnley ; but after his detection of the queen's infidelity he abandoned verse, and his later writings are all in prose. They comprise the *Detectio* (1571), a book which the Queen of Scots described with some justice as a defamatory libel ; the *De jure regni apud Scotos* (1579), in which the doctrine is laid down that the source of all power lies in the people, and that it is lawful to resist and even punish a tyrannical ruler ; and lastly the *Rerum Scoticarum Historia*, his most elaborate prose work, which his contemporaries seriously regarded as superior to either Cæsar, Livy, or Sallust.

Buchanan seems to have been a thoroughly unpleasant person, ill-tempered, pedantic and abusive ; but whatever we may think of him as a man, there can be no doubt that he was a writer of considerable talent. Dr Johnson, who had no great love for Scotchmen, considered Buchanan a very fine poet— ' the only man of genius his country ever produced ' —and in his own day he was hailed in every European country as a master, his Latin prose seriously compared to that of Livy, his Latin verse to Horace and Virgil. Modern readers leave him severely alone, for his longest and most characteristic poems, the Psalms, the tragedies, and the *Sphere* are little to our taste. This is not to say that they lack merit, or that they will not stand comparison with the minor classics. The two Biblical and the two mythological plays are quite equal to Seneca ; the *Sphere*, an elaborate account of the world in five books of hexameter verse, is fully as interesting as Manilius ; while the metrical version of the Psalms in the style of Horace—Psalm Eighty-two begins :

> ' Regum tremendorum in proprios greges,
> Reges in ipsos imperium est Jovæ,'

is a really wonderful achievement. But all these three suffer from their length and elaboration ; and it must be allowed that they are slightly dull. In Buchanan's occasional verse, however, as we have it in the Hendecasyllables, the Iambics, and the Epigrams, there are many pieces brilliantly written which deserve to be better known than they are. As an example we may take the Hendecasyllables, composed while he was still a faithful subject. Mary of Scotland was sending Elizabeth of England a present of a ring set with a heart-shaped diamond, and for it Buchanan wrote the following lines. The ring speaks :

> ' Non me materies facit superbum,
> Quod ferro insuperabilis, quod igni,
> Non candor macula carens, nitoris
> Non lux perspicui, nec ars magistri

Qui formam dedit hanc, datam loquaci
Circumvestiit eleganter auro :
Sed quod cor Dominæ meæ figura
Tam certa exprimo, pectore ut recluso
Cor si luminibus queat videri,
Cor non lumina certius viderent.
Sic constantia firma cordi utrique,
Sic candor macula carens, nitoris
Sic lux perspicui, nihil doli intus
Celans, omnia denique æqua præter
Unam duritiem.   Dein secundus
Hic gradus mihi sortis est faventis,
Talem Heroida quod videre sperem,
Qualem spes mihi nulla erat videndi,
Antiqua domina semel relicta.
O si fors mihi faxit, utriusque
Nectam ut corda adamantina catena,
Quam nec suspicio, æmulatiove
Livore, aut odium, aut senecta solvat !
Tam beatior omnibus lapillis,
Tam sim clarior omnibus lapillis,
Tam sim carior omnibus lapillis,
Quam sum durior omnibus lapillis.'

' 'Tis not my substance makes me proud,
Which neither steel nor fire can cloud ;
'Tis not the brilliance that you see,
Nor yet my flawless purity ;
'Tis not my artificer's skill
Who took and cut me to his will
And set me thus in talking gold
Bidding a ring my shape enfold.

No ; 'tis because in me you trace
An image of my lady's grace.
Displayed as clear as if your eyes
Could all her inmost thoughts surprise.
Her heart like mine is firm and sure,
Her flawless virtue is as pure ;
No guile has she, her light shines clear,
In all save hardness my compeer.

And in this too I must confess
Heaven has deigned my lot to bless.
I hope to see a warrior queen
Fairer than eyes have ever seen,
A virgin of heroic mind
Such as I hardly thought to find
When once my own great queen I left
And was of her fair face bereft.

Oh ! would that chance would grant to me
A link 'tween these two hearts to be,
Which neither age nor hate shall sever
Nor doubt nor envy's base endeavour.
Such happiness would then be mine
I should all other stones outshine,
As much more dear than all at length
As I surpass all stones in strength.'

John Owen (1560–1622)

From Buchanan the Scot we pass to Owen the Welshman, for it is a noticeable fact that the four chief Latinists of the northern Renaissance were men whose mother tongues were as yet unsuitable to the higher kinds of literature. John Owen, or in the Latinised form Johannes Audoënus, was born in the year 1560 at Llanarmon in Carnarvonshire. The paucity of Welsh names, which caused such confusion at Oxford in the case of Jones of Jesus, sometimes leads the unwary to identify him with the Bishop of St Asaph, who was his contemporary : but this, of course, is an error. Our John Owen was the son of Thomas Owen of Plas Dhu and Mary, sister of Sir William Morris. He was educated at Winchester under that famous pedagogue Dr Bilson, and thence proceeded to New College, Oxford, where he became Fellow in 1584. His first inclination was to the law, but in 1591 he decided on teaching as a profession

386

and after a brief essay in Monmouthshire was appointed in 1594 head master of King Henry the Eighth's School at Warwick. The facts of his life are not remarkable ; he never married and was of inconspicuous appearance ; as a schoolmaster he was only a moderate success, and his books brought him more monetary loss than gain. One of his uncles, a devout Roman Catholic, from whom he had great expectations, was so offended at his nephew's epigrams on the venality of the Roman clergy that instead of leaving him a handsome legacy he struck his name altogether out of his will.

On the other hand, like Martial before him, he found liberal patrons among the nobility who encouraged him in his literary efforts both with their critical approbation and with more substantial assistance. To most of them he renders his acknowledgements in dedications and in complimentary verse, but strangely enough he never mentions the most generous of them all, his kinsman Lord-keeper Williams, who maintained him during the latter years of his life. He died in London, 1622, and was buried in St Paul's Cathedral, where a memorial brass, bearing his effigy, was placed by Williams with the following inscription :

' Parva tibi statua est quia parva figura, supellex
    Parva, volat parvus magna per ora liber :
Sed non parvus honos, non parva est gloria, quippe
    Ingenio haud quicquam maius in orbe tuo.
Parva domus texit, templum sed grande : poetæ
    Tum vere vitam cum moriuntur agunt.'

' Small is your effigy ; your books were small,
And you yourself were not exceeding tall.
Small too your household, but not small your fame :
No bard can match the glory of your name.
Therefore you rest this mighty fane beneath ;
Poets in truth begin to live at death.'

Owen's first dated epigram is of 1596, on William Cecil, Lord Burghley ; and his first published volume appeared in 1606, followed by three more in the next seven years. The epigrams in these four volumes are divided into ten books, and there is a short appendix of posthumous verse. The first volume, containing the first three books, was dedicated to Lady Neville, daughter of the Earl of Dorset ; the second, *Liber Singularis*, which succeeded closely in the next year, was dedicated to Lady Stuart ; books five, six and seven, which make up the third volume, were dedicated to Henry, Prince of Wales, and Charles, Duke of York, and were published in 1672 ; the last three books, dedicated respectively to Sir Edward Noel, Sir William Sidley, and Sir Roger Owen, came out in 1613. The first collected edition of the complete poems bears on its title-page Amsterdam, 1624 ; the last was printed at Leipzig in 1824.

The success of Owen's poems was immediate and complete, and in a few years they were known and widely read, not only in England but all over Europe. In their Latin form they were the delight of men of letters and of the cultivated society which existed then in most European capitals, united far more closely than to-day by common standards of taste and mutual knowledge. But the epigrams also gained the ear of a second public in translations, for the seventeenth century marks the rise in importance of the man in the street, and those who found Latin a stumbling-block were for the first time becoming an important section of an author's audience. During the hundred years that followed Owen's death five different translations of portions of his books appeared in English, one in German, one in Spanish, and three in French, among these latter being the excellent version by

Le Brun (Paris, 1710), *Les pensées ingenieuses*, which gives the complete series in French and Latin. A full account of Owen's life and work appears also, with his portrait, in the *Elogii d'huomini letterati* of Lorenzo Crasso, published at Venice in 1666; and there are further notices in Anthony Wood, in Blount, and in Nicéron's *Memoires*. It is probable indeed that at the beginning of the eighteenth century most Europeans of literary tastes were fairly well acquainted with Owen : of Shakespeare, born four years later than the Welsh poet, they had only a vague and superficial idea.

And now perhaps it is time to try and give some impression of Owen's subjects and the manner of his treatment. While Martial is a realist, and excels in the vivid presentation of actual scenes and living characters, Owen is essentially a student and is occupied chiefly with problems of conduct and morality. He thus escapes Martial's worst fault of grossness which was forced upon him both by the conditions of the Roman life he pictured and by the taste of his Roman audience. Owen lived in gentler surroundings, and although he is often satirical his satire never offends. He was, as we have said, a confirmed bachelor, but many of his epigrams are concerned with the other sex. With him, as with many of his kind, a cautious timidity seems to have been one reason for his avoidance of marriage, and he remarks :

> ' The sage who said he needed naught in life
> Save what he carried on him had no wife.'

Another cause appears in a doubt of his own permanent attractiveness :

> ' Unless she loves, no wife will faithful be.
> Where there's no love, there is no chastity.'

A third, the diversion of spirit brought about by love, which is to scholars so distressing, is embodied in an ingenious comparison :

> ' As blind men wander in an unknown land,
> Led by a woman's or a stripling's hand ;
> So lovers in a maze must wander on,
> Led by fair Venus or by Venus' son.'

Strongest reason of all is the disbelief in woman's constancy which inspires two amusing pieces. One runs thus :

> ' The scripture tells us in a single day
> Thrice and again the good man goes astray.
> But though I've looked I nowhere find it written
> How oft by weakness is the good wife smitten.'

But although Owen had this general distrust of women, he was not immune against the charms of individual ladies, and he can turn a compliment with the best. To one damsel who had made him a present of a looking-glass he writes :

> ' You sent me a mirror, but in it I trace
> No glimpse of the giver : I see but my face.
> I wish you had given a different kind
> On whose shining surface your lips I might find.'

From a mirror again he points the old moral to his fair Caroline :

> ' When in the glass your sparkling eyes you see,
> Be not too proud of their soft brilliancy.
> Remember, fair as glass and as glass frail,
> Nor glass nor beauty against Time prevail.'

Owen's real strength, however, lies not in sentiment but in wit, and of that he gives us innumerable examples. There is the couplet on the spendthrift son at his father's tomb :

> ' " Rest, father, rest for ever ! " Peter cries
> And trembles lest he from the grave should rise.'

Another, on the double mania for didactic and complimentary verse, is equally clever :

> ' To-day a poet sings not of his lass,
> But much prefers to hymn the humble ass.
> The latest product of the tuneful lyre
> Is called " In praise of Thomas Jones Esquire." '

But in most of the pieces a solid basis of practical wisdom lies beneath the grace of their language. On the contrast between life and death Owen is especially good and it would be interesting to make a list of the epigrams that deal with death in its various aspects. The catalogue would be a long one, for on this topic Owen is the true precursor of Blair and Young in the next century, and his fancy is inexhaustible in the invention of metaphor and simile. At one time he cries :

> ' Death steals on life : old age on youth falls fast.
> We ask the hour ; and lo, the hour is past.'

The thought of life's frailty is ever present with him, and suggests many such a vivid comparison as this :

> ' Our life is like a spider's web,
> Its fabric frail by nature wrought :
> But the long toil of web and life
> One moment brings to nought.'

He has a subtle variant of the Greek complaint, ' The best thing is never to have been born ' :

> ' You wailed when you were born, and to draw breath
> Gave no delight. Why therefore shrink from death ? '

But he finds one comfort that rarely presented itself to the Hellenic mind :

> ' Make life a jest and at life's end
> Death has a bitter savour, friend.
> Make life a thing of sober zest
> And death is nothing but a jest.'

Owen was a born epigrammatist, and he finds in Latin a perfect medium for such a couplet as this :

> ' Ad mortem sic vita fluit velut ad mare flumen :
> Vivere nam res est dulcis, amara mori.'

He is very unequal, and is often puerile, often pedantic : but from the body of his works a competent selector could pick out three or four hundred epigrams which would be perfect specimens of concise wit.

Buchanan and Owen stand out from among the Elizabethan Latinists, as will be evident to anyone who peruses the collection of Latin verse published by Arthur Johnston at Amsterdam in 1637. Cheke and Ascham, author of the *Toxophilus*, were accomplished prose writers, and Elizabeth herself had surprising powers of eloquence in the Latin tongue. But most of the Elizabethans were too busy writing English to have much time for anything else, and the scholars among them found useful employment in translating the classics into their own language. One Latin poem, however, by John Lyly, the author of the *Euphues*, is so characteristic of his age that it deserves mention. Juno, Pallas, and Venus, meeting in heaven, all claim Queen Elizabeth as their particular charge. None will give way, so that the dispute is finally referred to Jupiter for decision, and the poem ends thus :

> ' Obstupet omnipotens " Durum est quod poscitis," inquit.
> " Est tamen arbitrio res peragenda meo.
> Tu soror et coniunx Iuno, tu filia Pallas,
> Es quoque—quid simulem ?—ter mihi cara Venus.
> Non tua, da veniam, Iuno, nec Palladis illa est,
> Nec Veneris, credas hoc licet alma Venus.
> Ergo quid obstrepitis ? Frustra contenditis," inquit.
> " Ultima vox hæc est, Elizabetha mea est." '

' Great Jove for long sat silent : then he spake :
"Hard is the judgment that you bid me make.
You are my wife and sister, you my child,
And you are triply dear "—fair Venus smiled—
"But still, forgive me, no one of you three
Can have the nymph, for she belongs to me.
Why cry in vain ? Your claims you must resign,
The judgment stands : Elizabeth is mine." '

Owen is one of the last authors who used Latin as their only medium. But during the first half of the seventeenth century a large amount of Latin was still being written all over Europe. In England we have Selden, Robert Burton, and Drummond of Hawthornden : in the Netherlands Heinsius, Grotius, Voss and Baruch Spinoza ; in France Saumaise, Du Cange, Rapin, and the brothers Santeuil; and further afield, Ferdinand von Furstenburg of Westphalia and Casimir Sarbiewski the ' Sarmatian Horace.' To give details of all these is here unnecessary, and this history must end with three Englishmen who were bilingual but are now better known for their English than for their Latin books.

Francis Bacon (1560–1626)

The first of these three is Francis Bacon Lord Verulam, that remarkable man who took all knowledge for his province and could rise as easily to the loftiest heights of sublimity in thought as he could sink to the lowest depths of meanness in action. The list of Bacon's works in Latin, as in English, is a long one, and their dates range from 1585 to 1626. The first, which is now lost, was the *Temporis Partus Maximus*, a fierce criticism of the early philosophers, in which Aristotle is described as *pessimus sophista*, and Plato as *cavillator urbanus*. Then came three books on natural science (1600–1605), *De Rerum Natura, De Scientia Humana,* and *De Interpretatione Naturæ.* In 1609 appeared the *De Sapientia Veterum,* which, after the *Essays* was the most popular of Bacon's works among his contemporaries and the one that best reveals his mixture of political caution and critical audacity. The *Novum Organum,* with its direct challenge to Aristotle and its analysis of the four chief causes of human error, the *Idola Tribus, Specus, Fori, Theatri,* after twelve revisions was published in 1620. In 1623 came the *De Augmentis Scientiarum,* an enlargement of the *Advancement of Knowledge,* and also the metaphysical *De Principiis,* while the last three years of his life Bacon devoted to the *Sylva Sylvarum,* an accumulation of a ' thousand prerogative instances '; facts, beliefs, fables, and conjectures ranging over all departments of nature. These are the more important titles in Bacon's great scheme, the *Instauratio Magna ;* and space will only allow this brief catalogue and one quotation from the *Novum Organum.*

' Præterea non abs re fuerit, tria hominum ambitionis genera et quasi gradus distinguere. Primum eorum, qui propriam potentiam in patria sua amplificare cupiunt ; quod genus vulgare est et degener. Secundum eorum, qui patriæ potentiam et imperium inter humanum genus amplificare nituntur ; illud plus certe habet dignitatis, cupiditatis haud minus. Quod si quis humani generis ipsius potentiam et imperium in rerum universitatem instaurare et amplificare conetur, ea procul dubio ambitio (si modo ita vocanda sit) reliquis et sanior est et augustior. Hominis autem imperium in res, in solis artibus et scientiis ponitur. Naturæ enim non imperatur, nisi parendo.'— *Novum Organum,* I, 131.

Abraham Cowley (1618–1667)

Cowley, like Bacon, began and ended his literary career as a Latinist, and in Latin verse essayed the epic, the lyric, the didactic poem, and the drama.

Born in London, Cowley was educated at Westminster School and Trinity College, Cambridge, where in 1638 he wrote for public performance the *Naufragium Joculare*. The *Naufragium* is a curious production; the scene is laid at Dunquerque, two of the chief characters are Captain Bombardomachides and Magister Gnomicus, the dialogue is partly in prose, partly in iambics and hexameters with songs in rhyme, and it is very difficult reading. This play was the beginning of Cowley's fame, and before he was thirty his English poems had gained him such a reputation that the folio which he published in 1656 passed through eight editions in one generation. In that volume Latin is represented by the first book of the *Davideis* :

> ' Bella cano fatique vices regemque potentem
> Mutato qui sceptra pedo Solymëia gessit '

a poem which, like Petrarch's *Africa*, was never finished and is now extant only in this one book of Latin and four books of English verse. The most considerable of Cowley's Latin works, however, is that which occupied the last years of his life, the *Sex Libri Plantarum*, a horticultural poem, of which the first three books are in elegiacs and lyrics, the last three in hexameters. It fills three hundred closely printed pages and is distinctly tedious : when it is read to-day, it is usually in the translation by Nahum Tate and other eminent hands, one of whom, Mrs Aphra Behn, begins the Sixth Book thus :

> ' Cease, O my Muse, the soft delights to sing
> Of Flow'ry Gardens in their fragrant Spring ;
> And trace the rougher paths of obscure Woods,
> All gloom aloft, beneath o'rgrown with Shrubs.
> Where Phœbus, once thy Guide, can dart no Ray
> T' inspire thy Flight, and make the Scene look gay.'

Cowley died in 1667, and the following inscription was placed upon his tomb :

> ' Anglorum Pindarus, Flaccus, Maro,
> Deliciæ, Decus, Desiderium ævi sui
> Hic iuxta situs est.'

John Milton (1608-1674)

Bacon only wrote Latin prose, Cowley only Latin verse ; Milton in his own day was equally well known for his Latin poems and for his Latin prose dispatches and treatises. The poems, mostly composed in his youth, extend to some sixty pages in the collected edition of his works. They consist of seven elegies, one, as usual, on spring :

> ' Ver mihi, quod dedit ingenium, cantabitur illo :
> Profuerint isto reddita dona modo ' :

thirteen epigrams, the three best addressed to an Italian lady Leonora Baroni, whom Milton met on his foreign tour : and a collection of very miscellaneous pieces, which includes hexameters on the Gunpowder Plot, iambics on the Platonic Idea in Aristotle, and a noble elegy on the death of Carlo Deodati :

> ' Himerides nymphæ—nam vos et Daphnin et Hylan
> Et plorata diu meministis fata Bionis—
> Dicite Sicelicum Thamesina per oppida carmen.'

The prose works are more extensive and cover a wide range of subjects. There are the state dispatches which he wrote as Latin secretary to the Commonwealth ; the pamphlets he composed against Saumaise and Alexander More, whom he supposed to be the author of ' *Regii Sanguinis Clamor ad Cælum*,' in which he undertook the defence of the English nation against Charles I ; the theological treatise *De Doctrina Chris-*

tiana ; the handbook to logic *Artis Logicæ Plenior Institutio ;* and lastly a collection of Latin letters addressed to his friends. Bacon and Cowley are true Renaissance types, Bacon a greater Machiavelli and Cowley a lesser Politian : Milton, like Dante and Virgil, stands above his age. But as Dante ends the medieval period, so Milton ends the Renaissance. By the close of the seventeenth century the attempt to make classical Latin the standard medium of literature had definitely failed, and the modern languages had won a decisive victory. Europe had already lost the bond of a common religion ; it now lost its common language ; and it has been suffering ever since from the lack of that unity which one religion and one language gave.

EPILOGUE

DURING the last two centuries Latin has just, but only just, maintained its existence as a medium for original literature. It is still the language of the Catholic Church, and for inscriptions, epitaphs, and prize poems it is still rightly held to be the most suitable vehicle. But those who write Latin with ease and those who read Latin with pleasure now form a very small class, and Guarino's dictum that the truly educated man must possess a sound knowledge of Greek and the ability to compose Latin verse now finds few adherents.

The decay has been progressive, for through the literature of the eighteenth century there runs a slender stream of Latin poetry, supplied in England by such men as Addison, Johnson, Cotton, and Vincent Bourne, in France by Cardinal de Polignac, in Spain by Juan de Yriarte, and in Germany by Christian Klotz. Even in the nineteenth century Landor, Kennedy, and Johnson-Cory were still using Latin verse with some success, and Baudelaire's *Franciscæ meæ Laudes* is not the least attractive of the ' Fleurs du Mal.' But it would be difficult to find any Latin poem written in the last fifty years that possesses great poetical merit ; and perhaps in that there is nothing much to regret.

The case of Latin prose, however, is different. Until the middle of the nineteenth century Latin was for all classical scholars a second mother tongue and served as an invaluable means of communication. It is true that Richard Bentley (1662–1742) preferred English for his *Epistles of Phalaris* ; but it was in Latin

that Newton composed the *Principia*, in Latin that
Porson and Dawes, Hermann and Wolf, Cobet and
Madvig lectured and wrote. Even as late as 1841 we
have Keble's *De poeticæ vi medica ;* but then an
organised effort was made to substitute German for
Latin as the language of scholarship, just as in the
eighteenth century French had taken the place of
Latin as the language of diplomacy. The attempt was
so far successful that Latin passed out of use, and
to-day it is necessary for a scholar to have a working
knowledge of English, French, German, and Italian.
But whether this is an advantage is at least doubtful.

SELECT BIBLIOGRAPHY

COLLECTIONS, HISTORIES, AND ANTHOLOGIES

Patrologia Latina. Ed. Migne. 222 Vols. Paris, 1857-1906 (P.L.).

Corpus Scriptorum Ecclesiasticorum Latinorum. 65 Vols. Vienna, 1866-1926 (V.C.).

Analecta Hymnica Medii Aevi. Leipzig, 1886 *sq.*

Monumenta Germaniæ Historica. Hanover and Berlin, 1877 *sq.* (M.G.H.).

Anthologia Latina. Ed. Buecheler and Riese. Leipzig, 1894.

Poetæ Latini Minores. Ed. Baehrens. Leipzig, 1910 *sq.* (P.L.M.).

Poésies populaires Latines. Ed. E. du Meril. 3 Vols. Paris, 1843 *sq.*

Bibliotheca Latina mediæ et infimæ ætatis. Fabricius. Padua, 1754.

Spätlateinische Studien. E. Löfstedt. Upsala, 1908.

Histoire littéraire de la France. Paris, 1733 *sq.*

History of Latin Literature. Teuffel and Schwabe. London, 1892.

Geschichte der römischen Literatur. Schanz. Leipzig, 1914 *sq.*

Geschichte der lateinischen Literatur des Mittelalters. Manitius. Munich, 1911.

Geschichte der Literatur des Mittelalters. Ebert. Leipzig, 1887.

History of Classical Scholarship. Sandys. Cambridge, 1913.

Decline and Fall of the Roman Empire. Gibbon. London, 1912.

Italy and her Invaders. T. Hodgkin. Oxford, 1892.

Cambridge Medieval History. Cambridge, 1911 *sq.*

The Mediæval Mind. H. O. Taylor. London, 1914.

Christian Latin Poetry. F. J. E. Raby. Oxford, 1927.

The Wandering Scholars. H. Waddell. London, 1927.

Notices et extraits. B. Hauréau. Paris, 1890.

Early Latin Hymns. A. S. Walpole. Cambridge, 1922.

Anthology of Medieval Latin. S. Gaselee. London, 1925.

SELECT BIBLIOGRAPHY

Oxford Book of Medieval Latin Verse. S. Gaselee. Oxford, 1928.
Mediæval Latin. K. P. Harrington. Boston, 1925.
Book of Latin Prose and Verse. F. A. Wright. London, 1929.
Einführung in das Mittellatein. 2nd ed. K. Strecker. Berlin, 1929.
Life in the Middle Ages. G. G. Coulton. Cambridge, 1928-30.

INTRODUCTION AND PART I

TERTULLIAN. Ed. Oehler. Leipzig, 1856.

CYPRIAN. Ed. Hartel. V.C. 3.

LACTANTIUS. Ed. Brandt. V.C. 19.27.

AMBROSE. *Opera.* P.L. 14-17.

SYMMACHUS. M.G.H. *Auct. Ant.* 6.

AUSONIUS. Tr. H. G. E. White. Loeb Library. London, 1919.

PRUDENTIUS. *Carmina.* Ed. Bergmann. V.C. 61.

PAULINUS OF NOLA. Ed. Hartel. V.C. 29.30.

CLAUDIAN. Tr. M. Platnauer. Loeb Library. London, 1922.

DONATUS, etc. Ed. Keil in *Grammatici Latini.* 7 Vols. Leipzig, 1880.

MACROBIUS. Ed. Eyssenhardt. Leipzig, 1893.

MARTIANUS CAPELLA. Ed. Dick. Leipzig, 1925.

VEGETIUS. Ed. Lang. Leipzig, 1885.

SULPICIUS SEVERUS. Ed. Halm. V.C. 1.

EUTROPIUS. Ed. Rühl. Leipzig, 1919.

AMMIANUS MARCELLINUS. Ed. Gardthausen. Leipzig, 1874.

DAMASUS. P.L. 13.22.71.

JEROME. *Opera.* P.L. 22-30.

—— *Epistulæ.* Ed. Hilberg. V.C. 54.55.56.

AUGUSTINE. *Opera.* P.L. 32-46.

—— *Confessions.* Tr. W. Watts. Loeb Library. London, 1912.

—— *De civitate dei.* Ed. Welldon. London, 1924.

Latin Christianity. P. De Labriolle. London, 1925.

Life and Letters in the Fourth Century. T. R. Glover. London, 1901.

Fathers of the Church. F. A. Wright. London, 1928.

SELECT BIBLIOGRAPHY

La fin du Paganisme. G. Boissier. Paris, 1913.

Roman Society in last Century of Western Empire. S. Dill. London, 1898.

PART II

 OROSIUS. P.L. 31. Alfred's translation. Ed. H. Sweet. E.E.T.S No. 79.

RUTILIUS. *De Reditu Suo.* Ed. C. H. Keene. London, 1907.

LEO THE GREAT. P.L. 54-56.

SEDULIUS. P.L. 19. V. C. 10. Ed. J. Huemer.

SIDONIUS. P.L. 58. Letters trans. O. M. Dalton. Oxford, 1915

—— *Collection des Auteurs Latins.* Nisard. (Lat. and Fr.).

SALVIANUS. P.L. 53. V. C. 8. Ed. F. Pauly.

BOETHIUS. P.L. 63, 64. *Boethius : An Essay.* H. F. Stewart. Edinburgh, 1891.

—— *The Theological Tractates and the Consolation of Philosophy.* H. F. Stewart and E. K. Rand. Loeb Classical Library.

CASSIODORUS. P.L. 69, 70. M.G.H. *Auctores Antiquissimi* 12. JORDANES P.L. 69.

GILDAS. P.L. 69. Latin and English. H. Williams. Cymmrodorion Society, 1901.

PRISCIAN. H. Keil. *Grammatici Latini* 2 and 3, and *Poetæ Latini Minores* 5.

MAXIMIAN. *P. L. M.* 5.

BENEDICT OF NURSIA. P.L. 66.

GREGORY OF TOURS. P.L. 71. M.G.H. *Scriptores Rerum Merovingicarum I.*

—— *The History of the Franks.* Trans. O. M. Dalton. Oxford, 1927.

—— *Le Latin de Grégoire de Tours.* M. Bonnet. Paris, 1890.

—— *Roman Society in Gaul in the Merovingian Age.* S. Dill London, 1926.

GREGORY THE GREAT. P.L. 75-79.

FORTUNATUS. P.L. 89. M.G.H. *Auctores Antiquissimi* 4, parts 1 and 2.

—— *Fortunat.* D. Tardi. Paris, 1927.

—— *Collection des Auteurs Latins.* Nisard. (Lat. and Fr.).

ISIDORE. P.L. 81-84. *Etymologiarum Libri XX.* W. M. Lindsay. Oxford, 1912.

COLUMBANUS. P.L. 80.

ALDHELM. P.L. 89. M.G.H. *Auctores Antiquissimi* 15.

TATWIN, EUSEBIUS, etc. J. A. Giles. *Anecdota Bedæ, Lanfranci et aliorum.* Caxton Society, 1851.

BEDE. P.L. 90-94. *Venerabilis Bedæ opera Historica.* C. Plummer Oxford, 1896.

The Dark Ages. W. P. Ker. Edinburgh, 1911.

PART III

The Schools of Charles the Great. J. B. Mullinger. London, 1877.

Life of Charlemagne. H. C. Davis. London, 1925.

Poetæ Latini Aevi Carolini. 4 Vols. Berlin, 1880 *sq.* (P.L.A.C.).

ALCUIN. *Carmina.* Ed. Dümmler. P.L.A.C. 1.

—— *Epistolæ.* Ed. Dümmler. M.G.H. 2.

ANGILBERT. *Carmina.* P.L.A.C. 1.

THEODULF. *Carmina.* P.L.A.C. 1.

PAUL THE DEACON. *Historia Langobardorum.* Ed. G. Waitz. Hanover, 1878.

HRABAN. *Opera.* P.L. 107-112.

—— *Carmina.* P.L.A.C. 2.

GOTTSCHALK. *Carmina.* P.L.A.C. 3.

WALAFRID STRABO. *Carmina.* P.L.A.C. 2.

SEDULIUS SCOTUS. *Carmina.* P.L.A.C. 3.

LUPUS SERVATUS. *Opera.* P.L. 119.

JOHN THE SCOT (ERIGENA). *Opera.* P.L. 121.122.

ERMOLDUS NIGELLUS. *Carmina.* P.L.A.C. 2.

ABBO OF PARIS. *Carmina.* P.L.A.C. 4.

ASSER. *Life of Alfred.* Ed. W. H. Stevenson. Oxford, 1904.

EKKEHARD I. *Waltharius.* Ed. Strecker. Berlin, 1907.

MONK OF ST GALL. *De gestis Karoli Magni.* M.G.H. Script. 2.

HROTSVITHÆ. *Opera.* Ed. P. de Winterfeld. Berlin, 1902.

ROSWITHA. *Plays.* Tr. C. St John. London, 1923.

SELECT BIBLIOGRAPHY

LIUDPRAND. Ed. J. Becker. Hanover, 1915.

—— Tr. F. A. Wright. London, 1930.

WIDUKIND. *Opera*. P L. 137.

FLODOARD. *Opera*. P.L. 135.

RATHER. *Opera*. P.L. 136.

GERBERT. *Opera*. P.L. 139.

PART IV

RICHER. P.L. 138. M G.H. *Scriptores III*.

EKKEHARD IV. *De Casibus Sancti Galli*. Ed. Ildephonsus of Arx. M.G.H. *Scriptores II*. Trans. (into German) G. Meyer von Knonau. Leipzig, 1878.

PETER DAMIANI. P.L. 144-145.

ABELARD. P.L. 178.

LANFRANC. P.L. 150.

ANSELM. P.L. 158-159.

WILLIAM OF MALMESBURY. P.L. 179. *De Gestis Regum Anglorum*. Ed. W. Stubbs. Rolls Series.

—— *De Gestis Pontificum*. Ed. N. E. S. A. Hamilton. Rolls Series.

GEOFFREY OF MONMOUTH. *Historia Britonum*. Ed. J. A. Giles. London, 1844. Trans. Aaron Thompson, 1718.

JOHN OF SALISBURY. *Policraticus*. Ed. C. C. J. Webb. Oxford, 1909.

—— *Metalogica*. Ed. C. C. J. Webb. Oxford, 1929.

—— *Opera Omnia*. Ed. J. A. Giles. 5 Vols. Oxford, 1848.

—— *Historia Pontificalis quæ supersunt*. R. L. Poole. Oxford, 1927.

WALTER MAP. *De Nugis Curialium*. Ed. T. Wright, 1856.

—— *De Nugis Curialium*. Ed. M. R. James. Oxford, 1914.

SAXO GRAMMATICUS. *Gesta Danorum*. Ed. A. Holder. Strassburg, 1886. Trans. (First nine books) O. Elton. London, 1894.

GIRALDUS CAMBRENSIS. Ed. J. S. Brewer. Rolls Series. 8 Vols.

CÆSARIUS HEISTORBACENSIS. *Dialogus Miraculorum*. Ed. J. Strange. Bonn, 1851. Trans. H. von E. Scott and C. C. Swinton Bland. London, 1929.

—— *Die Fragmenta der Libri VIII Miraculorum des C. von H.* Ed. A. Meister, 1901.

MATTHEW PARIS. *Chronica Maiora.* Ed. H. R. Luard. 7 Vols. Rolls Series.

—— *Historia Anglorum.* Ed. Sir F. Madden. 3 Vols. Rolls Series.

SALIMBENE OF PARMA. Ed. O. Holder-Egger. M.G.H. *Scriptores XXXII.*

ALBERTUS MAGNUS. Ed. A. and E. Borgnet and others, 38 Vols. Paris, 1890–99.

THOMAS AQUINAS. *Opera Omnia iussu impensaque Leonis XIII.* 13 Vols. Rome, 1882-1918; also Vivès edition, 34 Vols. Paris, 1871-80.

BONAVENTURA. *Opera Omnia ad Claras Aquas (Quaracchi).* 10 Vols. 1882-1902.

ROGER BACON. *Opus Maius.* Ed. J. H. Bridges. Oxford, 1897.

—— Trans. R. B. Burke. Philadelphia, 1928.

—— *Opus Tertium*, etc. Ed. J. S. Brewer. Rolls Series.

—— *Opera hactenus inedita.* Oxford, 1909-   (in progress).

DANTE. *Li Opere di Dante Alighieri.* Ed. E. Moore and P. Toynbee. 4th ed. Oxford, 1924.

PART V

Histoire de la poésie liturgique. L. Gautier. Paris, 1886.

The Abbey of St Gall. J. M. Clark. Cambridge, 1926.

The Cambridge Songs. Ed. K. Breul. Cambridge, 1915.

The Romanesque Lyric. P. S. Allen. North Carolina, 1928.

Die Parodie im Mittelalter. P. Lehmann. Munich, 1922.

NOTKER. *Liber Sequentiarum.* P.L. 171.

—— *Carmina.* Ed. Winterfeld. Berlin, 1890.

FULBERT. *Carmina.* P.L. 141.

COLUMBANUS. P.L. 80.

HILDEBERT. *Carmina.* P.L. 171.

MARBOD. *Carmina.* P.L. 171.

BAUDRI DE BOURGEUIL. *Œuvres Poétiques.* Ed. P. Abrahams. Paris, 1926.

BERNARD OF CLAIRVAUX. P.L. 182-185.

BERNARD OF MORLAS. A.L.S.

SELECT BIBLIOGRAPHY

ALAN OF LILLE. A.L.S.

ADAM OF ST VICTOR. *Œuvres poétiques.* L. Gautier. Paris, 1858.

The Flourishing of Romance. G. Saintsbury. Edinburgh, 1923.

Cambridge History of English Literature. Vol. I. Cambridge, 1925.

Latin Poems attributed to Walter Mapes. T. Wright. London, 1841.

Anglo-Latin Satirical Poets of Twelfth Century. T. Wright. London, 1844 (A.L.S.).

Les arts poétiques du XII et du XIII siècle. E. Faral. Paris, 1925.

Illustrations of the History of Medieval Thought. R. L. Poole. London, 1920.

Wine, Women, and Song. J. A. Symonds. London, 1884.

Carmina Burana. Ed. J. A. Schmeller. Stuttgart, 1847.

Vagantenlieder. Ed. Ulich and Manitius. Jena, 1927.

Fragmenta Burana. W. Meyer. Berlin, 1901.

PART VI

The Renaissance in Italy. J. A. Symonds. London, 1898.

The Civilisation of the Renaissance. S. Burckhardt. London, 1929.

Lateinische Dichter des XV-XVIII Jahrhunderts. Budik. Vienna, 1828.

Literature of Europe in the 15th, 16th, 17th centuries. Hallam. London, 1843.

PETRARCH. *Opera.* Lyons, 1620.

—— *Epistulæ.* Ed. Fracassetti. Florence, 1859.

POLITIAN. *Opera.* Basle, 1553.

POGGIO. *Opera.* Basle, 1538.

BEMBO. *Opera.* Venice, 1729.

The Early Renaissance. G. Saintsbury. Edinburgh, 1923.

Carmina Illustrium Poetarum Italorum. 7 Vols. Florence, 1719.

Deliciæ Poetarum Italorum. Ed. Gruter. Leyden, 1603.

Poemata Selecta Italorum. Oxford, 1808.

Deutsche Lyriker des sechszehnten Jahrhunderts. W. Ellinger. Berlin, 1893.

T. À KEMPIS. *Imitatio Christi.* Ed. Hirsche. Berlin, 1874.

ERASMUS. *Opera.* Ed. Leclerc. Leyden, 1703.

—— *Letters.* Ed. P. S. Allen. Oxford, 1906.

SELECT BIBLIOGRAPHY

MORE. *Utopia.* Ed. J. H. Lupton. Oxford, 1895.

Epistolæ Obscurorum Virorum. Ed. F. G. Stokes. London, 1925.

JOANNES SECUNDUS. *Opera.* Ed. Burmann-Bosscha. Leyden, 1821.

—— Tr. F. A. Wright. London, 1930.

BUCHANAN. *Poemata.* Amsterdam, 1676.

OWEN. *Epigrammata.* Paris, 1794.

BACON. *Opera.* Ed. Ellis, Spedding and Heath. London, 1857.

—— *Letters and Life.* Spedding. London, 1861.

COWLEY. *Poemata Latina.* London, 1678.

INDEX [1]

CAPITAL LETTERS *refer to the main articles on the writers or subjects dealt with. Incidental references are printed in smaller type, titles of books or parts of books, in italics.*

[1] The Index is the work of Mr W. Swan Stallybrass, to whom for this, and for much other help, the authors desire to record their deep obligation.

INDEX

INDEX

INDEX

GREGORY I (THE GREAT), 113–9; 67,
278
Gregory VII, Pope, 289
Gregory of Nazianzus, 15
Greek Anthology (The), 320, 370, 377
Grimani, Cardinal, 364
Grocyn, 352, 363
Groendael, 357
Groot, Gerhard, 358–9, 360
Grosseteste, Robert, 261
Grotius, Hugo, 393
Gruter's *Deliciæ Poetarum*, 354, 381
Guarino, 342, 343
Guibert of Nogent, 294
Guiscard, Robert, 289, 292
Gundobad the Burgundian, 91
Gunpowder Plot, 396
Gunther, King of the Franks, 174
Gunthram, King of the Franks,
154
Guuihtgaraburhg, 169

Hacquin, Nicholas, 376
Hadrian, Abbot, 123
,,   Emperor of Rome, 186, 273
Hagen, 173, 174
Hammerken, Gertrude, 359
HAMMERKEN, THOMAS—*v.* Kempis
(Thomas à)
Harald, King of Denmark, 168
Hartgar, Bishop of Liége, 162, 163
Hastings, Battle of, 295
Hatto, Bishop, 181
Hedwig, Duchess, 205
Hegius, 362
Heinsius, Daniel, 393
HEISTERBACH, CÆSARIUS OF—*v.*
Cæsarius
Heloïse, 216–9, 296, 297, 327
Henry I, 292
,,   II, 234, 235, 241
,,   III, 248
,,   IV of Germany, 292
Henry of Huntingdon, 226, 306
Heri mundus exsultavit, 319
Heribaldus, 205, 206
Hermann, C. F., 399
Hermann the Lame, 312
Herodotus, 344
Hessus, Eobanus, 374
Hilarion (hermit), 54
Hilary of Poitiers, 18, 274, 306

HILDEBERT, 292–3; 294
Hildebrand, 289
Hildegund, Princess, 173, 174
Hincmar, 159, 164, 165, 166, 202
Hisperica Famina, 125, 126
Hodie cantandus, 281
Homer, 12, 340, 341, 343, 352
Honorius, Emperor, 33, 69
Horace, 11, 282, 290, 384
HRABAN, 157–8; 159, 160, 161, 164
Hrodgaud, Duke of Friuli, 150
HROSWITHA, 183–90
Huadbert—*v.* Eusebius
Hucbald, 168
HUGH OF ORLEANS, 323–4; 326
Hugh de Sade, 337
Hugh of Arles, 175, 176, 193
Hugo of Montpelier, 250
Hugo of St Victor, 201, 232
Humanism, 336
Humphrey, Duke of Gloucester,
344
Hutten, Ulrich von, 372

In taberna quando sumus, 321
Innocent III, Pope, 241, 312
Iona, 123, 127
Irmingade, 163
ISIDORE OF SEVILLE, 119–21
Iso, 280

JACOPONE DA TODI, 316–7
Jado, Archbishop of Milan, 163
James IV of Scotland, 367
Janus Pannonius, 343
Jarrow, 127
JEROME, 49–55; 352
Joachim du Bellay, 381
JOANNES SECUNDUS, 32; 378–81
Jocelyn de Brakelande, 227
Joel (the prophet), 31
JOHANNES SCOTUS (ERIGENA), 165,
166
John XII, Pope, 172, 178, 179
,,   XIII, Pope, 196
,,   Prince (son of Henry II), 239
John de Hanville, 307
John of Fidanza, 260
,,   Hoveden, 314
,,   Ravenna, 342
JOHN OF SALISBURY, 227–32; 304–5,
336

413

INDEX

INDEX

415

INDEX

INDEX

417

INDEX

PRINTED IN GREAT BRITAIN BY THE EDINBURGH PRESS, EDINBURGH